VATICAN DIPLOMACY

A STUDY OF CHURCH AND STATE ON THE INTERNATIONAL PLANE

"... *the problem of sovereignty*
in its acutest phase—that of Church and State"

—HAROLD LASKI

Vatican Diplomacy

A STUDY OF
CHURCH AND STATE ON THE
INTERNATIONAL PLANE

BY ROBERT A. GRAHAM, S.J.

PRINCETON, NEW JERSEY

PRINCETON UNIVERSITY PRESS

1959

Publication of this book
has been aided by the Ford Foundation program
to support publication, through university presses,
of works in the humanities and social sciences

✧

Printed in the United States of America by
Princeton University Press
Princeton, New Jersey

TO THE MEMORY OF
MY FATHER AND MOTHER

ACKNOWLEDGMENTS

LIKE MOST BOOKS, this one owes much to the advice, encouragement, and inspiration of persons whose only compensation is their satisfaction of service to the cause of learning. The author, in appreciation, can only pledge to these unnamed but not forgotten benefactors, his resolve to do unto others what others have done for him in the fraternity of scholars.

Explicit mention, nevertheless, is certainly due to some of those who helped. My first thanks go to V. Rev. Joseph J. King, S.J., who in 1948 made available both the time and the financial means to begin a four-year research program in international relations, and to his successor in office, V. Rev. Joseph D. O'Brien, S.J., who from limited resources continued this support in the pursuance of a long-range policy to promote advanced research by members of the California Province of the Society of Jesus.

Then, for having provided the academic point of departure, my debt to the Graduate Institute of International Studies of the University of Geneva is great indeed. The co-directors of the Institute, Professors William E. Rappard and Paul Mantoux, both regrettably since deceased, welcomed the presence of a Catholic priest in their courses at the Institute. They and their professorial associates, Hans Wehberg, Maurice Bourquin, and Paul Guggenheim, devoted time to reading and scrutinizing not only my thesis but also the drafts of the full-sized book now before the reader. None of them Catholics, their professional attitude toward the progress of research on a Catholic subject by a Catholic priest was in the best traditions of objective scholarship.

The staffs of the foreign ministry archives in Paris, Brussels, London, Vienna, Munich, Berlin-Dahlem, and Rome will recognize throughout these pages my own indebtedness to their generous services. At the Vatican, Msgr. Giuseppe De Marchi provided for me not only guidance but precious documentation.

In those years of study abroad, the writer enjoyed the hospitality not only of St. Boniface in Geneva but also of l'Action

Populaire in Paris and, successively in Rome, of the Istituto Pontificio Orientali and *La Civiltà Cattolica*, in whose well-provided libraries fruitful avenues of inquiry opened before the delighted researcher. I must record my appreciation of the warm reception I found there as well as my deep thanks to other confreres in Munich, Frankfurt, Vienna, Berlin, London, Brussels, and The Hague.

Coming closer to home, I must acknowledge the generosity of Rev. John LaFarge, S.J., who as editor-in-chief of *America* graciously concurred in my long absence from editorial work, and of his successors, Rev. Robert C. Hartnett, S.J., and Thurston N. Davis, S.J., through whose considerate indulgence the tedious and time-consuming work of organizing raw research material finally culminated in a manuscript suitable for submission to a publisher.

To priest-historians, John F. Broderick, S.J., Florence Cohalan, and Joseph N. Moody, I should perhaps apologize for the impositions to which I subjected them. In fact, I am entirely unremorseful in view of the benefits gained from their reading my manuscript.

Finally, my thanks to William Dodd, who found time to type his way painstakingly through my crude originals, and to R. Miriam Brokaw, who tried nobly to render into more polished form the English of this book for whose shortcomings of any order I remain, of course, alone responsible.

Princeton University Press greatly relieved a financial problem by allocating some funds for the publication of this book from a grant received earlier from the Ford Foundation.

R.A.G.

NOTE ON DOCUMENTATION

All works cited in this volume, whether in the text or in the footnotes, are listed in the comprehensive Bibliography at the end, with their complete title and year of publication. Other books are also included in that Bibliography which, though consulted, have not been quoted. For the convenience of the reader, preceding the footnotes in each of the following chapters, are indicated the names of the authors whose writings have a specific bearing on the subject discussed in that particular chapter, but which are not mentioned in the footnotes. In most cases the title of book or review is abbreviated in the footnotes. It will be sufficient to consult the comprehensive Bibliography, under the name of the author, editor, or issuing agency, for the full title of the book or the exact source of an article or essay cited.

CONTENTS

Acknowledgments   vii

Introduction   3

1. Profile of Papal Diplomacy Today   17

PART ONE
THE ORIGINS OF MODERN DIPLOMATIC MISSIONS

2. The French Revolution. Prussia and the Protestant States   37

3. Imperial Russia. Great Britain. The New World. The United States (1848-1868). The Non-Christian World   65

PART TWO
THE ORGANS OF PAPAL DIPLOMACY

4. The Ambassadors   99

5. The Ministries   127

PART THREE
THE POPE AS SOVEREIGN

6. The Transition: Middle Ages to the 20th Century
   In the Company of Kings   157

7. International Law Aspects of Papal Diplomacy
   Right of Active and Passive Legation   184

8. Papal Sovereignty in Canonical Public Law
   Theoretical Foundations of Papal Diplomacy   215

9. Papal Sovereignty in Comparative Constitutional Law (1)
   Concurrence of the Two Jurisdictions   247

10. Papal Sovereignty in Comparative Constitutional Law (2)
    Free Church in a Free Society   276

CONTENTS

PART FOUR
TESTS AND CHALLENGES

11. Papal Diplomatic Relations in Time of War
1915-1918 to 1940-1945   305

12. United States-Vatican Relations
An Interpretation of the Mission of Myron C. Taylor   326

13. The Holy See and the Soviet Union
Catholic Church and Communist State   349

Conclusion   385

Bibliography   397

Index   421

VATICAN DIPLOMACY

A STUDY OF CHURCH AND STATE ON THE
INTERNATIONAL PLANE

INTRODUCTION

THE visitor to the home of Georges Clemenceau on the rue Franklin—now an official museum—finds a modest house kept just as it was when the "Tiger" left it. From here he went forth in 1917 to accept the call to form a government; here he lived when he was the dynamic force that rallied faint hearts in France's darkest hour of the First World War. Your guide will point out the ancient telephone which communicated directly with the General Staff headquarters.

The telephone is in Clemenceau's study, a ground-floor room walled with books. One volume lies on the desk. Undisturbed from the day when death made its visitation, it remains a source of reflection. This was the last book he read before the fatal illness struck him, says your guide, custodian of these souvenirs of a great Frenchman. "A political history of the Popes," he adds gravely, by way of description. You are not led to believe that it was anything more than a political work. It would not do for pilgrims to this shrine to infer that the old anti-clerical was in his last days getting religion.

But a history of the Popes nevertheless. To his dying day Clemenceau could not ignore the Pope. Devoted to separation, a notorious unbeliever, Clemenceau was fated as a government official to enter into negotiations with the Holy See in defense of French interests.

In him one finds almost the personification of the modern State. Despite its secular cast and its oftentimes positive hostility to the Catholic Church, the State finds itself going so far as to enter into direct contact with the papacy at the most formal, i.e., the diplomatic, level. Clemenceau reconciled himself to this line of policy. For him personally, no doubt, it went against the grain, but as a patriot he found it necessary; in the end, as a logical Frenchman, he found it not unreasonable after all. In the evening of his life the papacy was still the ancient institution that no statesman in office could pass over, still the institution that a statesman in retirement could study with profit and interest in his pursuit of wisdom in the art of government.

Church-State relations are too deeply rooted in human nature to conform to any single formula or any simple rule of politics.

Clemenceau no doubt thought, back in 1904-1905 when he supported diplomatic rupture with the Vatican and the law of separation, that France had introduced real separation of Church and State and that the problem was ended forever. In reality he had but backed a new kind of separation to replace another.

The Christian era is essentially the era of separation. In his epoch-making study of the ancient Greek and Roman civilization, Fustel de Coulanges, developing a point already made by Pope St. Gelasius I in the 5th century, showed that it was only with the coming of Christ that a distinction between religion and politics began to appear. The idea of separating divine worship from civil loyalty hardly entered the minds of the citizens of the most advanced city states. The *polis* was itself a religious community. The king was a pontiff, the magistrate a priest, and the law a holy precept; patriotism was the virtue of religion and exile was excommunication. What sense could it make to say that we must obey the gods rather than man, when each tribe had its own divinity which was a communal as well as a personal god? Christ split the Mediterranean world down the middle when he uttered his fateful command to render to Caesar the things that are Caesar's and to render also to God the things that are God's.

On this revolutionary Christian maxim, the French historian remarks at the conclusion of his *Ancient City* (v, 3): "It was the first time that anyone had distinguished God from the State so clearly. For, at that time Caesar was still the supreme pontiff, the head and principal organ of the Roman religion. He was the guardian and interpreter of beliefs; he held in his hands both worship and dogma. . . . But behold Christ smashes the alliance that existed between paganism and the Empire! He proclaims that religion is not the State and that obeying Caesar is no longer the same thing as obeying God."

In the new system that Christ introduced, man belonged to the State by only a part of himself. Such a duality, however, bore within it the seeds of inevitable and recurring conflict. Two imperious forces shared the innermost loyalties of one and the same human being who had to work out his other-worldly salvation while at the same time fulfilling his earthly tasks as a member of the civic community.

The claims of material existence could be, and often were, challenged by the claims of a higher destiny. The twenty centuries of the Christian era are studded with controversy between what is God's and what is Caesar's. The conflict has see-sawed, the advantage being now on the one side and now on the other. The *sacerdotium* has alternated with the *imperium* in positions of supremacy, with periods in between characterized by relatively stable if dynamic equilibrium. The State has in past times made of the Church its subordinate; the Church in its turn has dominated over the civil power. This pattern is particularly true of the relations between the Catholic Church and the State. The phenomenon did not, however, stop there. There have been periods and places in which Protestantism overshadowed and dominated the State, as there have been instances where the civil power has treated Protestantism as a branch of the government.

There is no reason to suppose that such a profound division reaching into man's inner being will ever cease to produce dramatic events in history. But if history is witness to the conflicts that arise from the duality of our civilization, it also testifies to the strivings for peaceful and harmonious collaboration inspired by that same Christian directive. In the background of every dispute there always lingered the mutual conviction that, in the end, a demarcation of spheres was not only possible but desirable. The prevailing spirit of the Christian era has been the belief that though there are two foci in man's life—God and country—these two apparently rival allegiances can somehow be reconciled to the common benefit of both Church and State.

Our age boasts of having "separated" religion from politics, as though this were something new and not, rather, a permanent feature of our Western civilization. What has happened, in reality, is that each succeeding age has developed its own distinctive system of relations between religion and politics. True, it is easy to see in such efforts of adaptation more the signs of hostility than the common desire to cooperate. It is easy to single out frictions while ignoring the framework of cooperation designed to confine this built-in tension within just bounds. But our society exhibits many monuments of constructive inventiveness called forth by the succeeding phases of the perennial challenge. Each of these creations reflects man's confidence that coordination can be achieved if due effort and good will are devoted to that end. The forces that work for such unity are inexhaustible and unfaltering, for they are the forces of life itself. When once-successful forms have outlived their usefulness, man bends his efforts once more to bring order into his affairs. In no area of human endeavor is this more true than in the relations between the sacred and the profane. Today, no less than a thousand years ago, man is still both citizen of a life below and pilgrim wayfarer in progress to a heavenly abode. But to the centrifugal drive arising from Christ's own acknowledged division, there corresponds the centripetal force faithfully working for unity.

If the recurring struggle is endemic even in a civilization united by common law, common ideals, and a common cult, what must be its complexities when all those factors, which tended to simplify Church-State relations, ceased to be operative? The Catholic Church, functioning in a world of eighty or more sovereignties, each with its own legal and political system, has a task much more difficult than formerly when there was but one emperor and one Christian commonwealth. The difficulty is mutual. If the Church which transcends political boundaries has problems, the states themselves have the challenge of adapting themselves to the religious needs of their citizens who belong to a universal Church. Pope Pius XII aptly described the new preoccupation in an address he delivered to the Foreign Correspondents' Association of Rome on May 12, 1953. The Balkanization of international society into very individualistic states has put a difficult burden upon the Mother Church:

"The Holy See is the supreme authority of the Catholic Church, and hence of a religious society whose goals are to be found in the supernatural and in the world beyond. Nevertheless, the Church lives in the world. Each of her sons and daughters—400 million Catholics—belongs to a particular state and people. It it always one of the essential tasks of the Holy See to see that, throughout the entire world, there reigns between church and state normal and, if possible, friendly relations, in order that Catholics may live their faith in tranquillity and peace, and that the Church may, at the same time, provide for the state that solid support which it constitutes wherever it is allowed to carry on its work in freedom."

When the parts of international civil society became so differentiated from one another in their ideals and institutions, thereby creating distinctive problems for the Church and for the faithful in each case, new instruments of action had to be developed. At that point papal diplomacy came into being.

That the Pope of Rome should be sending and receiving ambassadors in the late 20th century is a source of bewilderment to many persons, perhaps even to Catholics. In an age when Church and State are supposedly diverging more and more, the papacy has developed an ever-widening network of official relations with governments all over the world. There are those who reproach the State for complicity in sanctioning what seems out of tune with the spirit of the times. Yet the thoughtful observer cannot fail to be impressed by the fact that papal diplomacy is very much alive and modern. This is prima facie evidence that it serves some constructive purpose for all concerned. As will be discerned in the course of this study, the civil and the religious society face each other here in a modernized revival of an old drama. The official intercourse between the two authorities is but the contemporary form of an historic classic confrontation.

This ecclesiastical diplomacy is not less diplomatic for being ecclesiastical. The international lawyers term the Holy See *sui generis* in the sense that it is nowhere exactly paralleled. It is true that the Catholic Church is the only religious body which engages in direct relations with the various states. It is also true that papal diplomacy has cut its own course serenely and independently, leaving at more than one point the well-marked road that civil diplomacy is wont to follow. Nevertheless, in its broad outlines and in its essential function and operation, papal diplomacy conforms closely to the genius of diplomacy in general. It obeys, if in its own way, the basic precepts of diplomacy. That is why the states have found it feasible, despite points of divergence, to incorporate the Holy See in their own pattern of diplomatic relations. By so doing they implicitly avow that this relationship is proper and convenient. They acknowledge that this relationship is entirely compatible with their dignity as sovereign powers and serves in both theory and practice the interests of the State itself.

Because it is true diplomacy, papal diplomacy provides a peculiarly revealing key to the relations of Church and State. For if, as a close student of the institution says,[1] the new diplomacy of the Renaissance was the functional expression of a new kind of state, so the new papal diplomacy which emerged contemporaneously, under the same conditions, was the functional expression of the new position of the Holy See toward the political community. It is this factor which inspires the method followed in the present study. From an understanding of what papal diplomacy means in practice it is one short step to a clearer understanding of the general pattern of relations between Church and State as such, at least as far as the Catholic Church is concerned.

Before we proceed any further it is necessary to set forth some definitions. What is diplomacy? Clarification of this point is particularly necessary because of the many different, if related, meanings in which the term is used. The Oxford English Dictionary lists several meanings which Harold Nicolson prefers as broadly accurate. Diplomacy is "the management of international relations by negotiation; the method by which these relations are adjusted and managed by ambassadors and envoys; the business or art of the diplomatist." The word "diplomacy" is sometimes used as a synonym for "foreign policy." In this sense, for instance, it is said that "the Navy is the instrument of diplomacy." Diplomacy is sometimes also used when "international law" is really meant. These terms are employed because of their close connection with diplomacy as an institution. But their use in this sense is a loose and improper one.

The terms "diplomacy" and "diplomatist" are of fairly recent date and seem to have been introduced in the time of

[1] Mattingly, *Renaissance Diplomacy*, p. 55.

Richelieu. Previously, the preferred expressions were "negotiation" and "negotiator." Etymologically, the word is derived from the Greek word *diploma*, which, in turn, is derived from the root verb "to fold." It stands therefore for a document which, in ancient practice, was folded or doubled. It does not stand, as some cynics claim, for duplicity. (*Diplomatics*, the science of old documents, though of the same origin etymologically, has nothing to do with diplomacy.) This diploma, one might say, is symbolic of diplomacy as an institution. Through it the envoy, or diplomatist, is formally certified as one empowered to carry on negotiations in the name of the particular authority from whom it emanates. It is the letter of credence or visible warrant by which the envoy is recognized and without which he cannot enter upon his duties.

The Oxford definition just cited is a lexicographer's enumeration of permissible uses. Attempts at a scientific definition of diplomacy have never succeeded in gaining universal acceptance. For practical purposes that formulated by Carlos Calvo in the late 19th century may serve at this point. For Calvo, diplomacy is "the science of relations which exist between the various states, as they arise from their reciprocal interests, from the principles of international law and the provisions of treaties or conventions." The author reduced his own definition to an even more succinct form: "the science of relations or simply the art of negotiations." The essential object of diplomacy, according to Calvo, is "to assure the well-being of peoples and to maintain peace and harmony among them, while at the same time guaranteeing the security, tranquillity and dignity of each one of them."

Diplomacy is therefore the organ or channel of intercourse between the members of the international community. It is the ordered system by which governments enter into direct relations with each other, through the reciprocal exchange of formally accredited representatives. A product of long experience, diplomacy is an institution possessing its own principles and approved practices.

Ecclesiastical diplomacy can be fairly defined with almost the same terms as civil diplomacy. One principal difference is the fact that the relations are not between two states but between the State and a religious authority. The relationship is, therefore, not identical on both sides, though the techniques and outward forms may be the same. Unfortunately, efforts at defining ecclesiastical diplomacy have no more succeeded than efforts in the domain of purely secular diplomacy. Those who are best qualified and who have written treatises on the subject seem, in each case, to prefer their own phrasing. Msgr. Giobbio, long-time professor at the Pope's own diplomatic academy in Rome, defined papal or ecclesiastical diplomacy[2] as "the art of ordering, directing and following with full knowledge the relations between the Church and the political society." This definition is open to several criticisms. For example, it does not per se exclude the relations of the local or national hierarchy with their own government. Again, it does not exclude non-diplomatic, or unofficial, relations between the Holy See and the State. Yet these points are specially relevant in determining the essentially diplomatic character of Church-State representation.

A more detailed definition was formulated a few years after Giobbio by Pinchetti-Sanmarchi in his *Guida diplomatica ecclesiastica.*[3] Ecclesiastical diplomacy is "the science and art, based on the Apostolic Primacy and the consequent necessary relationship of the pontiff to the universal church, which is directed towards ordering the reciprocal rights and duties resulting from the coexistence of the church with the various states and which, while tending constantly to the advancement of the interests of the Holy See, at the same time promotes and preserves peaceful relations between the two powers." The author adds that if the mission of diplomacy in general is to promote peace among the nations, this mission is even more verifiable in the case of the Holy See, which seeks to promote peace not simply between the nations but between the Church and the various states.

This is admittedly an involved definition. More recently, in his own lectures at the Vatican's diplomatic academy Msgr. Paolo Savino[4] has defined papal diplomacy very briefly. It is

2 Giobbio, *Lezioni*, I, p. 9.
3 Pinchetti-Sanmarchi, *Guida*, I, pp. 299-300.
4 Savino, *Diplomazia ecclesiastica*, parte I, p. 10.

"the science and art of regulating, through official representatives, relations between the church and the states."

The use of the term "diplomacy" in papalist literature is just as varied and loose as it is in diplomacy in general. Rinieri's *La Diplomazia pontifica nel secolo XIX* is primarily a history of papal policy based on diplomatic dispatches. Giobbio's own *Lezioni di diplomazia* treats of the papal diplomatic missions only in the first volume. In the succeeding tomes of his published lectures under the same title he touches upon questions that really appertain to ecclesiastical public law and are, in fact, today treated in that special discipline. It is as though he were to write a textbook on international law and entitle it "Lectures on Diplomacy."

This present study does not treat of diplomacy in the loose meanings of (1) policy or (2) international law. There is therefore no intent here of outlining the course pursued by the Holy See in its relations with the many civil governments. Nor is this intended to be a study of international law. We do not touch here, for instance, the question of the privileges and immunities of diplomatic agents. On the other hand, the impact of diplomacy upon international law, and upon domestic law as well, is not to be denied. Hence in the coming chapters it will be necessary to examine the relationship between them.

We beg the reader not to look here for a study of ecclesiastical diplomacy as an art. This is best done by professional diplomats, writing from their own experience. Lastly, the reader should not expect to find in these pages a formal exposé of technical questions of form, procedure, and etiquette which are often linked with the art and science of diplomacy. These questions are treated in the "guides" to diplomatic practice, in the style of Martens and Satow, to whom the reader is referred. Where such matters of protocol as precedence are discussed in the present study, it is primarily because of the light they throw upon the Pope's standing in the diplomatic world.

For the purposes of this study, which is to explore Church-State relations, the term "papal (or Vatican) diplomacy" refers primarily to diplomacy as an institution. This is the system by which, through accredited public agents, the Holy See carries on stable, formal, and reciprocal intercourse with the states. It is the instrumentality by which the supreme authority of the Catholic Church communicates, within the framework of standard international practice, with the supreme authority of the states, in the transaction of current or special problems which arise on the part of either Church or State, for the resolution of which the common accord of the ultimate authority of both parties is required. This consensus may take the shape of treaties (concordats) or less formal understandings. The transaction of current business may involve the execution and interpretation of existing agreements, or the discussion of any matter which the two parties may deem worthy of taking up in the interest of good relations and joint advantage or for the welfare of the international community as a whole.

In short, by papal diplomacy is here meant the system of reciprocal permanent representation which the papacy has developed through the centuries to expedite through official channels any issue requiring negotiation or consultation with the several states. This representation includes not merely the envoys which the Pope accredits abroad (nuncios and internuncios), but also the envoys (ambassadors, ministers plenipotentiary, etc.) which the states accredit at the Vatican.

For various reasons to be explained, the method pursued in this examination of the institution so defined is primarily a posteriori. Before entering into theoretical considerations, this book establishes some material facts. These help to delineate, first of all, the external manifestations of present-day papal diplomacy. Next we make a survey of the origins of the diplomatic relations of some of the major non-Catholic countries with the papacy. This in turn invites a study of how and when the first envoys of the Catholic rulers began to assemble in Rome, with the corresponding inception of papal nunciatures abroad. The papal secretariat of state, which is the office to which the nuncios report, then comes under review. This is followed by a study of the papal congregations which comprise the administrative agencies of the Roman curia and perform a function analogous to the ministries or departments of civil governments. Only after these historical and organizational points have been set forth do we inquire into the high authority which stands behind this structure, namely, the Pope himself both as a temporal and as a spiritual sovereign. This question can and must be treated from three separate viewpoints: from the viewpoints, respectively, of the Church's canon law, of international law, and of domestic law. For, both civil and canon law operate here by their own autonomous principles, just as the diplomatic relations between two states must necessarily be viewed in part at least from the viewpoint of the respective independent legal systems. Our study closes with consideration of some supplementary questions concerning special issues, significant and important in themselves but not essential to a determination of the nature of papal diplomacy.

This work is essentially an essay of clarification. If there is a thesis it is, to use the words of Benedict XV, on December 6, 1915, to show that, even in our times, diplomatic representation is "the ordinary and particularly apt instrument" through which the Holy See is accustomed to carry on its negotiations with the foreign governments. Consistent with the inductive approach, in which we proceed from the concrete to the more theoretical, the initial emphasis in this study bears upon the simple facts of the problem area.

The case for such a method deserves to be developed for the benefit of those who, perhaps impatient with a mass of details, might have preferred a more theoretical approach. There are many advantages in approaching Vatican diplomacy from such a pragmatic point of departure. For one thing, diplomacy in general is itself the creation of experience and not the consequence of any preconceived theory. It grew up in response to certain exigencies. The form it takes was tested in fire. It existed as a technical organ of intercourse before theories and symbolic meanings began to attach themselves to it. The rulers of Europe adopted its precepts before it came to be integrated into a general system of law. Vatican diplomacy is no different in this respect. It grew up in its turn as a practical way for conducting the business of the universal Church in the existing state of international society. Even today it operates less on general principles than on a series of more or less abiding but basically practical norms whose real validity lies in their proved suitability for effectively resolving Church-State problems.

Furthermore, it is difficult to study in theoretical terms an object which is the only one of its kind. Confusion in abundance has already been generated by the efforts of writers to fit the papacy into preconceived patterns, instead of fitting the pattern to the reality. Vatican diplomacy does not fit snugly into the sometimes over-formalized categories found in textbooks on international law. It does not always match the criteria set up to judge ordinary diplomatic relations. As something unique, Vatican diplomacy should be expected to defy the rules, or what theorists have been too prone to think are the rules, of diplomacy. The best antidote to excessive speculative reasoning, in a subject which is so strongly pragmatic anyway, is to present it as it appears in reality rather than as a product of an ingenious theory.

Confusion and misunderstanding from yet other sources also dictate the inductive method. Our subject is obscured in an unusual manner by prepossessions in the minds of both scholars and laymen. For a long time the tendency has been strong on the part of governments and theorists to ignore the Pope's role in world affairs. Many factors have contributed to this attitude. Protestants, for obvious reasons, have anything but a natural sympathy for the idea of the Roman Pontiff entertaining official permanent relations with the heads of states. This is particularly true when the nation in question is Protestant in tradition. We see in coming chapters how Protestant objections for a long time prevented some European states from having diplomatic relations with the Holy See. In the late 19th century this instinctive Protestant reaction was seconded by the attitude of the anti-clericals whose objective was the elimination of the papacy from any role in public affairs. Finally, the secularization of international law and of public life generally is believed by many to outmode diplomatic intercourse between the governments and the head of a Church. To sum up, anti-Catholic sentiment, anti-clericalism, and the prevailing spirit of international law tended to the same effect, namely, to minimize Vatican diplomacy. This was done for the most part either by ignoring its existence or by interpreting the phenomenon in unreal terms.

The French constitutionalist Duguit alluded to this attitude that has for so long hindered a right evaluation of papal diplomacy. In his treatise on constitutional law (v, 461) he warned his contemporaries, after the First World War, against trying to ignore what he called "the Catholic fact." The statesmen who close their eyes to this reality, he said, commit a serious mistake and expose themselves to unpleasant surprises. Jurists and sociologists, he wrote, who do not perceive this are neglecting a fact of prime importance. This warning retains its validity today. A great many specialists, especially in the United States, are ill-prepared to understand the role of papal diplomacy. They have no theoretical framework or factual background in which to situate it. Too often, they are emotionally unready, as well, to pass a measured judgment upon it.

Distortions and misunderstandings do not arise only from the side of non-Catholics and the lay observer. Catholic writers, too, have tended in the past to stress some aspects of the world status of the papacy at the expense of others. For instance, much of the Catholic literature of the past century stressed beyond measure the temporal power of the Pope as the head of a state. This was natural in a period when the Roman question was a major preoccupation of the Holy See. Its effect, however, was to throw into a subordinate light the religious sovereignty. Our attitude here is to take at its face value the Lateran Treaty of 1929, which declared that the Roman question can be considered as "settled in an irrevocable manner." The Pope is, indeed, a temporal sovereign and by that title alone would be entitled to enter into diplomatic intercourse with the nations. Vatican diplomacy rests essentially, however, upon the spiritual sovereignty of the Holy See and not upon dominion over a few acres in the heart of Rome. The Pope's international position and his diplomatic standing derive from his religious authority. It is an error into which some Catholic writers fall too easily, though understandably, when they interpret Vatican diplomacy narrowly in terms of the temporal power.

Another source of confusion impeding full understanding of papal diplomacy is to make it excessively dependent upon the concordats which the papacy has with many states. Some readers may even be surprised at the relatively small place accorded here to this aspect of the international status of the Holy See. No doubt this is a subject of great importance, which has rightly absorbed the attention of canonists and lawyers. Nevertheless, the *jus legationis* should not be identified with the *jus foederis*. Vatican diplomacy is much older than the concordats and it embraces a wider field. Only since the past century have these conventions been regarded as binding contracts by either the canonists or the civil lawyers. The diplomacy of the papacy was not built to support the concordat system and does not depend upon it. Furthermore, there are many states having diplomatic relations with the Holy See which have no concordat and never anticipate having any. Finally, concordats are essentially legal instruments. But diplomacy is an extra-legal institution having its roots also in history, politics, religion, and the whole complex of human society. The diplomatic representation of the Pope demonstrates the international status of the Holy See in a manner independent of the concordats.

Our method here, therefore, is to treat papal diplomacy as a primary source, a social fact that speaks for itself. Theories and systems can depart from this abiding reality only at their own risk.

In reproaching others for distortions that have generated misleading conceptions of Vatican diplomacy, the author is not so hardy as to believe that he himself has etched a perfectly complete, balanced, and solid rationale of his subject. This book may perhaps succeed in laying bare some of the implicit laws of this remarkable centuries-old institution. In many respects, however, it is but a schematic outline by way of introduction. It will be the highest compensation for the author's efforts if others are provoked or inspired by these chapters to pick up where this hesitant beginning leaves off. This consolation will remain his even though those who come after him may perchance find much to correct in the glance afforded here at the long and fascinating history of papal diplomacy.

CHAPTER 1

PROFILE OF PAPAL DIPLOMACY TODAY

THE majority of states today maintain diplomatic relations with the papacy. Even many of those which do not entertain such official relations have at least in the past done so and their present absence is due to political situations that could alter in the future. In general, therefore, the right of the Holy See to take its place in the diplomatic life of the community of nations is fully recognized. As a concrete illustration of the extent of the Vatican's diplomacy may be instanced the mass renewal of credentials upon the accession to the pontificate of Pope John XXIII. In the New Year's audiences of 1959, 24 ambassadors, 10 ministers plenipotentiary, and 2 chargés d'affaires presented fresh credentials to the newly elected Pope. Since the relations between the Holy See and the states are reciprocal in most cases, for each representative who called upon the sovereign Pontiff there was a corresponding nuncio, internuncio, or chargé accredited at the seat of their own government.

A breakdown of the states represented at the Vatican reveals no political or religious homogeneity. It is noteworthy, first of all, that the list is not limited to what are traditionally termed "Catholic states." A significant number of the envoys at the Vatican represent countries which cannot be called Catholic in the remotest possible way. There is therefore no inherent confessional note in the fact of having diplomatic relations with the Holy See. Of itself, it is a purely diplomatic-political act. It is true that some Catholic states do tend to regard their formal relations with the head of the Catholic Church as a manifestation of their national and historic religious fealty to

Bibliographical Note: Four generally quoted studies of Vatican diplomacy are the works of Giobbio, Pinchetti-Sanmarchi, Wynen, and Savino. The standard "guides" to diplomatic practice include those by Bettanini, Charles de Martens, Nava, Pinheiro-Ferreira, and Satow. On general aspects of the diplomatic status of the Pope, see the following authors or editors cited in the Bibliography: Baumgarten, Benson, Brezzi, Eckhardt, Goyau, Charykov, Hollôs, Pernot, Pichon, von Lama, Sencourt, Sforza, Wallace, Williams, and Woodward. First-class sources, of course, are the memoirs of Consalvi, Pacca, Lambruschini, Ferrata, and Costantini, career papal diplomats, all but the last of whom became secretaries of state.

the sovereign Pontiff. Even these countries, however, do not imagine that to break diplomatic relations with the Pope is to go into religious schism. In fact, the record of the diplomatic relations of these countries with the Holy See is much more stormy and punctured with more frequent ruptures than is the case for the other states less intimately linked to the papacy by religious ties.

A second noteworthy fact about the group of governments that have taken the decision to exchange representatives with Rome is that only a small number of them have concordats with the papacy. A concordat is a formal treaty or agreement in legal form entered into between the Holy See and individual states for the purpose of defining the respective roles of the two parties in fields where conflict tends to arise. Usually such concordats close a long period of strained Church-State relations. In this case they can be compared with treaties of peace which lay down conditions of harmonious relationships. In other instances the concordats are the result of political divisions of old states. After the First World War, the new "succession states" of Eastern Europe lost little time in seeking explicit understandings with the Holy See in the form of concordats. Contrary to a widespread impression, however, the existence of diplomatic relations does not presuppose the existence of a concordat, either present or in prospect. In reality, the concordat states are in the minority in the present diplomatic corps at the Vatican.

The third and perhaps the most noteworthy feature of the group of states represented at the Vatican is that they include even those which at home officially espouse the principle of separation of Church and State. Manifestly, such states do not consider themselves inconsistent with their own principles when they maintain official agents at the court of a world religious leader. The constitutions of some separation countries are explicit on this point. Article 45 of the Portuguese constitution, for instance, requires the "regime of separation in relation to the Catholic Church" while in the same breath it calls for "diplomatic relations between the Holy See and Portugal, by means of reciprocal representation." But the classic example is France, which, though fiercely separationist, maintains a strong diplomatic mission at the Vatican at the same time that it permits the papal nuncio at Paris to act as the dean and spokesman of the diplomatic corps.

The separation issue plays hardly any role in the case of those few states which are not today represented in the Eternal City. Only in the United States is this considered a reason for not having relations. The overwhelmingly Protestant Scandinavian states of Norway, Sweden, and Denmark have union of Church and State. Canada, Australia, New Zealand, Burma, and Ceylon have no representative of their own, but their affairs, if any, are handled by the British minister to the Vatican. The whole bloc of Soviet-dominated states are conspicuous by their absence, but this has nothing to do with any objections on the score of separation. From time to time various Latin American states break off relations with the Holy See. But this has really little to do with separation. The long-standing estrangement of Mexico is a case in point. To judge from analogous cases in the past, even this stubborn conflict will someday be resolved harmoniously. When this happens, any separation provisions of the Mexican constitution will not stand in the way of a resumption of diplomatic relations.

A country-by-country breakdown in the above-mentioned three categories of states represented at the Vatican in the recent past shows the lack of any consistent pattern.

1. *Catholic states.* Taken in its broadest and loosest sense, this term can include any country which at least is considered as traditionally Catholic, regardless of its present legal or political relationship to the Catholic Church. The following states may be reckoned to fall under this broad term: Argentina, Austria, Belgium, Bolivia, Brazil, Chile, Colombia, Costa Rica, Cuba, Dominican Republic, Ecuador, El Salvador, France, Guatemala, Haiti, Honduras, Hungary, Ireland, Italy, Lithuania, Luxembourg, Monaco, Nicaragua, Panama, Paraguay, Peru, Philippines, Poland, Portugal, San Marino, Spain, Uruguay, and Venezuela. The Order of Malta should be added to this list.

The historical relationships of the above-mentioned states with the Holy See may account, at least in part, for the fact that they have had diplomatic relations with the Vatican. Such a consideration, however, plays no part in the case of many other states. These states can be considered as non-Catholic, that is, with no pronounced traditional tie to the Church: China, Ethiopia, the Federal Republic of Germany, Great Britain, India, Indonesia, Japan, Lebanon, Liberia, The Netherlands, Rumania, the United Arab Republic, and Yugoslavia. At this point should be mentioned Estonia and Latvia, whose absorption into the Soviet Union the Holy See has not recognized.

2. *Concordat states.* Under this classification can be included not only those states which have with the Holy See concordats, strictly speaking, but also those which have concluded less formal agreements such as a *modus vivendi,* or a convention. Some states have concordats or agreements applying to only a part of the territory. This is especially the case for European states having overseas possessions. In the category of concordat states thus broadly defined can be included: Austria, Dominican Republic, Colombia, Costa Rica, the Federal Republic of Germany, Haiti, Honduras; likewise, Nicaragua, Portugal, El Salvador, Spain, and Venezuela; Ecuador and Peru have each a *modus vivendi.* Belgium and France have partial concordats affecting the Congo and Alsace-Lorraine respectively. In Luxembourg the Napoleonic concordat of 1801 is theoretically in effect. Of those countries which do not at present have official relations with the Holy See, Poland, Latvia, Lithuania, and Estonia had concordats, Czechoslovakia a *modus vivendi,* and Rumania a convention.[1]

The rest of the governments represented diplomatically at the Vatican have no formal instruments of legal or quasi-legal force regulating Church-State problems. At the present time, thanks to the absence of the (mostly concordatory) states in East Europe, these form the majority in Rome.

3. *Separation states.* Separation of Church and State is evidently not a decisive factor. Only a minority of the countries now represented at the Vatican exercise at home any sort of union of Church and State, or any sort of preference of one religion over the other. Among the "non-separationist" countries may be cited, again taking the term in its broadest appli-

[1] For the list of agreements that governments have concluded with the Holy See, see Casoria, *Concordati;* Conci, *Chiesa e vari stati;* Perugini, *Concordata vigentia.*

cation: Argentina, Bolivia, Great Britain, Italy, Paraguay, Poland, and Spain. The Order of Malta belongs here also. Ireland goes only so far as to recognize that the Catholic religion is the religion of the majority of the people. Switzerland as a federal state is religiously neutral but it comprises cantons some of which have an official religion. Islam is the official religion, expressly or implicitly, in most of the countries of Muslim majorities.

The remainder are at least officially "separation" states. In many instances the constitutions declare this formally in one way or another; in others there is less explicit provision to this effect. Some of the former group include: Brazil, Chile, El Salvador, Guatemala, Honduras, Portugal, and Uruguay. Others have separation implicit in their institutions, such as Belgium, Luxembourg, and The Netherlands. The German Federal Republic can be considered a separation state. Japan abandoned Emperor worship after the Second World War. The Communist-controlled countries (during the brief time of their relations with the Vatican) claimed to follow the separation principle. In reality, they practiced all kinds of interference in internal Church affairs.

In the varied assortment of states represented at the Vatican in modern times, the only common denominator is that which is proper to diplomacy in general. The essential mission of these envoys is to defend and advance the interests of their nation in matters outside the jurisdiction of the country. These interests differ according to the contemporary situation, national history and traditions, and the political organization of the respective states. Sometimes they concern internal affairs. Sometimes they are linked with foreign policy. But in one case or the other they fall within the traditional scope of diplomacy. By negotiation and timely representations these envoys strive to obtain what their governments cannot achieve by the exercise of their own jurisdiction or unilateral action.

It is not surprising, therefore, that the governments look upon their relations with the Holy See as falling properly within the framework of their normal diplomatic activities. They assign their professional diplomats to this post. The staffs of the missions at the Vatican are not large.[2] There are no consuls, no commercial or military attachés. But apart from these and some other exceptions the post is considered by professionals as a genuine diplomatic duty which might well come their way in the course of their career. An appointment to this post is not considered by them a sinecure given to a political favorite. The high esteem of papal diplomacy by the professionals has long been a theme of writers. In his reflections on diplomacy, the Protestant Friedrich Kölle said in 1838 that "Rome was for a long time the best school of diplomacy, the post where apprentices should be sent at the beginning and ambassadors at the climax of their careers." Sentiments along these same lines are attributed to Bismarck.

The careers of some distinguished diplomats of non-Catholic countries might be instanced in support of this point. One of the earliest British representatives in Rome was Richard B. Lyons, who served as "semi-official agent" from 1853 to 1858. From Rome he went directly to Washington, where his brilliant work as British minister during the Civil War earned him the Paris embassy. As Lord Lyons he represented his country at that envied post for many years until his death. The man who succeeded him in Rome in 1858 was Odo Russell. In 1870 Russell left Rome for Berlin, where as Lord Ampthill he was British minister to the newly-founded German empire. His success there was often attributed by his colleagues in the diplomatic corps to his experience gained during his long years at the papal Court.

Exceptionally high, too, was the caliber of the Russian imperial envoys sent to the Vatican. The man who negotiated normal relations between the Czarist government and the Roman Pontiff after many years of tension was Alexander Isvolsky. From minister plenipotentiary to the Vatican he became foreign minister in St. Petersburg. He was Russian ambassador in Paris during World War I. His successor at the Vatican was Nicholas Charykov, himself also later acting foreign minister of the Czar. In his memoirs Charykov termed the Vatican di-

[2] The number of personnel on a mission affords no sure indication of its importance. Lord Strang develops this point with reference to the British Vatican legation, to which only three are assigned (*Foreign Office*, p. 108).

plomacy the "first in the world." The Czarist envoy at the Vatican named in 1906 was Sazonov, who had earlier served as secretary of the mission and who was foreign minister of the Czar at the outbreak of the First World War. Another diplomat sent on mission to the Holy See was Lobanov, chancellor and secretary of state in 1895. These were all career diplomats. Their tour of duty as envoys of the Imperial Russian Court to the head of the Catholic Church in Rome was part of their normal diplomatic work.

We have devoted our attention thus far to the Roman scene, where the civil powers have stationed their agents. The Pope, for his part, accredits his own representatives at the corresponding respective capitals in virtue of reciprocity. The papal envoys of ambassadorial rank are termed apostolic nuncios, or nuncios for short. The ranks of the respective missions usually match, but in Latin America all Vatican envoys are nuncios although not all the states concerned have embassy-rank missions in Rome. Those of rank corresponding to envoy extraordinary and minister plenipotentiary are called internuncios. The principle of reciprocity has a few exceptions, however. While there is a British legation to the Vatican, there has never been a nunciature or internunciature accredited to the Court of St. James in London. On the other hand, while the nunciature in Switzerland is one of the oldest, there is no permanent Swiss diplomatic mission to the Holy See.

The Vatican's diplomatic officers are today always ecclesiastics. The nuncio or internuncio is usually a titular bishop or archbishop,[3] while the personnel of the mission are usually monsignori. In a few rare instances bishops with residential sees are asked by the Holy See to serve the Pope. One of these was Bishop Aloisius J. Muench, of Fargo, N. D., who in 1951 became the first postwar nuncio in Germany.

The nuncio always enjoys the deanship of the diplomatic corps. That is, regardless of the date of presentation of his let-

[3] For further details on organization of the Vatican's diplomatic service, cf. Heston, "Papal Diplomacy." In May 1957 an American priest who was not in episcopal orders was appointed internuncio to Ethiopia. It was stated on this occasion that in accordance with a directive of the Pope only those papal diplomats would be made bishops or archbishops who would actually perform episcopal functions at their post.

ters of credence, the Pope's envoy acts as the senior member of the diplomatic body. He is their spokesman on ceremonial and other occasions, such as the New Year's reception by the chief of state, where the diplomats act in a body. This role is entirely honorary and carries no special powers. The nuncio's deanship is sometimes guaranteed by the terms of the concordat, such as in the German 1933 concordat. In most cases, however, the nuncio's deanship is recognized by the other diplomats as a long-standing custom confirmed by the Congress of Vienna. The deanship goes only to the nuncio and not to the internuncio. This subject is discussed at more length in Chapter 6.

By accrediting their career diplomats to the Vatican post, in the same conditions under which they send their regular envoys elsewhere in the national interest, the governments show they look upon the Holy See very much as they look upon any other state. That is to say, they treat with it as an equal. There are a number of authentic anecdotes current that illustrate in a particularly striking way how governments instinctively measure the papacy in terms of power, lacking any other means of expressing a reality that cannot be estimated in material terms. When Napoleon as First Consul sent François Cacault to Rome he was asked by the envoy what principle should determine his attitude toward the Pontiff. Napoleon told him, "Deal with the Pope as if he had two hundred thousand men at his command." The soldier mind calculated the moral influence of the Pope in military terms. A few years later, when the situation of the Church in Europe had improved somewhat, Artaud de Montor, to whom we owe this anecdote and who was Cacault's secretary in Rome, heard his chief recall Napoleon's injunction, this time mentioning the number of five hundred thousand. When twitted by his aide on this discrepancy, Cacault replied that in any case the position of the Pope had improved at least equivalently to the additional three hundred thousand men he had added to the papal "army."[4]

Stalin's famous question, "How many divisions has the Pope?" reflects this same line of thinking. This remark is vouched for

---

[4] Artaud de Montor, *Pie VII*, 1, c. vii, p. 117; c. xxiv, pp. 349-51.

by Winston Churchill in his memoirs.[5] The occasion was the visit of the French Foreign Minister Pierre Laval, who went to Moscow in 1935 for the purpose of discussing the extent of mutual assistance that could be mobilized in case of a Nazi attack. A Franco-Soviet mutual assistance pact was signed on May 2 of that year. When the military details had been discussed, Laval raised the question of religious persecution in the Soviet Union and the vigorous protests that were being raised by Pope Pius XI. It was at this point that the Kremlin chief drew on the previous subject for the theme of his now famous question. Churchill has commented: "Laval's answer was not reported to me; but he might certainly have mentioned a number of legions not always visible on parade."

Bismarck formulated the political principle underlying the imagery of military divisions in a more subtle and perhaps more accurate way. For him the intangibles were fully as important as the more material forces at the disposal of the State. "The *imponderabilia*," he used to say, "often have more influence in politics than gold or military force." The Iron Chancellor did not apply this maxim exclusively to the papacy but his experience with Rome in the course of the Kulturkampf helps to explain why it became such a favorite. The imponderables represented by the moral authority of the Holy See were an important factor in his ultimate decision to liquidate the Kulturkampf as a losing proposition.

The state of worldly humiliation of the papacy from 1870 to 1929 lent particular effect to the image of imponderable forces. There was something that could not be explained by any visible signs of power such as military prestige or wealth. The diplomatic corps accredited at the Vatican in 1870 not only was not dissolved but increased in number with the years. In 1890 there were 18 permanent missions at the Vatican. These had dropped to 14 on the eve of the First World War but rose again to 24 in 1921. At the time of the Lateran Treaty of 1929 there were 27 permanent diplomatic missions. Since most of these relations were on a reciprocal basis, as many papal diplomatic representatives were accredited at the corresponding foreign capitals.

[5] Winston Churchill, *Gathering Storm*, pp. 134-35.

The papacy is not entirely without at least apparent parallels in the diplomatic world. There are two other institutions which seem, at first sight, to occupy a position similar to that of the Holy See. These are the Order of Malta and the United Nations. Both of these institutions exercise the "right of legation" to a certain degree. Neither of them is a state and yet both are in many respects treated by the international community in ways analogous to the papacy. In reality the Holy See differs from these two instances in several important ways. An examination of the points of difference will prove illuminating.

The Order of Malta or, to give it its more complete title, "The Sovereign and Military Order of St. John of Jerusalem, of Rhodes and of Malta," once enjoyed sovereignty over the Island of Malta. In 1798 Napoleon seized the ancient seat of the Order on his way to Egypt. Subsequently the island fell into the temporary possession of England. The treaty of Amiens of 1802 provided for its restoration to the Order. This provision was not carried into effect and eventually the Congress of Vienna recognized this strategic island as a British possession. The Order went into exile and received hospitality from the Pope in Italy. It languished for many decades but the past half-century has witnessed a remarkable regeneration. The Order devotes its resources and energies today principally to the maintenance of charitable institutions throughout Europe. It also strives, in accordance with its traditions, to foster the ideals of chivalry. Full membership is limited to the nobility.

One of the most distinctive features of the Order is that it exchanges diplomatic representatives with various states. This has proved a valuable asset for the charitable work of the Order during time of war and world distress. The Order in recent years has accredited diplomatic representatives to the following: Argentina, Austria, Brazil, Chile, Colombia, Costa Rica, El Salvador, Ecuador, Haiti, Holy See, Italy, Lebanon, Nicaragua, Panama, Paraguay, Peru, Portugal, San Marino, and Spain. These agents had the rank of envoy extraordinary and minister plenipotentiary. At some times, the Order also had a representative in France who was legally authorized by the French Republic to bear the title of minister. But this representative did not present any letters of credence to the president. Reciprocity is limited for the Order. At its Roman head-quarters it receives the credentials of a smaller number of envoys. Most of these are at the same time accredited to the Holy See. Prior to the Second World War the Order had representatives in a number of East European countries. These relations were not usually reciprocal.

By what right does the Order of Malta carry on direct diplomatic intercourse with the states? Perhaps the simplest answer to this question is found in the Almanach de Gotha of 1860. This standard directory of the reigning houses of Europe and their courts said: "The Order of St. John of Jerusalem is always regarded as sovereign. Its diplomatic agents are recognized on the same basis as those of other sovereigns." In that year the Order had a representative at Vienna with the rank of envoy extraordinary and minister plenipotentiary who is listed as having presented his letters of credence in 1844. The Order also had chargés d'affaires in the Duchies of Parma and Modena but does not seem to have enjoyed any reciprocity. It therefore appears that the justification for the Court of Vienna to receive an envoy of the Order with the diplomatic rank of minister plenipotentiary was that the Grand Master of the Order enjoyed the rank of a sovereign prince, for purposes of protocol. Raoul Genêt states: "The Order is sovereign in this sense that its head is a sovereign European prince. By this title everyone before the Revolution, all the Powers, accorded to the Grand Master of the Order of Malta, Prince of the Holy Roman Empire, the precedence after the crowned heads."[6] Obviously, the question here is sovereignty in the ceremonial sense and not in the territorial sense. Despite the loss of the island the Master of the Order retained his standing as a prince of the Empire. The secularization decree which in 1803 took away from the bishops their position as princes of the Empire left the Master of the Order with his position in the Empire untouched.

The sovereignty of the Pope also, in its turn, is a product of the ceremonial hierarchy developed during the Middle Ages. The precedence of the Pope over the emperor and all crowned

6 Genêt, *Malte et son destin*, p. 104; Cansacchi, in *Diritto internazionale*, 1940; Breycha-Vauthier, in *Z.f.a.ö.R.V.*, 1956; Farran, in *International and Comparative Law Q.*, 1954; Guggenheim, *Traité*, II, p. 339, n. 2.

heads implied at the same time the precedence of papal nuncios over representatives of all other princes. Nevertheless, the diplomacy of the papacy even prior to 1929 was clearly distinguishable from that of the Order of Malta.

In the first place, those states which consented to have official relations with the Order appear to have done so essentially for reasons of form and tradition. It is not an accident that most of them are countries in which the old forms of the aristocracy are still in honor. Secondly, the function of an envoy of Malta was primarily ceremonial in nature. Even where questions of substance arose, these did not go beyond humanitarian and welfare activities. They had no political significance in the eyes of the State. Thirdly, the diplomacy of the Order rested on the fiction of the continuing territorial sovereignty which it once enjoyed over the Island of Malta, a sovereignty, be it added, which the Order in reality no longer claims against the present British masters.

On all these points the Holy See is in a distinctly more advantageous position. It might be noted that the international juridical personality of the Order is today seriously doubted, whereas the Holy See is generally acknowledged to enjoy personality independently of the State of Vatican City. Even today, the privileges and immunities of the Order's representatives appear to be based upon concessions of domestic law rather than a necessary consequence of the Order's international status. Such is not the case with the Holy See.

The United Nations is the other institution which has been compared with the Holy See. Some have contended that the world security organization enjoys the right of legation. This contention is based on the fact that most member governments maintain permanent official missions at the seat of the United Nations and usually confer upon the chiefs of such missions the diplomatic titles of ambassador or minister plenipotentiary. This practice began in the early days of the League of Nations. Indeed a certain logic would suggest that an international security organization can be properly assimilated to a state, since its responsibilities and mode of operation are so much similar to those of a state. This analogy was developed by some writers in the field of international law at considerable length.[7] It was argued that the League was empowered to enter into international agreements and was also able to impose military sanctions, two prerogatives that could be likened to the traditional sovereign rights of treaty-making and waging war. When the governments began to assign permanent representatives at Geneva with diplomatic titles it was quite natural for these writers to see in this the beginnings of a third sovereign prerogative, the right of legation.

The United Nations, organized at the San Francisco Conference in 1945, enjoys unquestioned international personality. Although such a status was not clearly set forth in the Charter, all doubt was removed on this point by an Advisory Opinion of the International Court of Justice of April 11, 1949. The Charter, for all that, remains vague on the exact extent of the privileges and immunities to be enjoyed by the organization. Among other things, there is no express mention of any right of legation.[8] Without going into a detailed contrast of the diplomacy of the United Nations with that of the Holy See, a few points suffice to indicate rather substantial differences. In the first place, it does not seem to be the present intention of the governments to deal with the United Nations in the same way that they deal with each other, i.e., through formal diplomatic relations. The United Nations is their own creature and an organ of their collective decisions rather than an entity entirely distinct from themselves. If the heads of permanent missions have diplomatic titles, this does not constitute them diplomatic agents in the usual meaning. These officials present no letters of credence to the United Nations; there is no qualified organ to receive such credentials. At most they communicate to the UN secretary general the fact of their appointment with such a rank. The organization is not consulted on these appointments and it cannot request their recall. That is to say, there is no *agréation* and there can be no question of being

[7] Schücking, in *Recueil des cours (La Haye)*, 1927, esp. pp. 366-67 Genêt, in *Rev. de dr. int. et de lég. comp.*, 1935.

[8] Kelsen, *Law*, p. 335; Oppenheim-Lauterpacht (*Int. Law*, par. 360) accords this right without qualification; Guggenheim (*op.cit.*, I, p. 489) says such international persons can acquire active and passive legation to the extent that they can pursue an independent foreign policy.

persona non grata to the United Nations. It is true that these representatives enjoy diplomatic privileges and immunities but this is in virtue of special agreements with the host country and not in virtue of their ambassadorial rank. Furthermore, these diplomatic "relations" are unilateral. Up to the present at least, the United Nations functionaries on service abroad do not carry diplomatic titles, including even the secretary general. In these respects the United Nations differs from the Holy See.

The diplomatic position of the papacy is therefore unique in international law. The states deal with the Holy See as they deal with one another and as they do not deal with any other non-state institution. They would continue to maintain this attitude even if the Pope were not the temporal ruler of the Vatican State. This was demonstrated from 1870 to 1929 when the Pope was not generally regarded as a temporal sovereign.

It must be admitted that the modern mind does not comprehend very easily the nature and function of Vatican diplomacy. For many people it seems a manifest anachronism that the Pope should exchange formal representatives with the civil powers, as though the modern world were some new version of a Holy Roman Empire on a vaster scale. It is inexplicable to them that the State in turn should support the anomaly by acquiescing in this system. For others it is a source of shock, even scandal, that the supreme head of the Roman Catholic Church should desire to maintain with the governments the same sort of relations that the temporal powers maintain among themselves. Vatican diplomacy, in their eyes, is a pure formality that should be discarded as outmoded; or, if not a formality then an abuse calculated to lead the Church to compromise its spiritual mission by involvement in the political affairs of nations.

From time to time even Catholics are heard to suggest the abolition of papal diplomacy and its replacement by other means of carrying on the business of the Church in any necessary relations with the princes of this world. The Church would gain, say these Catholics, if the apostolic nuncios were to renounce their privileges and prerogatives as diplomatic agents in the foreign capitals where they are stationed. By the same token, the governments would only be doing the Church a favor by closing their own embassies and legations at the Vatican. Any necessary business could be carried on through a secretary attached to the Italian diplomatic mission or by private persons enjoying the confidence of both parties.

That such objections are heard even in ecclesiastical circles has been acknowledged by no less an authority than a pro-secretary of state of His Holiness, Msgr. Giovanni B. Montini, later cardinal and archbishop of Milan. This Vatican official was the one with whom, for many years, the envoys of the states had their most intimate and most frequent contact, charged as he was (1944-1955) with the conduct of current diplomatic affairs. The then Monsignor Montini discussed the criticisms of Vatican diplomacy in a discourse delivered in Rome on April 25, 1951 on the occasion of the 250th anniversary of the founding of the Pontificia Accademia Ecclesiastica.[9] This is the institution which trains the young ecclesiastics destined for the papal diplomatic service. His audience included the members of the diplomatic corps accredited to the Holy See.

According to the pro-secretary of state the objections, which can perhaps be described rather as sources of perplexity, fall into three classes. These might be summarized in question form:

1. With the end of the temporal power in 1870, why did not the papacy discontinue its diplomacy, which had been so intimately linked with the papal states, especially in a day when different conceptions were beginning to prevail and Church affairs were more and more separated from political affairs?

2. Is not the very name of diplomacy, an art made notorious by Machiavelli, unsuited to the Church? Is not diplomacy in even its best sense too traditional and linked to etiquette and formalities belonging to the 17th and 18th centuries?

3. Is it right that the life and well-being of the Church should seem to rest upon such forms and such forces which savor too much of the merely human and not enough of the

[9] Savino, *Pontificia Accademia*, pp. xiii-xiv; Martini, in *Civiltà Cattolica*, 1951, pp. 372-73, citing Brezzi, *Diplomazia*, for one source of criticism. In 1890 Cardinal Manning, Archbishop of Westminster, himself an 1851 graduate of the same pontifical academy, wrote scathingly of the ". . . *tableaux vivants* of diplomatic relations, which were realities in the Middle Ages, but now, with nations estranged from the Faith, are a mere pageant, intensely provoking to a nation in schism and proud of its independence" (Leslie, *Manning*, p. 468). This is hardly a true portrait of Vatican diplomacy as it operates in the middle of the 20th century.

divine and supernatural? Can the prosperity of the Church depend upon having such links with the civil power, which is today for the most part secularist and a stranger to her, or even her enemy? Should not the Church rather put its hope upon its own interior strength and the means God himself has given her?

Monsignor Montini conceded in his discourse that these "objections" have a certain foundation of truth but that they do not translate the complete reality of the situation, and reveal, in fact, an inexact conception of diplomacy. This he defined as "the art of creating and maintaining international order, that is to say, peace." It is the art of establishing humane, rational, and juridical relations among the peoples of the world, not by means of force or the balancing of material interests but by means of open and responsible settlements. If this is the definition of diplomacy, said the Vatican official, then it is entirely appropriate to the Catholic Church, which strives to achieve true peace in the world. "If civil diplomacy," he commented, "tends to the unification of the world by making reason prevail over force, and to the growth of individual states in the harmonious concert of an ever larger international organization, it finds in ecclesiastical diplomacy almost a model towards which it can look with assurance; not so much because of any technical proficiency that the Church might display, or any success attending its efforts (for both of these elements may be lacking), as because of the ideal from which it takes its departure and towards which it tends, the universal brotherhood of men." The pro-secretary of state of His Holiness contended, in fact, that in a certain sense it would be a loss for diplomacy in general if, by some hypothesis, the Vatican's own diplomacy should disappear.

The hypothesis that the Vatican diplomacy may someday be dissolved cannot be excluded a priori, although it is evident that Monsignor Montini considered that prospect a remote one. There is nothing in either canon law or Catholic doctrine that imposes upon any Pontiff the obligation to carry on this institution. For one thing, diplomacy itself has existed as an institution for but a few centuries and the papacy was tardy rather than prompt in adapting its old methods to the new one.

The Pope will always, of course, have his own authorized representatives abroad as he has dispatched them to all corners of Christendom and beyond from time immemorial. It does not necessarily follow that these legates must per se also be members of the diplomatic corps in the capitals of the countries concerned. There is even less compulsion upon the Pope, doctrinally or canonically, to continue to receive a diplomatic corps accredited to himself at the Vatican. By mutual consent or even by unilateral decision of any state, the envoy of that country can manifestly be withdrawn from the Vatican without prejudice to Catholic principles.

It is said that the holy Pontiff, St. Pius X, once seriously considered the suppression of Vatican diplomacy. During his pontificate, in the decade just preceding the First World War, both France and Portugal ruptured relations with the Holy See, while Spain had entered a period of strained relations. As a result, of the four traditional "first-class nunciatures," three were closed or inoperative. With only Vienna left as the surviving pillar of the old diplomacy, would the whole structure come tumbling down? It was reported at that time that the Pope was just as well satisfied with having no nuncio in either Paris or Lisbon and resigned in advance to losing the one in Madrid, on the alleged grounds that the nunciatures were unnecessary for the conduct of the spiritual business of the Church and even harmful for her best interests. Those who gave credence to such reports did so in many cases out of admiration for the Pontiff, who upon his accession had been hailed as the "religious Pope" destined to follow a policy different from that of his predecessor, Leo XIII, who was considered a "political Pope." It was only logical that they should look upon the elimination of the nunciatures as a project that would come naturally to a "religious Pope." If the oldest papal nunciatures were thus permanently suppressed, the others would soon go by the board as a matter of course.

In reality, these rumors were highly tendentious, however complimentary to Pius X they seemed to be. At that stage of Church-State conflict in the three countries named, the renunciation of the nunciatures implied a capitulation all down the line on far more essential issues. For this reason it is safe to assume that the rumors had their source in the minds of those who differed with the Church and the Vatican on the basic issues and not on secondary and accidental questions such as the usefulness of the ancient nunciatures of Paris, Lisbon, and Madrid.[10]

Perhaps in the distant future it will no longer serve any useful purpose for governments to exchange envoys with the Holy See, or with each other, for that matter. Such a day is not yet in sight, although diplomacy has greatly changed in recent decades. As the chapters which follow will show, Vatican diplomacy is a quite spontaneous outgrowth of different factors operating over many decades and centuries. It was not the product of any one Pontiff and it is highly unlikely that any one Pontiff will ever eliminate it at one blow, however "religious" a Pope he may be. The existing system has succeeded in establishing a certain understanding and equilibrium between the Holy See and individual states. Its disappearance would induce confusion rather than clarity in the relations between the two parties.

[10] After his death, the August 21, 1914, issue of *Church Times* of London criticized St. Pius X for not having abandoned the "worldly methods of diplomacy" in favor of "evangelical directness."

PART ONE

THE ORIGINS OF MODERN DIPLOMATIC MISSIONS

CHAPTER 2

THE FRENCH REVOLUTION. PRUSSIA AND
THE PROTESTANT STATES

Papal diplomacy as we know it today can be said to date from the time when non-Catholic states, instead of only those states in communion with the Pope, began to be represented at the Roman Court. In his account of the pontificate of Pius VI (1775-1799) Pastor notes the growing number of Protestants who visited the Eternal City toward the end of the 18th century. What drew them were the art treasures to be found on the Italian peninsula as well as the relics of classical antiquity of ancient Rome. But the trend also coincided with the rising tide of toleration of that epoch. Among the most distinguished visitors of this period was King Gustavus III of Sweden, who passed many months in Italy for the sake of his health in 1783-1784. In the course of his frequent stays in Rome as the guest of the French minister plenipotentiary, Cardinal de Bernis, he was received in audience by Pope Pius VI. The ceremony was rendered less awkward for the masters of protocol by the fact that the Swedish monarch was travelling incognito. Several years earlier, in 1780, the Pontiff had thanked the king for his treatment of Catholics in Sweden. Gustavus issued an edict in favor of Catholics in 1781 that, by the standards of those times, was considered generous. Upon his departure, the king designated a member of the Piranesi family, who were well-known Roman artists, to be his agent in Rome for the purchase of antiques and other art objects. This agent, Francesco Piranesi, seems to have had only a minimal political function.

The number of Catholics in the Kingdom of Sweden was

Bibliographical Note: The Napoleonic era was as fateful for Germany as for France. This era has been fortunately well documented. In addition to the correspondence of Napoleon, there are also available the publications from the Prussian archives. The studies of Otto Meier are well-nigh classic in the field. Latreille's study of Napoleon and the Holy See benefits from long years of scholarly work. Cardinal Mathieu's work on the concordat of 1801 is essential, in conjunction with the memoirs of Cardinal Consalvi. For other authors not cited in the footnotes, the following may be usefully consulted for various aspects of papal relations with France and Germany: Bastgen, Friedberg, Göller, Hanus, Hegel, Kühn-Steinhausen, Prosch, and Van Duerm.

infinitesimal and the relations between King Gustavus and the Pope did not go much beyond the exchange of civil courtesies. It was another story for Prussia, Russia, and England, where large Catholic populations were subjects of non-Catholic princes. In 1783, as we shall see, the Pope sent Archbishop Archetti to St. Petersburg to negotiate with Empress Catherine II over the condition of Polish Catholics. Private negotiations were carried on by Monsignor Erskine with the ministers of George III in England. In May 1787 a representative of the new king of Prussia, Frederick William II, who succeeded Frederick II (the Great) at the latter's death in 1786, came to Rome to carry on negotiations on the vacant bishopric of Mainz.

In short, precedents were being broken by both the Protestant princes and the Court of Rome, even though the negotiations carried on were private and unavowed. Some of the Catholic powers, especially those who happened to be political rivals of the non-Catholic states, professed to be shocked at this traffic with heretics and schismatics on the part of the Pope. Prince Kaunitz, chancellor of Joseph II of Austria, for example, saw in certain of these negotiations a plot against the Hapsburgs. Writing to refute these suspicions, Cardinal Boncompagni, the secretary of state, declared to the nuncio Caprara in Vienna, under date of August 1, 1787, that Rome was not ashamed to admit the existence of these negotiations, which she considered legitimate and necessary: "We are negotiating, I do not deny it, with the King of Prussia, as well as with the Empress of Russia, with the King of England and with all the princes separated from us who have Catholic subjects, for the well-being of our brethren, for the good of religion and for the ecclesiastical affairs of the Roman See. . . ."[1] Nevertheless, the Court of Rome never consented to recognize, in Rome, the public and official standing of any representative of a Protestant prince. Nor did any Protestant prince formally admit an envoy of the Pope to take up residence in his capital.

Then came the French Revolution. Within a few years the Court of Rome found itself constrained to accept, for the first time, the credentials of an envoy whose government did not

[1] Montini, *La "Responsio,"* p. 92.

officially acknowledge the religious authority of the Roman Pontiffs.

The last representative of the Bourbons was Cardinal de Bernis. The envoy named to succeed him on March 29, 1791 was Louis Philippe de Ségur, but the designee was not acceptable to Rome, for he had taken the oath condemned by Pius VI. A few years later the National Convention dispatched François Cacault with a new mission. The instructions given to the envoy did not conceal that the new regime recognized no authority of the Pope in any matters, religious or civil, in France. In the eyes of the Convention, the Civil Constitution of the Clergy had eliminated any need to treat with the Roman Pontiff concerning the affairs of the Church in France. A *Mémoire servant d'instruction* given to Cacault on January 19, 1793, the eve of his departure for Rome, contained this declaration: "The French Republic recognizes the Pope only as a temporal sovereign. As the supreme head of a religion he has become a stranger to us. We no longer have a clergy. In the ministers of the various cults we recognize only citizens. . . ."[2] Cacault had only reached Florence when he was informed that he would be wasting his time going any farther, as the Pope would certainly not receive him.

It was not long, however, before the new regime, its revolutionary ardor somewhat cooled, saw the advantages of asserting claim to the not inconsiderable heritage of privileges that the old regime had enjoyed at Rome. As a result of more sober reflections in Paris, later negotiators were instructed to insist that the Holy See should consent to recognize in favor of the French Republic all the rights and privileges enjoyed by France previously, and in particular those concerning the ambassador in Rome.

The reason for this stipulation was explained in the instructions transmitted by the Directory to its representatives Garrau and Salicetti, dated October 3, 1796, before their departure for the negotiations which were to culminate at Tolentino. "The pontifical government [*reads the instruction*] has always refused to recognize formally the status of the diplomatic agents sent to it by the non-Catholic powers. The agents of Russia, Prussia and

---

[2] Hanotaux, *Recueil*, II, p. 534; du Teil, *Rome, Naples*, p. 22.

of Sweden at Rome are only recognized as charged with the interests of the Catholics living in those lands. The Pope receives their letters of credence only as 'residents' and nothing more. It was on account of this system that Ségur, ambassador of France, was not received. The Roman Pontiff, who knows well that we are no longer under his spiritual jurisdiction, would like perhaps to retaliate in his own fashion by treating us like the non-Catholic nations." As already stated, Ségur was rejected because he had taken the oath prescribed by the Civil Constitution of the Clergy. But the question of diplomatic protocol as practiced up to the moment at Rome no doubt also had its bearing in that refusal. Rome was not accustomed to receive with full diplomatic honors at its Court the envoys who were neither Catholics nor representatives of Catholic states. But the First Republic, while bold to declare its state of rebellion against the spiritual authority of the Popes, was willing to fight for the highly advantageous privileges enjoyed by France when the ruler was the "eldest son" of the Church. "Our prestige and our interests [*continued the instructions to Garrau and Salicetti*] compel us not to permit this assault upon the rights which have not ceased to belong to France. I order you, therefore, to stipulate formally in the treaty . . . that the representatives of the Republic in Rome, for political or commercial matters, will enjoy without restriction the titles, rights and prerogatives attached to their character and in the same way in which the ambassadors, ministers and consuls of France enjoyed these in the past."[3]

The desires of the Directory were accomplished, however illogical and unjustifiable they may have seemed to Rome. The Treaty of Tolentino of February 19, 1797 (1 Ventose, An V) shows how the French plenipotentiaries carried out their instructions. Article 5 of this treaty read: "The French Republic will continue to enjoy, as before the war, all the rights and prerogatives that France had at Rome, and it will be treated in everything as the major powers, particularly in regard to its ambassador or minister and its consuls and vice-consuls." What this meant was that for the first time, under the pressure of military force, Rome consented to receive at its Court, with

---

[3] Mater, *La République au conclave*, pp. 48-49.

the full honors of diplomatic agents, the envoys of a government that was not officially Catholic. Joseph Bonaparte, brother of the General, was named on May 6, 1797 minister plenipotentiary to the Holy See and, soon afterwards, ambassador. The Roman almanac *Notizie per l'anno 1798* gives the name of "Citizen Joseph Bonaparte" as "Ambassador of Paris." On May 31, 1797 the Marquis Camillo Massimi, a layman, was accredited as papal ambassador to the Directory. A new stage in the history of papal diplomacy was inaugurated.

In modern times, as Chapter 1 brought out, no distinction is made between the envoys of "Catholic states" and those representing Protestant or non-Christian governments, except on details of protocol. The Holy See does not limit its diplomatic relations to Catholic or Christian states. Even those countries whose traditions are alien to Catholicism or Christianity have found it quite compatible with their dignity to maintain official relations with the head of the Catholic Church in Rome. Today it is commonly accepted that no religious or theological connotations are necessarily involved in such exchanges.

This, we have seen, has not always been the case. Up until a century and a half ago, only Catholic envoys were permitted in Rome and the representatives, if any, of the Protestant princes were not accorded public recognition by the papal authorities. This attitude was mutual and no papal nuncio or other diplomatic agent was permitted to reside in the capital of a Protestant prince. The religious rupture of the Reformation implied a diplomatic rupture as well. If Rome would not recognize the representatives of what it continued to regard as its rebellious sons, those sons of the Reformation declined with equal vigor to go to Rome, where they would have to kiss the feet of the Pope.

An interesting testimony to the attitude of the Protestant princes of Germany is found in the warning given in 1728 to King Frederick William I of Prussia, by his minister of state Baron von Knyphausen. The Pope had, contrary to all precedent, addressed a letter to the king concerning a dispute over an ecclesiastical post in the realm. Consulted whether an answer should be made to this unexpected communication, the king's minister answered that such a thing had never been done before: "I must point out that there is no instance of the royal and electoral House of Brandenburg, from the Reformation to the present time, or of any Protestant King, Elector or Order of the Empire, having any correspondence with the Pope or wishing to have any, because no Protestant rulers, regarding him as the Anti-Christ, would have honored him with the title 'Most Holy Father,' or knowingly permit that he should exercise any papal jurisdiction in their lands."[4] The king himself, he added, exercised not only episcopal rights but papal ones as well. Frederick William annotated the recommendation in his own hand *"Gut FW."*

A similar attitude of systematic refusal to enter into any kind of communication with the Pope in Rome was expressed by a law of the reign of Queen Elizabeth. This enactment (5 *Eliz., cap. 1, sect.* 2) applied penalties provided by the Statute of *Praemunire* to any subject of the queen who should knowingly in his writings or other manner, directly or indirectly, attribute or imply any authority to the Pope in the affairs of the realm. This legislation, enacted in 1563, was interpreted rather strictly by the foreign office. Its language was so broad that for a long time the act was considered virtually to exclude any formal communication with the Roman Pontiff. It was thought impossible to write to the Pope without by that fact seeming to recognize the papal political or religious claims in England. This applied even more so to diplomatic relations.

Cardinal Consalvi himself tells us about the first Protestant minister to take his place in the diplomatic corps accredited to the Court of Rome. He was Baron William von Humboldt, of Prussia. "It was under Pius VII and at the time of my secretariat [*he wrote in his memoirs*] that a minister plenipotentiary of Prussia was first seen in Rome. This was Baron von Humboldt. Rome had never accepted the representatives of non-Catholic powers."[5] The French diplomat, Artaud de Montor, who has given us so many details about life in Rome, where he was secretary of the French embassy for many years, reported to his chiefs in Paris in May 1805, "We have just witnessed a new

---

[4] Lehmann, *Preussen, Erster Theil,* pp. 664-65.
[5] Consalvi, *Memorie* (ed. 1950), p. 184.

little minister slide in here without making any fuss."[6] The occasion was the reentry of Pius VII to Rome when it was discovered that in the ceremonies planned for the diplomatic corps the Prussian agent was to be included. Previously, reported Artaud de Montor, he had not been recognized publicly. The first indication of the new change occurred when Humboldt began to use stationery with the letterhead of "minister-resident."

Who took the initiative in this revolutionary departure? The opinion of the French secretary and therefore probably of the diplomatic corps generally seems to have been that it was the Prussian agent himself who thus forced an entry at last into the Roman Court. "The Secretary of State has thus far said nothing," he reported, adding, "The victory of M. von Humboldt is complete and we should not be surprised to find an English minister here before very long." On the other hand, the correspondence of Humboldt with his government at this period seems to show (or was meant to imply) that the step was made on the urgings of the cardinal secretary of state. On several occasions, he reported, Consalvi remarked to him that his letters-patent, or *ostensibile notificatorium*, was not accompanied also by a letter addressed to the Pontiff or to himself. "He added," wrote Humboldt, "that he thought that this formula came from the times when the Court of Rome was reluctant to recognize the agents of the Protestant courts; but that now, since this obstacle no longer existed, it seemed to him only right that the Protestant princes themselves should not make such a distinction." Consalvi said, according to Humboldt, that out of respect for His Majesty he had not wished to make any representations on this point, so insignificant in itself, but that he hoped the practice would not be imitated by the other courts at the present moment.[7]

Humboldt assured the secretary of state that the difference in form of the credentials had nothing to do with the difference of religion or anything that could be offensive to the Court of Rome but that he had no special information on the subject. It was only, he said, that those letters simply expressed the

6 Artaud de Montor, *Pie VII* (ed. 1836), II, p. 54.
7 Lehmann, *Preussen, Neunter Theil* (ed. Granier), pp. 37-38.

status that Berlin wished to attribute to its representative in Rome. What he meant was, of course, that the Protestant king of Prussia sought in this manner to avoid addressing a letter directly to the Pontiff.

Baron von Humboldt was evidently not personally averse to becoming the first Prussian diplomat at the papal Court. On March 9, 1805 he wrote to Prince Hardenberg, the Prussian chancellor, asking his approval for the use of the title "minister-resident." In the practice of that time, this was the lowest rank of full diplomatic agents. His chief approved the change but informed him that he needed no new credentials on the occasion. Within the year we find Humboldt advanced again in rank. He was named minister plenipotentiary by his government under date of April 10, 1806.[8] On this occasion, too, Berlin told him he needed no new letters of credence. Humboldt reported that he was presented in May.[9] Consalvi made no objections at this renewed lack of proper form. In any case, in the next month, June 1806, in a papal gesture of appeasement to Napoleon, he made way for Cardinal Casoni as secretary of state.

What had induced the leading Protestant power on the continent to abandon its former aloofness and enter into formal diplomatic relations with the head of the Catholic Church? And what had led the Roman Court to drop what Consalvi acknowledged was a long-standing refusal to recognize the agents of Protestant princes? The change was indeed a radical one for each party concerned. The almost surreptitious way in which both Berlin and Rome acted is sufficient indication that the move was one bound to shock traditionalists in both capitals.

[8] *Ibid.*, p. 511.

[9] That the absence of new letters of credence was deliberate on the part of Berlin is suggested by Humboldt's letter of May 12, following his accreditation: *"Auf diese Weise hoffe ich, dies Geschaeft meiner neuen Anerkennung mit nicht mehr Förmlichkeit vollendet zu haben, als E.K.M. mir dabei zu beobachten . . . anzubefehlten geruhten"* (*Ibid.*, p. 535).

The Roman almanac *Notizie per l'anno 1807 (Cracas)* lists Humboldt as "minister-resident" of Prussia and not as minister plenipotentiary. He was also listed as minister-resident for the Landgrave of Hesse. Since June 1803 he had represented at Rome the interests of the Prince of Orange and of Fulda, as well as the Landgrave of Hesse-Darmstadt. These had, about that time, come into possession of some of the secularized ecclesiastical principalities of the Holy Roman Empire. The same listing is repeated in *Cracas* for 1808.

According to Consalvi, the break in the former tradition really occurred earlier, in the case of the British consuls in the ports of the papal states. Before Pius VII not even the consuls of non-Catholic states were permitted to operate at Città Vecchia or Ancona. There had been a practice by which the papal government itself established two consuls in each of these ports, both of them its own subjects. The task of one consul was to represent the interests of ships from countries to the east, while that of the other was to represent ships of countries to the west. This curious division of competences had many inconveniences, not the least of which was that often enough the same consul had to represent the interests of rival ships at the same time. On the occasion of the occupation of Rome and Città Vecchia, records the cardinal, during the first revolution and the establishment of the Roman Republic in the time of Pius VI, the Neapolitans admitted at Città Vecchia some English consuls and those belonging to other nations. "Upon his return to possession of the Papal States," wrote Consalvi, "Pius VII found himself in the situation where the axiom applied, *turpius ejicitur quam non admittitur,* and it was in this manner that agents accredited by non-Catholic powers came to be recognized in the Patrimony of the Church."

What began by way of consuls, who were after all only commercial agents, was before long extended to formal diplomatic agents. The times were different, anyway, he observed: "In any case, the times had changed too much for the Pope to refuse to admit them without exposing religion to considerable harm in the schismatic and heretical countries. For this reason and for others about which I should not speak, it was thought opportune to soften the severity of the former procedure. The minister plenipotentiary of Prussia was, in consequence one of such representatives of non-Catholic powers permitted to function in Rome."[10]

From the viewpoint of Prussia, the assumption of formal relations with the Court of Rome was the natural culmination of more than half a century's experimentation. In 1728, as has been seen, Frederick William I of Prussia refrained from re-

[10] Consalvi, *Memorie* (ed. 1950), p. 185. Among the reasons that Consalvi could have mentioned was his desire not to complicate relations with England by expelling its consuls.

plying to a letter of the Pope on the grounds that such communication was unprecedented for a Protestant prince. However, political developments were shortly destined to put another face upon this situation. With the expansion of territory, large areas of predominantly Catholic population came under Prùssian sway. Frederick the Great won Silesia from Austria after three wars and in so doing he undertook certain obligations in regard to its predominantly Catholic population. The partition of Poland brought additional Catholics under the crown of Prussia. This was a very large bite for even an absolute ruler of that day to dispose of. Frederick realized he could not ignore the papacy.

In 1747 Frederick the Great decided to establish an agent in Rome, through whom he could carry on his business with the papal curia. The individual chosen for this role was an Italian nobleman, Giovanni Antonio Coltrolini, who had served the Catholic Elector of the Palatinate in the same capacity for many years. Coltrolini could not be given any public standing, yet he needed some sort of credentials which would enable him to carry on his work. We have evidence of Frederick's mind on this subject in a letter he wrote to his agent in Cologne who was arranging Coltrolini's coming functions:

"The only problem which now remains for carrying on this correspondence is the form to be given to the credentials Coltrolini will need at the Court of Rome. Since my religion and my status in regard to that Court do not permit me to follow the example of those princes in communion with the Pope and since I shall nevertheless be obliged to commission the said Chevalier in a way that will make him be accepted at Rome and put him in the position of being able to render me good service, you will please consult with the Count de Riario on this matter and draw up with him draft credentials that will be acceptable at Rome, which you will please send on to me."[11]

The formula which proved satisfactory to Frederick and his ministers constituted Coltrolini agent of the Prussian king in Rome. He was given letters-patent addressed "to those whom it concerned" (*omnibus has visuris*) and not to any person in particular, least of all the Pope. The letters-patent declared that

---

[11] Lehmann, *Preussen, Zweiter Theil*, pp. 669-70.

Frederick II wished that "entire faith" should be accorded "its bearer in everything that he will be authorized to propose or to represent on Our behalf."[12]

How justified were Frederick's precautions can be seen in the reaction that the news provoked in the Court of Vienna. The reports that the Prussian king had decided to station an agent in the Eternal City evoked mocking comments by his rivals to the effect that the Protestant prince was making his homage to the Pope of Rome. Stung to the quick, Frederick wrote promptly to his representative in Vienna under date of October 24, 1747. The new agent of Prussia was not, as Vienna mistakenly imagined, a diplomatic representative. Such a notion, he said, had never entered his mind. "Although I have authorized Chevalier Coltrolini, agent of his Highness, the Elector of the Palatinate, to assist my Catholic subjects in Rome, this has been without giving him any official standing on my part and without any letters of credence. . . . In any case, I consider it incompatible with my principles and with my situation in respect to this Court, to have a man there fully accredited and designated. Consequently such a thought has never come into my mind."[13]

The "special situation" of Frederick toward Rome was not simply that of the difference of religion but the fact that the Pope had never recognized that the kings of Prussia had the right to use the royal title or exercise prerogatives belonging only to kings. In 1701 the Elector of Brandenburg, Frederick III, assumed the title of king of Prussia, thus becoming King Frederick I. On April 16, 1701 Clement XI protested this action in communications to the emperor, to the king of France, and to other Christian sovereigns, alleging that no ruler could assume such a title without the consent of the Pope. He asked these sovereigns not to accord royal honors to the ruler of Prussia. But Emperor Leopold I had sanctioned this move beforehand and most sovereigns considered this sufficient to justify their recognizing the royal rank of the former elector. It was not until 1787 that Rome finally reconciled itself to the reality. In his memoirs Cardinal Pacca claims credit for having

12 *Ibid.*, pp. 684-85.
13 Lehmann, *Preussen, Dritter Theil*, p. 48.

persuaded the papal curia to yield on this point which had been a constant source of irritation to the Prussian king. Rome's change of mind was first indicated briefly but pointedly when the Roman almanac, *Cracas*, for that year carried the name of Prussia's ruler among the royal princes of Europe.

In 1783 an Italian priest, Matteo Ciofani, was given the post of Prussian agent upon the death of Coltrolini. When Rome finally decided to abandon its long-standing refusal to recognize the royal rank of the Prussian rulers, Ciofani received new credentials by which he was created not simply "agent" but "resident and agent at the Roman Court" (*residentem et negotiorum gestorem Nostrorum in aula Romana*). He was not, however, given letters of credence in the proper sense but only letters-patent in which the "Supreme Pontiff of the Roman Church and his ministers" were addressed in the third person and asked to "recognize and receive with benevolence the priest Ciofani as Our resident and agent." Prussia still shrank from addressing a letter directly to the Pope or to his secretary of state.[14]

The new credentials put the agent of Prussia in a slightly more definite official position, but he was not for all that recognized publicly in Rome in his official capacity. As the French Revolution was taking its course, Berlin began to think the time had come to be more directly represented in Rome. In 1798 it named the first Prussian subject as its resident, William von Uhden, who had lived several years in Italy as a student of art and had already previously assisted the aging Ciofani. Uhden's tenure was not very long. On May 25, 1802 Baron von Humboldt was named to the post of resident, arriving at his post on November 25 of that same year.

What brought Humboldt to Rome? The brother of Alexander Humboldt, the explorer and naturalist, William was a scholar in his own right, as his later career was to demonstrate. His own personal tastes attracted him powerfully to Rome, which at that period was profiting from the Romantic currents then being felt in Germany. But in naming a man of the quality

[14] *Ibid.,* p. 53. "*Rogamus quoque et requirimus hisce supremum ecclesiae Romanae pontificem, necnon ministros ejus, velint abbatum Ciofani tamquam residentem et negotiorum gestorem Nostrorum agnoscere et benevole admettere. . . .*"

of Humboldt, Berlin was showing that the Roman post had assumed an importance which it had not had when a simple Italian priest or Prussian art student sufficed. In recent years Prussia had become more and more preoccupied with questions of ecclesiastical policy. The Peace of Lunéville of February 9, 1801 had made some important territorial changes affecting Catholic populations. The reasons why Frederick II had an agent in Rome in the first place were ecclesiastical rather than political. Coltrolini's instructions dated Berlin, October 7, 1747, stated in part: "The ordinary object of your attention will be in general to watch for any intrigues which might arise at the Court of Rome against my interests and also to report on any complaints or other unpleasant insinuations that the Roman Catholic clergy in my provinces and particularly in Silesia might make against me. . . ."[15]

At the same time Coltrolini was to remember that the dignity of the king of Prussia did not allow him to accept any "decisions" of the Pope. Frederick was determined to do with his Catholic subjects as he saw fit but as a matter of practical prudence he saw positive value in having a representative in Rome even without official character. He could not entirely ignore the existence of the Pope's authority over his Catholic subjects. The stroke of the pen which had ceded him the former Austrian territories in Silesia could not wipe out centuries of papal authority there. Indeed the peace treaty imposed certain obligations of religious toleration upon the Protestant ruler. While pretending to exercise a policy of toleration, according to his lights, he named bishops as though they were his own officials and otherwise interfered in the internal organization of the Catholic Church. For its part Rome pretended to ignore the illegality of these procedures and frequently on its own accord sanctioned ex post facto the elections engineered by the heretic Frederick, without officially acknowledging his role in the affair.[16] And thus the anomaly arose of both king and

---

[15] *Ibid.*, pp. 19-22.

[16] "*Die römische Curie ignorierte officiel den von der preussischen Regierung auf die Besatzung der bischöflichen Stuhle ausgeübten Einflüsse. Sie betrachtete den ganzen Protestantismus als ein illegitimes Factum; so möchte sie auch nicht geradezu Recht protestantischer Fürsten anerkennen, welche sich auf die Kirche selbst bezogen, und welche diese doch nicht stark genug war, von sich abzuwehren*" (Friedberg, *Der Staat*, p. 45). On Frederick's policy in Silesia, see Hanus.

Pope ignoring each other officially and yet, in reality, constantly negotiating through an agent whose presence in Rome was unacknowledged publicly.

Humboldt's mission to Rome and his eventual assumption of formal diplomatic status was part of a general trend to normality in relations between Prussia and the Holy See. Yet, in that twilight of absolutism, Prussia had no intention of yielding an iota of the authority it considered itself to have in all Church matters, Protestant as well as Catholic. The long instructions issued to Humboldt under date of August 22, 1802[17] are in effect a treatise on relations between Church and State, as seen through Berlin's eyes. The post at Rome had its own particular role to play in this system.

In these instructions the Prussian king, Frederick William III, complimented himself on his tolerance. Although he personally recognized in the Pope only a "secular prince," he said, he allowed his Catholic subjects to reverence in the Pontiff the head of the Catholic Church. But this did not mean that he could abide any invasion of his sovereign prerogatives in religious matters within his realm, whether they concerned Catholics or Protestants. For one of the essential principles of his politico-ecclesiastical system was that papal decrees could not be published or take effect in Prussia without the royal knowledge and consent. In other words, the royal Placet must be given to each and every papal document before it could have validity.

In point nine of his instructions, Frederick William III tells Humboldt how this principle is to be applied in practice. Every communication destined for Rome by any Prussian subject, of whatever degree and whether lay or ecclesiastic, must first be brought to the *Cabinets-Ministerium*, where the document would be examined and then transmitted to Humboldt, if transmitted at all. The Prussian resident in Rome would, for his part, deliver directly to the same governmental agency all papal orders, decrees, enactments, and so forth, for the same kind of examination.

The point following indicated still more plainly the practical meaning of the royal Placet. It stated that the resident was to

17 Lehmann, *Preussen, Achter Theil* (ed. Granier), pp. 630-45.

report any instances in which any Prussian subject, of high or low degree, whether lay or ecclesiastic, should attempt to circumvent these provisions by going direct to Rome or to the resident, without first getting clearance from the government in Berlin. In other words, the Prussian system was that the Pope's religious authority could not operate normally in the country except to the extent that the government allowed it. Berlin set its own foreign ministry and ministry of worship, and its own resident in Rome, between the Prussian Catholics and the Pope. No distinction was made between matters purely of conscience and the broader, public expressions of the papal authority. In this way, while the authority of the Pope was not challenged, the effect of his decisions was conditioned upon governmental approval.

As will be seen in Chapter 9, this sort of policy was no new thing for Europe or for Prussia. Frederick II had exercised it before he ever had an agent in Rome. But the establishment of a permanent representative at the papal Court meant an extension and refinement of the system. It was rather to aid him in continuing this system that Frederick William III sent Humboldt to Rome. Contrary to some Protestant writers of a later epoch, the new move was no betrayal of Prussia's traditions. The learned Carl Mirbt, writing in 1899, exclaimed in anguish in recording this phase of Prussian-Roman relations: "The tradition of Frederick the Great betrayed! The agency for external (ecclesiastical) affairs has grown into a regular political legation—William von Humboldt the first Prussian minister to the Roman Court!"[18] Such an interpretation was a superficial one. The purpose of the Humboldt mission was to facilitate the preservation of the old royal Placet so dear to Frederick the Great.

That the supervision of intercourse between Rome and the faithful in Prussia was the heart of his mission at the papal Court was fully realized and heartily endorsed by Humboldt, if we can believe his own dispatches. Writing from Rome in 1805, he contrasted the Prussian system with the live-and-let-live policy of some other Protestant states which exercised no control whatever over the correspondence of what few Catholics

[18] Mirbt, *Preussische Gesandtschaft* (brochure).

existed within their boundaries. "Your Majesty's minister has always rightly considered the prohibition of all direct communications with the Court of Rome as the very foundation of the system that His Majesty has so wisely created for the relations of his Catholic subjects with the Court of Rome. And certainly, except with great inconvenience, we can follow only one of the two systems: either not to concern ourselves at all with these relations with Rome, which is the system followed by Denmark, Sweden, Saxony, and other lands, or to subject such intercourse completely and without limitation to the inspection of the government. No other point seems to me so important as this."[19]

One of the final points of the instruction tells Humboldt he is to keep Berlin informed on events in the Catholic Church generally, especially in Italy, the procedures of the Roman Court as a hierarchical power, and the activities and doings of the former members of the suppressed Jesuit Order. Clearly, Frederick William regarded the Roman mission as concerned principally with the Pope in his quality of religious authority. Yet at the beginning of these same instructions he declared, in point two, "We consider the Pope as a secular prince." The contradiction was apparent. It might have been continued as a concession to sentiment had not a major political event soon occurred to put it to the test. In February 1808 Rome was occupied by the French troops under General Miollis.

Humboldt had foreseen this development. As early as December 10, 1806, he was calling it "one of the most significant catastrophes of modern history, the stripping from the Holy See of every kind of sovereignty." For months before the blow fell the French troops under General Miollis, by their presence in the Eternal City, had taken away the Pope's de facto temporal power. The papal sovereignty had not yet been formally abolished by Napoleon's order but effective papal control was at an end. What then was the status of Baron William von Humboldt, whose own government considered the Pope only as a "secular prince"? Humboldt argued with his government that he should remain at his post as he in fact had dealings with the Pope for Church matters. As his biographer reports it: "Hum-

[19] Lehmann, *Preussen, Neunter Theil* (ed. Granier), p. 415.

boldt took as his point of departure that he was accredited to the Pope not as sovereign of the Papal States but as the head of the Catholic Church, a view that was not in harmony with the tenor of his instructions. Yet this view was approved by his government, which said that his diplomatic status in Rome had not been altered by the recent events, considering that his credentials appointed him only for ecclesiastical matters."[20] The reply of Berlin was dated April 1, 1808.

The occupants of Rome allowed the diplomatic corps accredited to the Pope to continue to function. Humboldt before very long, however, complained that his letters to Berlin were subject to censorship by the French. As early as April he wrote that the Pope as head of the Catholic Church could indeed still maintain a diplomatic corps around him but that the situation was very ambiguous when both the city and the State had gone into the de facto possession of another sovereign.

The situation was very like that which was to arise after the Italian soldiers of General Cadorna occupied Rome on September 20, 1870. In this case, however, there was to be a different outcome. Before long the Prussian plenipotentiary began to feel that his usefulness was coming to an end. On October 14, 1808 he left Rome "on vacation," having bade adieu to the Pope and leaving the conduct of Prussian affairs in the hands of a Roman prelate, an official of the Apostolic Camera. Humboldt was never to return to Rome. But in the six years of his mission, Rome and Berlin had come to learn to deal with each other face to face through normal diplomatic channels. The "heretic" in Berlin and the "anti-Christ" in Rome had entered into a new phase of their historic relationships.

The Napoleonic wars brought profound transformations in the situation of the Catholic Church in Germany. The medieval structure of the Church in Germany had been irrevocably shattered by the secularization. Reconstruction and reorganization of Church-State relations was the problem of the hour, felt just as keenly on the side of the Protestant and Catholic princes as on the side of the Holy See. The years immediately following the Congress of Vienna were characterized by unprecedented

[20] *Ibid.*, p. 615; Gebhardt, *Wilhelm von Humboldt*, I, p. 84.

{ 53 }

negotiations between the Protestant, as well as Catholic, rulers and the Court of Rome.

When Napoleon annexed the left bank of the Rhine to France he promised indemnification on the right bank at the expense of the Church possessions. Following the Treaty of Lunéville of February 9, 1801, an enactment of the Imperial Diet of Regensburg on February 25, 1803, known in history as the *Reichsdeputationshauptschluss*—ratified by the Empire on March 24 and by the Emperor Leopold himself on April 27— four prince-archbishoprics (Mainz, Trier, Cologne, and Salzburg) were secularized, along with eighteen bishoprics, as well as countless foundations, abbeys, and convents. Only the former prince-bishop of Mainz, Karl Theodor von Dalberg, a creature of Napoleon, retained any princely status. For him a special title and position was created.

The new masters of the secularized prince-bishoprics were in large part, though not entirely, Protestant. The incorporation of new territories radically changed the religious composition of those states. The old Grand Duchy of Württemberg had been completely Protestant. Its Catholic population was increased by the Paris treaty of July 20, 1802 and then by the decree of secularization. The new Catholic subjects of Württemberg had belonged to dioceses from all sides: Constance, Augsburg, Worms, Wurzburg, and even Speyer. This was a typical case, duplicated in the case of other Protestant rulers, such as those of Baden, Hesse-Kassel, Hesse-Darmstadt, Hanover, Nassau-Usingen, and Oldenburg. Prussia, as will be seen later on, was one of the states to profit the most from the secularization of ecclesiastical possessions.

A contemporary essay portrays on a broader canvas the new situation that the Court of Rome had to face in the aftermath of the Congress of Vienna. Its author is the rather original personality, Dominique de Pradt, once named by Napoleon to be Archbishop of Malines but whose canonical installation never took place. Pradt retired from public life after the fall of his protector and spent his remaining days writing political essays which had the distinction of being independent and informed, even if at the same time definitely individualistic. The author's discussion of the position of the papacy occurs in his two-volume *Du congrès de Vienne,* published in 1815:

"This court will find itself in a position that will oblige it to modify its ordinary practices. This arises from the nature of the changes that are taking place in more than one portion of Christendom. Catholic Poland is divided between two sovereigns, neither of whom is Catholic. Prussia's acquisitions on the Rhine have given it the subjects of the former ecclesiastical electors or princes. Belgium is ruled by a prince who is not of the same religion as the former sovereigns of this country. Yet the spiritual necessities of these provinces and the relations with Rome that are the consequence therefrom do not change like a new government or with one. It will be necessary to continue to have recourse to Rome. There will arise, therefore, between the Pope and the sovereigns relationships of a different nature from those that existed before. Consequently, the King of Prussia will no longer be considered at Rome as just the Marquis of Brandenburg. Holland will no longer be limited to a missionary status. The powerful sovereign of Russia, who has many millions of Catholic subjects, new and old, in Poland, can no longer be looked upon by the Pope as being nothing but the head of the Greek Church in Russia. The same holds for the Catholics of Ireland. These have become too numerous, too restless, too much supported by a part of England itself, not to have an importance that will give the English government occasion to deal often with Rome. The King of Württemberg is setting up dioceses and is founding universities for Catholics. The Grand Duke of Baden has come into possession of Catholic regions. Everything is then changed for the Court of Rome as regards its relations to a great many sovereigns who were complete strangers to it up to this time. This new situation is worthy of close observation and calls for close attention on the part of Rome, lest she offend those princes who have been brought up with ideas different from her own and who cannot but attach great importance to certain things that Rome herself is not in the habit of giving much weight to."[21]

The prognostications of Abbé de Pradt were fully verified in the aftermath. Even while Napoleon was at the height of his

[21] Pradt, *op.cit.,* 2 ed., II, pp. 156-58.

power it was realized that the secularization of the ecclesiastical domains in Germany had made necessary new negotiations with Rome. Proposals were already in the air in July 1805 for a concordat to be drafted in Paris for all Germany. In 1806 the foreign minister of Württemberg started discussions with Cardinal Della Genga, the nuncio at Regensburg. Later, in September 1807, the nuncio came in person to Stuttgart (the Swabians did not share Prussia's fear of nuncios), presented his credentials to the king, and proceeded to discuss the problem with the minister of cult and of justice. The negotiations were broken off abruptly, however, owing to Napoleon's objections.[22]

In 1817, with the death of Prince-Bishop von Dalberg, there occurred ipso facto vacancies in the sees of Constance and Worms, both situated in Württemberg. The succession presented a good many problems, not the least of which was that Rome refused to sanction the person elected by the Cathedral Chapter in Constance. The kingdom decided that it was useful to have a chargé d'affaires in Rome. Frederick Karl von Kölle, who already lived in the Eternal City, was named to this post and served from July 1817. Württemberg had previously had an unofficial agent in Rome, a certain Buonfiglioli whose credentials were withdrawn in 1808. Kölle served in Rome until 1833 and later published his reflections on papal diplomacy which were cited in Chapter 1.

Another kingdom had previously sent emissaries to Rome to negotiate on ecclesiastical questions. This was Hanover, whose prince regent appointed Baron von Ompteda and Court Councillor Leist to proceed to Rome for the purpose of negotiating a concordat. They were received by the Pope on May 3, 1817. This mission was to be successful in the end. The long negotiations terminated with the Bull of Circumscription *Impensa Romanorum Pontificum* of March 24, 1824.

But the most impressive delegation was that sent by a group of German states and principalities. In the spring of 1818 plenipotentiaries of the five Upper-Rhine states (Württemberg, Baden, Nassau, Hesse-Kassel, and Hesse-Darmstadt), along with

---

[22] Meier, *Römisch-deutschen Frage*, I, p. 258. The demands of Württemberg, typical of that age of Josephinism and Febronianism, included the Placet and surveillance of the bishops' correspondence with the Holy See. *Ibid.*, I, p. 269.

agents of Mecklenburg, Oldenburg, the ducal and grand-ducal Saxon states, the Prince of Waldeck, and the free cities of Bremen, Lübeck, and Frankfurt, met in the last-named city on the Main to plan for negotiations. A two-member mission empowered to discuss outstanding questions with the Pope was dispatched. One of the emissaries was Schmitz-Grollenberg, a Württemberg Catholic of Febronian tendencies; the other was Baron Türkheim, a Protestant of Baden. This delegation was received by the Pope on March 22, 1819, but it was not until after two years of discussions that even a partial agreement was reached, with the publication of the Bull of Pius VII, *Provida solersque* of August 16, 1821. This was followed by a supplementary Bull of April 11, 1827, *Ad dominici gregis custodiam.* Baden carried on its own negotiations independently of the other states through the mediation of the Austrian embassy in Rome, as it became dissatisfied with the progress made by the delegations sent in the name of the Frankfurt Congress.

The Netherlands, which then included Belgium, followed the trend of the times after the Congress of Vienna. In 1814 Johann Gotthard von Reinhold, a native of Aachen and a Protestant, had become the Netherlands "agent" in Rome. In 1826 Count de Visscher de Celles was sent with the rank of envoy to negotiate a concordat. His efforts proved successful only on June 18, 1827. In 1829 an internuncio was accredited to the Netherlands to assist in the execution of the agreement. However, difficulties arose and the concordat eventually was suspended.

The procession of official missions of the Protestant states succeeding each other in Rome after the Congress of Vienna definitely marked a new departure. It is true that only those of Prussia and the Netherlands were to assume a relatively permanent character, along with that of Bavaria, which, thanks to the secularization, had become the largest Catholic state in Germany. The other Protestant states maintained temporary missions at the papal Court as business required it. In endeavoring to explain the reasons why Protestant rulers found it useful and necessary to enter into this sort of transaction with the Pope, the learned Protestant scholar, Professor Carl Mirbt, who has already been cited, attributed it to the great political changes of the decades preceding. These transformations, he has written, had produced a disorder that was intolerable from the civil as well as the ecclesiastical point of view, at least as far as Prussia was concerned. It was necessary to eliminate the jurisdiction of foreign bishops from any part of Prussian territory and for this purpose a realignment of diocesan boundaries was a prerequisite. The seizure of the ecclesiastical property in the secularization also created, Mirbt pointed out, a moral obligation for the ruler to create new bishoprics. The negotiations with Rome were, finally, an act of prudence.[23] In fact, the Catholic and Protestant states which had profited by the secularization of 1803 could not have had a very easy conscience. The unseemly bargaining and bribery that went on in Paris, of which the chief beneficiary seems to have been Talleyrand, was not wiped out by the subsequent purely formal approval of the Holy Roman Emperor, in one of his last official acts. The German princes gained far more than they lost to the French in ceding their territories on the left bank of the Rhine. Prussia gained five times as much more, Bavaria seven times, and Württemberg four times, in pecuniary terms, according to one estimate. For the beneficiaries of this historic transaction a settlement with Rome on purely ecclesiastical problems resulting from the secularization was a small price to pay.

Reference has been made to the special gains of Prussia as a result of the secularization. After Napoleon's defeat and the second peace of Paris, it had regained also some of the left bank of the Rhine. It was master of the old prince-bishoprics of Paderborn, Muenster, and the Rhineland, as well as a part of the Grand Duchy of Warsaw (Posen). A state once exclusively Protestant, Prussia now had a population forty percent of which was Catholic. If Frederick II had found it necessary to negotiate with Rome, Frederick William III had even more compelling reasons to do likewise. In Paris in July 1815, following Waterloo and the occupation of the French capital, Prince von Hardenberg had already selected the man who was to succeed Hum-

23 Mirbt, *Preussische Gesandtschaft.* On the secularization in Germany see Edgar Alexander in *Church and Society* (ed. Moody), Part IV, "Church and Society in Germany," pp. 358-65, with bibl. Also Himly, *Histoire*, I, pp. 300-03, II, p. 90; Hertling, *History*, pp. 491-92. Partial text in Mirbt, *Quellen*, n. 560, p. 422.

boldt as Prussian minister plenipotentiary at the Court of Rome. The Prussian chancellor wrote on April 28, 1815 to Barthold Georg Niebuhr that he would be named Prussian envoy to go to Rome "in order to discuss with the Roman See the question of the organization of the Catholic Church in the Prussian state and to conclude an agreement."[24] It was not, however, until December 30, 1816 that the Prussian chancellor wrote to Cardinal Consalvi the following notification: "The King has decided to confer upon Niebuhr the rank of envoy extraordinary and minister plenipotentiary to give to His Holiness a proof of his highest esteem. I consider our relations as more solidly established than ever. The protection that His Majesty grants to his Catholic subjects, the attitude of the Holy Father and the broadminded conceptions that guide his venerable government mutually guarantee these good relations."[25]

Could such a letter have been written ten years earlier? This time there is no hesitation about addressing the Pope or his ministers directly or even in referring to Pius VII as "His Holiness" or as the "Holy Father." The new Prussian envoy found his position at the Roman Court far easier than had his precedent-breaking predecessor. Barthold Georg Niebuhr was no less a scholar than William von Humboldt and his assignment to Rome was congenial to his tastes, which were strongly in the classical tradition. His later career and writings demonstrated the use to which he put his many years' stay in the capital of classical antiquity.

Niebuhr arrived at his post in 1816 but it was four years before he received full powers from Berlin to negotiate with the secretary of state on the subject of a reorganization of the Church in Prussia. Meanwhile, however, he demonstrated the progress he was making with the Court of Rome by securing the right to have Protestant services in Rome and to maintain a Lutheran chaplain at the legation. In the course of his mission he conceived a warm friendship with Cardinal Consalvi, who reciprocated his regard. On July 16, 1821 the Bull of Circumscription, *De salute animarum*, redefined the boundaries of the dioceses

24 Meier, *Römisch-deutschen Frage*, II, p. 116.
25 Consalvi, *Mémoires* (ed. 1864), I, p. 94.

in Prussia, Prince von Hardenberg himself coming to Rome for the ceremony of signing.

Although Niebuhr was fully and formally accredited to the Pope in the normal way as minister plenipotentiary, this did not mean that Berlin had thrown all caution to the winds. The reestablishment of the Rome post after the Congress of Vienna provoked serious discussions in Berlin on points of principle and strategy. Some of the king's ministers declared against any kind of formal agreement with Rome, such as a concordat. Others warned of the danger that having an envoy in Rome might make reciprocity unavoidable. A memorandum dated September 8, 1814, prepared in the foreign office by Privy Councillor Carl Georg von Raumer, called for a representative at Rome but opposed a concordat. The choice of a representative to succeed Humboldt should be very carefully studied, said the councillor. Such an envoy should not be a Catholic prelate (such as Bishop Häffelin, who was minister plenipotentiary for Bavaria). He should not be a Catholic, nor even a too high-ranking Protestant. For the dispatch of an envoy too distinctly Protestant to Rome might provoke the reciprocal request on the part of Rome to send an equally too distinctly Catholic envoy to Berlin, i.e., a nuncio. This contingency Berlin sought at all costs to avoid.[26]

Niebuhr, essentially a savant, but not a mediocre diplomat, apparently fitted the description. His instructions were largely those given earlier to Humboldt. He was to observe and report on events. He was to be the intermediary, as before, for the business transpiring between the Prussian bishops and faithful on the one hand, and the Holy See on the other. This correspondence had to pass through the foreign ministry as well as through the minister in Rome. However, a benevolent exception was made in favor of the former prince-bishop of Paderborn, who was allowed to have unhindered and direct communication with the papal authorities.

In 1823 Niebuhr was succeeded by his secretary, Christian Karl Bunsen, as chargé d'affaires. In 1827 Bunsen became minister resident and served until 1838, when his usefulness came to an end at the height of the famous controversy over mixed mar-

26 Meier, *op.cit.*, II, 2, pp. 21f.

riages (the "Cologne Troubles"), which is discussed in Chapter 10.

The origins and background of the Netherlands mission have their own interest and significance. Mention has already been made of the early negotiations between the Netherlands and the Holy See, dating back as far as 1814. The revolt of 1830 leading to the formation of Belgium cost the Netherlands its southern provinces, with their predominantly Catholic population, and drastically altered the religious problem. Yet there remained a fair-sized Catholic minority in the Netherlands for whom a concordat already existed on paper. By 1848 a new policy of religious toleration was under way, a fact sufficiently proved when the Pope in 1853 restored the regular hierarchy by creating an archdiocese and four new dioceses in the country. In 1871, however, the Dutch legation at the Vatican was closed. Despite protests from the foreign minister, the Second Chamber voted on November 17 to cut off funds for the mission. The reasons given from the floor varied. Some said that the Pope had lost his temporal power and thus no reason remained for maintaining the legation. Another argument adduced was that of separation of Church and State. This was rather late in the day for such an argument and it was in any case challenged by the foreign minister, who testified, "Since I have been at the head of the department of foreign affairs I have had occasion to be convinced that even while strictly adhering to the principle of separation of church and state, the diplomatic intervention can have its usefulness in certain cases."[27] Despite the closing of the Vatican legation, the papal internuncio remained at The Hague. Consequently, diplomatic relations were never entirely interrupted.

Later developments present additional elements of interest. Diplomatic problems created by the outbreak of war in 1914 brought a Dutch envoy once again to the Vatican. The Netherlands was able to preserve neutrality but it was uncomfortably close to the scene of hostilities and menaced from day to day with the danger of being swept into the conflict. In addition, in a country with close economic, cultural, and other links with both Great Britain and Germany, an active policy of concil-

[27] Graham, *Rise*, p. 62.

iation was not only possible but imperative. After some exploratory inquiries the government came to the conclusion that its conciliatory role would be well served by close liaison with the Vatican through a Dutch envoy formally accredited to the Holy See on a "temporary and special mission."

The government's proposal when first outlined before the Second Chamber on May 19, 1915 met with opposition from some Protestant circles, as might have been expected in a country usually considered traditionally Protestant. Mass meetings of protest were held. Delegates of Protestant parties prepared to subject the plan to severe scrutiny. The debates in the Second Chamber opened on June 10, 1915 and the speech of Prime Minister Cort van der Linden adverted to the objections raised on religious grounds. In his opinion the objections drawn from the Protestant character of the nation were irrelevant to diplomatic action. Reminding his hearers in passing that Catholics, too, made up an important part of the population, the prime minister declared: "But even if we grant the Protestant character of the nation it is still difficult to imagine how this Protestant character could suffer from any diplomatic action initiated by the Government. I ask: did not our country have a Protestant character during all the time that we had not simply a temporary or special envoy, but a permanent minister to the Holy See? Does not our country have a Protestant character at this very moment when an agent of the Pope [*i.e., the internuncio*] is accredited to our Government?"

The papacy, he went on to say, was an important international power; few neutral centers were more important at that time than the political center of the Vatican. He pointed out the inadequacy of trying to carry out the aims of the Netherlands through some unofficial contacts. One of the deputies named Tydeman had asked why a commission of some sort would not suffice. To this the prime minister replied that the Netherlands was in no position, as a small power, to treat lightly the requirements of protocol: "The Dutch occupy a modest place in the ranks of the Powers and the Pope, whether one likes it or not, belongs to the great Powers, even though he is not a temporal sovereign. Mr. Tydeman can be assured that the doors of the Vatican do not open so easily as he imagines. The commission envisaged by him would be no doubt admitted as far as the antechamber of the Pope, but he can be sure that it will not learn anything important for the mission it has before it."

The government's proposal was adopted by a vote of 82-10. The Upper Chamber approved the measure a few days later and on July 10, 1915 I. H. W. Regout, a Catholic, was named envoy extraordinary on "temporary and special mission to the Holy See."[28]

The legation was discontinued in 1924 when the opposition chose this item on the budget as the issue on which to precipitate a cabinet crisis. As a result, the Netherlands found itself again without representation at the Vatican in 1940 at the moment of the Nazi invasion. Once again the government moved to make up the deficiency, made more acute by the fact that, this time, the Netherlands was not only a belligerent but entirely occupied by the enemy. The decision was made in London by the cabinet in exile.

We are fortunate in having a concise and authoritative summary of the specific reasons why diplomatic relations were resumed with the Vatican. In his report on the government's policy in London, the wartime prime minister, Professor P. S. Gerbrandy adduces five considerations that entered into the decision:

"1. During the war the Holy See became an observation post of great diplomatic interest.

"2. A number of Holland's allies had normal diplomatic relations with the Vatican and a similarity of policy in this respect was desirable.

"3. Because of the strengthening of diplomatic relations in 1942 between the Holy See and Japan it was desirable that representatives of the Allies whose interests were threatened by Japan should not be lacking at the Vatican.

"4. It was essential to consider the attitude of the Roman Catholic clergy in the Netherlands and of the Netherlands Catholic population who had been very disappointed at the time that the Vatican legation had been closed.

"5. Besides, after a careful survey, it was found that the

[28] These details of the 1915 debate are drawn chiefly from Goulmy, *Nederland naar het Vatikan*, where the parliamentary proceedings are given *in extenso*.

Protestant section of the Netherlands population would rather see relations with the Vatican restored than not."[29]

It is not hard to read between the lines of this enumeration. The Dutch envoy was to be an observer and listener, but he was to be more than that. He was to join hands with the other representatives of the Allies in presenting the common cause to the Holy See. He was also to counter the diplomatic maneuvers of the Japanese representative whose country had overrun the Dutch East Indies (now the Republic of Indonesia). Then, too, home-front morale and solidarity were matters of special importance for a government-in-exile. The gesture was bound to stimulate the confidence of the Dutch Catholics under Nazi occupation in their absent queen and ministers. The same consideration applied to the Protestants, who at that moment were working in close cooperation with the Catholics in the resistance.

The first appointee to the Vatican was not actually able to reach his post until after the Allied occupation of Rome had made it possible for him to make the journey. After the war, the legation was continued on a permanent basis.

[29] Gerbrandy, *Eenige Hoofpunten,* pp. 115-16; Vandenbosch, *Dutch Foreign Policy,* Ch. x, pp. 140-48.

CHAPTER 3

IMPERIAL RUSSIA. GREAT BRITAIN.

THE NEW WORLD.

THE UNITED STATES (1848-1868).

THE NON-CHRISTIAN WORLD

THE partition of Poland by the rulers of Austria, Prussia, and Russia, two of whom were not in communion with the papacy, produced serious problems for the Church. Some of these have already been touched upon in the discussion of Prussian policy. The Catholics in that part of Poland taken over by Czarist Russia were in a more serious predicament than those in Prussian Poland. Rome found it necessary to dispatch at least three special missions to St. Petersburg. In time the question arose of a permanent Russian envoy in Rome but nothing materialized until after the Congress of Vienna. The history of these relations in the 19th century comprises some of the most stormy chapters of papal diplomacy.

Catherine II took inspiration from Frederick II, with the difference that she and her successors carried out the Prussian method to its worst logical consequences. Czarist Russia was still operating on the Prussian system until the very last days of its existence, at the end of World War I. Like Berlin, St. Petersburg strove to prevent the coming of a nuncio to its own capital while welcoming the chance to station its own envoy at Rome. Roman envoys on special mission managed to get to St. Petersburg during the reigns of Catherine II, Paul I, and Alexander I (Archetti mission, 1783; Litta mission, 1797-1799; Arezzo mission, 1802-1806). But these were temporary missions (Consalvi termed these emissaries "extraordinary nuncios") and the Czar-

Bibliographical Note: For background material on the wide scope of events sketched in barest outlines in this chapter, the reader may find it useful to consult the following authors whose works are cited in the Bibliography: *Russia*: Adamow, Charykov, Rouët de Journel, Winter; *New World*: Accioly, Artaud de Montor (*Léon XII*); Bannon-Dunne, Coleman, Holloran, Leturia, Mecham, Paz, Vargas Ugarte, Shiels, Watters, Wright; *Great Britain*: Albion, Ashley, Broderick, Ellis, Gasquet, Lucas, Newton, O'Reilly, Randall, Gaselee, Miko, Meier, Temperley; *United States*: Hamilton, Farrell, Goss, Marraro.

ist regime refused to recognize them officially as "nuncios" and regarded them only as "ambassadors."

In his treatise on international law written for Russian students, F. F. Martens says: "The Empress had adopted as an invariable rule to consider her new Catholic subjects as being in a situation exactly equivalent to that of her other subjects and as subject exclusively to Russian jurisdiction in their rights and duties. All the proposals of the Court of Rome in view of a concordat were rejected by Catherine."[1] Catherine's immediate successors, Paul I and Alexander I, continued this policy. In 1808, Archbishop Count de Bernis was named nuncio at St. Petersburg. The nuncio-designate, however, got no farther than Vienna. Alexander I refused to receive him under that title. On this occasion the Russian point of view was expressed in a diplomatic dispatch sent by the chancellor of the Empire, Count Rumiantzev, to Prince Kurakin, his envoy at Vienna. "Your Excellency knows," wrote the chancellor, "that the Court of St. Petersburg has always striven to eliminate as much as possible the influence of the papal Court and it has not consented to recognize, in Russia, any other supremacy than that of the Emperor in everything touching the Roman Catholic religion."

"In virtue of this principle," Rumiantzev went on, "the envoys of His Holiness have always been received here in the character of ambassadors and not, as in the Catholic Courts, in the character of nuncios. It follows that the request of Count de Bernis cannot be taken into consideration for it conflicts with the above-mentioned principle."[2] It should be noted that the Russian system did not exclude the maintenance of a regularly accredited minister in Rome—in other words, outside Russian territory. Neither the Russian nor the Prussian absolutist rulers sought to deny that the Pope had any authority over their own subjects. They sought means rather to keep this influence under control by various legislative and procedural means. This feature of 18th century constitutional law is further discussed in Chapters 9 and 10.

In 1802 rumors arose in St. Petersburg that Alexander I

[1] Martens, F. F., *Traité de droit international*, II, p. 162.
[2] Martens, F. F., *Recueil des traités et conventions conclus par la Russie*, III, pp. 22-23. (Not to be confused, though it often is, with the *Recueil de traités* edited by G. F. Martens.)

would establish an imperial legation in Rome. Soon after there arrived in Rome not one but two Russian representatives, an Italian, Count Cassini, and a Russian subject named Lizakevitz. They did not have any formal diplomatic rank. Indeed, according to Consalvi, they caused only trouble for the papal government, chiefly because of their efforts to prevent the secretary of state from laying his hands upon a Russian naturalized citizen of French birth, whose arrest Napoleon was demanding. In the following year, St. Petersburg went so far as to designate officially a full diplomatic representative in the person of one Buturlin, who was not a Catholic. The appointee never took up his duties in Rome. Only on February 1, 1817, after the Congress of Vienna, did the first Russian diplomat present his letters of credence as envoy extraordinary and minister plenipotentiary of the Czar. He was Andrei J. Italinsky, who had served as the Russian envoy at Constantinople.

What was Italinsky's mission? The operating principle of Russian policy, as we have already seen, was to prevent the papacy from exercising its religious authority directly upon Church affairs in Poland. This did not mean that Russia was indifferent to the Pope—far from it. The Poles were proving difficult to govern and numerous revolts were destined to punctuate the history of Russian domination. St. Petersburg could not ignore Rome, even though it would not permit a nuncio at the Russian capital. In sending Italinsky as a formal diplomatic officer, the Russian cabinet had its own interests very definitely in mind. Like Prussia, Russia sought to remove papal influence as far away as possible by stationing its own man in Rome itself, where all necessary negotiations could be conducted. The instructions that were given to Italinsky by his government in this respect reflect the influence of Prussia. The Russian plenipotentiary was instructed to state on behalf of the Czarist government that the relations between the faithful and the Pope could "never take place except through the regular and uniform intermediary of the government." The Czar would not accept a nuncio but only a representative exercising "functions strictly appertaining to His Holiness' temporal government."

The instructions, dated January 15, 1817, reveal how the

Russian government envisioned the procedure by which the Roman Pontiff would exercise his religious authority over Russian subjects: "The procedure goes by stages. The Primate of the Catholic Church in Russia addresses himself, whenever the intervention of the Pope's authority is called for, to the Ministry of Foreign Denominations. This office, after having presented the subject of the proposition to His Imperial Highness, informs the Ministry of Foreign Affairs, which, conformably to higher orders, dispatches the petitions to the Russian envoy to His Holiness, instructing him to carry on the necessary negotiations on the subject. The replies, decisions or explanations, of whatever nature, emanating from the See of Rome, should follow the same channels."[3] In short, the Russian minister in Rome was to be the channel by which all ecclesiastical business was to be conducted. If the government saw fit to do so, it could, so to speak, strangle in its cradle any initiative of the Pope which displeased it.

The Holy See never accepted the legitimacy of these attempts to maintain an embargo upon direct relations with the faithful in Russia. In its reply to this exposé of the Russian attitude, it declared that "Jesus Christ had constituted the Church free and independent of every other power." In the end, Rome had to acquiesce in this procedure, as a matter of practical necessity. But, on the principle, Rome and St. Petersburg never saw eye to eye.

The convention of 1847 under Nicholas I was a revolutionary departure in Russian policy. It did not, unfortunately, have a long life, and its application was a source of constant complaints. The concordat became inoperative in November 1866. A diplomatic break became inevitable after the Russian chargé d'affaires Meyendorf, on the occasion of an audience in December 1865 with Pius IX, blamed the Pontiff for the Polish insurrection of 1863-1864. He was unceremoniously ordered out of the Pope's presence.

Rapprochement between Russia and the Holy See began again when in 1878 Leo XIII wrote to Alexander II announcing his accession. Significantly, the Czar replied. In 1883 there took place the coronation of Alexander III. The future Cardinal

---

[3] Boudou, *Saint-Siège*, I, p. 85; Pierling, *La Russie*, v, p. 388.

Vannutelli represented the Pope at this occasion. The end of Bismarck's Kulturkampf provided additional encouragement for a reconciliation. Negotiations carried on in Vienna between the nuncio and Russian envoys at the Hapsburg Court proceeded so well that they were transferred to Rome in 1888, at which time a semi-official Russian agent was appointed. The imminent restoration of formal diplomatic relations was foreshadowed in 1893 with the appointment of Alexander Isvolsky as semi-official agent of Imperial Russia. In the following year he became envoy extraordinary and minister plenipotentiary. The relations thus reestablished after such a long time and with such pains continued until the Russian Revolution of 1917. The relations between Rome and St. Petersburg were never very easy, especially in questions relating to Russian Poland.

ENGLAND AND THE HOLY SEE

The state of relations between England and the papacy at the end of the 18th century can be judged from an episode that took place in 1793, after Great Britain had joined the war against the French. In the course of blockading the port of Toulon in the Mediterranean, Admiral Hood found himself obliged to replenish his supplies of food and water in ports of the papal states and to enter into negotiations with the Roman government for that purpose. This act, though of a purely civil nature, was unprecedented. It soon caused those responsible to worry that they had violated the law of Queen Elizabeth and perhaps even incurred the penalities of *praemunire*.

Writing on October 3, 1793 to Sir John Coxe Hippisley, Edmund Burke scoffed at the scruples of his friend. Hippisley, an Englishman living in Rome, had been a prime actor in negotiating the purchase of supplies from the papal government and had promoted closer relations with Rome. "Nobody can be so very squeamish," wrote Burke, "as to refuse Benefits (nothing else will ever be offered by His Holiness) because they come from the Pope." The writer went on to enunciate the pragmatic outlook which, in his opinion, should dictate England's dealings with Rome in the existing circumstances, making an ironic allusion to some aspects of Catholicism which loomed large in the thinking of many of his countrymen:

"He would be an Admiral of wonderful Theological Talents, but not of quite such splendid Military Qualities, who should scruple the receipt of those Indulgences called *Munitions de Guerre et de Bouche* from a Prince Prelate that believes in Purgatory. I should not think a great deal better of a statesman at home, who from a disposition to Polemick Divinity, was so indifferently qualified for the conduct of any other kind of Warfare."

The English statesman thought that the circumstances did indeed call for "more distinct and avowed political connections" with the reigning Pontiff, Pius VI. If this were declined, he wrote Hippisley, the bigotry would be on England's part and not on that of His Holiness. "Some mischief had happened," he commented, "and much good has, I am convinced, been prevented by our unnatural alienation. If the present state of the World has not taught us better things, our errour is very much our fault."[4]

Even if the law had not been violated by the purchase of papal grain for His Majesty's Navy, the situation was not ripe for the assumption of formal diplomatic relations and Burke's recommendations in that sense were a long time waiting acceptance. It was a hundred years after the Congress of Vienna before Great Britain finally established a permanent mission accredited to the Pope. The intervening years were a long story of subterfuges and evasions as the great world empire of Great Britain sought to close its eyes to the existence of the Pope even as a secular ruler. As one English historian of Britain's relations with Rome, H. A. Smith, has written, "For internal and domestic reasons dating from the sixteenth century the government of Great Britain was forced into the false position of pretending to ignore a European state which in fact existed."[5]

There is extant in the foreign office archives of the Public Record Office a survey of British-papal correspondence which fully substantiates the aforementioned curious record of evasions and subterfuges. Signed by the foreign office archivist,

---

[4] Burke, *Correspondence*, pp. 63-64.
[5] Smith, H. A., in *The Law Quarterly Review*, 1932.

L. Hertslett, under date of July 16, 1846, it is in printed form, marked "private and confidential" and bearing the title, "Memorandum respecting the Relations of Great Britain with the See of Rome."[6] There is a supplementary handwritten report carrying the record up to 1875, signed by E. Hertslett, under date of February 5, 1881.

The foreign office résumé shows that as early as April 1, 1814, before he had resumed possession of the papal states which had been in principle restored to him, Pius VII wrote to the prince regent, soliciting England's support in the task of assuming full control. The Pontiff expressed his desire of seeing an English "resident" in Rome and also stated his hope of being able to send a "minister" to London. Three other letters were written by Pius VII to the regent in 1814. None of these appears to have been answered. The first communication of which there is record is a note from Lord Castlereagh to Cardinal Consalvi on July 9, 1814. This letter contained a draft treaty for the abolition of the slave trade that the British foreign secretary had proposed at Paris. The note earnestly requested assurances that the influence of His Holiness would be actively exerted on the Catholic nations of the continent to awaken them to a sense of the enormity of traffic in human beings and to procure, if possible, the early and complete abolition of the slave trade. No reply to this communication from Cardinal Consalvi is extant. The papal secretary of state was then a visitor in London, where he had a friendly welcome, regardless of the law of Queen Elizabeth.

The first instance of a formal letter sent directly to the Pope by the prince regent was on December 4, 1815 in replying to the Pontiff's expression of thanks for help in the restoration

---

[6] *Public Record Office. General Correspondence. Italy. F.O. 45/661.* One bid for diplomatic relations by Cardinal Consalvi to Castlereagh, dated May 17, 1817, depicts the situation of the non-Catholic courts at that time in Rome: "*Que le Saint-Père tâchera toujours de son côté de témoigner aux yeux du public, dans toutes les manières les plus solennelles, son dévouement à Son Altesse Royale et à la Nation Anglaise; et qu'il ne peut renoncer à l'espoir que l'Angleterre, voyant que la Russie, la Prusse, et autres Puissances non-Catholiques, ne trouvent point de difficulté à avoir à Rome leurs Représentants et Ministres Plénipoten-tiares, pourra trouver les moyens dans sa bienveillance pour le Gouvernement Romain d'en faire autant; en donnant par là à Sa Sainteté une satisfaction à laquelle Elle ne saurait mettre un plus grand prix, celle de posséder un Ministre anglais dans sa capitale*" (*ibid.*).

of works of art. Several communications subsequently passed
between the Pope and the king on subjects connected with the
situation of papal subjects, on the state of the Church in the
Ionian islands and Canada and Malta. On these occasions
Cardinal Consalvi frequently raised the question of an exchange
of representatives. There was no evidence that the law of Queen
Elizabeth was being thought of.

But when Pius VII died in 1823 and the election of Leo XII
was announced by a letter sent to the king on September 28,
1823 worries began to put in an appearance. The secretary,
Mr. Canning, sought the advice of the attorney and solicitor
general as to whether it was lawful to answer such a communication. The law officers replied that they thought any answer
to those letters might in fact involve a violation of *Statute 5
Eliz. cap. 1, sect. 2.* Consulted upon this opinion by Canning,
Lord Chancellor Eldon thought that the construction of the
law was probably correct, even though it might be doubted
that effect would be given to the law at that point. Canning
found it possible, however, at least to reply to Cardinal Somaglia, the new secretary of state, "as one individual to another,"
while pointing out that the laws of the country prevented him
from replying officially.

A new phase of Anglo-Roman relations arrived when an
attaché at the British mission at Florence, Mr. Aubin, was
ordered by Lord Palmerston on August 22, 1832 to take up
residence in Rome and to report to his chief in Florence anything that might be of interest. This order followed by two
days receipt of another answer of the law officers that it would
be permissible to accredit a diplomatic agent to the Court of
Rome. No reasons for the reversal were given. From 1832 until
the death of Aubin in May 1844 communication between
London and Rome was carried on through this agent. Aubin
enjoyed the status of semi-official representative of Great
Britain. The position of Mr. Aubin was further solidified by
an opinion of Sir John Campbell, solicitor general, who informed Lord Palmerston on April 24, 1833 that he thought a
minister might be safely sent to Rome, accredited in the manner
proposed by the foreign office, but that he must be careful not
to bring home with him any bulls or relics; otherwise, he might

incur the penalities of *praemunire* or be guilty of high treason.

Although the intent of these inquiries was obviously to clear the ground for the dispatch of a fully accredited diplomat, this step was not taken. In September 1844 a Mr. Petre succeeded Aubin. Richard B. Lyons took over this post in 1853, to be succeeded by Odo Russell in 1858. The last "semi-official" agent in Rome was Clarke Jervoise, who served from 1870 to 1874. In that year Clarke Jervoise was notified by the Earl of Derby that his mission was terminated and that the files of his office (which consisted of six cases) were to be turned over to the British minister to the Quirinal, who had transferred from Florence in 1871. This did not, however, entirely close the history of Anglo-papal relations prior to World War I. On August 8, 1889, Sir J. Lintorn A. Simmons was given full powers to go to the Vatican to settle problems arising over religious affairs in Malta. The object of the mission, said Lord Salisbury's instructions, was "to consider questions affecting the internal government of that dependency in respect to which it is necessary to enter into communication with the highest ecclesiastical authorities in Rome."[7] He was given the rank of envoy extraordinary and minister plenipotentiary.

It is legitimate to conclude from the survey of Mr. Hertslett that the British government seriously thought for a long time about entering into formal diplomatic relations with the Pope. It had even reached a point where the law officers had approved a formula for credentials of a diplomatic agent accredited to the Holy See. In the years immediately following the Congress of Vienna in 1815 the matters of common concern were principally of a temporal and political nature. Later on, however, religious matters began to assume the major proportion, especially as the temporal domains of the papacy began to diminish in both size and importance.

The 1846 memorandum of the archivist of the foreign office, Mr. L. Hertslett, was drawn up at a time when the issue of formal diplomatic relations was being revived. Just what the immediate preoccupation of the government was might be judged from Hertslett's own account:

"In October 1844, in consequence of a protest of certain

---

[7] *Tablet,* May 31, 1890.

Roman Catholic prelates in Ireland against the operation of the Act of Parliament which had been recently passed for the more effectual application of charitable donations and bequests in that country, Mr. Petre was directed to communicate to the Government at Rome such explanations as to the real character and object of that Act and the intentions of Her Majesty's Government as would, it was thought, induce the Papal Government to pause before deciding upon the *ex parte* statements which in a spirit of factious and political hostility were advanced against this measure.

"It was stated to Petre that the British Government were desirous of securing the cooperation of the Roman Catholic Hierarchy in carrying the Act into execution; and that the explanations which he was instructed to give to the Court of Rome were given in the full confidence that the influence of that Court, so far as it could be made available, would be exerted to further the cause of religious concord and good government."

When, shortly afterward, some of the Catholic bishops had in fact expressed their acceptance of the Charitable Donations and Bequests Act, Petre was instructed to thank the Pope for his salutary influence on that occasion. London was increasingly aware of the part that the Pope's own authority could have in resolving its own political difficulties in the government of Ireland. However, this same influence was not forthcoming as desired on behalf of another Act of Parliament, for the founding of university colleges in Ireland. On November 25, 1845 Petre was again told by his government that there was every confidence, to use Hertslett's paraphrase, "that in any step which the Court of Rome might think it necessary to take with reference to these proceedings, that Court would be anxious and careful to support the cause of good government, and would discountenance every attempt made by factious parties to render abortive, measures which had been adopted solely with a view to the benefit of Her Majesty's Irish subjects."

However, the Pope's views on the new law, which set up an educational system contrary to the Church's policies, did not correspond to the hopes of the government. A decree of the Congregation of the Propaganda of October 9, 1847 expressed

Rome's desires to have in Ireland university colleges like those recently established in Louvain and not the kind proposed by Parliament. The British government was sorely disappointed at this action, which made its own plan virtually unrealizable. Bishop Wiseman, who had long favored more close and formal relations with the Pope, took the occasion to argue that it was the absence of regular and official contact with Rome that had led to this decision contrary to the views and interests of London. If the English government thought that the Pope was ill-informed on the real situation in Ireland, it had only to send its own fully qualified representative and to receive the Pope's own envoy in turn.

We learn of Wiseman's position from the memoirs of Lord Greville, who reports under date of December 7, 1847:

"A few days ago I met Dr. Wiseman and had much talk with him about Rome and the Pope's recent rescript about the colleges in Ireland. He said it was all owing to there being no English Ambassador at Rome, and no representation of the moderate Irish clergy; Irish ecclesiastical affairs were managed by MacHale, through Franzoni, head of the Propaganda, and Father Ventura, who has the Pope's ear, and he strongly advised that Murray and his party should send an agent to Rome, and that Lord Minto should communicate with Father Ventura, who is an able and good man, deeply interested in Irish affairs and anxious for British connections. . . . I am going to speak to Lord John Russell about these things, and to try and persuade him to send Normanby as Ambassador to Rome."[8]

Lord Russell had in fact already ordered a bill drawn up explicitly to authorize diplomatic relations with the Holy See. Although the law officers on several occasions had declared they thought such relations were permissible, it is evident that the prime minister did not want to leave any doubts and consequently sought to have a formal bill passed authorizing the move. In 1848 such a bill was proposed and eventually passed, with the title, "An Act enabling Her Majesty to establish and maintain diplomatic relations with the Court of Rome." In the course of debate, however, an amendment was adopted that virtually rendered the authorization useless. As passed on

[8] Greville, *Memoirs*, III, pp. 108-09.

September 4 (*11 et 12 Victoria, c. 108*) the Act included this proviso: "That it shall not be lawful for Her Majesty, her heirs or successors, to receive at the Court of London, as ambassador, envoy extraordinary, minister plenipotentiary, or other diplomatic agent accredited by the Sovereign of the Roman States, any person who shall be in holy orders of the Church of Rome, or a Jesuit, or a member of any religious order, community or society of the Church of Rome, bound by monastic or religious vows."

The amendment prohibiting the receiving of ecclesiastics in London as envoys of the Pope would have been unacceptable at Rome, as the invariable practice had been to send only ecclesiastics on such missions abroad. But, above all, the attitude of hostility manifested by the amendment was not one calculated to inspire the confidence necessary for the success of a diplomatic mission. A leader in the *Tablet* of September 9 scoffed at the generosity and toleration that the Act's supporters claimed for it. "Certainly," it commented, "this is a new way of conciliating princes: to begin diplomatic relations by a wilful insult and an act of deliberate hate to the very class of which the Pontiff is the head." The *Tablet* had its own reasons for denouncing the Act, with or without amendments. Its editors saw in the move an effort by the government to use the Pope's influence for its own purposes. A mass rally organized in London by Catholics, mostly Irish, denounced the plan to send a British envoy to Rome. One speaker quoted Lord Russell as having told a visitor: "We have tried to govern Ireland by coercion and have failed; we have tried to govern it by conciliation, and have failed also. No other means are now open to us except those we are resolved on using, namely, to govern Ireland through Rome." Whether or not the prime minister ever uttered such words, there is no doubt that they fairly depicted the state of mind of the government. The Act remained a dead-letter and was repealed on July 12, 1875 (*38 et 39 Victoria, c. 66*).

The outbreak of general war in Europe in 1914 created an entirely new situation. In December of that year Great Britain at last decided to end its self-imposed aloofness. For among the weak links in the political defenses of the Triple Entente, the Vatican was one of the most conspicuous. The Central Powers out-represented the Allies in number and quality of their diplomatic missions. Imperial Russia, although represented at the papal Court, was at the nadir of influence on account of Czarist religious policy in Russian Poland. France had, of course, broken off relations in 1904. All through the war it had an unofficial representative in the Eternal City but this person's influence was necessarily reduced. Belgium alone could be counted on to circumvent the maneuvers of the Central Powers, unless Great Britain moved in to fill the breach.

The election and coronation of Pope Benedict XV gave London the occasion to mend the situation in the Eternal City. Pope St. Pius X died on August 20, 1914, within three weeks after the declaration of war. The British government sent Sir Henry Howard, member of a distinguished English Catholic family, to present the congratulations of His Majesty to the new Pope. But Sir Henry had more than a merely ceremonial mission to perform. He was given the task of laying before the Pontiff "the motives which compelled His Majesty's Government, after exhausting every effort in their power to preserve the peace of Europe, to intervene in the present war, and of informing him of their attitude towards the various questions that arise therefrom." The instructions issued to Sir Henry by Sir Edward Grey, dated December 16, 1914, recalled that in the recent months the government had exerted itself to present the case of the Allied Powers to the unbiased judgment of neutral governments and their public opinion by the circulation of diplomatic documents. Such a procedure had not been possible in the case of the "high authorities of the Roman Catholic Church," owing to the want of a representative of His Majesty at the Vatican. "You will therefore, in presenting your letters of credence to His Holiness and offering him the cordial congratulations of His Majesty the King on the occasion of his election, intimate to him that His Majesty's Government are anxious to put themselves into direct communication with him for the purpose of demonstrating the motives which have governed their attitude since the first moment that the normal relations between the Great Powers of Europe began to be disturbed, and of establishing that His Majesty's Government used every effort to maintain the peace of Europe which His Holiness' venerated predecessor had so much at heart. You will also be in a position to give His Holiness from time to time exact information of the events which have already occurred and may occur during the period of your mission."[9]

The British envoy established himself in Rome as envoy extraordinary and minister plenipotentiary "on special mission." During the war Sir Henry was replaced by the Count de Salis, also a Catholic.

While Great Britain had many other reasons for diplomatic relations with the Holy see, the imperious necessities of war finally broke through the centuries-long tradition. The Pope was an important neutral who could not be ignored. Though he had no military or material forces to affect the tide of battle one way or the other, his moral authority could well tip the balance in a struggle where the imponderables could be decisive. Britain had nothing to lose and much to gain by sending Sir Henry Howard to Rome in 1914. The "special mission" was made a regular one after the war. Announcing the government's decision on November 11, 1920, Lloyd George stated, "I think the general opinion is that it is in the interest of the country that the British envoy should remain."[10]

[9] Issued as a Command Paper, *Despatch to Sir Henry Howard containing Instructions respecting his Mission to the Vatican, presented to Both Houses of Parliament by Command of His Majesty, January 1915. (Cd. 7736).* Miscellaneous. No. 1 (1915).

[10] British-Vatican relations are not reciprocal, since there is no nunciature in London. The reason for this is not entirely the opposition of the foreign office. Cardinal Manning has left on record his vigorous antipathy to the coming of a nuncio. In his mind it would serve to import strange and unwelcome Latin traditions. A nuncio would be useless and even harmful to the Church in England. Purcell, *Manning*, II, pp. 742-43; Leslie, *Manning*, pp. 463-71. One of the Latin traditions which Cardinal Manning thought inapropos in Anglo-Saxon countries was the inclination to adopt coercive measures against non-conformists. He considered this a relic of an era that was past. In a note left for his successor, dated July 6, 1890, he wrote: "But if Catholics were a majority, would they proceed to oppress those who forsake or oppose the Catholic Faith or Church? I think not. The medieval or dynastic period long maintained itself by coercion. Heresy and schism were political crimes punished by the public coercive law. This has been swept away by multiplied heresies and schisms, making coercion odious and morally impossible. So far as we can see, the new world will never be mathematically Catholic; nor will the Public law ever again be applied to enforce belief by coercion, or to maintain it when once the religion of the majority is in power. This policy has been tried and found wanting" (Leslie, *op.cit.*, ed. 1921, p. 467).

THE NEW WORLD

The revolt of the Spanish and Portuguese colonies in the New World (1811-1822) had for one consequence the extension of papal diplomatic activity to the young states that arose there. It was natural that the new governments, all of them officially Catholic, should have sought direct relations with the Holy See and natural that Rome should welcome such relations. There were a vast number of ecclesiastical matters that required communication and negotiation between Rome and the young republics. The new regimes considered themselves the heirs of all the rather extensive rights of the *Patronato real* previously enjoyed by the kings of Spain in the New World in Church matters, such as the right of episcopal presentation. But there was, from the first, a more paramount consideration and that was to get the Holy See to recognize the new governments. This proved to be a long and painful process.

It was many decades before Madrid was able to reconcile itself to the loss of its rich overseas domains. During that period its influence was strong enough in Rome to hold off papal recognition of these new states. The Spanish government also sought to deter the other European states from such recognition. It was in 1823 that England recognized the independence of the Latin American states, an act celebrated in Canning's boast in the Commons, "I resolved that, if France had Spain, it should not be Spain with the Indies. I called the New World into existence to redress the balance of the Old." Unfortunately for the Holy See, analogous action toward Spain's ex-colonies did not become possible for yet many years to come. A better situation prevailed for the former possessions of Portugal. King John VI of Portugal recognized Brazil's independence in 1821. This action facilitated the appointment of a nuncio in 1829 (internuncio in 1840), this date therefore marking the beginning of diplomatic relations between the New World and the Holy See. However, the exchange was not immediately reciprocated. *Notizie* for 1834 records the presence of a Brazilian representative in Rome with the rank of chargé d'affaires. This is the first time a Brazilian envoy is noted.

The first indication in *Notizie* of an envoy from Spanish

America at Rome is in 1836, when a chargé d'affaires represented New Granada. This was Ignacio de Tejada, who had
come to Rome in 1824 bearing the credentials of minister
plenipotentiary. He was not received until recognition in 1835.
In 1836 Gaetano Baluffi went to New Granada as "internuncio
and apostolic delegate." In 1837 *Notizie* for the first time gives
the name of a representative of Mexico, with the rank of envoy
extraordinary and minister plenipotentiary. The Holy See
recognized Mexico in December 1836. A representative of
Mexico, Canon Pablo Francisco Vásquez, had left for Europe
in 1825 with credentials as minister plenipotentiary to the
court of Rome. Failing, however, to get advance assurance of
welcome, he did not go to Rome. It was not until 1830, and only
after he had resigned his commission as minister, that Canon
Vásquez was able to see Pius VIII about the problem of the
vacant sees in Mexico. He was only partially successful. Except
for the time of Emperor Maximilian (1864), the Holy See has
never had a permanent diplomatic mission in Mexico.

New Granada, or as it is now known, Colombia, was the
first of the Spanish colonies to revolt, and Spain found it harder
to admit defeat in this case than in that of any of the other lost
provinces. In the Conclave of 1831, Spain, using its *exclusivum,*
vetoed the candidacy of Cardinal Giustiniani, who had urged
the late Pope, Leo XII, to go ahead and appoint bishops in
New Granada in defiance of Spain's protests. Spain had continued to regard its right of *patronato* as unchanged by the new
political independence of its colonies. As a consequence, no
episcopal sees could be filled in New Granada for years since
that government would naturally never allow a Madrid-named
prelate to carry on his functions.

The memoirs of Cardinal Lambruschini, nuncio and eventually secretary of state, indicate the nature of the problem and
the solutions proposed. According to him, in 1826 the Court
of St. Ildephonsus contended that Rome should not give any
bishops to the people of Colombia, as they requested, because
refusal would be an excellent means of constraining that government to recognize the authority of the (to Madrid's eyes)
legitimate sovereign. The pontifical advisors, on the other hand,
while disclaiming any intention of prejudicing the rights of the

Most Catholic King, insisted that the Pope also had to consider the interests of the faith and of souls. The protracted delay in filling the sees of New Granada was becoming a serious danger to the Church. Rome told Madrid that if the requests were deferred much longer a schism could very well result. From Rome's point of view the crucial problem was how to nominate a new bishop without officially recognizing the government of Colombia and without, on the other hand, offending Colombia by asking Spain's formal approval.

Lambruschini, who was consulted on this problem by Leo XII, argued that if those civil governments which had not themselves recognized the new republics were nevertheless able to maintain consuls in those countries for the protection of the commercial interests of their subjects, certainly the Holy See could with all the more justification take like action for the protection of the spiritual interests of the population and the rights of the Holy See.[11] This line of argumentation was not sufficiently convincing to the Spanish Court. But at the end of 1835, after the death of Ferdinand VII, Gregory XVI finally recognized New Granada. As already noted, the first diplomatic exchanges between New Granada of Central America and the Holy See took place at this time.

Even after the opposition of Spain was overcome, the relations of Rome with the new states of the New World were affected by the political instability of the regimes of those countries. This is reflected in the listings given in the Roman almanac, *Notizie*, and in its successor, the *Annuario pontificio*. The name of Ecuador appears for the first time in 1839 with a chargé d'affaires, while the name of Chile appears in the following year. Though Brazil at one time accredited an envoy

---

[11] Lambruschini, *Mia nunziatura*, pp. 17-19, 67-79. Moody, *Church and Society*, pp. 746-51. Leo XII finally declared in consistory May 21, 1827 that he had to proceed to fill the long-vacant sees regardless of Spain. The role of the Spanish crown in the Church affairs of the New World had been virtually complete. No papal legates were allowed to function there. The Propaganda Congregation was excluded. Hertling, *History*, p. 471. For the Church, the lesson of the Spanish colonies was that legitimacy should not be the sole criterion of its policy toward new regimes. Gregory XVI, in his encyclical *Sollicitudo ecclesiarum* of August 5, 1831, enunciated for the first time the general principle that, in entering into relations for Church matters with regimes in de facto control, the Holy See did not necessarily imply any judgment on the claims of the respective contestants. *Acta*, I, pp. 38-40.

extraordinary and minister plenipotentiary, not even Mexico after 1840 had a minister. All missions were confided to chargés d'affaires for a number of years. And even these posts were often vacant. However, on the eve of the annexation of the papal states, according to the *Annuario pontificio* of 1870, the representation of Latin America stood as follows: Bolivia, minister plenipotentiary; Brazil, minister resident; Costa Rica, chargé d'affaires; Ecuador, chargé d'affaires; Guatemala, minister plenipotentiary; San Salvador, minister plenipotentiary. The same individual, Senor de Lorenzana, a familiar figure for long years in Rome, represented Bolivia, Guatemala, and San Salvador at the same time. It is probable that reasons of economy, as well as lack of sufficient business to transact, were responsible for the duplications and vacancies of long-standing, not to speak of the frequent changes of government at home.

Papal representation in the New World itself was almost as sporadic, with the possible exception of Brazil. It was actually not until after the end of the papal states in 1870 that the Holy See organized its diplomatic representation in Latin America on a fairly broad and stable basis. In 1877 two papal envoys were sent with plural missions. One was accredited to Bolivia, Chile, Ecuador, and Peru; the other to Argentina, Paraguay, and Uruguay. In 1881 a third envoy was accredited to San Domingo, Haiti, and Venezuela. These diplomatic representatives bore the title not of nuncio or internuncio but the now discontinued designation of "Apostolic Delegate and Envoy Extraordinary."

THE UNITED STATES

The young republic of North America also appeared on the Roman scene for a brief period of two decades, 1848-1868. In his Message to Congress on December 7, 1847 President James K. Polk announced that the secretary of state had submitted an estimate to defray the expenses of opening diplomatic relations with the papal states. The president declared: "The interesting political events now in progress in these States, as well as a just regard to our commercial interests, have, in my opinion, rendered such a measure expedient." The appropriation was approved by a wide margin in the House (137-15) and the Senate

(36-7). The first appropriation called merely for a chargé
d'affaires. Later, a minister-resident was assigned to the post.
This is a diplomatic rank higher than that of chargé but lower
than that of envoy extraordinary. In 1867 the budget for the
mission was refused by Congress and the current titular of the
Rome legation, Rufus King, was informed that although the
mission itself had not been closed no more funds would be
forthcoming for its support.

As indicated in President Polk's message, the motives that
argued for representation in Rome were political and commercial. They did not concern any religious questions. It was
acknowledged that the federal government had no concern
with the ecclesiastical affairs of the Catholic Church and had
no right to interfere in such anyway. The United States mission
to the papal states was the rare, probably unique, instance of
diplomatic relations with the Pope purely in his capacity of
temporal sovereign. As has been seen, many governments claimed
to deal with the Pope in his capacity of civil ruler when in fact
their primary interest was his religious authority. The debates
that took place in both House and Senate reflect agreement
that while the Pope enjoyed a double character—that of religious chief and political sovereign—the United States mission
necessarily would deal with the Pope solely in his latter capacity.
The instructions of Secretary of State Buchanan to the first
chargé d'affaires under date of April 5, 1848 set the line of
conduct for the duration. It is an important statement of
principle that should be presented *in extenso*:

"There is one consideration which you ought always to keep
in view in your intercourse with the papal authorities. Most,
if not all, the governments which have diplomatic relations at
Rome are connected with the Pope as head of the Catholic
Church. In this respect the government of the United States
occupies an entirely different position. It possesses no power
whatever over the question of religion. All denominations of
Christians stand on the same footing in this country, and every
man enjoys the inestimable right of worshipping his God according to the dictates of his own conscience. Your efforts
therefore will be devoted exclusively to the cultivation of the
most friendly civil relations with the Papal government, and

to the extension of commerce between the two countries. You will carefully avoid even the appearance of interfering in ecclesiastical questions, whether these relate to the United States or any other portion of the world. It might be proper, should you deem it advisable, to make these views known on some suitable occasion, to the papal government, so that there may be no mistake or misunderstanding on this subject."[12]

There is no evidence in the record that these instructions were departed from in the following twenty years. The prestige of the new Pope, Pius IX, was high in the United States in 1848. The young Pontiff seemed the man destined to take the lead in promoting political reforms throughout Italy and the rest of Europe. The commercial stake of the United States at that time seems to have been relatively insignificant. But the view was taken in Washington that Rome was a good center from which the United States could develop wider commercial contacts not only in Italy but in the whole Mediterranean.

During the Civil War the Confederacy made efforts, through a special delegation, to win papal sympathy for its cause. The United States legation in Rome was able to counter this effort. But the papal states had declined in political and commercial importance through their losses of territory and seaports. The fate of the mission was already sealed. In 1939, seventy years after the departure of Rufus King in 1868, the United States and the papacy were to meet again under entirely different circumstances.

THE NON-CHRISTIAN WORLD

Non-Christian states did not begin to establish permanent diplomatic missions at the Holy See until relatively late. The large representation of Muslim, Hindu, and other non-Christian states accredited at the Vatican is a relatively new phenomenon that does not antedate the Second World War. This is not to say that no official contact existed between the Pope and the heads of such governments. In the course of the First World War, the Japanese minister at Berne, Switzerland, represented the Emperor at the coronation of Benedict XV. This was rather a ceremonial mission, even though the envoy had diplo-

12 Stock, *United States Ministers*, pp. 2-3.

matic rank. In the 19th century occasional official contacts were made with the Sultan of Turkey, the Emperor of China, or the Shah of Persia. Thus in 1847 the Turkish envoy in Vienna, Chekib Effendi, was sent on a special mission to Rome. In addition, a papal envoy was received by the Sultan in Constantinople on January 21, 1848. Sultan Abdul-Hamid II sent an envoy extraordinary on the occasion of the golden jubilee of Leo XIII. In May 1875 the Shah of Persia sent Nazar Aga as envoy extraordinary to the Pope. In 1942, within a year after the outbreak of war in the Pacific, first Japan and then China agreed to exchange representatives with the Holy See. These were the first states of the East with which the Vatican ever had permanent relations.

This lag on the part of the non-Christian states is not attributable to religious reasons so much as might be imagined. For a long time the Sultan of Turkey and the Emperor of China were not recognized as having the right of diplomatic representation. International law was considered to be limited to Christendom and therefore inapplicable to the heathen world, where different rules applied. Not until the beginning of the 19th century was it generally customary for European states to admit the Sultan into treaty relations. In 1856, by the treaty of Paris, the Sublime Porte was admitted "to participate in the advantages of the public law of Europe and the system of concert attached to it." Subsequently China, Japan, Persia, and Siam were accorded similar recognition. This did not, however, immediately signify admission on a plane of full equality. The system of capitulations or extra-territorial privileges imposed on these countries by the European powers graphically emphasized the subordinate position occupied by the non-Christian world in international law.

One of the consequences of this inferior position was that the diplomatic rights of such rulers as the Sultan of Turkey or the Emperor of China were limited. In that age of expansion the European powers had no desire to see the rulers they dominated in a position to deal independently with the international community. For this reason, among others, they did not want the papacy to have any direct relations with these rulers. France, in particular, for many decades fiercely opposed the establishment of formal relations of the Holy See with either the Sultan of Turkey or the Emperor of China. So important did this issue appear to France that on several occasions its foreign ministers threatened rupture of relations should an envoy of Turkey or China ever be admitted to the papal Court. In short, it was due primarily to the opposition of the colonial powers, and especially France, that the non-Christian states were so late in being represented diplomatically at Rome.

The rather paradoxical role of the "Eldest Daughter of the Church" in blocking papal efforts to widen its diplomatic contacts to include the non-Christian states is simple enough to explain. Since the time of Francis I (d. 1547) France had increasingly exercised in the Muslim world the role of protector of the Latin Christians. In the course of time this proved to be an extremely useful instrument in the extension of French influence in the Middle East. For all intents and purposes France became the official representative of Christianity, and of the Pope, as far as the local rulers were concerned. For long years the only communication, if any, between the rulers of the Ottoman Empire or the Celestial Empire passed through the French representative in Constantinople or Pekin. The interdiction of direct communication between Rome and those two capitals became and remained until as late as this century one of the basic points of French policy in the Near and Far East.

The preoccupations of France over its position as intermediary for the Pope in the Ottoman Empire were registered in 1871. During the Franco-Prussian war Rome had resolved to send a special representative to Constantinople with the rank of envoy extraordinary. This was Archbishop Franchi, who had been previously nuncio in Madrid and whose mission was simply to patch up a schism that had developed among the Armenians in union with Rome. Franchi presented his credentials to the Sultan on April 24, 1871.

Jules Favre, foreign minister of the new provisional government in Paris, manifested the keenest anxiety at this step taken by Rome. In his eyes it might portend the beginning of the end of France's role as protector of Catholic Christendom in the Orient. He ordered his newly-appointed envoy to Constantinople, Count de Vogüé, to pass through Rome en route and there confer with the Vatican concerning the real import of Archbishop Franchi's mission. The French envoy arrived in Rome on May 1, 1871, where he went into immediate consultation with Count d'Harcourt and with papal officials. "If we could only be assured," Favre wrote him on May 8, a week later, "that, under the appearance of a temporary mission designed to settle a religious question, this is not a serious effort to substitute the direct and official action of the Holy See in place of our centuries-old protectorate."[13] Whatever the original intentions of Rome, France received assurances that the mission of Franchi was no more than what it was declared to be. He had been sent on this temporary mission, the Vatican said, only because of the urgency of the schism and the fact that France's hands were tied for a long period on account of the war with Prussia and its aftermath.

France's jealous vigilance over its valued prerogative as the only spokesman and intermediary of the Christians erupted again fifteen years later. This time it concerned not Constantinople but Pekin. In January 1886 a secret mission appeared in Rome, in the person of an Englishman, one John George Dunn. He bore credentials from the government of the Celestial Empire and from the office of foreign affairs (Tsungli Yamen) and the viceroy, Li Hung-chang. In the name of the empire he proposed to the Pope a mutual exchange of diplomatic agents. The Holy See was invited to send a nuncio to Pekin, while a Chinese representative would come to Rome as minister.

Rome was more than pleased at this unexpected development and even went so far as to select the prelate who was to go to Pekin. But the reaction of France, as soon as the facts became known, was sharp and categoric. If Leo XIII should go through with his plans he would have to reckon with a possible diplomatic break with France. The language of Foreign Minister de Freycinet, writing on August 12, 1886 to Ambassador Lefebvre de Béhaine at the Vatican, was emphatic: "As soon as the Pope names a diplomatic delegate at Pekin you will go off on indeterminate leave. It will be well if these instructions become known to everyone about you." For the Quai d'Orsay the papal

---

[13] *Paris. Affaires étrangères. Correspondance politique. Rome. 1871, mai-juin,* T. *1051, f. 25.* Unpublished.

decision, if carried out, would be an intolerable blow to French prestige in the Far East, in the eyes of the Chinese as well as for the other rival powers. The move had to be combatted with vigor. Wrote Freycinet: "Such a thing would be for France, in the eyes of the nations, a diminution of prestige and consequently of influence. If there are any doubts on this point, you need only to consider who those are who are already rejoicing at the decision of the Pope. Are they the friends or the enemies of France?" The foreign minister did not gloss over the seriousness of the reprisals that might ensue in France: "This act of defiance of us will be zealously played up by the enemies of the Church and these are many. The suppression of the Vatican embassy will be the first reprisal. Those who think the reaction will stop there are deceiving themselves. I refrain from going more into detail."[14] This was an obvious reference to the repudiation of the Concordat and the expulsion of the religious orders and congregations, which anti-clericals even then were demanding.

The Vatican gave way to this pressure and canceled the plans for a representative in Pekin. However, in his subsequent reports the French ambassador to the Holy See, Lefebvre de Béhaine, warned his government that this did not mean that Rome recognized France's claims to the privilege of the protectorate as a right that could not be withdrawn when Rome saw fit. Writing on September 13, 1886 following the definitive abandonment of the plan, he warned that he did not share the optimism that the Quai d'Orsay apparently felt. Only the present embarrassment had been overcome; there would be others to follow. The Vatican's notification announcing its decision had a "ton sec," he pointed out. Nevertheless, His Holiness, added the ambassador, "after having asserted his rights, will not use them."[15]

On May 22, 1888, the Congregation of the Propaganda, which had jurisdiction over the missionaries working in the Near and Far East, issued instructions to them to conform their actions to the wishes of France, that is to say, to undertake all the démarches with the local government through the intermediary

---

[14] *Ministère des affaires étrangères. Documents diplomatiques français.* 1ère série, VI, p. 287.
[15] *Ibid.,* p. 310.

of the French representative, to the exclusion of the other agents. The Holy See, however, always took the position that its own order was revocable at its own discretion. Rome did not recognize France's strict right to this privileged position in relation to the missionaries.

What was the objective of the Chinese government in this proposal which struck such a sensitive point in French diplomacy? The immediate provocations of the secret mission were not of great political moment. The Catholic Church in Pekin was located virtually within the precincts of the imperial grounds, and, in fact, overlooked the palace. It was a continuing source of annoyance to the imperial household. But nothing could be done about it, as the French representative was adamant against any change of location. It was apparently the Englishman, Dunn, who suggested a direct appeal to the Pope. This individual, a Shanghai businessman, seems to have acted on his own, and not as a British agent. This conjecture is supported by the surprise that the news of his arrival in Rome brought in London. *Punch* quipped, "Evidently there is a great deal doing, but who is Mr. Dunn?"

It is probable that the proposal for inviting a nuncio was also the Englishman's, as the imperial court did not at once understand the meaning of the cables that began to come from Rome, until they had reread the instructions they had themselves approved. The Dowager Empress seems to have been one of those who grasped the significance of it all, and she had Dunn cabled to send on the papal envoy without delay. She was one of the few who understood what it meant to have the Catholic Church in China represented by a Church officer, without an army or navy behind him, rather than by a French diplomat with political purposes in view. A comment appearing in a Chinese newspaper at this time shows that this consideration was clearly before their minds. It noted: "As the Pope has no troops and no territory, but is merely a kind of Dalai Lama, there is no danger to China from opening direct relations with him. The affairs of the missionaries can then be dealt with in an open and straightforward manner, as no fear of political traps will lurk behind."[16]

[16] Michie, *Englishman in China*, I, p. 350; Cordier, *Histoire*, II, pp. 591-604;

There is no doubt that France's colonial rivals would have been delighted, for their part, to occupy the same privileged position at the Court of Pekin or elsewhere, enjoyed by France as the protector of the Christians and of Christian missionaries. Their efforts in this direction not being very successful, they adopted the next best plan of trying to undermine France's protectorate. One means to this end was to encourage the Emperor of China, the Sultan of the Ottoman Empire, or any other prince in like situation, to seek direct relations with the Vatican, a proposal welcome to those rulers. The reactions of Foreign Minister de Freycinet showed that France realized full well the loss of prestige and therefore of influence that would be entailed should it be by-passed in this manner.

With the end of the First World War the era of capitulations or extra-territorial privileges enjoyed by the Western powers in China appeared on the way out. But it is interesting to note that as late as 1922 France invoked her traditional role as protector of Christians in order to prevent the Republic of China from having diplomatic relations with the Holy See. This was on the occasion of the appointment of Archbishop Celso Costantini as apostolic delegate. A few years earlier, in July 1918, the Republic of China had proposed formal relations with the Vatican and the papal envoy had already been named for the *agrément* of China before France again made her objections felt. The Allies secured a promise from China to defer the dispatch of a pontifical envoy until the end of hostilities. That government subsequently stated it wished to receive only a religious representative and not a diplomatic one. The mission of the Apostolic Delegate Celso Costantini in 1922 was the result.

Even the dispatch of a non-diplomatic agent like the apostolic delegate annoyed the French government and proposals were made in the Chamber of Deputies to reduce the budget of the newly-established Vatican embassy as a token of displeasure at the Vatican's procedure. But speaking in the Senate on June

---

Aureli-Crispolto, *Leone XIII*, pp. 183-85. A similar project was in the air at this time with reference to Greece but with like objections from France (Aureli-Crispolto, p. 398). On the China episode, see also Renault de Moustier, in *Correspondant*, 1886; Alcock, in *Nineteenth Century*, 1886; Anon., in *Revue des deux mondes*, Dec. 15, 1886.

19, 1922 Raymond Poincaré, at that time premier, said that he had been assured by Rome that the archbishop's mission was a temporary one, occasioned by the impending synod of 1924. In any case what was essential in France's eyes was that the mission could not have a diplomatic character. "This prelate," Poincaré told the senators, "cannot, in the view of France, have any diplomatic standing. He should be accredited only to the clergy and he does not have the right to enter into communication with the Chinese government except by the intermediary of our legation or in the presence of one of our representatives. We have insisted on these points at Rome and at Pekin and we do not have any reason to suppose that they will not be followed." France's sensitivity about its traditional, if outmoded, rights was respected by the Vatican and it was not until World War II that formal and direct Vatican-China relations were at last achieved.

A special interest naturally attaches to the relations of the Ottoman Empire with the Holy See. The ancient struggles between the Muslim world and Christendom, and notably the leading role played by the Roman Pontiffs in the wars against the Turks, could conceivably have made official relations between the two capitals more difficult than in the case of China. Yet the same pattern applied for the Ottoman Empire as for the Celestial Empire. It was due not to the natural reluctance of a Muslim ruler but to the formal opposition of Western states that Rome and Constantinople never established formal direct relations with each other as long as the Ottoman Empire existed. And whereas in China, Italian and British influence was instrumental in stimulating the Chinese to ask for such an exchange, in the Turkish Empire it was Germany which played the leading part in urging the Sultan along this road, again at France's expense.

It was inevitable that, as Germany sought to extend its influence in the Near East focus of imperialistic rivalries, the question of the protectorate of Christians would come up. Germany, too, sought to have some of the prerogatives enjoyed by France (and Italy), with respect at least to German missionaries. Failing that, or as a means to that end, Germany's strategy was to loosen France's own hold in the field. The German ambassador in Constantinople worked zealously to promote a diplomatic exchange between Pope and Sultan.

On March 4, 1898 the German ambassador to the Sublime Porte, Baron Adolf Hermann von Marschall, reported to Berlin that according to information confidentially communicated to him by the foreign minister Tevfik Pasha, the Pope had inquired if the Sultan was disposed to send a diplomatic representative to the Holy See. The Sultan, said Marschall, was favorable to the proposal. The German ambassador pointed out the significance of this new development, from the viewpoint of the powers having interests in the Middle East: "As is known, on account of France's claim to exercise an exclusive right of protectorate over the Latin rite Christians of Turkey there are no direct diplomatic relations between the Holy See and the Porte. Archbishop Bonetti, the papal delegate at Constantinople, does not himself have any diplomatic character and does not enter into communication with the Porte except through the French embassy. The dispatch of a Turkish envoy to the Holy See would be of great significance for the situation of the Latin Church and would be a hard blow to French claims."

The opportunity thus offered to exercise an act of independence in the European diplomatic society had a powerful attraction to the Sultan. It would at one time release him from some supervision by the French and would render his international position more acceptable to the Christian world. The German ambassador did all in his power to confirm the Muslim ruler in his initial reactions. Meanwhile, as might be expected, France was working at both Rome and Constantinople to force a halt to the proceedings. On April 18, 1898, as the Sultan began to show signs of weakening under French pressure, Ambassador von Marschall drafted, and sent to Berlin for approval (which was granted), a communication he might usefully present to the Sultan. In this case, Germany was not directly involved, which permitted an air of disinterested concern for the prestige and independence of the ruler of the Ottoman Empire. The German ambassador's draft throws light upon the factors at play in the diplomacy of the Middle East at the turn of the century and the relationship of the Vatican to this situation:

"The government of His Majesty has taken particular interest in the nomination of a Turkish representative to the Holy See. The Sultan, by thus having himself represented diplomatically to another sovereign, has only exercised a right which is inalienably inherent in his sovereignty rights. The very opposition that the move has encountered makes it obvious that the Sultan has gained thereby in power and in independence, to the extent that it limits for certain powers the occasions to interfere in Turkish internal affairs. The Government of His Majesty the Kaiser therefore believes it its obligation to advise the Sultan to maintain his decision unchanged because all direct or indirect concessions in the matter of his relations with other sovereigns will profit only those powers which have announced their intention of raising in the near future the question of reforms."[17]

The reader will read between the lines the barbed attacks upon France by the Kaiser's envoy in Constantinople. That is one side. There is another. A rather melodramatic account of the ultimatum given to the Holy See by the French ambassador is found in the *Journal des débats*, for July 23, 1909, signed "M.P." (Maurice Pernot). According to the writer, Leo XIII had a vain desire to multiply his diplomatic relations and proved this in the Turkish affair of 1898. He reports that Gabriel Hanotaux, the foreign minister at the time, issued instructions to Poubelle, the Vatican ambassador, that posed a dilemma: either a French or a Turkish ambassador at the Vatican. According to this version, Poubelle called upon the secretary of state, Cardinal Rampolla, at the customary day and hour for their weekly meetings but first discussed indifferent or secondary matters until the moment of departure. Rising then from his chair, the French ambassador recalled to Rampolla the good relations he had always had with him, stating he sincerely hoped that the Vatican was not going to sacrifice him, the representative of France, for an ambassador

[17] *Die grosse Politik, XII. Die Orientreise Kaisers Wilhelm II und die Protektoratsfrage 1898-99. Doc. n. 3351—Doc. 3395* (pp. 589-638), *esp. Doc. 3358, 3362.* Anon., in *Revue des deux mondes*, 1898; Anon., in *Civiltà Cattolica*, 1904.

of Turkey. The secretary of state, says the writer, understood at once that this pleasantry contained France's ultimatum and he acted accordingly. The project was called off, and shortly afterwards the worries in Paris that a new Vatican policy on the protectorate was envisaged were alleviated somewhat by a letter written to the Archbishop of Reims by Leo XIII on August 1, 1898 in which France's special role in the Near and Far East was acknowledged. The Pope's letter was vague, however, on the question of future direct relations with the rulers of those areas.

Indeed, the question was far from closed. With the accession of Pius X changes were noted. When a delay ensued in the choice of a new apostolic delegate to succeed Bonetti, who died in August 1904, the post was removed from the hands of the Congregation of the Propaganda and handed over to the Secretariat of State, under Cardinal Merry del Val. The new apostolic delegate was Archbishop Tacci-Porcelli, who arrived in Constantinople in the following April, where he was formally presented to the Sultan by the French ambassador, Constans. But the change in jurisdiction from the Propaganda (where French influence was stronger) to the Secretariat of State (headed by the supposedly anti-French Merry del Val) was bitterly noted in Paris. In 1909 a Turkish delegation arrived in Rome to announce the accession of Mohammed V. This delegation was received by the Pope on July 4 and it naturally aroused renewed talk of forthcoming closer relations between Sultan and Pope. The contemporary Catholic press suggested that the purpose of the mission was primarily to counterbalance the impression among Catholics that the new regime of the Young Turks were under the influence of the anti-clerical enemies of the Church.

What the Young Turks thought at this moment of the idea of diplomatic relations with the Holy See can be judged fairly authentically from an article published in the semi-official *Young Turk* which we find cited in the French journal *l'Eclair*, October 22, 1910. This editorial points out the value of having direct relations with the Pope in order to avoid the interference of the powers enjoying the privileges of the capitulations in the Ottoman Empire: "In order to put an end to this situation so absolutely contrary to the law of nations, would it not be good for the Imperial government to entertain direct relations with the Holy See, instead of having a thousand annoyances with the powers which in reality are pursuing purely political aims even when purely religious questions are at issue? For example, can anyone have confidence in Italy where public opinion does not even try to conceal its designs upon the Adriatic and in Tripoli?" (In 1905, France had conceded to Italy some role in the protection of Italian missionaries.) It was because the Holy See did not have relations with Turkey, continued the writer, that the powers are now interfering in Turkey's affairs.

The farthest that these proposals ever got, however, was the naming of a minister resident, named Chery-Bey, who was never able to present his credentials at the Vatican. At least one more effort was made in Turkey. At the outbreak of the war, while the Sultan was still neutral, the same proposals were put in motion. This time, with France still absent from Rome, it was the newly arrived British minister, Sir Henry Howard, upon whom it fell to prevent the realization of these plans. The Vatican's reaction was a compromise. An apostolic delegate was sent, in the person of Archbishop Dolci, whose instructions were to explain to the Turks why, in the existing circumstances, the Pope could not receive a Turkish minister in Rome. This was considered at the time a victory of the Allies over the Central Powers. "England can therefore register the first success of its representative," as Guglielmo Quadrotta commented, writing during those months.[18]

After the French representative had to retire from Constantinople upon Turkey's entrance into the war on the side of the Central Powers, the Pope's representative was more than careful not to give France cause for alarm. As Favre in 1871 feared that the Vatican might take advantage of the disturbed conditions to set up direct relations with the Sultan at the expense of France, so the Quai d'Orsay in 1915 was on the alert to prevent a comparable development. But to the last days of the Ottoman Empire, the Apostolic Delegate adhered to all the formalities. In his dealings with the government he

[18] Quadrotta, *Il Papa, l'Italia et la guerra*, pp. 106-07.

addressed himself first to the minister of the Netherlands, to whom French interests had been confided after the rupture brought on by the war. As Father de la Brière, writing in *Etudes* for June 5, 1919, reports the situation: "The Apostolic Delegate was always careful to recall that he was officially recognized by the Turkish Government, not as one accredited diplomatically by the Holy See but as one formerly introduced to the Grand Vizier by the Ambassador of France and as the religious client of France."

Thus during World War I Turkey and the Holy See were carrying on their mutual relations through an intermediary power which had ruptured diplomatic relations with each of them separately! When France broke with the Vatican in 1904 this made no appreciable difference in the conduct of the protectorate. It never seemed to occur to anyone in France at the time, or was not considered important, that the logical consequence of a rupture at Rome implied a rupture likewise all over the Near and Far East where France had traditionally exercised the role of representative of the Pope. The Holy See, had it wished to, could legitimately have declared the protectorate at an end and proceeded to enter into direct relations with the governments of those regions. Logic, however, is not the last law of politics. Neither France nor the Vatican saw any utility in pushing matters to their ultimate conclusion.

Japan initiated diplomatic relations with the Holy See during the Second World War. The circumstances of this move are recorded in Chapter 13.

PART TWO

THE ORGANS OF PAPAL DIPLOMACY

CHAPTER 4

THE AMBASSADORS

THE ENVOYS AT THE PAPAL COURT

P APAL diplomacy was an established institution before the
Holy See began to receive Protestant envoys. Let us now
study its beginnings.

Historians usually fix the birth of modern diplomacy around
the second half of the 15th century. Ambassadors were, of
course, by no means unknown before that time. The practice
of sending legates abroad for the purpose of forming alliances
or concluding peace is as old as war itself. But these were occasional emissaries on specific, limited missions. They did not
take up their post abroad on a permanent basis, empowered to
represent their sovereign in any category of question affecting
their master's interests. When their ad hoc task was accomplished they returned home; there was no provision for
regular succession. A milestone in political history was reached

Bibliographical Note: Scholarly interest in diplomatic representation as a
permanent institution owes much to several studies made at the end of the 19th
century, the reports of Krauske, Schaube, and Maulde-la-Clavière. Similar research was done by Pieper on the origins of the permanent nunciatures. This
study was supplemented by researches by Biaudet and Karttunen, before the
First World War.

Although diplomatic representation is inseparable from the person of the
envoys, the courts did not for a long time issue formal diplomatic lists. The
Almanach de Gotha did not publish the names of the envoys at the courts
before 1803. For Rome, the *Notizie*, though founded in 1716, did not begin to
list either the nuncios or the envoys accredited at the papal Court until after
the French Revolution. The most complete source of diplomatic lists has recently been made available in the two-volume Bittner-Gross-Hausmann *Repertorium*. This *tour de force* gives the names of all the envoys at all the courts
from 1648 until 1763, with their title, dates of arrival, and dates of the end
of mission. For modern times, the official *Annuario pontificio* may be usefully
supplemented at times by the *Annuaire pontifical catholique*, edited by Battandier. General Church histories, such as that of Pastor, give the names of
nuncios and ambassadors only incidentally to their role in events narrated. German representation in Rome is described in part by Noack and Hudal in their
studies on cultural life on the Italian peninsula. For the nuncios, the lists drawn
up by Biaudet and by Karttunen have been continued by De Marchi from
1800 to 1956.

In addition to Moroni's *Dizionario*, the special section on encyclopedias in the
Bibliography may be consulted for articles. Most of these give details concerning
the historical origins of the reciprocal representation.

when these occasional missions developed into full-time representation through a regular succession of envoys stationed at the courts of foreign rulers with a general mandate to handle the interests of their respective sovereigns. The institution of permanent diplomatic representation is closely linked with the system of sovereign independent states which has formed the basic structure of international society for the past four centuries and more.

Credit for establishing the first permanent diplomatic mission is generally attributed to the Italian republics. Venice took the lead. One of the first permanent diplomatic posts was that of Rome. The Venetian annalists, recording their conflict with Paul II (1464-1471), remark that these quarrels prevented the republic from maintaining ambassadors at the papal Court "according to its custom."[1] This implies that the practice was in existence before the time of Paul II. The first "permanent" envoy of Spain to the Apostolic See, as far as the official records tell us, was one Don Inigo Lopes de Mendoza. He went to Rome during the pontificate of Innocent VIII (1484-1492) and remained during the first year of the next Pope, Alexander VI.[2] From that time the succession of Spanish ambassadors is regular. Ferdinand the Catholic, king of United Spain (1479-1515) and husband of Isabella, believed in having his own men at foreign courts even as "official liars" or "licensed spies."[3] His contemporaries, Henry VII of England and Louis XI of France, were slow in following the example but they or their immediate successors conformed in the end. Modern diplomacy never really established itself until the suspicious sovereigns ceased to look upon the ambassadors as espionage agents, honorable or other than honorable—or at least before they had calculated that it was a fair price to be paid for having their own spy in another king's court. Before that point was reached the relations among the princes were limited to extraordinary embassies on special business.

[1] Richard, in *Dictionnaire d'histoire et de géographie ecclésiastiques*, citing Schaube, "Zur Entstehungsgeschichte des ständigen Gesandtschaften" (*Mittheilungen des Instituts für oesterreichische Geschichtsforschungen*, x [1889], p. 519n).

[2] Hinosa, *Despachos*, i, p. 37-39. This mission was primarily political, in connection with the dispute with France over the Kingdom of Naples.

[3] Mattingly, *Renaissance Diplomacy*, p. 239.

Venice and the other Italian republics did not make a sharp break in tradition and this makes it difficult for students of that transition period to draw a clear-cut line of demarcation. We know from various indications that envoys from all over Christendom were present at Rome on certain occasions, sometimes in considerable number. The embassies sometimes included two or even four members. In 1444 the presence of a large group of foreign *oratores* or *ambaxiatores,* as they were termed, is revealed by a quarrel over precedence.[4] The contending diplomats were the representative of King John II of Castile and Leon and that of King Alfonso V of Aragon who fought over their places in the papal chapel. The latter claimed a position farther up front on the grounds of the greater number of realms possessed by his sovereign, enumerating these to be Sicily, Sardinia, Corsica, and others. Pope Eugene IV, however, decided in favor of his rival from Castile and Leon.

These were not permanent missions in Rome. The episode shows, however, that even before modern diplomacy existed, the presence of the envoys of kings was not unfamiliar to Rome. The incident also proves that questions of precedence were already apples of discord among the fledgling diplomats. Like Esau and Jacob struggling in the womb for seniority, the diplomats were fighting for precedence before modern diplomacy was born.

By 1500 Rome had become a recognizable diplomatic center, as far as we can deduce from the documents that have come down to us. In that dawn of modern diplomacy there were no official "diplomatic lists," no *Annuario pontificio,* no regularly organized foreign service, to tell us what rulers or governments had permanent representatives in the Eternal City or what were the names of their envoys. Our knowledge of these missions and their permanency depends not upon titles but rather upon indirect indications, such as the instructions which the envoys received for their guidance. P. Richard, who examined the pertinent archival material, has summarized his findings on the beginnings of the diplomatic corps in Rome with these words: "Under Alexander VI [*1492-1503*] there were political agents who appeared one after the other regularly at the Roman court.

---

[4] Moroni, *Dizionario, s.v.* "Ambasciatori presso la Santa Sede," I, pp. 299-309.

The contemporary documents, the *Diarium* of John Burckhardt, Master of Papal Ceremonies, and the diaries of Marino Sanuto, official historian of the Venetian republic, establish this at every turn. The Emperor, France, Spain, England, in a word, the great powers, not to mention the Italian princes, were permanently represented at Rome."[5] The papacy was an early participant in this new form of international intercourse. It was a charter member, so to speak, of the society of sovereigns which, in 1500, was in the process of formation.

The rise of permanent diplomatic representation reflects the profound changes that were transforming European political organization at that very moment. A quiet revolution was ushering out the feudal system and introducing a new pattern of society. The unitary, hierarchical structure of medieval life was yielding ground to another in which independent units dealt with each other on the plane of equality and not along an elaborate ladder of dignities. A world that had known only one Emperor, theoretically the temporal head (*dominus mundi*) of all Christendom, was dissolving in favor of another order comprising a multiplicity of rulers who saw themselves as little emperors, enjoying a status equal or analogous to that of the Emperor. *Rex est Imperator in regno suo*. The king entered into his own, overshadowing duke and count who in the past, though lower in the feudal hierarchy, often were insolently independent, if not actually more powerful. The lesser nobility were reduced to real as well as to theoretical obedience within the national, centralized state under the new royal absolutism. The king took care that his view of his own status was recognized at the courts of the other crowned heads, as well as at home by his own subjects of whatever rank. Master at home, he recognized no superiors abroad but only equals. His ambassador in the new diplomacy became the herald of his sovereignty. Toward Rome, this attitude of independence was spurred, at the end of the 15th century, by the disorganized state of the papacy. When Pope Martin V (1417-1431) brought the seat of Church administration back to Rome after the Council of

[5] Richard, in *Revue d'histoire ecclésiastique*, 1906. Same author in *Dictionnaire d'histoire et de géographie ecclésiastiques*, II, col. 1015-1030, s.v. "Ambassadeurs auprès du Saint-Siège."

Constance, the princes were very conscious of their part in the extinction of the great schism of the West and wanted their reward. Rome was no longer in a position to adopt any but a conciliatory attitude.[6]

The official known as "ambassador" was not, originally, the envoy of what we would today call an independent sovereign. It was a general term indicating any sort of envoy sent by one civic community to another. At Rome the Pope received representatives of his own vassals, as well as of semi-independent princes. These were termed ambassadors none the less. What distinguished these envoys among themselves was not their title but the protocol with which they were received. At the top was the protocol for the representatives of emperors and crowned heads. To be received with "royal honors" became the touchstone of the real ambassador.

The actions of rulers and republics that were not entitled to these honors show how prized they were. The Italian republics petitioned the Pope that their agents, too, should be received in the Roman Court with the same ceremony granted to those of kings. This favor was first granted to Venice. The jealous Republic of Genoa, according to Moroni,[7] thereafter ceased to have in Rome any agent at all, since their man would suffer from comparison with his opposite number from rival Venice. Genoa preferred under such circumstances to perform its business through a countryman who was a cardinal or through some Roman nobleman whose own princely dignity covered, so to speak, the nakedness of the un-royal republic. The Duke of Savoy, finding it intolerable that his "ambassador" could not receive the same royal honors, maintained only an agent with the title of resident. Even the Pope's own dependencies, such as Ferrara and Bologna, sought and obtained some special recognition.

From the earliest days modern diplomacy was therefore marked by the jealousy of the kings for their independence.

---

[6] Martin, Victor, *Cardinaux et curie*, pp. 147-48. The process by which, in the 14th century, the kings arrived at both *de jure* and *de facto* independence from the emperor is described by Ullmann, in *English Historical Review*, 1949; Von der Heydte, *Geburtsstunde*.

[7] Moroni, *Dizionario*, *loc.cit.*

They were jealous for their new-found power and status not only vis-à-vis their fellow kings and the emperor, but particularly toward the Roman Pontiff. The fate of the special missions known as the "embassies of obedience" eloquently illustrates the evolving attitude of the rulers as the centuries of the new era moved along.[8] Since at least the time of Gregory VII (1073-1085) the secular princes of whatever rank, including the emperor, had been accustomed to send special embassies to Rome on the occasion of the election of a new Pope. The practice reached the peak of its importance perhaps at the end of the 15th century but it had practically died out completely by the end of the 18th. Among the brilliant embassies recorded in papal history were those of the kings of France and England in 1504, following the election of Julius II (1503-1513), as well as the one sent by the Republic of Venice on the same occasion. Francis II of France sent one to Paul IV in 1560 and Louis XIII to Urban VIII in 1633. A particularly spectacular embassy of obedience was that of David, emperor of Abyssinia, sent to Clement VII in 1533. One of the last was the mission which came to Rome in November 1802 in the name of Maria I, queen of Portugal.

As their name suggests, these extraordinary *legationes obedientiae* were, at the beginning, gestures of homage and allegiance. They implied also not merely a religious affiliation but even a certain dependence upon the papacy in political matters. This was particularly true of the emperor of the Holy Roman Empire. Until the declaration of Rense in 1338, the Pope's confirmation was necessary for the definitive validity of the imperial elections. But even after that date the missions continued to be sent. As the Hapsburgs grew stronger, they sought to omit the traditional embassies, or at least to play down their significance. Leopold I (1658-1705) and his son Joseph I (1705-1711) omitted them. Charles VI (1711-1740) and Charles VII (1742-1745) resumed the practice but their representatives used

---

[8] Buder, *De legationibus obedientiae*. Also Maulde-la-Clavière, *La Diplomatie*, I, pp. 110-18. The reception of such missions was the best possible act of recognition and hence highly prized. Roger's *Obedience of a King of Portugal* contains an analysis of the address delivered in 1485 before Innocent VIII by the ambassador of John II of Portugal.

non-committal language in presenting to the Pope their master's announcement of their election. After the one sent by Francis I (1745-1765) they fell into desuetude as far as the Empire was concerned.

But long before that they had lost any real political meaning. When Rudolph II (1576-1612) sent the usual embassy to Gregory XIII following his own election, he instructed the envoy to omit the word "obedience" and to employ rather the term "homage." The emperors were willing to profess their respect for the Pope but not their political dependence. The French kings, in the traditions of their Gallicanism, were even more guarded in their terminology. It should be noted that one reason why the emperors continued to send their extraordinary embassies of obedience was because Rome's express consent was still necessary for certain prerogatives of the emperor in the ecclesiastical field. Chief of these was the "right of expectancy," or *jus primarum precum.* This customary renewable privilege put into the emperor's hands the right to choose successors to episcopal sees not yet vacant. But he, or his envoy, had to go to Rome in order to get this renewal.

The missions of obedience set the tone for the ordinary missions. The permanent ambassadors lost no occasion to manifest the independence of their sovereign master. Modern diplomacy is nothing if not a vehicle of sovereign powers. It was so at the Roman Court, as well as elsewhere, from virtually the earliest days.

Despite the many reverses that the papacy experienced in the period which coincided with the first centuries of the new diplomacy, the Eternal City grew to be a brilliant and vibrant center of international life. The Protestant revolt in the 16th century and the Treaties of Westphalia in the 17th century failed to alter notably the international importance of the Holy See. Various factors contributed to this. One of the most important was the intense competition between the rival Catholic houses of the Bourbons and the Hapsburgs. The religious stake in the wars of that period was another factor. It was advantageous for the Catholic kings to stress at Rome their role as defenders of the Faith—as it was also a necessity for them to explain themselves at Rome when reasons of state aligned them on the side of Protestant princes. Within that part of Europe which remained faithful to Rome, the papacy was still strong. The great monarchs of Europe were Catholic. There were only a few Protestant rulers in Christendom enjoying royal rank and thereby entitled to send ambassadors to the major courts of Europe.

A memorial prepared for the French king by an experienced official of the Roman embassy at the time of Louis XIV indicates how the papal Court was regarded in the period of classical diplomacy.[9] "This mission outranks all others in dignity [*said the writer*] because its object is the pope to whom the Christian princes wish to show their respect as the highest dignitary of the Church, in addition to the fact that its seat is Rome which is a center whither all important matters converge, for study and decision, including issues affecting the kings of France." Two factors, therefore, according to this memorialist, combined to make the Rome post so important. On the one hand, the Pope's own Court was necessarily important in the eyes of a Catholic monarch who made official profession of his devotion to the supreme Pontiff. This applied particularly to the king of France, who made the most of his title of "Eldest Son of the Church." But this was not all, as the old Roman hand went on to add immediately: the papal capital was still a busy diplomatic center and France had its stake in what transpired there.

The elaborate ceremonies that punctuated diplomatic life in Rome are evidence of the papacy's importance. It was necessary, for prestige reasons, to make a good showing here, virtually in the eyes of all Europe. The arrival or grand *entrée* of an ambassador grew in time into an occasion that would not soon be forgotten. The magnificence of the event was judged by the number of carriages and horsemen who took part. Much of the expense of this solemn moment was borne by the king himself, but even so the ambassador's own personal expenses were so great that he had to think seriously before accepting the flattering nomination to represent his liege Lord in Rome. Saint-Simon reports in his diary how he was once informed

---

[9] Cited by Lesourd, *L'Ambassade de France*, p. 3.

that Louis XIV had chosen him as ambassador and that his resources had been examined to determine whether he could take the post without financial ruin. Saint-Simon was able to beg off the dubious privilege of bankrupting himself for the glory of being the king's ambassador at the papal Court.

The occasion of a conclave or papal election provided the kings with a particularly compelling occasion to parade their glory. Under the existing system the Catholic princes had means to influence the elections, or at least to intimate the wishes, of their sovereign. In addition, Paris, Vienna, and Madrid possessed the important *exclusivum* or veto. In the absence of a Pope, *sede vacante*, the college of cardinals was the appropriate authority to which the special credentials were presented. The ambassadors strove to leave nothing undone to impress them. Lucius Lector has given us a description of the sight that met the eyes of the Romans as the ambassadors proceeded to the place of conclave in order to present their special letters and, at the same time, make their little speech, which they hoped would serve some good purpose, from their royal master's point of view. A detachment of papal troops led the way. The de luxe coaches of the embassy, duly polished and shined, came after them, to the number of twelve or fifteen. In these rode the ambassador, his staff, and the members of his household. Then, upon special invitation, the carriages of all the cardinals (sans cardinals, of course, since they were already in the conclave). There followed the carriages of the other members of the diplomatic corps, colleagues of the ambassador who wished to show their solidarity, and, finally, the carriages of the Roman princes and patricians. The long train was closed by the papal troops. The Roman populace, according to reports, dearly enjoyed this spectacle, a pleasure that was no doubt augmented when at times coins were thrown into the crowds en route. It is not recorded whether music or trumpet calls accompanied the procession to the conclave. Nothing else was neglected, it seems, to heighten the glory of the monarch whose ambassador was on his way to salute (and try to influence) the cardinals in conclave.

For the election of the successor of Clement XIII (1758-1769) preparations were begun four years before the Pope actually died. The Marquis d'Aubeterre, ambassador of France, was leaving nothing to chance. But even his preparations did not keep pace with those of his arch rival, the Hapsburg ambassador from Vienna, Kaunitz. He alerted Versailles to the danger that the French king might be outdone if more funds were not forthcoming to finance a demonstration worthy of France. "Kaunitz," he wrote to the king in April 1769, "has a magnificent cortege in readiness. Tomorrow he will make his solemn entry to the conclave with a succession of sixteen carriages. Everything else is in proportion. And Sunday he will return again, this time in the name of the Empress. Here in Rome they estimate that his extraordinary embassy will cost the Court of Vienna at least five hundred thousand pounds." The marquis asked for at least 120,000 pounds which he alleged to be absolutely indispensable to counteract the splendor of the Hapsburg display. Versailles hesitated between its desire to save money and its solicitude for French prestige. While temporizing it instructed the ambassador to allow the rumors of his bad health to circulate around Rome a little longer. This would quiet the impatience of those who wanted to see how Versailles would meet the challenge flung by Vienna. The French king and his ministers thought, or hoped, that there were less expensive ways of influencing a conclave.

At a later date the rivalries among the ambassadors were not so pronounced, at least as far as the magnificence of the processions was concerned. Cooperation (and economy) reigned among the diplomats in Rome. In 1830 the Marquis de Latour-Maubourg, ambassador for Louis-Philippe, borrowed the carriages of his predecessor, the representative of the older but deposed branch of the Bourbons. The horses he got on loan from the Austrian ambassador. On this occasion, however, reports the Marquis, "My cortege was very large and seems to have satisfied the curiosity of the public who are very avid for this kind of show which suggests more than one oriental custom."[10]

The diplomatic life of the ambassadors of foreign courts stationed in Rome was not always featured by elaborate and expensive exhibitions designed to impress the Roman curia. The

---

[10] These details of the time of a papal election are based on the matchless study of Lucius Lector on the conclaves.

European monarchs had many ways of influencing the course of events in the Pope's councils.[11] Although, to read the solemn protestations of both king and ambassador, the royal houses of Catholic Europe had nothing but respect and affection for the common Holy Father, these pious sentiments sometimes took strange forms. Louis XIV was second to none in his professed attachment for the Apostolic See but he could use strong-arm methods against the Pope when he found it useful or necessary. In 1687 he seized the two near-by papal provinces of Avignon and the Venaissin when the Pope refused to receive his ambassador, the Marquis de Lavardin. He also put the papal nuncio under house arrest for eight months. The French ambassador had entered Rome on November 16, 1687, like an invading general, with a retinue of 800 men, defying the local authorities and threatening to cut off the ears and noses of the papal customs officers who wanted to inspect their baggage. The Pope excommunicated the ambassador and put the national Church of St. Louis of the French under interdict.[12] The crisis blew over, however, aided by the timely death of the Pope, the saintly Innocent XI, beatified in 1956. But this was all too typical of the peculiar relations that at times existed between the Christian monarchs and the Pontiff to whom they were professedly so devoted. The history of the absolute sovereigns of Catholic Europe amply demonstrates that what the political rulers had in mind first and foremost was an increase of their power and prestige. Their reiterated protests of filial loyalty were probably quite sincere most of the time, but their feelings were potently aided by the realization that it was politically useful for them to maintain their diplomatic missions in full strength at the Court of Rome.

In the early phases of modern diplomacy the sovereigns manifested a preference for churchmen as their representatives at the courts of other princes.[13] This practice gradually disap-

---

[11] Many cardinals owed their red hat not so much to the favor of the Pope as to the favor of the king. In addition, their sympathies, and that of lesser Church dignitaries, were easily won over in many cases by the pensions and benefices which were at the disposal of the royal munificence for bestowal upon those whose gratitude could be counted on.

[12] Adair, *Extraterritoriality*, pp. 220-22.

[13] Degert, in *Revue d'histoire de l'Eglise de France*, 1923.

peared. But up to a hundred years ago ecclesiastics were not entirely missing from the diplomatic corps accredited to the Pope. The last envoy of the old regime was Cardinal de Bernis, who represented Louis XVI. At the same time Cardinal Herzan von Harras was the envoy of the Empire. At one time all three Bourbon courts were represented by clerics. Thus, in addition to Cardinal de Bernis, Cardinal Domenico Orsini represented the Kingdom of Naples and Monsignor Thomas Azpuru y Ximenes was the diplomatic agent of Spain. In 1803, Napoleon sent his uncle, Cardinal Joseph Fesch to represent him in Rome. After the restoration of the papal states this custom was not entirely interrupted. In 1818 Cardinal Casimir Haeffelin represented Bavaria. On various occasions in later years Latin American countries were represented by ecclesiastics.

It should be noted that cardinals never took the title of ambassador. At most they were ministers plenipotentiary. The explanation of this practice lies in the fact that, according to the protocol of the Roman Court, cardinals were considered part of the Pope's own household. Since the Council of Basel in the 15th century the rank of ambassador was not granted to a cardinal.[14] This regulation did not cause the king any particular inconvenience for, as cardinal, the royal envoy was already a prince of the Church and as such not only enjoyed precedence over the ambassadors but also could penetrate farther into the councils of the Roman See.

Today the Vatican does not accept an ecclesiastic as the diplomatic representative of a state. The reasons for this date back to 1870. The circumstances that led to the adoption of this rule may be briefly described. After the army of the king of Italy occupied the Eternal City on September 20, 1870 the diplomatic status and immunities of the envoys accredited to the Pope remained unaffected. The new occupants of Rome hoped that, with the passing of time, these diplomats would be merged with the envoys accredited to Italy. Or, at least, the Italians hoped to see the Pope's envoys transformed into a purely ecclesiastical group. They therefore dropped broad hints to the governments concerned that it would, no doubt, be just a matter of time

[14] This practice seems to have dated from as far back as the time of Pope Julius II.

before only churchmen would be assigned to the Vatican post. This would be a tangible indication that the temporal power was really at an end.

The very reason why the changeover was welcome to Italy was naturally the reason why it was unwelcome to the Pope. The Vatican sought to counteract this tactic. For reasons of their own the foreign states complied with the Vatican's wishes. For one thing, they had professed a hands-off attitude in the Roman question. To make any change in the status quo (in 1870 there were, as it so happened, no ecclesiastical envoys representing foreign governments in Rome) would be implicitly to take a stand on an issue they wanted to stay out of. France was one of the first to give a blunt refusal to the suggestions whispered in its ears. "For nothing in the world," wrote Foreign Minister Jules Favre in his memoirs on the Roman question, "would I have consented to an ecclesiastical representation at Rome, which would get out of our control and expose us to religious conflicts." Favre referred to the controversy that had divided the French hierarchy in the months preceding the definition of papal infallibility at the Vatican Council on July 18, 1870. He felt he would be rashly involving the new regime in such disputes by appointing a churchman as France's envoy. Besides, France was in no mood at that time to cater to Italian preferences. With grim satisfaction, Favre named a layman, Count Bernard d'Harcourt, as the new French ambassador at the Vatican.

In Germany a half-hearted effort by the Iron Chancellor to nominate a high ecclesiastic as his envoy in Rome was abandoned. In April 1872 Bismarck sent the name of Cardinal Gustav Adolf zu Hohenlohe to be the ambassador of the Emperor William. The decision was naturally greeted with enthusiasm in Italy but sprang more from domestic policy. It was a maneuver of this original statesman to seem to appear a friend of the German Catholics and to present himself in their eyes as a man of toleration and compromise. As Bismarck confided to the Italian minister, Count de Launay, "In choosing for representative to the Pope a Prince of the Church we give ourselves a certificate of good conduct, and we shall prove to the good peasants and others that we are not so black as we are painted and that we want to live in peace with sincere Catholics who do not mix religion with politics."

Bismarck was prepared for either of the two eventualities. If the Pope agreed to receive his nominee this would split Catholic opposition on the home front. If the Vatican refused to give its *agrément,* the Chancellor could adduce this as a sign of how little the Vatican was prepared to meet his gestures of appeasement. He told the Italian minister: "If the Pope says No, we shall play up his refusal with the blowing of trumpets and the beating of drums. Intelligent people will absolve us of all blame. His Holiness will take all the responsibility. We shall cry from the house-tops that we could not do anything better than to choose a representative from among the members of the Sacred College."

On May 2 the papal secretary of state, Cardinal Antonelli, replied that Cardinal Hohenlohe could not be accepted as the emperor's envoy "in the existing circumstances." No other explanation was offered. This naturally ended the case of a high churchman as prospective Prussian envoy in Rome. As he promised, Bismarck had the inspired press in Berlin play up the refusal. From then on, there was no more talk in Germany or elsewhere of nominating cardinals or any other grade of churchman to the Vatican post.

It is interesting to note that Bismarck did not seem to be impressed by the arguments used in France against the employment of ecclesiastics on diplomatic missions to the Vatican. He had complete confidence that Cardinal Hohenlohe would be a pliable instrument in his hands. Part of this was based on his knowledge of that person's character and past record. A good man but not gifted with great talents, Hohenlohe had rendered himself unpopular in Vatican circles. Even prescinding from personal factors, the very nature of diplomacy was sufficient to assure the useful functioning of the Prussian legation in Rome. As Bismarck again remarked to Count de Launay, he could do no harm: "On the contrary, he will be able to get important information, as was never possible under the reign of Frederick the Great. This monarch got reports directly from a priest. Anyway, a representative acts in virtue of his instructions and, if he should depart from them, the phantasm will disappear at the first breath from Berlin."

The refusal of the Vatican was motivated, as already seen, both by the knowledge of the trap Bismarck was setting and by the desire to thwart the Italian hopes that all the diplomats sent to the Pope would be henceforth exclusively ecclesiastics. But there was another consideration in the minds of the Pope and his advisors, a broader, more impersonal one. A day or two after the Hohenlohe case had been closed, Cardinal Antonelli told the Hapsburg minister plenipotentiary, Count Kalnoky: "If you cite precedents of former centuries . . . in which different powers were represented at the Holy See by ecclesiastics, even by cardinals, this does not prove that what was possible then and which was even at that time not without many disadvantages, is possible today in our own times when everything is changed and especially when ideas on modern law differ so much from the principles of the Church which ought to be the principles of every good priest. Besides all that it is also to be noted that Prussia is a thoroughly Protestant power. . . . How can a cardinal be able to represent it and place himself in the perspective of its policy?" In representing a Protestant state the ecclesiastic would, in short, be in danger of finding himself in a false position.[15]

Such a difficulty does not present itself in the case of a Catholic layman. Non-Catholic countries have frequently accredited lay Catholics to be their diplomats at the Holy See. No difficulty in such appointments is felt by either of the two parties concerned. It is not beyond the realm of possibility that clergymen may once again appear in the Vatican diplomatic corps. Many of the particular circumstances that induced the current interdiction no longer exist. There seems today no objection in principle to the accrediting of churchmen.

Do Catholics or Protestants make better envoys at the Vatican? This is a question on which opinions can differ. Outside of the case of the old Catholic countries, no particular preference for one rather than the other seems to be felt by the Holy See.

[15] The story of the Vatican's fight to prevent the employment of clerical envoys by foreign governments is told more fully by the present author in *The Rise of the Double Diplomatic Corps in Rome*, pp. 32, 38-49.

Much depends upon the personality of the envoy or the particular kind of business which he must transact in Rome. The essential criterion is whether the envoy is able to function effectively. The role of a diplomat is to act as a bond of friendship and understanding. In some cases this is more easily done by a Catholic, in others by one who is not a Catholic.[16]

THE NUNCIOS AT THE ROYAL COURTS

The Court of Rome was slow in adopting for itself the custom inaugurated by the Italian republics. For many years after Venice, Florence, and the other cities on the peninsula had begun to be regularly represented at Rome, the papal authorities refrained from taking corresponding action. The Popes did not have their own envoys, or apostolic nuncios, at the foreign capitals until the practice was well established in Europe. Biaudet tells us, "The permanent nunciatures cannot be considered as definitively established until the second half of the sixteenth century."[17]

This does not mean that the papacy had no system by which it was represented in some fashion throughout Christendom. On the contrary, the Apostolic See long exercised its universal authority through special agents, either designated from among those on the spot or dispatched from Rome. The legates of the papal see are familiar figures in the history of the Christian era. These envoys foreshadowed what we today term the nuncios. They were not, however, diplomatic agents. They were not necessarily sent to negotiate with civil rulers. They were not sent for permanent duty, and there was no regular succession. They are proof, nevertheless, of the very deep roots which contemporary papal diplomacy has.

The envoys representing the Pope in the course of the pre-

---

[16] Except for the first two envoys, the British minister to the Vatican has always been a non-Catholic. On the other hand, in Germany, though the first Vatican envoy of the Federal Republic after World War II was a Protestant, his successor (1956) was a Catholic. This action was taken despite the contention of some that, in line with the prewar custom, the envoy should always be a Protestant. To this it was answered that the so-called tradition was rather a Prussian custom. In February 1956 the foreign minister of the Netherlands declared that the government was free in its choice of envoys. A Catholic in this instance was named to succeed a Protestant envoy at the Vatican.

[17] Biaudet, *Nonciatures permanentes*, p. 94.

nuncio period had various names and their functions varied. Leo the Great (440-461) stationed his own representative, called *apocrisarius* or *responsalis*, at the imperial court in Constantinople.[18] This official became a regular figure at the court after Justinian but he disappeared, both from Constantinople and from papal practice, after the dispute on the holy images in the middle of the 8th century. This papal agent, or observer, as far as the meager sources enable us to determine, reported on the news of the court and acted for the Pope on matters touching not merely questions of faith and discipline but also problems affecting the Italian peninsula. Several of those who had thus served in Constantinople later became Popes. Other bishops also had their own *apocrisarii* at the Imperial Court. At a later date, officials with this title were sent from time to time to the Frankish court, especially in the time of Charlemagne and Louis the Pious, but these were not maintained on a permanent basis. For the rest of Christendom, the Roman See was represented by *Vicars Apostolic* (not to be identified with missionary bishops of the present time). These agents in time became what were termed *legati nati*. They were the principal residential bishops of a region who, in addition to their powers as local ordinaries, were endowed with special faculties from Rome as the permanent delegates of the Pope. This role was attached to the see itself. Among the *legati nati* were the Archbishops of Salzburg, Cologne, Prague, Graz, Canterbury, Reims, Toledo, York, and others. The role survives today in part in the "primate." Today the title of apostolic legate attached to any ancient see is purely honorary and carries no special jurisdiction. These legates were not sent from Rome, being always local bishops. Their relations with the civil power in that capacity were incidental and hence they cannot be exactly termed diplomatic agents of the Pope. Their function was essentially in the field of Church jurisdiction.

The time came when it was necessary for Rome to send its own specially chosen representatives, instead of relying on local bishops. These were the *legati missi* (literally, *legates sent*, to distinguish them from the residential legates). This form of

[18] Batiffol, in *Revue apologétique*, 1928; also in *Recherches de sciences religieuses*, 1926.

papal envoy appears around the time of Gregory VII (1073-1085). He was dispatched to the courts of the princes as well as to the local church authorities. The principal type of the *legatus missus* was the *legatus a latere* (literally, *legate from the [Pope's] side*), because he came from the papal Court. He was usually a cardinal. This category of *legatus missus* was gradually supplanted by the nuncio as the chief papal emissary. The *legatus a latere* encountered opposition from both the local hierarchy and the civil potentates, who often enough charged that the legates were acting *ad instar proconsulum*, just like the proconsuls of the old imperial Rome. The papacy had to insist upon its right to send legates wherever it was necessary. But the princes retained their distrust of this type of envoy. William the Conqueror threatened to hang from the highest oak in his kingdom the first legate who came to England. Other rulers were not so strongly minded on this subject, but the legates were usually looked upon with dislike and suspicion (unless, of course, as in the case of Cardinal Wolsey, the chancellor was himself the legate). The Council of Trent cut their canonical jurisdiction.[19] The last legate *a latere* sent on an important mission was Cardinal Caprara, who went to Paris in connection with the execution of the Concordat of 1801. The title is today given to cardinals performing ceremonial functions, such as representing the Holy Father at international eucharistic congresses.

Such legates were not on permanent missions. The first instance of a permanent mission that can be identified with some exactitude is that of a certain agent, one Barzio de Barzii, who received from Sixtus IV (1471-1484) the order to reside in permanence (*ut ibi permaneat*) at the Court of France. This person remained, however, only six months.[20] The claim is now made, following recent research, that the first papal emissary on permanent mission was Francisco des Prats, who served in Spain for Pope Alexander VI from 1492 to 1503. Another sometimes regarded as the "first nuncio" is Angelo Leonini, bishop of Tivoli, who arrived in Venice in May 1500. Ludovico di Canossa, who went to Paris in 1513, is listed as the first permanent nuncio to the king of France.

[19] *Sess. xxiv, cap. 20, de Reformatione; Sess. xxii, cap. 7, de Reformatione.*
[20] Biaudet, *Nonciatures permanentes,* passim; Richard in *Revue des questions historiques,* 1905, p. 126.

Other permanent nunciatures began to appear as the 16th century advanced. Leo X (1513-1521) seems to have realized the importance of this spreading practice, but it was Pius IV (1559-1565) and especially Gregory XIII (1572-1585) who gave the nunciatures their definitive status. These are the other nunciatures set up during this century, with their approximate date of foundation: Warsaw (1500), Lucerne (1510), Vienna (1513), Lisbon (1513), Naples (1514), Milan (1560), Florence (1560), Cologne (1582), Brussels (1577). The Cologne nuncio exercised jurisdiction for the Rhineland, the nuncio of Brussels for the Low Countries. Subject to the Lucerne nuncio was southwest Germany as well as the Swiss cantons. The nuncio in Vienna to the Imperial Court also included Bohemia and Lusatia in his area of responsibility. To the Warsaw nunciature was added the territories of East and West Prussia as well as Poland.[21] It will be noted that not all the nuncios were accredited to a single court. The nuncios in Cologne, Brussels, and Lucerne were accredited to a multiplicity of minor princes.

The immediate antecedents of the nunciatures are shrouded in the fogs that beset the history of institutions.[22] Diplomatically the nuncios had the same origins as the other ambassadors of the latter half of the 15th century. Ecclesiastically, however, they had roots of their own. The exact process of their evolution as papal organs is still obscure. One theory with the virtue of simplicity is that the nuncios developed from the *legati a latere*, just as the *legati a latere* developed from the *legati nati*. When the Holy See began to feel that the appointment of residential bishops as the special papal representatives on the spot was unsatisfactory and a source of bad feeling among other bishops, Rome began to send cardinals from its own curia with ample powers but on short-term missions. When these legates in turn outlived their usefulness the nuncio came upon the scene—a papal envoy with fewer powers but at least permanently stationed in the field and, what is more significant, with closer relations to the local civil authorities.

In reality, according to those who have made a close study

[21] Meier, *Propaganda*, I, pp. 180-323; II, p. 184.
[22] What follows on the origins of the nunciatures is based chiefly on the researches of P. Richard.

of the origins of the nuncios, these papal agents appear to derive not from the legates but from another category of envoys: the papal fiscal officials who covered Europe in the Middle Ages bearing the title of *nuntii et collectores jurium, reddituum et omnium bonorum Camerae apostolicae.* Their mission was to procure the means for the support of the Roman See and especially for the expenses of the Crusades. Such *nuncii et collectores* were found in the Kingdoms of Poland, Sweden, Norway, and Denmark; in England, Scotland, and Ireland. There were others in Sicily, Portugal, Castile, Burgundy, at Venice, Naples, and elsewhere. They were established on the most formal basis in France, the Rhineland, and Germany. Such agents were officially in contact with the local political authorities and were on occasion able to transact papal business with such rulers. In the main, however, their role was chiefly financial. Their political and especially their ecclesiastical function was limited. At the end of the 15th century the *nuntii collectores* were rapidly losing their importance. For one thing, the local clergy and princes began more and more to retain for themselves the disposition of these funds, sometimes with papal consent, sometimes without it. In Spain the fund was applied directly to the war against the Moors. It is quite possible that this network of *nuntii collectores* provided the name as well as the pattern of the *nuntii ambassadores.*

The term *nuntius* (messenger, envoy) meant any emissary, exercising some function in the name of the curia outside Rome. It was used in a general sense therefore and this makes it difficult to determine at just what point the nuncios become ambassadors. A more reliable criterion than the mere title are the instructions the nuncio received and the manner in which he was dispatched. The tenor and scope of the letters appointing him and the terms of his accreditation to the prince indicate whether the nuncio in question is a real ambassador in the diplomatic sense. The papal officer was a diplomatic agent if he was: (1) sent to a foreign court, (2) with the mandate of remaining at his post until recalled, and (3) with the authority to oversee not one or other special question but any matter which might arise between the Pope and the prince. To the permanency of his mission was added the generality of his man-

date. The nuncio's instructions began to take this form when
the papacy consciously adopted the new practice already introduced by the Italian cities. The formula appeared with the
case of Barzio de Barzii, already mentioned, and came into
general use with Julius II (1503-1513). Up to that stage the
nuncio was delegated for such and such specific negotiation.
The letter which sent him off simply stated that he was sent
for some, or various matters of interest to the Pope (*pro non-
nullis nostris atque S. Sedis negotiis, pro magnis, pro diversis
negotiis*). To make the transformation from an extraordinary
to an ordinary mission it was enough to suppress the adjectives
restricting the mandate.

It is sometimes said that the institution of the nunciatures
was a papal reaction to the Protestant revolt. As the above account of the origins of this papal diplomatic instrument shows,
this is not quite correct. The permanent nunciatures already
existed in Vienna, Paris, Madrid, Lisbon, and on the Italian
peninsula and elsewhere before the Reformation had assumed
any serious proportions. Their primary purpose was not, therefore, that of combatting Protestantism. On the other hand, the
creation of the new series of nunciatures in the north, at Lucerne, Cologne, and Brussels were definitely in response to the
religious threat. The letters of the papal legates sent to Germany and to other danger spots where religious rebellion was
rife testify eloquently to the need for direct and constant action
by the papacy through permanent agents at the courts of the
princes, above all those whose orthodoxy was shaky. The princes
who still remained loyal needed to be stimulated to take action
against the heretics. The same could be said for the local
hierarchy. Both the civil officials and the higher clergy, drawn
from the ranks of the nobility, appointees of their own relatives,
powerful princes, were only too often on the verge of apostasy.
Furthermore, the decrees of the Council of Trent needed to be
carried into execution. For the next hundred years the nunciatures were a major instrument in the counter-Reformation. In
1648 the Treaties of Westphalia ended the stage of religious
wars. But, as time was to show, the nuncios still had their mission to perform in the age of classical diplomacy that ensued.

In general, the diplomatic practices followed by the Court of

Rome were the same as those that the other courts of Europe adopted on the basis of experience and custom. The diplomatic law of Europe developed along the lines of a unified system in which precedent and tradition played a great role. The papacy developed, however, some distinctive features of its own. For one thing, its own envoys were not termed ambassadors but nuncios. The nunciatures were divided into two groups, first class and second class. The internunciature is an innovation of the 19th century. The first-class nunciatures were those at the great Catholic courts. These were distinguished by certain privileges that the receiving monarch possesssed or, better, managed to extort. One of the valued rights possessed by the major Catholic powers was that the nuncio who had been accredited to that power should, upon completion of his tour of duty, be named a cardinal. In other words, appointment as nuncio to a major court was virtually a guarantee of the red hat. It was not long before the Catholic monarchs asked to have the privilege of knowing and approving in advance the man to be designated as nuncio at their own court. Today we know this as the process *agréation*. Before the name of a new ambassadorial appointment is published, the receiving government is asked confidentially if he is acceptable. Rome, however, did not at first take kindly to the idea of asking prior approval for the nuncio it wished to send.

The issue came to a head in the time of the short pontificate of Alexander VIII (1689-1691). At a time of particular tension between Rome and Vienna, the Pope named Lorenzo Corsini (later Clement XII) to be nuncio at the court of Leopold I. The emperor refused to receive him and demanded, in return, the right to have a list of possible candidates submitted to him beforehand. This would have the advantage, contended Vienna, of avoiding the rejection of the nuncio when he arrived to present his credentials and the resulting ruffled feelings on both sides. In the light of current diplomatic practice requiring that the envoy be always *persona grata*, this demand was quite reasonable, but Alexander VIII rejected it as an innovation. Corsini was given another post, but not a nunciature, as if to demonstrate that the appointment to Vienna still held good. The rupture continued until the new Pope, Innocent XII (1691-

1700), yielded and granted Leopold what he wanted by sending him in 1692 a list of three names, or *terna*, of possible nuncios. From this list the Emperor chose Sebastiano Antonio Tanara.[23]

Naturally such a favor could not be limited to the house of Hapsburg. It was not long before Paris and Madrid sought and received the same privilege. Saint-Simon is witness to this privilege. He also notes that when the nuncio finished his turn of duty he was automatically created a cardinal. Writing as of the year 1705 he recorded: "The three great crowns, that is, the Emperor, the King [*of France*] and the King of Spain, have this privilege that the Pope proposes to them three or four subjects and the one who is chosen is named to the nunciature accredited to them, and from that nunciature it is certain that they will leave as cardinals."[24]

While penning the above words, the chronicler of Versailles was not thinking of John V of Portugal, who was watching the situation with rising envy and anger. Up to this time, as Saint-Simon's enumeration reveals, Lisbon was not reckoned one of the first-class nunciatures. By the same token Portugal was not considered by either Rome or the three crowns to be a great power. The king of Portugal was determined to exact from Rome at least the formal recognition of Lisbon as a first-class nunciature. In 1709 Clement XI sent King John V a list of possible nuncios, from which the Portuguese monarch chose Vincenzo Bichi, who had been nuncio at Lucerne. That this concession did not satisfy the jealous king became evident when Rome sought to recall Bichi. His service in Lisbon was not up to Rome's expectations. But John V demanded that, before his departure, Bichi should be made a cardinal, just as was done in the first-class nunciatures. Clement XI rejected the petition made on behalf of a nuncio whose performance seems not to have deserved such recompense. The king's answer was to forbid the nuncio to leave Portugal.

Bichi tarried in the country for a number of years while the nunciature managed to carry on under emergency conditions. Finally in September 1720 Rome peremptorily ordered him home. A successor, Giuseppe Firrao, was sent to take his

23 Bischoffshausen, *Papst Alexander VIII.*
24 Saint-Simon, *Mémoires*, XIII, p. 190.

place. But the ambitious Portuguese king, seeing his demands ignored, refused to allow Firrao to exercise his functions and continued to regard Bichi as the legitimate papal nuncio. Faced with this open defiance, the conciliatory Roman Court compromised by naming Bichi auditor of the nunciature, even though that ex-nuncio was still ignoring his orders to return home. Clement XI bequeathed this problem among others to his successor, Innocent XIII (1721-1724). The new Pope found that the Portuguese king, with greater life expectancy than the Pontiffs, persisted in his demands that Bichi should get the red hat, with the implication, of course, that all succeeding nuncios would also be named to the Sacred College, in line with practice obtaining at the other three courts. The next Pope, Benedict XIII (1724-1730) in his turn found the problem still very much alive, very much unsolved, and Bichi still in Portugal awaiting his hat. The cardinals whom Benedict consulted advised strongly against according such a privilege to . either Portugal or to Bichi. They argued—and few could fail to see their point—that the Pope should be able to recall his own envoys at his own pleasure. Then there was the question of precedent of which other princes, with fine plans for themselves, might wish to avail themselves.

The deadlock continued. In 1728 John V ordered his own ambassador from Rome. Shortly afterward, Firrao, who had never been recognized or received anyway, was ordered out of Portugal. A decree of July declared the existence of diplomatic rupture with the Holy See and forbade subjects of the Pope to live in the realm. Even Bichi, still hoping for his princely robes of cardinal, was told to get out. Portuguese subjects were forbidden to petition Rome for benefices and the king's subjects in Rome, lay as well as clerical, were ordered by him to leave the Pope's domains. At this point Benedict XIII himself died in turn, happy no doubt, in leaving this world, to leave the stubborn Portuguese monarch behind him.

The new Pope, Clement XII (1730-1740), the fourth to be involved with the robust King John V, finally yielded in 1730, for the peace of the Church. The Lisbon nunciature was raised to the state of equality with that of Paris, Madrid, and Vienna. As for Bichi, in 1731, eleven years after his "recall" from his post, he was made cardinal. He received but a routine reprimand and passed off the stage.[25]

It may be wondered if any similar case exists in secular diplomacy of an envoy who was not only *persona grata* to the sovereign but so satisfactory that the government to which he was accredited actually broke with the accrediting government for trying to recall him. To modern eyes the dispute seems trivial. Obviously, however, it involved important points of prestige and therefore of power. In the tightly-knit if quarrelsome society of Catholic monarchs it was highly advantageous for Portugal to be thus recognized in the same class with the other major crowns. The fears of Benedict XIII and his advisers soon proved well grounded. In the next pontificate, that of Benedict XIV (1740-1758), the king of Sardinia put forward a similar demand in the interests of the red hats of the nuncios at his capital of Turin. Poland, Venice, and Naples stood by, ready to make like demands. This time Rome answered with more decisiveness. In 1753 it deliberately passed over the nuncio in Turin, reckoning that it was better to lose one nunciature there than three later. This happened, for the king closed the nunciature, although he did not recall his Rome envoy.[26]

From the beginning the nuncios were, almost without exception, ecclesiastics and not laymen. Some of them were mere deacons, or members of religious orders; most were of episcopal rank. They were not cardinals except in special cases. In the earliest days of diplomacy even the secular rulers exhibited a marked preference for clerics as their representatives. Too often the noblemen at their courts were more skilled in horsemanship and wielding a mace than in conducting negotiations in Latin. The Court of Rome generally refrained from the use of laymen. In the whole history of papal diplomacy the number of laymen employed on diplomatic missions is infinitesimal. One case cited is that of Bernardino Pimentel, who was not merely a layman but married and the father of a family. The conclave of 1522 elected the Dutchman Adrian VI (1522-1523) while he was in Spain as papal legate. Prior to his departure for Rome

[25] Pastor, *History*, XXXIV, pp. 37, 181-89, 403. For Bichi's biography, see *Dictionnaire d'histoire et de géographie ecclésiastiques*. h.n.
[26] Pastor, *op.cit.*, XXXV, pp. 50-51, 431-34.

to take the tiara, the newly elected (and short-lived) Pope named Pimentel, who was his aide, to be nuncio. The next Pope, Clement VII (1523-1534), sent another layman to Charles V in 1524. He was Balthasar Castiglione, author of *El Cortesano*. Another instance cited is that of one Cavaliere Antonio Bussi, major of the papal militia who was sent on a purely political mission to Milan after the Treaty of Tolentino in 1797. But this was in very unusual circumstances and Bussi did not carry the title of nuncio in any case.

A curious case is that of "Count" Pieracchi, who went to Paris in 1796, after the armistice of Bologna, with the rank not of nuncio but of minister plenipotentiary. Pieracchi was in reality an ecclesiastic. Had he come as a clergyman the Directory would not have received him. Yet negotiations were imperative. This course was advised by the Spanish ambassador at Paris, the Marquis de Campo, who acted as intermediary. His recommendations on this occasion describe sufficiently both the situation and the motives that led to the sending of a cleric in the guise of a layman. "This minister," he wrote, "should be a layman, for it has been stated that they would not receive an ecclesiastic, and such a one would be exposed to insult. . . . It seems to me that Pieracchi would be the most worthy of this appointment. . . . It would suffice to have him put on secular garb and to call him Count Pieracchi."[27] This advice was adopted and even Pieracchi's secretary, a priest, went by the name of Sieur François Evangelisti. After the Treaty of Tolentino the "Count" was himself succeeded at Paris by a real layman, Marquis Camillo Massimi, who had the rank of ambassador.

It is natural that the Pope's representatives should themselves be ecclesiastics, since the person whom they represent is himself first and foremost a religious authority. The nuncios' quality should correspond to that of their chief. Another reason why the nuncio was from the start an ecclesiastical officer is that he had to conduct ecclesiastical affairs as well as political negotiations. In many cases he possessed canonical jurisdiction delegated by the Pope. It was therefore appropriate that the envoy should be in clerical orders. There were exceptions, as

[27] du Teil, *Rome, Naples*, p. 196.

already noted. In addition to the lay nuncios occasionally sent on mission, it may be recalled that in earlier times kings were given the title and powers of legate. St. Stephen, king of Hungary, was a papal legate and his successors were at least honorary legates. Alexander III (1159-1181) gave Henry II of England the powers of papal legate, although as it turned out the terms were unsatisfactory to Henry and he rejected the role.

The ecclesiastical and political business of the papal envoys has, consequently, practically always been confided to an ecclesiastic. Theoretically it should be possible for the Pope to have two representatives in one country. In this case, one envoy would be accredited to the sovereign while the other would confine his relations to the local clergy and faithful. It appears that, in fact, an experiment along this line was once attempted when the Jesuit Possevino was sent in 1577 on a "political" mission to Sweden, the reconciliation of John III.[28] Another Jesuit, Lauritz Nilsson, was put in charge of purely religious matters. This division of competences did not work and the experiment has not been followed.[29] One reason for the cumulation of functions of envoy and religious agent was the simple fact that no ruler would permit a papal representative to operate on his territory independently of the crown. A permanent papal envoy with a non-diplomatic role such as an apostolic delegate was a practical impossibility until rather recent times. The change in this respect is discussed in Chapters 9 and 10.

The nuncio today has, therefore, a double function. He represents the Pope before the civil government and also before the Church of the country. He has what is appropriately styled both an *external* and an *internal* mission. According to canon law (n. 267) the mission of the papal envoys known as nuncios and internuncios embraces these points: (1) To foster, according to the usual rules of the Holy See, good relations between the Holy See and the civil governments to which they are permanent envoys. (2) To watch over the state of the Church in the territory assigned them and to report to the Roman Pontiff thereon. Besides these powers and duties, the papal representatives receive from the Pope certain special delegated

28 Pastor, *op.cit.*, xx, p. 421.
29 Biaudet, *op.cit.*, p. 10.

ecclesiastical powers which vary according to the circumstances of time and place.

There is another kind of papal envoy who is likely to be confused with the nuncio but who is, nevertheless, not a diplomatic agent. This is the apostolic delegate to which reference has just been made. Formerly, a papal representative with this title had, like the nuncio, both a diplomatic and a canonical mission. According to present curial practice, however, the apostolic delegate is never a diplomatic representative. To clarify a confusion existing between the titles of internuncio and of apostolic delegate, an administrative order of the secretary of state of May 8, 1916 established[30] that thereafter papal envoys known as apostolic delegates would not, even though they, too, represent the person of the Pontiff, any longer have diplomatic status. The delegate performs today an exclusively internal mission. He is not accredited to the government and his relations are restricted to the hierarchy and faithful of the country.

The difference between the two kinds of papal representatives is sometimes explained by saying that the nuncio has a "political" mission whereas the delegate has a "religious" one. Such terms are likely to be misleading, but in the context they are perfectly clear. The nuncio has a political mission to the extent that, unlike the apostolic delegate, he is accredited to the civil authorities. But he does not cease to be an ecclesiastical officer for being an ambassador. The nuncio can and does represent the highest Church authority before the government as well as before the local prelates. On the other hand, the nuncio also has the same powers as the apostolic delegate. He has the same commission to concern himself with the Church problems of the region, directly and without reference to the government.

---

[30] *AAS*, VIII (1916), p. 213. The title of "internuncio" was given in the 17th century to papal representatives sent to nunciatures where for some reason a nuncio could not be sent at that time. The internunciature as a separate category of papal diplomatic mission is a rather recent introduction.

CHAPTER 5

THE MINISTRIES

THE CARDINAL SECRETARY OF STATE

ALL diplomatic agents, including nuncios, are docile instruments of a higher authority. The foreign minister (or his equivalent) gives tone and direction to the work of the envoys, who merely report to him and execute his orders to the best of their ability. Important as the envoys are in symbolizing the institution of modern diplomacy, they are overshadowed in the conduct of that diplomacy by their chief, who remains at home setting policy and coordinating the work of his foreign representatives. In the case of the Holy See, the cardinal secretary of state of His Holiness is charged with the conduct of the Vatican's relations with the civil governments. He, more than the nuncios, represents papal diplomacy, at least in the popular mind. The personality of this official dominates the course taken by the Holy See in these relations, perhaps more so than in the case of the ordinary foreign minister, for the papal secretary of state is more than just a foreign minister.

Moroni, physician of Gregory XVI, whose *Dizionario* is a vast storehouse of papal lore, says of the office of secretary of state: "This high charge is exercised by a cardinal of rare talents, who is distinguished by his energy and successful experience in all sorts of matters and who enjoys the full confidence of the Supreme Pontiff who selects him for this high office from among the ablest cardinals." The cardinal secretary of state of His Holiness has been and remains the most intimate collab-

Bibliographical Note: Richard's 1910 study of the origins and development of the secretariat of state is still the best work, although it has been refined more recently (1950) by Serafini. Many of the topics covered in this chapter are to be found in the standard religious encyclopedias, beginning with Moroni's *Dizionario*, under the heading of "Roman Curia," "Congregations," or "Secretary of State." The organization of the Roman curia is the subject of lengthy books by canonists. In addition to the sources mentioned in the footnotes to this chapter, the following authors found in the Bibliography may be consulted: Bangen, Berutti, von Kienitz, La Brière, Heston, Hugues de Ragnau, Paro. Also relevant are the memoirs and biographies of Consalvi, Ferrata, Lambruschini, and Pacca. Giovanni Carga's 1574 study of the secretariat, edited by Hugo Laemmer in 1861, is an informative memorandum.

orator of the Pope. More than a foreign minister, he is also more than a prime minister. The secretary is identified with the policy of the Pope. The names of Pacelli, Gasparri, Merry del Val, and Rampolla, to mention only the secretaries of Pius XI, Benedict XV, St. Pius X, and Leo XIII, are inextricably linked with the history of the papacy of their times. Yet this official is more than a passive instrument. The fact that Pope Pius XII in the last half of his pontificate refrained from naming a secretary of state, preferring to keep the handling of foreign affairs in his own hands, shows that this post is more than that of a mere "secretary."

By all odds the secretary of state is the most conspicuous and most familiar personage at the Vatican, after the Pope himself. Perhaps one reason for this prominence is that the secretary is the first object of criticism from within as well as from outside the Church. Upon him falls the burden of complaints from those who disagree with the course of papal policy. The lot of the secretary, convenient target for those who do not wish to attack the Pope himself, is not always full of human rewards. Credit for success is not proportionate to the condemnations that are his when failure comes. He has no illusions that his tribulations are a sort of preparation for the tiara upon the death of his patron. On the contrary, he is fairly certain that he will never rise higher than the post to which he has already risen, and that he will probably not retain even that. History may indeed raise him higher in the estimation of men, but he will be lucky if his contemporaries put him on a pedestal. The cases of cardinal secretaries who have afterward become Popes are rare indeed. When Eugene Cardinal Pacelli, secretary of state under Pius XI, ascended the throne of Peter in March 1939, this broke a tradition of centuries. The last secretary to be elected Pontiff was Cardinal Rospigliosi, who became Clement IX (1667-1669) after having served his predecessor Alexander VII in that capacity. On the other hand, if the post of secretary is difficult and thankless, the incumbent can at least console himself with the thought that the first person who seems to have occupied a similar post was a saint, Charles Borromeo, nephew of Pius IV, who came to Rome in 1560.

The historians of the papacy and its institutions have traced the origins of the secretariat of state to a double source. One of these was the *camera secreta,* or private staff of the Pope. The other was the system of "cardinal nephews." Related to both of these offices was the secretariat of letters of princes and the secretary of briefs. The official correspondence of the Pope was prepared in the Pontiff's own personal quarters, in his *camera secreta.* The end of the Western schism in 1417 enormously increased the amount of written communication between the Roman authorities and Christendom. Rulers and even universities sought concessions and guarantees as rewards for their services to the Pope. The answers called for great skill as well. This was no longer the time of Boniface VIII. "The Pope needed first-class secretaries," writes Martin, "skilled in all the finesses of the Latin language, able to employ its nuances so that its remonstrances and reproaches should be sufficiently visible, under the compliments with which they were wrapped, to move without wounding. For the Vicar of Jesus Christ could no longer count upon the old faith and respect."[1]

Out of this group of secretaries around the Pontiff it was inevitable that one should emerge as the chief. Innocent VIII (1484-1492) gave the first formal existence to this office when he created the apostolic secretariat with twenty members in 1487. His order on this occasion sanctioned the *secretarius domesticus* and outlined his duties as follows: to live at the Pope's own residence, ready at his beck and call, and to serve as liaison with the other secretaries. In the nature of things such a secretary was bound to have great influence. It is not surprising that in the time of Alexander VI and Julius II, the next Popes, the Venetian ambassadors, ever alert to opportunities as becomes diplomats worth their salt, report him as a man whom the foreign representatives visited often and cultivated diligently because they knew he had the confidence as well as the ear of the Pope.

When permanent diplomatic missions began to assume importance in the operation of the papacy's own affairs, a further development was inevitable. Nowhere was the trend of the times more appreciated at its true value than at Venice or Florence. Is it surprising that a scion of the Medici, Leo X, son of

[1] Martin, *Cardinaux,* p. 148. I have drawn heavily on this excellent study.

Lorenzo the Magnificent, brought such an awareness with him to the Apostolic See and took steps to activate it? One of his innovations was the introduction of Italian as the medium of communication not only with the princes but also within the Pope's own administrative machinery. He also brought in one of his countrymen, one Pietro Ardighello, and assigned to him the task of editing the Italian-language dispatches.

What was to develop into the cardinal-nephew system began at this time. If earlier Popes had enriched their relatives, they did not bring their nephews into the Church's central administration. Leo X brought with him, not his nephew, but his cousin, Giulio de' Medici, whom he made cardinal and upon whom he relied heavily for advice and action. From 1519 he saw the Pope every day, took his instructions, dictated the outlines of diplomatic dispatches, reviewed the draft, and finally signed the definitive version. It is interesting to note, however, that this secretary was not himself a serious believer in the system, for when he in turn became Pope with the name of Clement VII (1523-1534) he did all this work himself, leaving only scraps of work for his secretaries. But the system of cardinal nephew, to which Leo X had given the first impulse, was destined to take hold. From the time of Paul III (1534-1549) until the system blew up in the explosion of 1676 the cardinal nephew generally held the real power in his hands in most pontificates.

After Paul III, if the cardinal nephew does not appoint the nuncios himself, he at least selects them and it is he who has them removed when they cease to suit him. He transmits to them the Pope's orders, as interpreted by himself. He directs them. In short, he is their "patron." The nuncios address him in fact by this title (*Illustrissime e Reverendissime Signore mio padrone colendissimo*). He is, in addition, the administrator of the sacred palaces; he distributes jobs, patronage, honors, money. He is the intermediary of the Pope with the other departments of the pontifical government. After the creation of the Holy Office, however, he ceased to have anything to do with questions of doctrine. From then on, his role was the administration of political matters.

In the heyday of the cardinal nephew, what became of *secretarius domesticus*, whose duties had been outlined by Innocent VIII? Though overshadowed by a vigorous cardinal nephew, the domestic secretary was still on the scene. In the reigns of Popes St. Pius V (1566-1572) and Gregory XIII (1572-1585) cardinal nephews played no role in the general affairs of the Church. It was the domestic secretary who, in this interval, signed the dispatches and took orders directly from the Pope. After 1592, however, following the accession of Clement VIII (1592-1605), the term though not the office disappears from official documents. It is replaced by a new title, secretary of state.

The cardinal nephew, however, continued for a long time to be the Pope's right-hand man for diplomatic matters.[2] At length in 1644 Innocent X was elected at a conclave that had manifested its sharp discontent with the abuses of the cardinal patron. The new Pope continued the custom of making his closest relative a cardinal, but at the head of diplomatic affairs he placed the experienced Cardinal Pancirolo, no relative, whose hand became freer very soon when the cardinal nephew, who was not even a priest, put aside the purple in order to marry. From this time on, while the newly elected Pope continued to make his favorite nephew or other relative a member of the sacred college, it was to an experienced diplomat who had himself served as nuncio to whom the conduct of foreign relations was entrusted. The result was that Rome for a while became accustomed to seeing the papal policy directed by two pairs of hands. The change was not entirely to the displeasure of the nephew, who found it more interesting and profitable

---

[2] Baron von Heubner calls attention to the instructions alleged to have been given by Sixtus V to his nephew, Cardinal Montalto. The authenticity of this memorandum is not certain but since it was printed in 1602, twelve years after the death of the Pope, its observations on the role of the cardinal nephew have a certain validity of their own. Sixtus V is presented as alluding to the special links of blood relationship that bind the cardinal nephews to their Pontiff and then describes their duties as the right hand of the Pope: *"C'est avec eux que traitent les envoyés des princes, tant ceux qui résident ici que ceux qui sont venus en mission spéciale à cette cour; c'est par leur organe que le pape apprend à connaître les désirs et les besoins de toute la Chrétienté; c'est à eux qu'écrivent les nonces et les autres ministres du Saint-Siège; c'est par leur entremise qu'est gouverné l'Etat Ecclésiastique; c'est par leur intervention et à la suite de leur intercession que beaucoup d'emplois et de bénéfices ecclésiastiques sont conférés, et, ce qui importe d'avantage encore, par eux se fait la promotion des cardinaux. Enfin, c'est par eux que le pape manifeste sa pensée et qu'il distribue des grâces; leur assistance, plus que tout autre, l'aide à porter le lourd fardeau du pontificat"* (Huebner, *Sixte-Quint*, II, pp. 391-92, app.).

to attend to internal details of administration while the tedious drafting of dispatches was left to professional hands.

There remained only the elimination of the cardinal nephew for the secretary of state to enter into his own as sole aide and confidant of the Pope. This was not long in coming. Although the Roman Court had long patiently suffered the grasping and arrogance of the cardinal nephew and seemed indeed to consider his plundering of the papal resources a quite natural thing, even this long suffering had its limits. The eruption of indignation took place under Clement X (1670-1676), whose "nephew" (in reality, the uncle of the Pope's niece's husband) by his blunders and petty taxations finally made the Romans explode in resentment. The next Pontiff, Blessed (beatified on October 8, 1956 by Pius XII) Innocent XI, broke the tradition and named none of his family to the purple, much less put them in positions of power. The secretary of state now had the field unchallenged. What is more, he took over in part some of the functions that had been previously performed by the cardinal nephews in the general conduct of the Pope's business. In 1692 Innocent XII abolished nepotism completely, with the bull *Romanum decet pontificem.*

The development of the secretary of state from one who drafts and signs diplomatic dispatches to a general counselor of the Pope was a natural one, in the case of a sovereign who rules as well as reigns. For such sovereigns the difference between personal affairs of the Court and public business was very slight, if any existed at all. To be secretary to the Pope meant not simply to be his "foreign minister." The secretary of state of the Pontiff supervised the apostolic palace. Not only did he live in the same palace with the Pontiff, but he was responsible also for its administration, from the servants to the museum and library. If this "housekeeping" aspect of the secretary's duties seems today entirely alien to the "prime minister" or even of a "foreign minister," it is only because sovereigns in former days saw no distinction where we see one. The government of the prince's household was not different from the government of the prince's subjects. The papal government is not a government alone; it is also a royal court. That is why today the cardinal secretary of state, if he is not responsible today for the temporalities of the Vatican palace, resides there nevertheless as head of the papal family under the Pope.

The evolution of the secretariat of state throws light on another distinction, one of great importance, the difference between the Pope as a religious Pontiff and as a temporal sovereign. Theoretically, the separation of the two roles is easy. In practice, as the history of the secretariat shows, it is difficult if not impossible to draw a hard and fast line between the two.

As long as the Roman Pontiffs were lords of the papal states, political questions absorbed much of the attention of the cardinal secretary. There was not one secretary for political affairs and another for ecclesiastical matters. From the viewpoint of the modern mind a division of competences would seem appropriate and even necessary. From the Roman viewpoint, however, the separation was impractical. The two roles could not be separated in the Pope's first minister any more than they could be separated in the Pope himself. An incident that occurred during the Napoleonic era may serve to illustrate the double function of the cardinal secretary as seen in the eyes of the papacy.

On June 11, 1809 two French officers belonging to the army of occupation in the Eternal City forced their way into the papal residence on the Quirinal and proceeded to the apartments used by the secretary of state. They sealed the files of the secretariat, stationed a sentinel at the door, and gave the incumbent, Cardinal Gabrielli, two days to leave Rome. The cord was tightening closer about the Pope. In a month the Pontiff himself, Pius VII, would be carried away by the emperor's orders. Poised to annex Rome to the Empire, Napoleon was for the moment satisfied to strike the Pope's first minister.

The protest which Cardinal Gabrielli, who was actually pro-secretary (his predecessor, Doria Pamphili had already been expelled from Rome), dispatched to General Miollis, French commandant in Rome, in the name of the Pope stressed the double character of the secretary. The order of expulsion to the Pope's own minister, in the Pope's own personal residence, and the sealing of his official papers, was not merely a brazen violation of the principles of public law. It was, in addition, protested Gabrielli, a supreme affront to the dignity of the supreme head of the Catholic hierarchy. "This minister," said the Pope through his secretary, "is not only the political minister of a temporal prince but also the minister of a sovereign whose primary attribute is to be head of the Church." This minister, the protest continued, "is not merely responsible for the administration of the temporal concerns of this sovereign but also of the spiritual interests of the whole Catholic world." In short, complained the Pope, a double injury was committed by the emperor, who pretended to have so much regard for the liberty, independence, and safety of the head of the Church which in reality he trampled underfoot.[3]

After the restoration of the temporal power in 1815 following the Congress of Vienna, the question of the distinction between the two roles was destined to gain prominence. The movement for constitutional reform of the papal states, amounting to the secularization of the papal administration, gained momentum as the 19th century advanced. On May 21, 1831 the powers who were intervening in the peninsula at that disturbed epoch presented a memorandum to the Holy Father urging a certain number of constitutional reforms in line with the trend in governments generally in Europe. The new Pope, Gregory XVI (1831-1846), did not welcome this interference, but changes did ensue in the papal administration, one of them concerning the secretary of state. Up to that time the secretary was in effect also minister of the interior, responsible for the internal administration of the papal states as well as for its foreign interests. In a decree of February 20, 1833 the Pope created two secretariats, that of the secretary of state proper

---

[3] Pius VII, *Correspondance authentique*, p. 66. The protest of the Austrian representative followed the same line of argument. In his answer, dated the same day (June 11, 1809), to General Miollis' order to leave Rome, the chargé d'affaires of Austria, Louis von Lebzeltern, said that he could not leave Rome except under constraint for, both as a temporal ruler and as the head of the Church, the Pope was entitled to the treatment of a sovereign: *"Une des prérogatives les plus essentielles du Pape, soit en qualité de Souverain temporel, soit comme Chef de l'Eglise, est d'avoir près de sa Personne sacrée des ministres des cours catholiques, qui entretiennent avec le Saint-Siège les rapports nécessaires au bien être de la religion et des fidèles, et l'interruption de ces communications—qui ne pourrait avoir lieu qu'au préjudice du catholicisme dans les Etats respectifs—serait la plus forte et inconcevable atteinte portée à la souveraineté spirituelle du Pape"* (Lebzeltern, *Mémoires*, p. 77).

and a secretary of state for internal affairs. The heavy burdens upon the cardinal secretary were adduced as reason for the change. Cardinal Bernetti remained as secretary of state proper while Cardinal Gamberini became the first papal "minister of the interior."

Under the reorganization of Gregory XVI the secretary of state was to have the following responsibilities: (1) relations with the diplomatic corps resident in Rome and with the ministers of the courts abroad; (2) relations with the papal nuncios, pontifical diplomatic agents, and the consuls; (3) relations with all the other representatives of the Holy See, insofar as this was necessary in matters touching foreign affairs, or internal matters of the papal states having implications for foreign governments. In addition, the cardinal secretary was responsible for the issuing of passports. He was ex officio member of the Congregation for Extraordinary Ecclesiastical Affairs and he was the designated official to give effect to the decisions of that congregation as approved by the Pope.

In addition to the above attributes, which parallel those of foreign ministers generally, the cardinal secretary retained certain prerogatives in domestic matters. Among others, the governor of Rome as director of police depended upon him for matters of *alta polizia*, or general direction of policy. Certain military matters, notably the movement of troops, was subject to the secretary. He was also to be responsible for censorship of the press, whether in the city of Rome or outside it.[4]

We need not tarry over the reorganization of Gregory XVI, for it was soon superseded by other reforms of his successor who, among other things, promptly (August 1, 1846) reunited the two secretariats. The decree of February 20, 1833 is one of the first clear official delineations, in contemporary terms, of the duties and functions of the secretary of state in the sphere of diplomacy. But there is no thought of separating the political from the ecclesiastical work of the secretary of state, at least on the foreign level. That question arose in the first years of Pius IX, who came to the See of Peter in 1846.

Cardinal Mastai-Ferretti was hailed at his election as the

---

[4] Gregory XVI, *Acta*, I, pp. 229-31. On Cardinal Bernetti's situation at this time, see Morelli, *Politica estera*.

Pontiff of the long-awaited constitutional reform. But the new Pope soon found out, if he did not already know, that it was not easy to graft 19th century political institutions and forms upon the ancient administrative machinery which is the Roman curia. Nevertheless, the attempt was begun. Among the earlier reforms affecting the secretariat of state was a *motu proprio* of June 12, 1847 by which Pius IX established a council of ministers comprising seven members. Of this council the secretary of state was declared "president." He retained, with some exceptions, the same diplomatic functions assigned to him in the decree of Gregory XVI. The *motu proprio* stressed the key role of the cardinal secretary: "The secretariat of state is the center of all the matters that are treated by the various ministers; it is the organ for the publication of the laws and for the transmission of the orders emanating from the sovereign, as well as for relations with the Sovereign himself on appeals against the acts and decisions of the various dicasteries (papal organs)."[5]

The establishment of a council of ministers along the model of the constitutional governments did not entirely please advocates of reform. The portfolios were all held by ecclesiastics. But the cry of the day was, "Let the Church be run by churchmen and the state by laymen." The general admissibility of the laity to the higher posts of the papal states was one of the central points of the desired reform. In answer to the complaints, a new *motu proprio* of December 29, 1847 set up nine ministries.[6] These included a "foreign ministry" and a ministry of the interior. The president of the council would always be a cardinal. But the other ministries (except foreign affairs) could be held by laymen. The powers of the cardinal secretary were outlined in these terms (art. 14): "It belongs to the cardinal secretary of state, foreign minister (in addition to the intervention proper to him in ecclesiastical matters, for which he deals directly with the Supreme Pontiff), to establish and maintain relations with the other powers and, as needed, in dealing with these governments, to defend the dignity and integrity

[5] Pius IX, *Acta, seconda parte,* I, p. 52.
[6] *Ibid., seconda parte,* I, pp. 191-215.

of the domains and the territory of the Holy See as well as the rights and claims of the pontifical subjects."

As it turned out, the first cabinet based on the new *motu proprio* was comprised entirely of ecclesiastics. Cardinal Ferretti, the secretary of state, assumed the title of "foreign minister." Soon after, however, a new cabinet was formed, with Cardinal Bofondi as secretary of state, president of the council, and foreign minister. In this new council of ministers four laymen held portfolios. On March 10, 1848 Cardinal Antonelli succeeded Bofondi. But the greatest (and the last) of the constitutional reforms was quickly to follow. On March 14, Pius IX promulgated the "Fundamental Statute for the Temporal Government of the States of the Holy Church."[7] This provided for the constitution of two chambers or councils. While this document chiefly concerned the parliamentary structure, several articles affected the conduct of foreign policy. Article xvi declared that correspondence with the representatives of the other courts belonged to the competence of the secretary of state, as well as the negotiation of treaties, concordats, commercial treaties, boundary questions, the protection of papal subjects, and the issuance of passports. Article xvii subjected the civil guard of the whole papal states to the secretary of state. Article xxxiii inhibited the two councils from discussing the "diplomatico-religious" relations of the Holy See with foreign states.

These provisions reflect the Pope's determination to keep foreign affairs securely in ecclesiastical hands. By the same token he was opposed to the creation of two foreign ministries, one political, the other ecclesiastical. But the turbulence of succeeding months led him, much against his will, to a momentary experiment in this direction. Forced in the beginning of May 1848 to ask Terenzio della Rovere Mamiani, a former revolutionary, to head a government, he yielded to several demands. One of these was the creation of a "ministry for foreign secular affairs" (*ministero degli affari esteri secolari*) whose titular would be a layman. This strange new portfolio was taken over by Count Giovanni Marchetti, a poet, while Mamiani became minister of the interior and, in reality, head

[7] *Ibid.*, *seconda parte*, I, pp. 222-38.

of the government. Cardinal Ciacchi became secretary of state and nominal president of the council, retaining foreign ecclesiastical affairs for himself. A layman was thus in charge of the foreign policy of the papal states.

This new kind of papal official was particularly unwelcome to the Pontiff. There were objections to this arrangement on grounds both of principle and of practice. Mamiani made no secret of his aim to make of the Pope a sovereign who reigned but did not rule. In his own words, the Pope's role should be "to pray, to bless and to forgive" (*pregare, benedire e perdonare*) and not, as Pius IX retorted, "to bind and to loose" (*sciogliere e legare*). The creation of a "foreign ministry for secular affairs" could be the opening wedge leading to a complete alienation of the Pope from the destiny of the papal states. As Spada points out, to accept the full consequences of the separation of the two domains would have been deliberate "suicide" on the part of the papacy. The danger was quite proximate, for Mamiani wanted to get the papal states into war with Austria, and he expected to be able to do so regardless of the opposition of Pius IX. For this end it was convenient to have a minister for foreign secular affairs. Naturally, this was another reason for the Pope to suspect the work of Count Marchetti.

The practical difficulties of such a separation of religious and secular competences can be imagined. How could a cardinal secretary of state entertain good relations with a given state, on the religious plane, when the papal foreign minister for secular affairs was aiming to wage war with that same state? How could he carry on negotiations with an ambassador on Church matters, if the foreign minister expelled the said envoy from Rome? This latter contingency was not a hypothetical one. The Austrian ambassador, von Luetzow, having consulted the cardinal secretary as to whether his continued presence was desired in Rome, despite the tension, was assured that the Pope wished him to stay. Despite this, Marchetti's ministry handed him his passports and the Austrian ambassador felt himself constrained to leave on May 16. The confusion of the foreign governments can also be imagined. For centuries they had been accustomed to deal with the cardinal secretary. Now they found themselves faced with a lay minister. Should they have two envoys in Rome, corresponding to each of the two new foreign ministers? The nuncios, all ecclesiastics, now took their instructions from Marchetti and reported to him. Should a new lay foreign service be organized to represent the secular minister abroad?

Even the majority of the foreign ambassadors in Rome, while they kept up the appearance of communicating with the office of the lay minister, in reality stayed close to the cardinal secretary of state. The Duke d'Harcourt, the new French ambassador, presented himself to the cardinal before he went to see Marchetti. "Foreign nations," attests Farini, "attach great weight to diplomatic intercourse with Rome, not certainly as a temporal sovereignty, but as the universal Catholic sovereignty. Their envoys naturally chose to be on good terms with the head of the Catholics rather than with a tottering administration."[8]

The division of foreign ministries made sense only in the hypothesis that in the near future the Pope was to lose complete real control of the affairs of the papal states. But this is not what Pius IX intended. A new secretary of state, Cardinal Soglia, put an end to this confusion by instructing all the nuncios to take their orders from him and to furnish him with all their past correspondence with Marchetti. When there were protests to be made against Austria's military actions, it was Soglia and not Marchetti who made them. On August 3 the Mamiani cabinet resigned. Pius IX abolished the *ministero degli affari esteri secolari* when Fabbri, on August 6, took over the new government. A circular of August 12 emphasized that the secretary of state should have all the attributions of the foreign minister, in conformity with the *motu proprio* of December 29, 1847. All were ordered to send their dispatches and reports to the secretary.[9] With the ministry of Pellegrino Rossi (September 16, 1848), Cardinal Soglia retained the title of secretary of state, president of the council, and foreign minister. The experience, while painful, was brief; it convinced the Pope and his advisers of the necessity of keeping both

---

[8] Farini, *Roman State*, II, p. 252.
[9] Spada, *Storia*, II, p. 456.

political and ecclesiastical affairs in the hands of the cardinal secretary.

The revolution of Rome and the Pope's flight to Gaeta at the end of 1848 ended the reform phase of the pontificate of Pius IX. The experience convinced the Pope of the incompatibility of the constitutional state with the exigencies of the Holy See in its worldwide religious role. At the restoration the secretariat of state returned to its old position of predominance. Cardinal Antonelli, who had resumed his former post, in an edict of September 10, 1850 redefined the position of the secretariat of state: "The relations of the government of the Holy See with the other powers are always entrusted to a cardinal of the Holy Church, who bears the name and the attributions of secretary of state." This cardinal, continued the statement in succeeding paragraphs, is the organ of the sovereign, "including the publication of legislative acts." The secretary corresponds with the governments or foreign representatives. Matters that have or could have some concern to foreign governments, even though within the scope of the other sections of the papal curia, should be cleared through the secretary. There is no mention of a "minister of foreign affairs," let alone of a minister for foreign secular affairs. The secretary also retained other functions accorded him in earlier papal decrees.[10]

Giacomo Cardinal Antonelli was the last secretary of state of the papal states. Continuing in office after 1870, his negotiations with the civil governments on "secular" matters were limited to whatever protests he could make against the annexation of the papal domains to the Kingdom of Italy. Today, the State of Vatican City has no foreign ministry or foreign service of its own. Its foreign affairs are completely subject to the secretary of state of His Holiness, who is not, however, "foreign minister" for the Vatican State. The papal authorities after 1929 made many studied efforts to dramatize the restoration of the temporal power of the Popes. They issued stamps, coins, and took other steps to this end. But what would be the most tangible demonstration before the whole world—the creation of a Vatican foreign ministry—is conspicuous by its absence. For an explanation perhaps the most illuminating

10 Pius IX, *Atti, seconda parte,* I, pp. 613-27.

clue lies in the short months of the Mamiani government in 1848. The Holy See does not want any "foreign minister for secular affairs." It might be added that the civil governments, for their own part as a consequence of their own experience in 1848, probably do not want to have to negotiate with two authorities in the Vatican.

As can be discerned in the description of the powers of the secretary of state before 1870, much of his responsibilities were of a purely temporal nature. He had to administer the affairs of the papal states. It is not surprising, therefore, that commonly enough the cardinal secretary was not a priest, much less a bishop. In the 19th century three of the best-known secretaries were only deacons. Cardinal Consalvi, the famous negotiator, was not even a sub-deacon when he was chosen to be the first minister of Pius VII. Although made cardinal when appointed in 1800, he was ordained sub-deacon and deacon only after his return from negotiating the concordat with Napoleon in 1801. He never received the priesthood and consequently was not a bishop. Cardinal Thomas Bernetti served as secretary to two pontiffs, Leo XII and Gregory XVI. Cardinal Giacomo Antonelli was, except for the first few years and the last few months, the secretary of Pius IX during the long pontificate of that Pope who died in 1878. Bernetti and Antonelli, like Consalvi, were not priests but deacons.

Since the loss of the papal states took from the papacy the burden of the temporal concern for some three million or more papal subjects, the cardinals secretary have all been bishops. But the custom had been quite in line with the Roman practice of conferring the clerical status upon papal civil administrators. Even those who were not in orders were accustomed to wear clerical garb. It was, so to speak, the uniform of the civil administrator. This practice gave rise to misunderstandings in the minds of visitors to Rome not familiar with the situation. In his 1864 edition of the memoirs of Consalvi, Crétineau-Joly cited in this connection the example of the governor of Rome. Often this high official was neither priest nor in orders. Nevertheless, he wore the robes of a monsignor. On the day after Christmas it was his duty to make a formal appearance at the opening of the *Nobile theatro di Apollo*. Although the Romans had long been accustomed to this and understood it, Crétineau-Joly bears witness that it caused surprise and scandal among visitors from the rest of Europe.[11]

The secretariat of state of His Holiness at present operates under the form given to it by Pope St. Pius X, in the general reorganization of the Roman curia effected by the apostolic constitution *Sapienti Consilio* of June 29, 1908. The new Code of Canon Law (n. 263) introduced some additional details on this office. It consists of three sections, all of course under the cardinal secretary:

1. *Section for Extraordinary Ecclesiastical Affairs.* Here are referred all questions discussed by the Holy See through the nuncios or internuncios or with the diplomats accredited at the Vatican itself and which are related to or connected with civil laws. Other questions are referred to the competent Roman congregation. The section prepares and dispatches documents for matters taken up by the Pontiff on his own initiative for the faithful of the entire world or for any specific region. The secretary of the Congregation for Ecclesiastical Affairs presides over this section, whose work is closely coordinated with that of the congregation.

2. *Section for Ordinary Ecclesiastical Affairs.* The routine business of the secretariat is handled by this section, such as the appointing and recall of nuncios and internuncios and their staff, and the preparation of instructions and the analysis of reports sent in from the various nunciatures and internunciatures. This section prepares official notifications of appointments to papal offices; it replies to testimonies of respect sent to the Holy Father; it awards papal honors to the laity as well as to the clergy.

---

11 Consalvi, *Mémoires* (ed. Crétineau-Joly, ed. 1864, II, p. 241, n.). Of Cardinal Giacomo Antonelli, the last of the secretaries of state who exercised civil authority, his biographer in the *Catholic Encyclopedia* (revised and enlarged edition of 1936, I, pp. 627-28) has some harsh things to say: "Without taking up all the calumnies that were brought against him, it can be admitted that he made himself a fortune and enriched his relatives, that he left his large estate (estimated as high as $4,000,000) to his natural children. His private conduct gave good cause for criticism and to a certain extent cast a shadow on the person and pontificate of Pius IX." With the passing of the papal states, this type of papal civil administrator who entered the ecclesiastical state for mainly career purposes, also passed from the scene.

3. *Section for Apostolic Briefs.* This section transmits apostolic indults granted by other congregations. It is responsible also for transmitting letters of felicitation to distinguished men on exceptional occasions.

When the Pope dies, the secretary of state *ipso facto* loses his mandate. Until the next Pontiff is elected, this function is assumed by the secretary of the Sacred College, or by the assessor of the Consistorial Congregation.

THE PAPAL INTERNAL ADMINISTRATION

The foregoing portions of Part II trace in their broadest outlines the genesis of the essential organs of papal diplomacy. The nunciatures and the secretariat of state are the products of fairly recent centuries and the result of modern conditions. Their coming into being reflects graphically the challenges presented to the papacy by the political and religious events that have transpired since the close of the Middle Ages. The princes, proud of their independence, increased their diplomatic representation at all the courts of Europe, including the papal Court. The Popes for their part found themselves likewise obliged to station their own public agents at the major points of Europe's political power. At Rome itself a special office had to be created in order effectively to handle the business transacted by the nuncios and ambassadors.

What differentiated the Pope's envoys from those of kings and emperors was the primarily religious nature of their commission. A complete study of papal diplomacy in its origins would really require a thorough description of the nature of the authority wielded by the Roman Pontiffs as religious leaders. For if the nuncios are, as we have said, the docile instruments of the cardinal secretary of state, the latter is himself but the loyal minister of the Pope. The Pope, to paraphrase Canon n. 218, is the head of the bishops, the bishop of all the dioceses and the bishop of all the faithful. His authority is "immediate," that is to say it is exercised directly upon the individual and not merely through the intermediary of the local bishops or through ecumenical councils. In matters of faith and morals and of Church discipline the Pope enjoys jurisdiction throughout the world, without regard to diocesan lines, and without regard to distinctions of rite. It is his prerogative to enact ecclesiastical law, indeed, even to codify canon law entirely, by his own initiative and authority, as Pope St. Pius X and Benedict XV did. He establishes lesser regulations or ordinances, orders visitations and dispenses from Church laws, even those established with his sanction by ecumenical councils. He is the court of last appeal in all canonical disputes. He himself is not subject to any court. He combines in his own person the fullness of legislative, judicial, and executive power in the universal Church.

These are large powers for one mortal, and they may seem to open the way to abuse. Tradition, however, has operated as an effective brake on the actual exercise of the papal authority over Catholics. For, in practice, the details of Church affairs are not administered by the Pontiff personally but by officials endowed with well-defined authority in their respective domains. These officials and their departments constitute what is known as the *curia Romana,* or Roman curia. This administrative complexus has, like the nunciatures and the secretary of state, a long history during which it evolved into its present form. It is beyond the scope of a study of papal diplomacy to trace this evolution, or even to describe in detail the functions of the various organs of the curia. Yet these are the administrative bodies through which the Pope transacts his business. Their operations can, in some instances, be of concern to the political powers and can be the object of diplomatic conversation and negotiation in the secretariat of state of His Holiness. For just as sometimes a purely internal policy of a state—e.g., the fixing of a rate of currency exchange—can be of concern to a foreign power, so the decisions of a Roman congregation in what is per se a purely religious or ecclesiastical matter, can, and often do, have a political impact which the governments cannot ignore. In fact, almost any decision of a Roman organ has a relevance to the faithful of at least one country and therefore perhaps to their government. The history of papal diplomacy is replete with instances in point, as is shown throughout this book. A brief glance at the evolution and, in particular, the present state of the papal administrative machinery is therefore pertinent.

The principal advisers of the Roman Pontiffs have long been the cardinals who in olden times were the clergy of the Roman diocese. Canon 230 terms its College of Cardinals the "senate" of the Roman Church. In early times these aides of the Pope assisted him through the Roman council or synod. At a somewhat later date, around the 12th century, the council was replaced by consistories. In the 16th century appear the Roman congregations, which were permanent bodies better organized to give continuing help and advice to the Pontiff.

The difference between the councils and the consistories has been the object of considerable study by Church historians who have brought out the character of the various forces that influenced papal administration. According to Victor Martin, the Roman council was essentially a Western European institution, similar to the *Champs de Mai* held by the Carolingian princes, in which the nobles were called by the king and their advice sought. This embodies the concept of a central power more or less patriarchal in nature but where the sovereign relies upon a large aristocracy which shares the administration of public affairs. On the other hand, says the authority cited, the consistories appear rather to follow the model of the Byzantine courts. The Christian emperor was absolute monarch, vicar of God, sole depository of His power. The emperor presided at the meetings of the great dignitaries, spoke last, and his opinion decided the matter. The analogy between the two consistories is too close to be an accident, according to Martin. Some think that Gregory the Great (590-604) was particularly influential in this development. He had lived long years in Constantinople as apocrisarius of his predecessor Pelagius II (579-590). In any case, when Alexander III (1159-1181) determined to dispense with the council and to reserve to the cardinals the task of assisting him in the government of the Church he had at his hand, all prepared, the instrument he needed. It was sufficient to extend the field of its activities.

The consistories took an intimate part in the government of the Church from the 13th to the 16th century. Innocent III is said to have conferred with the cardinals three times a week.

Today they meet only when the Pope calls them into session. At the present time the consistories have become simply a cere-mony or solemn occasion for special announcements. The Pontiff asks simply, *"Quid vobis videtur?"* (What is your opinion?) The question is rhetorical. Today the cardinals par-ticipate in the real government of the Church to the extent that they are members of congregations or of the other organs, called tribunals or offices. The congregations are composed exclusively of cardinals whose number varies in each case. They head most of the offices and two out of the three tribunals, namely, the Sacred Penitentiary and the Apostolic Signature. The third tribunal, the Rota, is not comprised of cardinals. Under Pope John XXII (1316-1334) there were only twenty cardinals. The total number was fixed in 1586 by Pope Sixtus V, who invoked the picture of the seventy wise ancients whom Moses, upon order from God, surrounded himself with as his special counsellors.

Paul III (1534-1549) established the first congregation when he set up in 1542 a special group of cardinals on the Inquisition. Other similar groups for various tasks, such as the Congregation for the Council of Trent, were shortly afterward instituted. But it was Sixtus V who in 1588 really inaugurated the system of congregations when he formed a dozen such committees, each responsible for a definite area of the papal business.[12] What he established is still essentially that which is in operation today, although some congregations have been suppressed and others added.

The congregations can be compared to the ministries or de-partments to be found in modern governments. They are stand-ing commissions among which are divided the various categories of affairs that the Holy See transacts. Although the members of these organs are cardinals, they are assisted by other ecclesias-tics of lesser rank and in some cases by laymen. The congrega-tions at the present time operate under legislation set down by St. Pius X, who defined their prerogatives and responsibilities in the Apostolic Constitution, *Sapienti consilio,* of June 29, 1908. The subsequent new code of canon law left these pro-visions largely intact (canon n. 243, 1). In general the congrega-

12 Huebner, *Sixte-Quint,* II, pp. 1-18.

tions have no territorial limitations. In some cases, however, they have a limited jurisdiction in certain areas, notably mission areas and regions in which the non-Latin rite is predominant. The so-called decrees of the congregations, however, always have the express approval of the Pontiff himself. The congregations do not enact laws in their own name.

Canon law recognizes eleven congregations. Giving them their full names, these are: The Supreme Congregation of the Holy Office, The Sacred Consistorial Congregation, The Sacred Congregation for the Oriental Church, The Sacred Congregation of the Sacraments, The Sacred Congregation of the Council, The Sacred Congregation of Religious, The Sacred Congregation for the Propagation of the Faith, The Sacred Congregation of Rites, The Sacred Ceremonial Congregation, The Sacred Congregation for Extraordinary Ecclesiastical Affairs, The Sacred Congregation for Seminaries and Universities.

Most of the congregations are headed by one of their members with the title of cardinal prefect. However, for three of them, by reason of their special character, the title of prefect is reserved to the Pope himself. These three are, using their more familiar shorter names, the Holy Office, the Consistorial Congregation, and the Congregation for the Oriental Church.

The Holy Office is reckoned the highest in dignity among the congregations, for it has the guardianship of faith and morals. It has a doctrinal as well as a disciplinary function. It is charged with the defense of orthodoxy against erroneous doctrines and temerarious opinions in matters of faith or religious practice. Certain categories of marriage questions—such as dispensations involving the Pauline privilege—belong to its jurisdiction. The Index of Prohibited Books is confided to this Congregation. Cases of offenses against the faith and unity of the Church—such as apostasy, heresy, schism, and profanations of the Holy Eucharist—come under its jurisdiction for judgment and action. On account of the character of its duties a rigorous secrecy is observed in its transactions.

The Consistorial Congregation prepares the agenda to be presented to the Consistory of Cardinals, hence its name. It therefore has for its mission the examination of the nominations of bishops and other ecclesiastical dignitaries of high rank whose names will be announced later in the consistory. For those instances in which the nominations involve (by reason of a concordat or other kind of agreement) the consultation or consent of civil governments, the Congregation for Extraordinary Ecclesiastical Affairs takes responsibility. The creation of new dioceses and the redistribution of old boundaries are also the function of the Consistorial. It is to this body that the bishops submit their reports. In short, the Consistorial Congregation is charged with matters directly relating to bishops and dioceses of the Latin Church not under the Propaganda (the Congregation for the Propagation of the Faith). Under Pius XII the congregation received responsibility for the religious welfare of the (Latin rite) postwar migrants.

The Oriental Congregation has existed as a distinct organ since 1917, when Benedict XV dissolved its links with the Propaganda. The move was necessitated by the special problems of the faithful of the non-Latin rites. The change was particularly appropriate because these peoples have been Christian virtually from apostolic times and cannot be considered missionary churches. The jurisdiction of this organ is considerable since it exercises alone powers that for the Latin rite are divided among several congregations. The Oriental Congregation exercises upon the dioceses, the bishops, the clergy, and the faithful of the non-Latin rites, in whatever part of the world they may be found, all the faculties that the Consistorial, Council, Religious, and Universities and Seminaries Congregations share among themselves in respect to the Latin rite. It is also responsible for all Church matters, whether of Eastern or Latin rite, in Egypt and the Sinai peninsula, Eritrea and Northern Ethiopia, Southern Albania, Bulgaria, Cyprus, Greece, the Dodecanese Islands, Iran, Iraq, Lebanon, Palestine, Syria, Transjordania, Asiatic Turkey, and Turkish Thrace. With certain exceptions, it exercises for those of the Latin rite in these regions the powers that the other congregations exercise for the Latin rite elsewhere.

The Pontifical Commission for Russia is in a category by itself. Russians of all rites still living in the Soviet Union are subject to this body. It came into being on June 20, 1925 under the Oriental Congregation. The commission was reorganized in March 1927 and became an independent unit on April 9, 1930. On December 21, 1934 it was attached to the Congregation for Extraordinary Ecclesiastical Affairs.

The Congregation of the Sacraments watches over not only rite or doctrine but the proper *administration* of the sacraments, especially matrimony and sacred orders, except for those cases reserved to the Holy Office and the Congregation of Rites. It has jurisdiction, territorially, over all regions of the Latin rite, including mission lands otherwise under the Propaganda.

The Congregation of the Council accomplishes, on the lower level, for lesser prelates and canonical institutions, what the Consistorial does for bishops and dioceses. First created in 1564 with the mission of interpreting and promoting the practical application of the decrees of the Council of Trent (hence the name), it now watches over the discipline of the clergy and the faithful, including religious instruction. It reviews the acts of provincial councils and episcopal conferences.

The Congregation for Religious has jurisdiction over questions principally involving religious orders and congregations. It examines the statutes of new foundations.

The Congregation for the Propagation of the Faith, known also simply as the Propaganda (not to be confused with the Society for the Propagation of the Faith, founded at Lyon, France, in 1822 by Pauline Jaricot), was created by Gregory XIII as a commission of cardinals for the reconciliation of Eastern schismatics. After 1622 it assumed responsibility for the lands of the New World. Territorially, it functions today where there is no regularly constituted hierarchy, that is to say, in what are frequently called "missionary countries." Its task is essentially that of spreading the faith where it does not exist rather than safeguarding it where it does. Its role ends, in principle, at the moment that the Church in the given country is organized on a regular basis and passes under the regime of general canon law, with formally organized dioceses and residential bishops. The powers of the Propaganda are broad, reflecting the wide variety and unusual character of the regions to which it gives its attention. It is limited only by the special jurisdiction of some of the other congregations, for certain categories of questions.

The Congregation of Rites, as its name indicates, deals with questions of liturgy and worship. One of its most absorbing occupations is the examination of causes for beatification and canonization, and allied matters.

The Congregation for Ceremonies is charged with questions of protocol, particularly where the Holy Father or the cardinals are concerned. Of interest from the viewpoint of papal diplomatic practice is the fact that this commission decides matters of precedence affecting the diplomatic corps at the Vatican. On July 8, 1925, for instance, the Ceremonial Congregation established two separate protocols to govern the manner in which ambassadors and ministers, respectively, were to present their credentials to the Pontiff. A distinction was made in some instances for the case in which the ambassador or minister plenipotentiary is not a Catholic. A non-Catholic makes three profound bows on approaching the Pontiff, instead of the three genuflections made by a Catholic diplomat. But neither kisses the feet of the Pope, as was once the custom.

The Congregation for Seminaries and Universities endeavors to maintain and promote high standards of education in ecclesiastical institutions. It authorizes Catholic institutions to confer pontifical degrees. In some countries, as in Germany, the (Catholic) theological faculties of the state universities are, by concordat, subject to this congregation as to professors and courses.

Of the congregations whose functions have been quite summarily described in the preceding pages, two present a special interest from the diplomatic point of view. These are the Propaganda and the Oriental Congregations. The 19th century colonial powers learned from experience that they could not be indifferent to the missionary policy of the Catholic Church. They sought in consequence to minimize the dangers that lack of coordination and liaison could produce. In many regions the colonial governments depended in part upon the missionaries for the success of their policies in the cultural field. The importance of the Oriental Congregation for the governments arises naturally from the fact that the Near East has long been one of the perpetually disturbed regions of the world. The wide authority of this congregation over the non-Latin Catholics has not been ignored by the European powers with political interests in these regions.

There is one papal organ not yet described, which is expressly charged with questions directly involving relations with the civil governments. This is the Congregation for Extraordinary Ecclesiastical Affairs. According to Canon 255, as interpreted by Pius XI on July 5, 1925, this body has the task of creating or dividing dioceses, and of filling vacant sees, in those instances where the civil government has some right of participation or consultation. It also holds itself ready to examine any question submitted to it by the sovereign Pontiff through the secretary of state of His Holiness, especially those which have some relation to the civil law or to concordats entered into, or to be entered into, with various states. A review of the problems in which this congregation was called upon to give advice shows that its range of jurisdiction is wide. The congregation does not itself have any direct relations with the governments. Its function is to advise the Pope. This organ is sometimes known as the "Grand Council" of the Pontiff. Cardinal Lega called it a *parvum consistorium* or "small consistory."

The history of this congregation may best serve to illustrate its role in the government of the Church.[13] Prior to the French Revolution the Pope had occasionally sought out the advice of a limited number of chosen counsellors for special problems involving relations with governments. But there was no need for a standing body. If it is true that the Catholic princes were seldom without some difference with Rome, sometimes going to the point of war, at least these quarrels were conducted within the framework of a legal system in which canon law and civil law were fairly harmonious and coordinated. The Revolution drastically affected this foundation. In 1793 Pius VI set up a special commission to study the course to be followed toward France in view of the overthrow of the monarchy and the rejection of religion. Known at first as the *Congregatio super negotiis ecclesiasticis regni Gallorum,* this commission was later regrouped by Pius VII for the preparation of the Con-

---

[13] Magnin, E., in *Dictionnaire de droit canonique,* "Affaires ecclésiastiques, Congrégation des"; Moroni, *Dizionario,* xvi, pp. 156-58; Richard, in *Revue d'histoire ecclésiastique,* 1910.

cordat of 1801 with Napoleon. On this occasion it bore the name *Congregatio a negotiis ecclesiasticis extraordinariis,* but it ceased to function in 1809 when the Pope was spirited away into captivity and the cardinals were dispersed.

The real foundation of the congregation dates from Pius VII's return from captivity and exile. On July 19, 1814 he established the *Congregatio extraordinaria praeposita negotiis ecclesiasticis orbis Catholici* for matters affecting the "liberty and dignity of the Church throughout the world." In 1827 the commission assumed its present name and its formal status as a congregation. The harrowing experience at Fontainebleau, where Pius VII was isolated, deprived of counsel, and subject to pressure, undoubtedly served to convince the Pope and his successors of the need for able advisers. In any case the territorial and political changes of this historic period not only in Europe but in the New World as well, to say nothing of the changing spirit of the times, called for bold decisions in the field of Church-State relations.

The first task of the new congregation was the question of concordats with Sardinia, Sicily, Prussia, and the provinces of the upper Rhine. The recently revolted colonies in New Spain were also a source of dispute. Spain brought pressure to bear upon Rome in its own favor. The congregation was called upon to resolve the unusual problems of this impasse. It was consulted at a later date preceding the condemnation of *l'Avenir* and the theories of de Lamennais in 1829. For many decades relations with Russia were in a lamentable condition. The congregation was often called upon to give its recommendations in the crisis provoked by Czarist policy, especially in Poland.

The Congregation for Extraordinary Ecclesiastical Affairs differs from the others in that its conclusions are usually in the form of recommendations to the Pontiff. It rarely issues "decrees" as do the other congregations. This does not mean that its mission is any less important. On the contrary, it collaborates in a special way with the Pope in some of his most difficult decisions. A French writer has noted the high qualifications and the influence of the cardinals who comprise this congregation. It is often said, remarks Maurice Pernot, that the Roman congregations are composed of two elements: competent consultors who study the problems but do not have the powers to resolve them, and incompetent cardinals who resolve the problems without having studied them. This is, of course, a caricature, but in any case, admitted the writer, it is not true of the Congregation for Extraordinary Ecclesiastical Affairs whose members have both the capacity and the authority to resolve the problems put before them. They include, ex officio, the heads of the most important other Roman organs. If this congregation is divided at all into two tendencies, a division suggested by another French writer may be more illuminating and to the point. Georges Goyau once wrote that the essential problem of the Congregation for Extraordinary Ecclesiastical Affairs is to reconcile principle with expediency. Within this organ are found men of both practical and theoretical bent, those whose natural inclination is for an immediate solution and those who hold to principle regardless of consequences. The congregation's job is to seek a balance between these two approaches, so that the practical-minded cardinals do not sacrifice principle to the demands of the civil powers out of expediency, while on the other hand those who pride themselves as standing on principle do not in their intransigence rashly fly in the face of grim reality.[14]

Consistent with its function of consultant to the sovereign Pontiff, the Congregation for Extraordinary Ecclesiastical Affairs does not come in direct or immediate relations with any government. When its advice has been sought it submits its recommendations to the Holy Father through the cardinal secretary of state who is ex-officio prefect of the congregation. The organ serves as advisory board not simply for the Holy Father but also for the secretary himself. Canon law (n. 255) states that the congregation considers questions presented to it by the cardinal secretary.

---

[14] Cardinal Mathieu has drawn attention to the differences of opinion that can and do arise between the theologians and the diplomats of the Church: "*Il doit arriver, dès lors, que ses théologiens ne s'accordent pas toujours avec ses diplomates. Les uns, en effet, habitant les hauteurs sereines et planant au-dessus des champs de bataille, s'appliquent par-dessus tout à étudier et à proclamer les principes, en italien la* massima. *Les autres, mêlés aux affaires et aux mouvements des sociétés, voient surtout la difficulté de les appliquer et la nécessité de se plier aux circonstances*" (*Concordat*, pp. 270-71).

In addition to the Roman congregations, there are two other categories of Vatican organs: the tribunals and the offices. These do not concern us, except the secretariat of state of His Holiness, one of the three offices. We have already discussed the cardinal secretary. He is normally the only direct contact that governments have with the Holy See but, as can be judged from the description of the congregations, the governments can be concerned, sometimes vitally, with decisions taken by these bodies in the prosecution of their routine Church business.

PART THREE

THE POPE AS SOVEREIGN

CHAPTER 6

THE TRANSITION: MIDDLE AGES
TO THE 20TH CENTURY

IN THE COMPANY OF KINGS

D IPLOMACY comes easily to a high religious authority
whose traditions embrace a millennium and more of
eminence and even predominance in the affairs of
Europe. It is hardly necessary to stress the influence of the
papacy upon the formation of Western civilization. From the
decline of the Roman Empire the bishops of Rome assumed an
ever greater part in the destinies of the many races which
coalesced into Christian Europe. In that period of formation
the Popes were more than religious leaders. They were civ-
ilizers and often, by default of other leaders, political leaders
as well. The papacy is inextricably linked with the temporal
and political history of Europe, no less than with its religious
and cultural traditions.

In brief, the papacy was exercising a form of sovereignty long
before that word took on the clear-cut political and juridical
meaning it was later to have. When the rudiments of contemporary diplomatic institutions began to crystallize around 1500,
the papacy was already a major diplomatic force.

Rome's direct involvement in the public affairs of Europe derived from two factors. The first was that, from the 8th century,
the bishop of Rome was suzerain of territory on the peninsula
of Italy. As such, he had the concerns of a temporal ruler. At
times the Pope himself led the papal armies in defense of his
territorial interests. The other factor, much more significant,
was the supremacy which the Holy See began to claim over the

Bibliographical Note: The literature on the two-fold role of the Popes in the
Middle Ages is too abundant to need detailed mention. Almost any study of
the Middle Ages discusses papal supremacy, e.g., Ullmann and Rommen. For
material on the temporal power strictly so-called—that is, the Roman question—
the following authors mentioned in the Bibliography may be consulted for
various aspects of the issue: Bastgen, Bianchi, Binchy, del Giudice, Halperin,
Jacini, Mollat, Parsons, Piola, Salata, Steed, and Toynbee. Yves de la Brière has
created the most comprehensive doctrinal and historical exposé of the Vatican's
viewpoint on the temporal power and the Roman question.

other rulers of Christendom, even in temporal matters, in virtue of its overriding religious authority. In the 13th century, indeed, the papal spokesmen proclaimed that, granting that there were "two swords" by which the world was ruled, the temporal and the spiritual, it remained that both swords were in the hands of the Pope. This was an extremist formulation of the theory of papal supremacy, but there was no mistaking the practical effect of the papal theory, regardless of how it was formulated. Excommunication was a strong weapon to bring recalcitrant princes to heel. More drastic was the declaration absolving subjects from their oath to king or liege lord and by which even kings were deposed. It is true that this latter measure was employed only rarely. Nevertheless, it hung constantly over the heads of princes as a threat to their crowns. Religious in form and in motivation, it was no less political in effect and nature.

The papacy's international status today rests upon essentially the same twofold foundation: the temporal power and the papal religious authority. The first remains, though much altered, in the papal sovereignty over the State of Vatican City. The second presents itself in the coexistence of the two sovereignties of Church and State. Here, the papal supremacy has been exchanged for a partnership of two equally autonomous powers, each supreme in its own sphere.

Part III examines, in four chapters, the principle of sovereignty which animates the external organizational structure depicted in the preceding two sections. First it is necessary to bridge the gap between the medieval and the modern status of the Pope, in his relation to the civil rulers. The vicissitudes of the temporal power, which culminated in the Lateran settlement of 1929, are examined in the second half of this chapter. Once again, with that treaty, the Pope is an acknowledged temporal sovereign in his own right, even though on an essentially symbolic scale. Quite different was the fate of papal supremacy. Running into increasingly successful resistance from the princes, the papal power *in temporalibus* was gradually diminished until today the papacy is content to proclaim the existence of two independent spheres of authority.

The theory of papal supremacy, especially as manifest in the power to depose princes, was the fruit of the particular circumstances of the ages of faith. It is now abandoned by the Roman Pontiffs. Though the primacy of the spiritual over the temporal remains central in papal theory, the form this primacy took in the Middle Ages is recognized as anachronistic. At the time of the Vatican Council of 1870, some European statesmen interpreted the solemn definition of papal infallibility as an effort to revive papal "pretensions" over the political allegiance of their own citizens and to interfere in the life of governments. Gladstone, for example, vigorously stated his alarm at what he feared were its implications. To him, the council's decree was a bid to reassert the papal claim to "universal monarchy." In Germany, Bismarck, for another, even urged the European powers to concert together at the time of the next conclave for the purpose of exacting from the new Pontiff a pledge of non-interference in civil matters.

This concern was in some cases based on a misunderstanding of the meaning of infallibility; in others it was politically motivated. Pius IX himself adverted to the misconceptions or, rather, tendentiousness of the council's critics in an address he delivered to a Catholic group on July 20, 1871. Infallibility, he said, had nothing to do with the right to depose sovereigns and to release subjects from allegiance. This right, he recalled, was sometimes exercised in extreme cases in the ages of faith, when the Pope was revered as the supreme judge of Christendom and when his arbitration between nations and their rulers was admitted. Its exercise, he said, was sanctioned both by the prevailing public law and by the common consent of the nations. The Pontiff concluded, "Our own times are quite changed and only bad will can confuse two things so different: infallibility in matters of Revelation, and the right that the Popes once exercised in virtue of their authority when the good of society required it."[1] More recently, Pius XII reaffirmed the circum-

[1] Cf. *Civiltà Cattolica*, 5 agosto 1871, pp. 485-86. On the papal position in the Middle Ages see de Maulde-la-Clavière, *Diplomatie*, 1, pp. 22-45. The text in *Civiltà Cattolica* is the one usually cited, but it is a journalistic résumé of the Pope's remarks. For the verbatim text see de Franciscis, *Discours*, 1, pp. 202-03. In 1826 Leo XII told Lambruschini that the doctrine of the "indirect power" was of no advantage to the Church, as it was interpreted by the theologians. The only ones for whom it was any benefit, he said, were the secular princes, who used it as a pretext to justify usurpation and rebellion (Lambruschini, *Mia nunziatura*, p. 17).

stantial origins of the medieval system. In an address to the Congress of Historical Sciences on September 7, 1955 he alluded to statements of Boniface VIII on the complete dependence of the temporal upon the spiritual, and added the comment: "This medieval conception was conditioned by the age. Those who know its sources will probably agree that it would undoubtedly have been still more surprising had it not appeared."

The history of the relations of the Catholic princes with the see of Rome in the post-medieval age of absolutism is the story of the attempts by the civil power to attain independence from the papacy in political matters. The theory of papal supremacy in temporal matters was, as Pius XII pointed out, medieval and passing. Nevertheless, its practical and theoretical effects carried over into later centuries. In his famous revision of papal theory, for instance, the Roman theologian St. Robert Bellarmine (d. 1621) greatly reduced the papal claims of power in purely temporal matters. But even he upheld the Pope's right to excommunicate and depose Christian princes. From this there arose a conspicuous susceptibility on the part of the Catholic kings in their official relations with the papal curia. If they were jealous of their independence from all other rulers, they were all the more anxious to assert their independence in regard to the Pope, of whose earlier record of predominance they were only too mindful. In time, the new diplomatic institutions provided an excellent vehicle by which the absolutist rulers expressed, exhibited, and exercised their complete independence. This applied above all to diplomatic relations with the Holy See. The Pope's nuncios were received with highest honors at the Catholic courts. It was made plain to them, however, that these distinctions were understood to prevail only within the framework of diplomacy and implied no subordination to Rome affecting the royal power as such. The nuncio enjoyed precedence over the other visitors to the Court, but he remained for all that an ambassador.

It should not be imagined that the Popes easily reconciled themselves to this changed relationship, but their policy in these centuries tended inexorably toward acceptance of the new system of independent political sovereigns. In their reaction to the new state of affairs the Roman Court multiplied permanent

and special diplomatic missions. They put more and more re-
liance upon bilateral negotiations with princes. Whereas in the
Middle Ages the messengers of the Popes carried orders, now
special negotiators went out from Rome with a mission of ex-
hortation and persuasion. The former direct and peremptory
intervention in the affairs of kings gave place to indirect intervention, in an ever-narrowing scope, through the more conciliatory methods of diplomatic representation.

In no case was this changed relationship more evident than
between France and the Holy See. The Gallicans, while continuing to profess religious fealty to the Popes, were not far
behind the Protestant princes in asserting their political independence from the Holy See. The kings of France drew their
sovereignty from God and from their sword and not from the
Popes. Article Six of the *Liberties of the Gallican Church* expressed the attitude of the French kings with great accuracy:
"The Most Christian anointed King, eldest son and protector
of the Catholic Church, when sending his ambassadors to the
newly-elected Pope to congratulate him on his elevation and to
acknowledge him as spiritual father and head of the militant
Church, has not been accustomed to employ terms of such
precise obedience that many other princes employ, who have
some special duty or obligation to the Holy See of Rome, as
vassals or under tribute, but they only recommend themselves,
the kingdom which God has given to them in sovereignty and
the whole Gallican church to the good favor of his Holiness."
Though Louis XIV did not go so far as the most extreme Gallicans, nevertheless the above-cited article of Pierre Pithou's
famous formulation, published during his reign, reflects quite
faithfully his policy toward Rome. The standing instructions
issued to the French ambassadors in Rome at the close of the
ancien régime express in more official terms the viewpoint
of the royal power. The orders given under date of October 30,
1763 to the Marquis d'Aubeterre prior to his departure for the
embassy in Rome express supercilious disdain for the Roman
Court: "The court of Rome for many centuries had a very
great influence in the conduct of general affairs and the capital
of the Christian world was at that time the center of negotiations where were discussed the public interests of Europe, whose

sovereigns still embraced and professed the Catholic faith. Religion and education inspired the secular princes with reverence for the papal authority and this rendered the Popes ambitious and adventurous. Some of them conceived the idea of subjecting the crown of the kings to the Tiara. The injustice and abuse of such a claim became evident and joint efforts were made to keep the Roman power within its proper limits. Success has been so complete in this respect that there is hardly left to the sovereign pontiffs, even in the Catholic states, but a respected name, the power to grant indulgences and the right, often challenged, to dispense from the prescriptions established by the canons and the discipline of the Church."[2] Almost identical terms are contained in the instructions prepared for Cardinal de Rochechouart and other French envoys of this period.

This unflattering vision of the papacy (drawn up, it appears, by a cleric in the royal ministry) clearly shows the independent attitude which the kings of France had developed toward the Holy See even at the moment, or rather especially at the moment, of sending an ambassador. The Court of Versailles sought to convince itself and the world that the embassy implied no political subjection to the Pontiff. But why, if the Pope was so weak and unimportant, should France wish to be represented at Rome? The instructions proceed to justify the apparently inconsistent attitude: "However, despite the fact that the Court of Rome has lost more power than it had ever usurped, the King, following the example of his august predecessors, has preserved the greatest veneration and the most inviolable attachment to the Holy See and for the Vicar of Jesus Christ. He has always earned by his expressed sentiments and by his conduct the title of Eldest Son of the Church. His Majesty has in consequence always given great importance, since the beginning of his reign, to maintaining in ordinary mission to the Holy See, ministers of the highest order, equally recommendable by their ancestry, their rank and their personal qualifications." What this elaborate language means is that, regardless of what one professed to believe at Versailles concerning the low state of papal authority and influence vis-à-vis the royal power, it was

[2] Hanotaux, *Rome*, xx, p. 544.

still necessary to defend the royal independence by maintaining a strong mission in Rome. The other Catholic monarchs in Christendom, emboldened by the example of the French king, made a point of displaying the same independence. The humiliating and fruitless journey that Pius VI made in 1782 to Vienna is ample indication of the low position into which the papacy had fallen. At the same time it never entered into the heads of the Catholic monarchs to deny to the Pope the right to participate in the diplomatic intercourse of the European community. In a day when the right of embassy was jealously reserved to crowned heads or sovereigns of equivalent standing, the Holy See enjoyed full diplomatic privileges.

The Pope was, of course, the temporal ruler of fair-sized territories on the Italian peninsula and in the south of France. Under this heading alone he was entitled to the rating of sovereign in the European community. Even the Protestant princes acknowledged his sovereign capacity as an Italian prince. But the Catholic rulers, the only ones who had official relations with the Pope, did not find it necessary to regard the Pope exclusively in this light. They sent their ambassadors or ministers to the Pope both as head of the Church and as a temporal ruler. From their point of view it was equally advantageous to treat the Pope, diplomatically, under both aspects. The instructions to the French ambassadors in the 18th century habitually carried this remark, or something else of similar tenor: "He [*the ambassador*] is too well-informed not to know the distinction which it is important to make between the Church and the Court of Rome, between the Pope as common father of all the faithful and the Pope as possessor of states in Italy. . . . It is under these two aspects that an ambassador of the King must alternately negotiate with the Holy Father and with his ministers."[3] The special honors of precedence which the papal nuncio received at the Catholic courts proves that, of the two aspects under which the Pope could be considered sovereign, that of his religious character was the most characteristic. In sum, the Treaty of Westphalia excluded the papacy from a direct role in the great decisions of the European political community but it did not entirely laicize diplomacy.

[3] *Ibid.*, p. 437.

The Congress of Vienna ushered in a new phase of international relations and one of its monuments remaining in force today is the regulation concerning the classification of diplomatic agents and the manner of determining their precedence. In this regulation, whose purpose was to put an end at last to recurring disputes over first places in the diplomatic corps, the papal representative was given full recognition. More important, the Vienna Congress recognized the deanship which the papal nuncio had up to that time enjoyed in the Catholic courts. For, up to the French Revolution the nuncio of the Pope automatically took precedence over any other ambassador in the diplomatic corps. Even the envoys of the Protestant kings acquiesced in this form of recognition of the special dignity of the nuncio. At the Congress of Vienna the continuance of this custom was guaranteed. The regulation of 1815 (altered slightly at the Congress of Aix-la-Chapelle in 1818) recognized that the papal legates and nuncios are diplomatic agents in the same class as ambassadors. As regards precedence, Article IV of the Vienna regulation stated that seniority within each category of envoy (ambassador, minister plenipotentiary, minister resident, chargé d'affaires) was to be determined by the date of the official notification of their respective arrivals. But there was one express exception: this requirement did not affect the position of the nuncio. "The present rule," in the words of this article, "does not effect any change relative to the representatives of the Pope."

This is the first instance of the European concert of Protestant as well as Catholic powers expressly recognizing the papal legate and nuncio as diplomatic agents in the framework of the contemporary practice of modern states. Since this pact guaranteeing the deanship of the nuncio has never been superseded, a rather lengthy account of this decision of the Vienna Congress is particularly indicated here. The reports sent back to Rome during the discussions on this subject by Cardinal Consalvi provide at least the papal side of the negotiations, as well as an authentic firsthand account of the reasoning that entered into the solution. These reports were published in Rome, 1899, in a 63-page brochure by the secretariat of state.[4]

---

[4] *Segreteria di stato. Il Congresso di Vienna.* Rousset, *Mémoires* (1746), con-

Consalvi's first letter to Rome on this subject, dated December 17, 1814, can serve to introduce the question: "I have learned to my surprise that the Congress will also take up the question of precedence. There has been formed a committee of eight members, chosen from among the alternate plenipotentiaries of the eight powers which signed the Peace of Paris, for the purpose of examining this question. I have just had some words with one of these, making him to understand that of course there could be no question of depriving the nuncio of the prerogative which he has enjoyed for so many centuries, that of preceding all the others, out of respect for the spiritual dignity of the person whom he represents. I was told in reply that 'as far as the Catholic powers were concerned there was no doubt, but that there could perhaps be some as far as the non-Catholics were concerned.' I replied that even in the non-Catholic courts where there is a nuncio, they have enjoyed this precedence up to now and I added one other reason even stronger, namely, that since it cannot be imagined that the nuncio should not keep his precedence in the Catholic courts, it would be absurd for the non-Catholics to accord precedence to the nuncio outside their own house and not accord it in their own, and that therefore it would be better to leave things as they stand."

Thus the issue was clear. The powers were to attempt to eliminate once and for all the vexing problem of precedence. The attitude of the papal secretary of state was that no change should be made in the Pope's existing status. These papal prerogatives, as Consalvi pointed out, dated back many centuries and were accorded in deference to the spiritual dignity of the Pope. As for the objections that could be raised by the non-Catholic powers, Consalvi's contention was that they could not complain since they had already conceded the precedence of the nuncios over their own representatives at the Catholic courts, namely, in Vienna, Paris, Madrid, and Lisbon. Moreover, even at some non-Catholic courts the nuncios had been granted the precedence. In later correspondence Consalvi cites only the

---

firms that the Pope's precedence was freely acknowledged by the Catholic rulers. But he did not fail to stress that these gestures of respect for the Pontiff implied no political subordination, pp. 5-7.

case of Russia, which would seem to prove that he could discover no other example. Nuncios sent on extraordinary missions to the Czar, particularly to treat of the affairs of Poland after the partition, had been accorded precedence over the other diplomats at the Court of St. Petersburg. These missions were those, mentioned earlier, of Msgr. Archetti to Catherine II in 1783, of Msgr. Litta to Paul I in 1797, and of Msgr. Arezzo to Alexander I in 1803. In these cases, however, the precedence of the nuncios seems to have been more in principle than in reality.

Consalvi's argumentation throughout the discussion on precedence at Vienna in favor of the nuncio's prerogatives shows how much the position of the Pope had evolved as a European sovereign in the new diplomacy. On the one hand the secretary of state, by emphasizing the religious character of the Pope, avowed that the precedence was purely honorific and therefore implied no political claims. Of course, had this claim been susceptible of any other interpretation neither the Catholic nor the non-Catholic powers would have entertained it for one moment. No one knew better than Consalvi that the old medieval role of the papacy was gone. His primary mission at this same Congress of Vienna was to secure, by the grace of this mixed gathering of Catholic, Protestant, and Orthodox plenipotentiaries, the restoration of the papal temporal power destroyed by Napoleon. Consalvi succeeded in this primary mission but not before he had made what was a formal admission that the Pope's international honors no longer had the political meaning of bygone centuries. The cardinal's declarations on this occasion did not constitute a new change of policy but, as a recognition of a long-existing state of affairs hitherto never acknowledged, they mark a significant stage in the development of papal diplomacy.

The papal envoy's line of thought also indicated that when Protestant princes consented to yield precedence to the nuncio, even in deference to the religious character of the sovereign he represented, their gesture involved no recognition of the theological claims of the Pope nor any religious subjection to Rome. Past experience with the Czarina and the Czars of Russia had impressed the Roman authorities with the prudence and utility of not giving unnecessary religious and theological significance to diplomatic relations.

In short, while insisting on the one hand that the Pope's dignity as a religious authority entitled him to special deference even by non-Catholic sovereigns, and on the other hand that in so doing the Protestant and other non-Catholic sovereigns did not necessarily imply any judgment on the theological or canonical claims of the Popes, Consalvi established the basis for the future relationship of the Holy See with the whole international community, Catholic and non-Catholic. In this formula he safeguarded the spiritual mission of the Popes and respected at the same time the viewpoint of non-Catholics.

The first drafts drawn up prior to any formal intervention on Consalvi's part recognized the special position of the Pope due to his religious dignity. It was contemplated that the nuncios would be counted among the representatives of the first-class powers, although as a temporal sovereign the Pope belonged to the second-class powers. Consalvi reported on December 21, 1814 what had been told him of the intentions of the plentipotentiaries: "Although the pope as a temporal sovereign is somewhat inferior in force and power by comparison with almost all the other princes, nevertheless, out of regard for his spiritual dignity . . . it has been decided that he should be put in the first class, in company with the emperor and the kings." In the second class would be placed the envoys of those rulers not having the title of king, such as the Prince of Orange, grand dukes, and the two republics of Switzerland and the United States. Precedence of the envoys would be determined by their seniority.

While naturally pleased that the spiritual dignity of the Pope was thus formally recognized in the projected regulation, which ranked him among the major sovereigns, Consalvi objected that this arrangement would nevertheless leave the Pope in a worse position than before. The nuncio's automatic precedence was not provided for. He therefore proposed that the nuncios should be considered in a class by themselves in which the rule of seniority would not apply.

In his subsequent conversations with the members of the committee charged with the precedence question (the representative of Pius VII, not being formally a participant at the congress, was merely on the fringe of the discussions as an interested party), Cardinal Consalvi pleaded that no change should be introduced in the existing status of the nuncio. He put his views formally to the committee in a note dated January 8, 1815 in which he suggested the following phraseology: "As concerns the pope, who in his person has a religious dignity as well as the character of temporal sovereign, and by that fact does not belong in the same category as the other princes, the new system shall make no innovation relative to his representatives."

In this memorandum Consalvi argued that it was the religious authority of the Pope they represented which constituted the distinctive character of the nuncios and that for this reason these diplomats could justifiably be considered in a category by themselves. As he said, the size of the papal states and the Pope's real power as a temporal sovereign should really rate him a second-class ruler, but, he added, "It is by reason of his religious character that the question becomes a different one and of greater importance. From that point of view, he is placed, so to speak, outside the ordinary line, and it is because of this preponderant consideration that the precedence has always been accorded to the Pope as well as to his representatives." From the very weakness of the temporal power the resourceful Consalvi drew another argument in support of his position by saying that this sign of deference supplies the place of the external brilliance that temporal sovereigns gain from their military and political power: "Since the Pope does not possess that great temporal power which makes other princes respected even outside their own domains, he should not be deprived of the external marks of respect and deference which produce consideration and it would appear that the Catholic governments, or those which count a large number of Catholics among their subjects, have no less concern in not denying the Pope in their eyes of this consideration which can be of value to the state in some circumstances." According to Consalvi, therefore, the place of honor for the Pope should come to him precisely because of his spiritual office. Even the non-Catholic governments might find it to their interest to treat the Pope with these marks of respect. It should be noted that the cardinal secretary of state does not adduce before the congress the argument of tradition. This was deliberate. In one of his letters to Rome Consalvi stated: "My petition is that an exception should be made for the representatives of the pope, not however for the reason that they have enjoyed this precedence for so many centuries, for the past gains no one's votes (*il passato non suffraga a nessuno*), but by respect for his religious character."

The memorandum, which was presented to the committee of eight equally divided between representatives of Catholic and non-Catholic powers (Austria, France, Spain, Portugal; England, Prussia, Russia, Sweden), took pains to state clearly that what was at stake was a mark of deference and nothing more. Wrote Consalvi: "When the precedence is accorded to the pope and to his representatives this is done only to his religious dignity, without this implying any consequence for all the other aspects. This is why it has already been noted that the representation of the pope is outside the ordinary line."

What was the reaction of the eight powers to the plea for special treatment for the nuncio? As might have been expected, the Catholic powers, for whom this involved no change either in practice or in principle, could be counted upon for approval. Of the non-Catholic powers, only Great Britain made serious objections. Russia had already on several occasions adapted itself to this rule, and its Vienna representative was satisfied by some verbal changes. The Prussian representative was none other than Baron William von Humboldt, savant and diplomat, who a few years before had been the first Prussian minister plenipotentiary to the Roman Court. His experiences at that post evidently left him with pleasant memories, for he supported Consalvi throughout. The Swedish representative was apparently willing to follow what the majority agreed to. It was Lord Castlereagh, the British foreign secretary, who provided the greatest worries for the cardinal. On January 4 Consalvi reported that he was to see the British chief on the next day on "*il doloroso affare della precedenze*" but that he had "not the slightest hope" of convincing him. Unless Castlereagh was willing to go along there was no chance for the papal hopes, for the decision had to be unanimous.

In his interview with Castlereagh, the cardinal related subsequently, he found himself in a most difficult situation. He, a "papist," was telling an Englishman, "We want to take precedence over you." The British secretary must have appreciated the unusual challenge this presented to the papal diplomat and it could well be this interview of January 5, 1815 which inspired Castlereagh later to express his great admiration for the diplomatic skill of the Roman emissary, although Consalvi gave many other occasions in his career to justify such a compliment.

As far as can be judged from Consalvi's résumé of Castlereagh's views, the foreign secretary had no particular objection to the deanship of the papal nuncio in itself. The chief obstacle was a legal one. The English law made it punishable, "even by death," for any royal subject to have any relations of whatever kind with the Pope of Rome. The government would have the whole Parliament, the Anglican Church, and the entire nation against it, if it should formally recognize in this way the religious dignity of the Pope. Castlereagh therefore proposed, as an alternative, that it would be left to each court to negotiate directly with the Pope on the precedence of the nuncio. In that way even the non-Catholic courts might eventually agree to the precedence, since the same legal difficulties did not exist for them. In the foreign secretary's view, the formula stating that there would be "no innovation" was equivalent to saying that the nuncio would continue to have the deanship. The British representative could not legally accept such a *positive* confirmation of the papal prerogative, he declared.

Cardinal Consalvi left his long conversation with Lord Castlereagh feeling more encouraged than at the start. There is no indication in the correspondence here drawn on how the English delegation at Vienna came around to the view of the majority. It is evident, however, from the outcome that Castlereagh and his associates decided that they could, after all, subscribe to the suggested formula without violating the law. But for many days the position of the English caused anxiety to Consalvi. Finally, on January 25, he reported with great satisfaction that the cause had been won. On the preceding day the committee of eight, or rather the plenary session of twenty representatives of the eight powers, had acceded to Consalvi's petition and expressly excepted the Pope's envoys from the new system based on seniority. The decision was unanimous. Prussia and Russia spoke in specially cordial terms. Even the English followed suit: "The English representatives were also most favorable, since the situation already exists in fact. Because of their existing laws they found themselves obliged to oppose making an express and positive exception in writing for the Pope, and therefore admitting the precedence in principle. But they yielded in the end, Milord Castlereagh saying with great courtesy that he would take the responsibility upon himself before his nation and government."

The victory of Consalvi was sealed in the second paragraph of Article IV of the *Règlement sur le rang entre les agents diplomatiques* of June 9, 1815 which has already been quoted. This meant and has continued to be interpreted to mean that the papal nuncios exercise the deanship of the diplomatic corps regardless of their seniority in point of service at their post.

The Holy See has always contended that the Vienna regulation holds for all nuncios. It also holds that precedence belongs to the internuncios, within their class. The terms of the Vienna measure seem to support this interpretation. The British viewpoint, however, has been that it applied only to the status quo of 1815. In 1849, on the occasion of a dispute between the British minister and the internuncio at The Hague, Lord Palmerston took the position that the Vienna regulation applied only to the nunciatures then existing and not at all to inter-nunciatures.[5] (The first permanent internunciature, that of Holland, was created in 1829.) In practice, the Holy See has been able to strengthen the Vienna decision by provisions in its recent concordats. The Lateran Treaty provided for the nuncio's deanship in 1929. The precedence of the nuncio in Berlin was confirmed in the concordat of 1933. Other recent concordats contain similar provisions. It should be added that these cases involve governments which reserve to themselves the right to establish rules of seniority in their own capitals.

[5] Satow, *Guide*, p. 169 (par. 290); Binchy, *Church and State*, pp. 704-05, relates details of the acceptance of the papal nuncio's precedence as dean in Berlin.

Some countries, such as the United States, leave such questions to be decided by the diplomats themselves.

The same congress which was so obliging in recognizing the special position of the Pope in the diplomatic cortege as a religious dignitary was not equally benevolent in more important matters. The powers were dilatory and evasive when it came to recognizing the Pope as the ruler of the papal states. The much-stressed principle of legitimacy was not always the overriding consideration when selfish interests interposed themselves. Consalvi had to deploy all his diplomatic skill, and to rely on more than one lucky turn of events, before the congressists on June 9, 1815 agreed to restore to the Pontiff his former possessions. Even this act was incomplete. France and Austria found sufficient pretexts to retain for themselves certain long-coveted segments of the papal domains. Nevertheless Pius VII was once again, in fact as well as in right, a temporal sovereign.

What Vienna restored reluctantly was received by hands no longer strong. The secretary of state had cause to know that the Revolution had sown seeds in the minds of men which were growing into a coming challenge. Neither Waterloo nor the Congress could restore Europe or the papal states to what existed before. The papal subjects, for their part, were in no mood to return to the former regime. Consalvi wrote to Pacca in Rome on June 12, 1815 that the recovered territories could not be held for six months if the right policy was not followed. Even in those provinces which had been lost for only eight years, and not merely those which were ceded to France twenty years earlier in the Treaty of Tolentino, the spirit was entirely different. Practices, customs, and ideas were all changed in those provinces, he said, adding: "The younger generation does not take well to the idea of a pontifical government or at least to that idea they have of it as corrupt and detestable. They are even ashamed of being subjects of priests. With no prospect of advancement under an ecclesiastical government they return to papal sovereignty without enthusiasm. I do not say that the older generation thinks along these lines or that the common people do, but these are not the ones who sooner or later wind up dictating the law."[6] One of the challenges to papal control was the demand for the constitutional form of government. To this challenge no answer was ever discovered. Consalvi's clairvoyance was not enough to conjure away the coming new dangers to the temporal power.

For a century before the Revolution the temporal power of the papacy had been unchallenged and unaltered. But the peaceful possession of its realm was rudely disturbed by the political collapse of 1789. Even before the French Revolution greedy eyes were looking upon the papal domains. It was conveniently argued that the temporal should be separated from the spiritual. The revolutionists at Paris who adopted the Civil Constitution of the Clergy in France were just as inclined to extend secularization to the papal power. As the republic's military force spilled over into the Italian peninsula, even Catholic princes sought to benefit from the situation. During the Directorate, the crown of Spain unashamedly promoted, in conjunction with Paris (1796-1798), a plan which envisaged the elimination of the Pope as a temporal ruler. The scheme, whose purpose was to satisfy dynastic ambitions, was to put the heir to the duke of Parma, brother of the queen of Spain, upon the throne of a kingdom of Rome. The death of Pius VI which then seemed imminent was judged the propitious moment to end the temporal power. This particular project fell through. Instead, the Roman Republic came into being, at the instigation and with the help of the Directorate, to interrupt briefly the papal sovereignty.

After Napoleon made his peace with the Church in 1801, his ambitions began to include the papal territory. Another break with the Pope, Pius VII, was rendered inevitable with the refusal of the Roman authorities to drop their neutrality and expel the English, the Swedes, and the Russians from the papal states. The Pontiff refused the emperor's demand to consider France's enemies Rome's enemies. Napoleon's troops occupied the Eternal City. The blow fell on May 17, 1809 with an imperial decree from Schoenbrunn Castle in Vienna. The states of the Church were declared annexed to France, with the city of Rome declared to be an "imperial and free city" under a

6 Rinieri, *Corrispondenza inedita*, p. 731.

special regime. Provision was made for the Pope, who, though no longer a temporal sovereign, would continue to enjoy certain immunities and financial advantages.[7] What happened in the end was that, on the night of July 5, French soldiers invaded the Quirinal and carried the Pope, Pius VII, off into captivity.

Napoleon took this drastic step under pressure of the current political and military situation. Nevertheless the move fitted into the emperor's grand conception of his role as successor not of Louis XIV but of Charlemagne. To him would be reserved the temporal affairs of the new Christian empire, while the Pope was left to attend to purely spiritual matters. The Schoenbrunn decree argued that the union of the two powers, spiritual and temporal, under one head had been and was then "the source of continual discord." The sovereign Pontiffs, said the decree, "have only too often used the influence of the one to support the claims of the other." Furthermore, "spiritual matters which are by their nature unchangeable are confused with temporal matters which change according to the circumstances and the politics of the day." To these arguments of principle, Napoleon on other occasions added practical arguments. The personal formation of the clergy, he said in a discourse of October 27, 1808, rendered them less capable of handling practical affairs: "The theology which they learn in their youth provides them with sound rules for spiritual government, but gives them none for the government of armies and for administration, and consequently they should confine themselves to the government of the things of heaven."[8]

Such a line of argument, whose net effect was to undermine the idea of the temporal power, awakened sympathetic echoes in the first decades of the 19th century. The old familiar patterns of union of both temporal power and ecclesiastical jurisdiction in one and the same person were undergoing significant evolution. There was a time when it was taken as a matter of course that a bishop could also be a prince and even command forces in the field. The suppression (referred to in Chapter 2) of the ecclesiastical principalities of the Holy Roman Empire in 1803 closed this era. In this process, the bishops and more

---

[7] Pius VII, *Correspondance authentique*, pp. 103-04.
[8] *Ibid.*, p. 86.

than forty exempt abbacies and prelacies ceased to exercise the temporal jurisdiction they had enjoyed up to that time in the Holy Roman Empire. The areas involved in this mass secularization contained an estimated three million inhabitants.

These bishops and abbots exercised civil jurisdiction as well as ecclesiastical jurisdiction. The liquidation of these principalities, however small, was a high-handed procedure, to say the least. The unseemly scramble of both Catholic and Protestant princes to enrich themselves by plundering Church lands shows how much greed entered in as a factor. Years later at Vienna, Consalvi registered a solemn protest in the name of the Holy See against this spoliation and suppression. But his words fell upon deaf ears. The powers were eager to undo the work of the Revolution but not where they themselves had benefited.

By 1815 the Pope was the only prince-bishop in Europe. Would he succumb to the same fate? Consalvi could not have been misled by his success in the nuncio affair. Napoleon, too, in the moment of annexing the papal domains was willing to allow the Pope to send and receive diplomatic agents with the usual privileges and immunities. He willingly incorporated a provision to this effect in the so-called concordat of Fontainebleau of 1813. He had no reason to object to the nuncio's precedence as the representative of a religious dignitary. This was entirely within the line of his policy. It would have facilitated his use of the Pope as an instrument of his own control over the faithful not only in France but in the universal Church.

The Pope would certainly have gone the way of the prince-bishops of the Holy Roman Empire if his situation had been comparable to theirs. But the bishop of Rome was in a class by himself, both as bishop and as prince. As civil ruler he was a major independent sovereign and not a petty prince of the Holy Roman Empire. Kings, too, are dethroned but not with the ease with which the spoliation was executed in Germany after 1802. But, more pertinently, as bishop: there was no inherent link, in the case of the prince-bishops, between their ecclesiastical and their temporal jurisdiction. A combination of historical circumstances and not the nature of their episcopal authority as such had resulted in this institution. A local bishop can exercise his functions under the political subjection of another without any essential limitation of his freedom to act within the scope of his religious mission. The geographical area of responsibility of such a prelate is comparatively limited, almost always within one single state or province. He does not need political independence in order properly to fulfill his charge as "ordinary of the place." His political loyalties to the civil ruler cannot jeopardize his religious authority among his flock since both shepherd and sheep are under the same political allegiance.

The episcopal authority of the bishop of Rome, however, is universal. The supreme head of the Church recognizes no territorial boundaries in the scope of his mission and his religious role is liable to be suspect to any given portion of his flock by being himself the political subject of any one prince. In order to be free in his religious work he had also to be politically free. It was necessary that the whole world should have means of knowing that the head of Catholicism was free. It was not enough for him to *be* free; he also had to *be seen to be* free. He had, in short, to be a territorial sovereign in his own right.

Such, in its barest essentials, was the basis of the papacy's claim to the right to possess the temporal power. To the modern mind of the second half of the 20th century, such reasoning may seem irrelevant and far-fetched. The Pope was asking the European community of states to acknowledge at this late date that the head of the Catholic Church has the right to be a territorial sovereign precisely because he is the leader of a universal religion.

Nevertheless, the papacy's standpoint on the necessity of the temporal power is deeply registered in the history of Christendom. Perhaps the classic formulation of the papal thesis was that of the eloquent Bossuet, Bishop of Meaux (d. 1704). The temporal power, he declared in his famous *Discours sur l'unité de l'Eglise*, was, in God's providence, the means by which the supreme Pontiff, in the midst of so many political rivalries, could retain his position above all contending parties, in order the better to carry on his spiritual functions as shepherd of the whole Christian flock, regardless of nation. Bossuet wrote: "God,

who wished that this Church, the common mother of all kingdoms, should not be dependent upon any one of them in temporal matters and that the See through which all the faithful
should preserve their unity should be above all partisanship that
the conflicting interests and jealousies of state could cause—
God, I say, laid the foundations of this great plan through the
instrumentality of Pepin and Charlemagne. As a felicitous consequence of their liberality the Church, which in her chief is
independent of all temporal powers, is in the position of exercising this divine power to rule souls more freely for the
common good and under the common protection of the Christian kings, so that, holding upright in her hands the scales of
justice, in the midst of so many empires so often enemies one
with the other, she maintains unity in the whole body, sometimes by inflexible decrees and sometimes by wise compromises."
Bossuet's description of the grounds for the papal claim was all
the more impressive because of the known Gallican tendencies
of the author. But his argument was not original, and it is
hardly necessary to discuss it at length. Many writers and public
men, both clerical and lay, have testified their conviction that,
considering the religious authority of the Pope, it is in the
interests of both Church and government that the Pontiff should
be his own sovereign. In an interview with an English visitor,
Lord Augustus Loftus, on November 2, 1867, to cite one instance, Bismarck said that the Pope must be an independent
sovereign were he possessor of only ten or one hundred acres
of ground. The head of the Catholic Church could never be
the subject of any prince.[9]

The thoughts of an eminent churchman imprisoned by
Napoleon at the moment of the liquidation of the papal states
may reveal the real issues better than any theoretical analysis.
Cardinal Bartolomeo Pacca was pro-secretary of state when
Pius VII was arrested by the officers of the Emperor on July
5, 1809. He was one of those most responsible, among the
cardinals, for the Pontiff's firm refusal to accede to Napoleon's
demands that the Pope surrender the temporal sovereignty
and thus become virtually a vassal, a prince liege of the French
empire. He joined Pius VII in arrest, imprisonment, and exile.

---

[9] Loftus, *Diplomatic Reminiscences*, I, pp. 197-98.

Writing later, when the storm was over and the Emperor's star had set forever, the veteran diplomat confided that in prison he at times wondered whether the "catastrophe" of which he had been a witness and a victim was not, in reality, a blessing of God. He had the opportunity in his solitude and inaction to reflect upon the old thesis of the necessity of the temporal power.

Pacca was more than casually familiar with Bossuet's defense of the temporal power. It was quoted often in Rome as Napoleon's attacks, in word and action, foreshadowed what was to come. On March 10, 1806 the overwhelming majority of the cardinals, consulted by Pius VII, pointed out how accurately the predictions of the French orator were being fulfilled in their own time. Napoleon wanted the Pope to side with France in the war, to expel from the papal states the British, Russian, Swedish, and Sardinian subjects found there and to close his ports to their shipping. Neither as a temporal prince nor, *a fortiori*, as head of the Church, could the Pope accede to such demands, agreed the cardinals. For the Pope to become thus aligned with the politics of the French Empire would be fatal to the independence of the Roman Pontiff.

In prison at Fenestrelle from 1809 until 1813, Cardinal Pacca confesses that although in moments of calm he never lost hope in the ultimate restoration of the papal domains and therefore in the Providence which had seemed to confer them upon the Holy See for the Church's freedom, he did not have such an optimistic outlook on all occasions. Indeed, reflecting upon the very words of Bossuet, he at times drew a different line of thought from that which had inspired him in encouraging the Pope to resist. For if, as Bossuet alleged, the multiplicity of kingdoms was a reason why the Pope had to have his own sovereignty so as not to be subject to any one of them, what need would there be for such in the case where all Christendom was once more united under one ruler, the French emperor? The Church prospered and spread for the first eight centuries, even though the Pope was a subject of the Roman emperor. To one who was a prisoner of Napoleon, the success of the Corsican general was very impressive and, from the "little window" of Fenestrelle, nothing seemed to stand in the way of French domination of all of Europe. Could it be that Providence destined Bonaparte to eliminate that multiplicity of sovereignties and thus destroy the presupposition upon which Bossuet based his argumentation? Writing in retirement to his brother in 1816, Pacca explained his moments of doubt:

"Everything seemed to point to the imminent establishment of a great monarchy which would mean the end of this plurality of states and of principalities which, according to Bossuet, render the position of a pope-citizen incompatible with the exercise of his apostolic ministry. I thought that in permitting the fall of the pontifical sovereignty, God, in the secret designs of His providence, was himself laying the foundations of this monarchy in the midst of all these great European upheavals, so that for a second time the popes might rule the universal church without hindrance, despite the fact that they were themselves subjects."[10]

There were other compensations, too, for the loss of the temporal power. For one thing, to continue with Pacca's meditations, the end of the papal states would end or weaken the blind jealousy or antipathy which existed in so many places against the clergy and Court of Rome. The sovereign Pontiffs, freed from the heavy burden of temporal affairs, could devote all their time henceforth to the spiritual good of their flock. The Church, shorn of the attraction that wealth and honors conferred upon it, would recruit its clergy only from those of right intentions. The Popes would no longer have to pay heed to considerations of nobility or birth or to the recommendations of the princely courts in the selection of their own aides and their advancement, recommendations which often left much to be desired. Finally, to complete the enumeration of Cardinal Pacca, there would no longer be need to fear that Church decisions were unduly influenced by political or material considerations.

Napoleon was not destined to be the new Charlemagne, to bring Europe once more under a united rule. With the fall of the First Empire all of Bossuet's arguments regained their validity, with their force enhanced by the bitter experiences

---

[10] Pacca, *Oeuvres*, I, pp. 70-71, *"Lettre du Cardinal B. Pacca au Marquis Joseph Pacca, son frère."*

of the Napoleonic era. Bonaparte's meteoric passage across the European sky was a brief one, but it seemed to illumine with particular sharpness the necessity of the temporal power of the Popes. The lessons of those years give the key to the course followed by the Roman See in the turbulent decades after the Congress of Vienna when the successive Pontiffs fought with dogged determination to maintain or recover their status as independent territorial sovereigns.

The history of the death agonies of the papal states after the Congress of Vienna is too much part of the history of Europe and of the movement for Italian unity to require any lengthy account. Despite the restoration of the temporal power by the Congress, Consalvi and his successors learned how much the times had changed. As the century progressed it became increasingly difficult for even the most outspoken ultramontanists to see how the papal states could sustain the attacks made upon them, or how the papacy could adhere to its claim concerning the necessity of the temporal power. In 1831 grave internal disorders in the papal domains led to the intervention of the powers. France, Austria, Prussia, Russia, Sardinia, and England sent plenipotentiaries to Rome to consult among themselves. They submitted a memorandum to the Pope recommending widespread reforms. The election of Pius IX in 1846 seemed to promise a solution to the problem of these reforms. But riots in 1848 compelled the flight of the Pontiff to Gaeta in the Kingdom of Naples, while in the Eternal City the constituent assembly of February 9, 1849 declared that the papacy had "forfeited, in fact and in right, the temporal government of the Roman state." But once again foreign intervention, this time particularly the French troops under Oudinot, put the papal flag back on top of Castel Sant' Angelo on July 15, 1849. This rescue of the papal sovereignty was but a reprieve. The cause of Italian unification finally found its leader in the Kingdom of Sardinia, after the Pope had shut the door against proposals for him to become titular head of a united Italy. Count Cavour at the Paris conference to wind up the Crimean War in April 1856 achieved the feat of putting the "Roman question" for the first time before the European powers in the form which suited most the designs of the House of Savoy. In 1860 the provinces of the Marches and of Umbria, the most flourishing part of the papal states, were united to the kingdom of Sardinia after the battle of Castelfidardo in which the papal army was defeated. In 1861 the King of Sardinia took the title of King of Italy. Cavour's death that same year did not bring a halt to the ambitions of the Piedmontese.

In an agreement of September 15, 1864 Italy pledged to France not to attack what was left of the Pope's territory, the Patrimony of St. Peter. But in 1870 the withdrawal of the French garrison from Rome, necessitated by the disasters of the Franco-Prussian war, presented the long-awaited opportunity. Royal troops marched upon Rome. On September 20, 1870 the city's walls and gates were battered by cannon. Pius IX gave the order to capitulate. Italy was at last united. But the Pope, protesting the usurpation of which he had been the victim, withdrew into the Vatican palace and refused to admit the legitimacy of the *fait accompli*. The second phase of the Roman question had begun. Once again the Roman Pontiff had to fight for recognition of his right to be a territorial sovereign. His efforts were rewarded with success only in 1929 when the Lateran Treaty made him acknowledged master of the State of Vatican City.

The 1929 Lateran Treaty ended the Roman question. For the first time in almost a century and a half, the temporal power was secure and unchallenged. The Pope was a temporal sovereign, territorially independent. But the recovery and peaceful possession of this civil sovereignty was more than a simple paragraph in international chronology. It was a vindication of the papal claims that such sovereignty was due it in virtue of the special mission the Holy See must perform in the world. For, during the long years of conflict, the issue had become glaringly clear: the papacy wanted back the temporal power, not as any dethroned prince seeks the restoration of his crown unjustly taken from him, but in the name of the independence it needed as the organ of a universal Church. International law, by recognizing the statehood of the State of Vatican City, recognizes implicitly the legitimacy of this claim. At least it reconciles itself to acknowledge as inevitable a situation it does not fully understand and to which it is not fully sympathetic.[11]

True, what is left of the old papal states is meager, if the present 108.7 acres of Vatican City can be considered a continuation of the papal states. But the size of the Pope's territory is inconsequential. What is important is the international juridical status of that territory, be it large or small. In the Lateran Treaty the Kingdom of Italy recognized the "full possession and exclusive power and sovereign jurisdiction of the Holy See over the Vatican, as at present constituted. . . ." (art. 3). This was a bilateral treaty and did not, of course, directly engage other parties. No effort was made, in fact, to solicit outside of Italy the formal approval or recognition of the new entity. But the governments implicitly accepted the treaty at its face value. International law today accepts the State of Vatican City as a state in the strict meaning of international law, enjoying the legal personality and prerogatives inherent in territorial sovereignty.

By formally acknowledging the liquidation of the Roman question and renouncing all further claims, the Holy See admitted that its post-1929 situation is compatible with the conditions described by Bossuet. The minimum essential was at least a speck of real territorial independence. Even in 1871 Pius IX told the French ambassador: "All that I want is a small corner of earth where I am master. This is not to say that I would refuse my States if they were offered me. But so long as I do not have this little corner of earth I shall not be able to exercise in their fullness my spiritual functions." A fair question to ask at this point is why the Holy See did not make a settlement long ago on such terms. This would have prevented the expenditure of so much energy, avoided the exciting of so many passions and hatreds, with the damage to the cause of re-

---

[11] Yves de la Brière expressed the papal thesis in terms of customary international law with this formulation: *"Le titre fondamental du Saint-Siège apostolique à exercer, dans la communauté internationale, une prérogative d'indépendance temporelle, juridiquement reconnue et garantie, n'est autre que son pouvoir religieux de suprême Pasteur de l'Eglise catholique. Non pas, à vrai dire, le pouvoir religieux et pastoral considéré en lui-même, mais le rayonnement historique, social et temporel, de ce pouvoir religieux et pastoral"* (La Brière, *Recueil. La Haye*, 1930, p. 161). In other words, the papacy's international situation in the community of nations is not per se a confessional issue, yet this position would be unexplainable prescinding from the Pope's high mission as the supreme head of a universal Church.

ligion occasioned by the protracted dispute over the Roman question. Such a question cannot be answered by judging the past in terms of the present. In 1871 the vision of Pius IX was beyond practical realization. The great issue of the temporal power was not simply a question of "how" but also of "when." What would that "small corner" of earth have meant, in international law, in the latter half of the 19th century? Even in 1929, despite the clear language of the treaty, some doubts were initially raised whether the new creation was really a state. Could such an obvious legal fiction, it was asked, be really a state when it could not provide its own public utilities, let alone defend itself from attack? In 1871 such a tiny bit of territory would have extra-territorial privileges. Such extra-territoriality was pledged by Italy in the 1871 Law of Guarantees. But this unilateral and revocable act was not sufficient. The Pope rejected it.

The political and juridical atmosphere had to mature further before the settlement was possible. A Lateran Treaty under the conditions of the post-1870 decades would have been as unthinkable as it was impractical. What was easily given could be just as easily taken away. Besides, it was far more honorable for the Holy See to remain in its position of apparently fruitless protest than to be put in the position of accepting as a gift from the usurper a tiny remnant of its own domains.

Sixty years passed before the time for settlement was ripe. The contest of strength between the Vatican and the Quirinal was in a sense indispensable as a means of demonstrating to the world the real relationship between the two Romes. Without the dramatization of the Roman question over a sustained period of time the present tiny territorial sovereignty would lack much of the authenticity now conceded to it. It was necessary during those years not only to justify the claim in theory but also to impress its merits first upon Italy and secondly upon the other states. The Pope had to act as a king before the world community would recognize him as one. The ultimate triumph of the papacy is all the greater because it had to convince a modern world cool and even hostile to the sight of a prelate at the head of any temporal government, especially when that temporal government is entirely subordinated to the needs of a world religion.

CHAPTER 7

INTERNATIONAL LAW ASPECTS
OF PAPAL DIPLOMACY

RIGHT OF ACTIVE AND PASSIVE LEGATION

THE long dispute over the Roman question has left its mark in international law. The issues—whether political or religious in origin—tended to express themselves in juridical terms. One of the consequences of the quarrel between the Vatican and the Quirinal after 1870 was to stimulate inquiry into the question of the legal position of the Holy See. Such a question transcended the problem of the temporal power. Even without a state of his own, the Pope remained an international figure with an undefined standing of some special kind in the world community. This was a fact beyond all denying. It could not be ignored by students of the law of nations, much as many would have liked to. But it was a fact that was subject to various interpretations. Today hardly a textbook on international public law does not devote a section or paragraph to the Holy See. An abundant bibliography of monographs

Bibliographical Note: The status of the Holy See in international law, as well as the juridical character of the State of Vatican City, are discussed in a myriad of writings, some of which are more likely to confuse than to enlighten. Many are theoretical exercises composed for thesis purposes; others are manifestly sharply partisan pieces. The Lateran settlement removed the political source of the conflicting opinions, but the coming into being of the Vatican State was the signal for a new rash of theoretical writings. Modern manuals on the subject leave much to be desired. The treatment of Oppenheim-Lauterpacht, for instance, is confused.

Most treatises contain bibliographical references from the vast literature. Consult, for instance, Oppenheim-Lauterpacht, *International Law*, I, p. 226, or Anzilotti, *Corso di diritto internazionale*, ed. 1955, pp. 136-37. For an evaluation of recent studies, see Josef L. Kunz in the *American Journal of International Law*, XLVI (1952), pp. 308-09.

The most exhaustive treatise on the legal nature of the concordats is that of Henri Wagnon, *Concordats et droit international*. In addition to the authors cited in the footnotes of the present chapter, the following writers, whose works are identified in the Bibliography, may be usefully consulted: Balladore-Pallieri, Bluntschli, Cumbo, Despagnet, Fauchille-Bonfils, Genêt, Guggenheim, Hackworth, Hershey, Higgins, Hochfeld, Hyde, Von der Heydte, Imbart de la Tour, Ireland, Le Fur, Miruss, Moore, Odier, Pasquazi, Pierantoni, Pradier-Fodéré, Rivier, Sereni, Siotto-Pintor, Vali, Wright.

testifies to the interest aroused by this perplexing and unique phenomenon.

The present study of Vatican diplomacy would be going too far afield if it attempted to develop in detail the question of the personality of the Holy See in international law. Diplomacy is not dependent upon international law. On the contrary, historically it has developed according to its own laws. Diplomatic practice is a source of international law rather than one of its creations. As we shall see later, Vatican diplomacy is one of the touchstones of the legal status of the papacy. At the risk of seeming to enter too casually onto terrain in which so many nuances of opinion exist, let us try at least to establish some basic points with an eye to their relevancy for diplomacy.

The treatment of the question in the standard manuals usually occurs at the point where the author is asking what entities can be considered as international persons or, as the phrase is given, "subjects of international law." Such persons or subjects are those institutions which are capable of international rights and duties. The fully independent state is the normal instance of such a legal personality. On this there is no dispute. The difficulty arises when there is question of semi-independent states or of international institutions lacking a territorial basis. What non-state institutions can posit juridical acts recognized by international law? Can non-territorial entities be endowed with international personality? The question presents itself in connection with organs of international cooperation among the states, such as the United Nations and the specialized technical agencies. It also presented itself with growing acuteness after 1870 in reference to the Holy See. Could the papacy, the highest organ of a worldwide Church, be properly regarded as a member of the international community of the law of nations? This was tantamount to asking whether the papacy had "international personality." To express the same concept in yet a third way, the problem was whether the Pope is a "sovereign" and therefore entitled to the inviolability and other prerogatives of sovereigns, including the right of active and passive legation.

Two important issues are directly related to the international personality of the Holy See. One of these is whether the concordats are treaties or conventions in the sense of international law. Such a question is obviously of great importance for a "concordat country" as well as for the Vatican. It makes an essential difference in the interpretation and application of the Church-State agreement whether the concordat is an international convention or simply an understanding without formal international juridical character. In the one case the concordat has legal force of treaty, while in the other it is per se revocable by either party at any time for any reason. Naturally, if the Holy See has no international juridical personality it has no capacity to conclude legally binding agreements with the several states. In that case, the concordats do not fall under the heading of international pacts. But if, on the contrary, the Holy See does have such personality, if it is a subject of international law, then the concordats are as valid and obligatory as any legal commitment ratified between two states. The legal nature of the concordat, upon which so much depends, has naturally given rise to a copious amount of speculation.

The other issue closely related to the personality of the Holy See is whether the papacy's right of diplomatic representation falls within the framework of international law. To put it another way, the question is asked whether the right of active and passive legation exercised by the Vatican is a legal right in the strict sense.

The present state of the debate can be summarized in a few words. The view seems to be dominant today—and this is assumed here—that the Holy See does, in fact, enjoy international personality. Furthermore, this personality of the Holy See is distinct from the personality of the State of Vatican City. One is a non-territorial institution, the other a state. The papacy as a religious organ is a subject of international law and capable of international rights and duties.

From this contemporary verdict two corollaries emerge: (1) *The concordats are international conventions.* Here, in other words, two subjects of the law of nations, one of whom is a religious, non-territorial institution, enter upon a legally binding contract. (2) *The Pope's right of active and passive legation is a right of international law.* The envoys sent and received by the Holy See are diplomatic agents in the full sense. The title of ambassador, or envoy extraordinary and minister plenipotentiary, given to the representatives whom the governments send to the Vatican are not merely honorary titles. They designate a public minister accredited as a diplomatic envoy within the meaning of international law and entitled to the privileges and immunities of diplomatic agents. The same holds for the nuncios and internuncios sent by the Pope.

Such, at least, seems to be the present prevailing opinion among writers in international law. This was the culmination of a long development of thinking in international law, marked by some well-defined turning points. These we shall now try to trace. To conform to the scope of our present study, we shall in the following devote primary attention not to the concordats but to the right of legation.

For many decades prior to 1914 the accepted conception of the international community was that of a society comprised only of sovereign independent states. The "European concert" was an exclusive club of sovereign states. In this system, institutions and individual persons were without any personality. They were incapable of performing any juridical act in international law. The law of nations was the law *inter-gentes*, between states. Up to the First World War this theory worked well and seemed to correspond to the needs of Europe. For a century after Napoleon, Europe experienced no general war. Wars there were, but brief and, above all, limited to a few states. It was still possible for a state to remain neutral. The rights of neutrals and the right to be neutral were respected by the belligerents. The cataclysm of 1914-1918 ended that phase. No longer did the sovereign State suffice as the only organ representing men on the world juridical plane. Other instrumentalities for international action had to be created.

The "classic" conception (which, if the truth be told, was never completely verified in practice even in its heyday) is today punctured by many exceptions. The creation of the League of Nations was one of the first breaches in the old system. This organization enjoyed some degree of juridical capacity. The creation of the International Labor Organization in the Versailles Treaty was another instance of this trend. Today the United Nations and the numerous specialized agencies coordinated with it enjoy uncontested international juridical personality. Such institutions were unthinkable to 19th century international lawyers. The wind has changed today and, as one result of this shift in doctrine, international law has become more disposed to accord to the Holy See, another non-territorial entity, the juridical status so contested after the loss of the temporal power in 1870.

But it was a long and hard-fought struggle. The continuance of Vatican diplomatic representation was an open defiance of the prevailing conception. After 1870 the Holy See continued to send and to receive agents who bore at least the titles of diplomatic officers. The question that arose was whether these representatives were really public ministers in the strict sense of international law, or merely by courtesy. Two approaches to this situation were possible. On the one hand it could be argued that the Pope was no longer sovereign of the papal states and therefore could not send or receive real diplomatic envoys. On the other hand, the reverse reasoning could apply: these representatives were indistinguishable from real diplomatic agents and, consequently, the Pope was still a sovereign. It was a question of theory versus practice.

It must not be imagined that this controversy was entirely scientific and detached on either side. The issue of sovereignty has seldom, if ever, been debated, in any of its aspects, purely with an eye to theory. Lord Bryce testifies to this effect in his *Studies in History and Jurisprudence.* Concluding his analysis of sovereignty, the historian of governments said he was struck by the fact that the historic controversies in this field had been at bottom political rather than philosophical, "each theory having been prompted by the wish to get a speculative basis for a practical propaganda."[1] Frequently enough the effort ended in a purely academic theory to which the facts refused to conform. The period between the fall of the papal states and the beginning of World War I was one of intense Church-State partisanship in many parts of Europe. It was inevitable that these conflicts should impinge even upon legal theory. The writers of manuals were caught with the fever.

Much of what passed for international law in that debate

[1] Bryce, *op.cit.*, p. 552.

was, in reality, highly colored extra-legal interpretation influenced by the personal sympathies of the publicist in question, clerical or anti-clerical. So far as the juridical question of the Holy See is concerned this was not a distinguished phase in the history of writing in international law. Politics, law, and religion crisscrossed the entire issue and impeded clear-cut legal thinking.

An extreme instance may be cited here which will convey in a particularly striking way both the essential points at issue and the atmosphere in which the controversy was conducted. In September 1904, shortly after the rupture of diplomatic relations between France and the Holy See, there took place in Rome a world congress of free-thinkers. A featured speaker of the occasion was one Gustave Hubbard, a well-known anti-clerical deputy from Paris, who delivered a paper and presented resolutions on the subject of "Diplomatic Relations between the States and the Churches." The orator was the editor of a quarterly known as *La Justice internationale*, subtitled a "review of questions of cosmopolitan law." Of his sympathies for the cause of free thought he made no secret. Religion he defined as "the blind, sentimental and unreasoning confidence that popular imagination gives to the priests and to the dogmas they teach." But, as he assured his audience, the question should be approached in what he called the "juridical and objective spirit." The speaker then proceeded to give short shrift to the diplomatic prerogatives of the Holy See and to the international position of the papacy generally.

Said Gustave Hubbard: "The supreme Pontiffs of all the religions, whatever they are, are merely the responsible directors of the different associations and religious hierarchies, national or international. As such they cannot be reckoned among sovereign moral persons—republics, empires, confederations, kingdoms, principalities and free cities—whose mutual relations have alone the nature of diplomatic relations." He went on immediately to draw the desired conclusions from this premise. "Consequently," he said, "the present relations existing between these states and these Pontificates should be assimilated exactly, from the juridical point of view, to those which common law within each internal legislation prescribes for the relations between the state and the various national or foreign associations grouping in one and the same state a given number of individuals."[2]

The drift of these remarks was all too clear to the contemporary audience, free-thinkers or others. From the viewpoint of international law the Catholic Church is at most an association of private law. The Pope is a private person as far as international law is concerned and the several states are entitled to take whatever measures they choose in his regard, as they feel their own interests dictate. This was an obvious reference to the Italian Law of Guarantees, which unilaterally regulated the status of the Pope in Italy. The logic of these premises leads to another conclusion: "There is no essential difference, from the juridical point of view, between any religious group, whatever it be, the Roman Catholic or any other, on the one hand, and those other societies which share a common moral, philosophical or intellectual point of view."

The theses stated by Hubbard involved, in his mind, some practical consequences which can be summarized in five points:

1. The rupture of diplomatic relations or the suppression of reciprocal diplomatic representation currently existing between any church and the various states, constitute social progress and is "in harmony with the purely human and positivist international law, and with the modern international legislation exclusively inspired by the totality of the positive sciences."

2. In particular, the Pope of Rome is merely the head of the "Roman Catholic Association" and should not be considered as a sovereign in the juridical meaning of the word.

3. The conventions called concordats should not have the character of international treaties.

4. The envoys of the Pope, of whatever rank, legates, nuncios, etc., and the officials sent by states to the Pope, should not be considered as real diplomatic agents.

5. The mutual reciprocal relations of the Pope and the states belong entirely to the domain of the internal law of each of those states and are not subject to the norms that should regulate "cosmopolitan law."

The views of Gustave Hubbard express in accurate form the

2 *La Justice internationale*, août-déc. 1904.

issues at stake in the debate on the international status of the Holy See even if the anti-religious bias shows through the affected objectivity of this so-called juridical analysis. Other writers of that period wrote to the same effect but succeeded somewhat better in clothing their partisanship with legal language. In France the central object of anti-clerical attacks was the concordat of 1801. It was easier to repudiate and destroy the concordat if it could be proved that the papacy was not a subject of international law in any sense of the word, and had no diplomatic rights. The rupture of diplomatic relations between France and the Holy See was therefore a preliminary to the abolition of the concordat. To this purpose it was necessary to show that the sovereignty of the papacy was not real. A work widely quoted in anti-clerical circles and published in 1888 by Raoul Bompard makes a line of argument that indicates the political objective in view: "If the Holy See is an international sovereignty, if it belongs to this community of rights, obligations and interests, then the legislative abrogation of a concordat, the refusal to receive nuncios, the recall without cause of a representative at the Vatican constitutes on the part of a government a violation of its international obligations, an action that can and should arouse the concern of the other powers. But if, on the contrary, the Pope is outside the law of nations and if his relations with the various powers, although clothed in diplomatic form, depend upon their internal legislation, their own public law and constitutions, then in that case the conduct of every government should be dictated solely by the wishes of the country and the circumstances of internal policy. Foreign nations could not be alarmed or affronted by the refusal to consider the nuncios as diplomatic agents, or by the abrogation of a concordat."

For Bompard, the Pope had lost all his sovereignty. Whatever immunities the Pontiff enjoyed were a free concession of the Italian royal government upon whose territory he lived: "[*The Pope*] not having today any territorial sovereignty, the representatives of the powers accredited to the Vatican are not diplomatic agents. Their status, as regards privileges and immunities, depends upon the good pleasure of the government on whose territory the Pope resides." The writer reiterates an idea he has already expressed: "Any state can recall its agent at the Holy See without being obliged to allege any complaint. The recall can result particularly from the adoption of separation of church and state by the constitution of a country."[3]

The standpoint represented by Bompard was the common one in anti-clerical circles in France. It was not merely in Italy that political and anti-clerical objectives inspired attacks upon the international personality of the Holy See. In Italy the Pope's claims to continuing sovereignty over the papal states had to be countered by reducing his international status to zero. In France the ground had to be laid for the long-sought termination of the concordat. The campaign began in France with the elections of 1877, which returned a republican and anti-clerical majority. It culminated in 1905 with the repudiation of the concordat, preceded in late 1904 by the rupture of diplomatic relations.

In Belgium an analogous situation developed during this same period. The Liberal ministry of Frère-Orban came to power in 1878, the same year which closed the long pontificate of Pius IX. The program included a school reform project which had been vigorously fought by the Catholics with the encouragement of the Holy See. The bitterly anti-clerical program also included the demand for rupture of relations with the Holy See. The advent of a new Pope, Leo XIII, suggested to the new government, however, the prudence of waiting until it could be ascertained whether a modification of the opposition was imminent. This apparent hesitation did not please some of the extremists of the party who feared that it portended a drawing back from the electoral platform. They pushed for immediate rupture with the Vatican. A brochure published at this stage in 1879 by one of this group laid down arguments that were thought good in that situation. The author of the small study, a Brussels lawyer named Theodore Wilbaux, entitled his work "The Vatican question from the viewpoint of the right of diplomatic representation." The Italian Law of Guarantees, he declared, could not attribute to the Pope or anyone else the right of embassy, any more than purely internal law can attribute the rights of international sovereignty. The

3 Bompard, *Le Pape,* pp. 59, 71-72.

envoys at the Vatican were not public ministers in the strict sense but, "by way of exception and thanks to a fiction created by a unilateral will, for reasons of convenience and courtesy," they should be treated as if they had this character. Wilbaux concluded his thesis by saying: "The law of nations proclaims and history confirms that the Pope has not the right to receive ambassadors, nor the right to send them." The basic reason, he said, was that the Pope had lost his (territorial) sovereignty.[4]

The pamphleteer's worries that the Frère-Orban government was softening on its campaign demands were unfounded. It was soon established that Leo XIII was just as insistent on the school issue as his predecessor had been. Accordingly, on June 5, 1880, Frère-Orban as foreign minister ordered the Belgian envoy at the Vatican, Baron d'Anethan, to notify papal Secretary of State Cardinal Nina that he was being recalled. Notification of rupture was made to the apostolic nuncio in Brussels on June 28, and he was handed his "passports," as the expression was in those days.

In Belgium, however, the issue did not terminate as it did in France. The execution of the school reform so aroused public opinion that in 1884 the Liberals were swept from power and the Catholic party was returned with a greater majority than before. The new government wasted no time in reestablishing diplomatic relations with the Holy See, as well as in repealing the repudiated school legislation. Funds for the Vatican mission were approved in August 1884, carried by a vote of 73-44 in the Chamber.

The opposition party took the occasion of the debate on the Vatican budget to renew the juridical arguments against the international personality of the Holy See. One of the Liberal deputies, Gustave Rolin-Jacquemyns, who had himself been a member of the preceding cabinet, based his protest chiefly on legal grounds. The relations that had been terminated by the Liberals and whose restoration was proposed by the Catholic party, he contended in a speech delivered on August 7, could not be justified from the viewpoint of international law. "The Pope," he said, "has neither territory, nor civil authority. He is not a sovereign in the sense that international law attaches

4 Wilbaux, *La Question du Vatican* (brochure).

to that word. He has no subjects, no judiciary, no armed forces. In a word, he has nothing of a temporal sovereign. The soil on which he stands, or where he lives at this moment, is Italian territory. He himself is an Italian today, as he would be a Belgian, a Frenchman, tomorrow, if on the present Pope's death, the conclave should elect as his successor a Belgian or a Frenchman. In the case of death the inheritance of the Pope would be apportioned according to Italian laws." The Chamber turned a deaf ear to this argumentation. Nevertheless the points were urged from that time forward in Belgium, especially by the Liberals. One of Belgium's leading legal minds, Professor Ernest Nys of Brussels University, in his *Treatise on International Law*, adopted this as his own. It was, in general, the position of the Liberals throughout Europe.

It is not difficult to trace the source of a line of legal theorizing which today seems so arbitrary but which had great vogue between 1870 and 1914. The fundamentals of this school of thought were first outlined in Italy by Pietro Esperson, in an interpretation of the Law of Guarantees. This theory was expounded in the first of a three-volume work published in 1872-1876, *Diritto diplomatico et giuridizione internazionale Marittima col commento dell' disposizione della Legge Italiana del 13 Maggio sulle relazione della Santa Sede colle Potenze stranieri*. The author was the friend and associate of the Leftist parliamentarian, S. Mancini, who was conspicuous in the Chamber of Deputies in 1870-1871 when the Law of Guarantees was being debated. Mancini introduced many amendments whose effect would have been to reduce the Pope to an even less satisfactory position than was contemplated in the original draft. The Rightist cabinet of Lanza and Visconti-Venosta was able to beat down most of Mancini's amendments. But in March 1876 the conservative government of Cavour's disciples which had been in power since 1849 was overthrown. In its place came a government of the Left headed by Agostino Depretis, with Mancini as minister of justice. What had before been the opposition and minority interpretation of the Law of Guarantees soon became the official one. The headlong anti-clericalism of the new regime, strengthened by the elections of November 1876, soon showed what that meant in practice.

According to Esperson, whose theoretical writings thus found a means of practical expression after 1876, the status of the Pope was determined exclusively by the internal legislation of Italy. The Pontiff had only such privileges and immunities as the Kingdom of Italy chose to accord. These privileges and immunities could therefore be abolished or altered by the unilateral action of the Italian parliament. In international law the Pope was only an individual, that is, without any international juridical personality whatever. One corollary of this interpretation of the status of the Pope in relation to the Law of Guarantees was that the so-called right of embassy was not a true right in the sense of the law of nations. The nuncios sent by the Pope derived their status only from the concession of Italy. They were not real diplomats in the sense of international law. The same held for the ambassadors and ministers received by the Holy See.

Because the Pope was no longer temporal sovereign of the papal states he was not a real sovereign in any sense at all. Said Esperson: "For the same reason, according to the same principles, the ministers that the powers should wish to send to the Pontiff cannot be considered true diplomatic agents, unless they are at the same time accredited to the Italian government. It is true that they represent their own country but that is not sufficient for diplomatic status, since it is in addition indispensable that they be charged with representing their country to another country. The putative juridical situation of the envoys of the foreign governments accredited to the Holy See does not differ from that of the representatives of the Supreme Pontiff accredited to the foreign governments."[5] It was not, according to this interpretation, the intention of the Law of Guarantees to confer any international juridical standing upon the Pope. This would have been beyond the powers of the Italian parliament, even if such had been its desire. The law merely wished to confer privileges and immunities identical in form perhaps, but not in substance, with those enjoyed by diplomatic agents. These granted by the law derived from internal legislation and were revocable at the will of the legislator. Thus far the Esperson thesis. It was an attractive position

[5] Esperson, *op.cit.*, I, p. 37; cf. *ibid.*, pp. 50-51, 79-80, 125-26, 153-54, 167-69.

elsewhere in Europe also, particularly in France and Belgium, as an anti-clerical instrument against the Catholic Church.

What sort of arguments were offered by Esperson and those who came after him to prove that the papacy could not, as a non-territorial entity, enjoy international personality? On what grounds was it asserted, over and over again, that "only states" could be subjects of international law? Mention has already been made of the "classic" conception envisaging a world juridical society composed exclusively of sovereign states. In addition, two specific reasons alleged were applicable to the case of the Pope. These were: (1) *The religious and spiritual function of the papacy.* International law was designed to establish order in the temporal and political field. But the Church and State operate in entirely different spheres and there is no occasion for them to enter into contact with each other. There was "no point of contact," no common ground. The business of nuncios was purely religious and ecclesiastical and they could be "diplomats" only by analogy. (2) *The internal nature of Church affairs.* Anything that the Holy See wished to discuss with the State necessarily concerned the State's own internal affairs. The religious affairs of its own citizens cannot be considered proper objects of "international" negotiations. Furthermore, the Holy See cannot enforce fulfillment of any agreement without appeal to revolt by the Catholic citizens. But international law forbids such interference.

These general arguments were supported by a variety of collateral considerations. For instance, it was pointed out that the Pope could not go to war to redress wrongs inflicted on him. Therefore, he could not claim the status of sovereign, for the touchstone of sovereignty lies in the ability of a ruler to wage war. If this argument seems a curious one at the present time it had a certain appeal in the state of international law in the second half of the 19th century. Another argument was that the Pope could not guarantee immunity to the ambassadors accredited to him in Rome, since they necessarily lived on Italian territory and depended upon the good will of the Italian government for their diplomatic privileges.

These and other such arguments were plausible in the abstract, but they lost most of their effectiveness when confronted with the actual practice of the European states. The weakness of the Esperson school was that it preferred to start from a theoretical hypothesis, such as the one that "only states" can be subjects of international law, or from a gratuitous supposition that religious affairs could not possibly be conducted through the instruments of the law of nations, such as diplomatic representation or bilateral conventions. This doctrinaire construction, unsupported at any time by diplomatic practice, finally collapsed of its own weight.

It is sometimes stated, as an explanation for the analysis of the Esperson school, that the idea of spiritual sovereignty was new and strange at that time. In reality, Esperson was consciously challenging the concept of spiritual sovereignty which underlay the Law of Guarantees. This idea of spiritual sovereignty was not only not unknown at the time Esperson wrote but it was the preferred view. In proof of this, it is only necessary to cite the criticism that no less a person than Rolin-Jacquemyns made of the Esperson book when it first appeared. In a review appearing in the *Revue de droit international et de législation comparée* of 1873, Gustave Rolin-Jacquemyns (1835-1902) challenged the basic assumption of the Esperson interpretation of the Law of Guarantees. "While we entirely approve of this law," said the reviewer, "we are not completely in accord with Esperson in the explanation which he gives of it, in this sense that the law does not seem to us to have been a purely voluntary act on the part of the Italian government but rather a consequence of the special character that the Popes have enjoyed in modern international law, and which already distinguished them from all the other sovereigns, even from the purely diplomatic point of view, prior to the suppression of the temporal power."[6] In other words, the Law of Guarantees conferred nothing upon the Pope which he did not already possess in virtue of international law. This law merely gives the force of internal legislation to prerogatives that it was beyond Italy's power to take away. Rolin-Jacquemyns, no friend of the papal cause, saw nothing incongruous in the Pope's enjoying the strict right of active and passive legation even after 1870. He changed his mind later, as already seen.

[6] *Loc.cit.*, v (1873), pp. 300-01.

Writing in the same international law review a few years later, another contributor took exception to the idea that diplomatic representation can take place exclusively between states. Reviewing the pamphlet of Wilbaux, already cited, Prof. E. R. N. Arntz declared that this fundamental thesis was "entirely erroneous." It was not true, he declared, that only states could receive ambassadors. Such a statement applied to the papacy, he argued, ignored the constant practice of the European community. "The law of nations," wrote Professor Arntz, "has for principal source history and the usages and the practice of civilized nations. International law has not been created by general and broad formulae nor can it be summarized by such."[7] The Pontiff, he pointed out, did not send his nuncios as the prince of a small Italian state nor did he receive ambassadors as such. He was accorded exceptional diplomatic honors and entered into treaties and concordats as a spiritual ruler and not as an Italian prince. Other citations can be found which show that, before Esperson, European writers recognized that the Pope enjoyed his position in international law primarily as a religious leader and only secondarily as a temporal ruler.[8]

Time has proved the mistake of limiting international juridical personality to the states alone. Today, many non-territorial entities enjoy such personality. The thesis so widely espoused

[7] *Loc.cit.,* xi (1879), pp. 659-60.

[8] The shift in opinions coincided with the advent of ministries of the Left throughout many European countries after 1877 and the growth of anti-clericalism. Heffter, in his 1873 edition, declared that the relations of the Pope with the states could not be denied and that the Law of Guarantees did not change this. This author died in 1880 and the 1881 edition carries a vigorous dissent by his own editor, Geffcken (Heffter, ed. Geffcken, 1881, p. 96n.). Another writer who changed his outlook was Emile Brusa. In his notes on Casanova, *Diritto internazionale,* published in 1878, he sanctioned the criticism by Rolin-Jacquemyns of the Esperson thesis: "*Sarebbe troppo lungo il discutere qui la questione, ma sembra impossibile negare ciò che non è che un fatto storico, vale a dire appunto il carattere sovrano che sempre riconosciuto al papa anche in que'soli rapporti che'esse aveva cogli altri sovrani in materia ecclesiastica. Ora colla caduta del poter temporale non poteva percerto intendersi cessato anche questo carattere nel pontefice Romano*" (II, pp. 7-8). Contrast this view with that developed by the same author a few years later apropos of the Martinucci case (in *Rev. de dr. int. et de lég. comp.,* 1883). Here Brusa holds that the Pope's standing cannot appertain to international law because his role is religious: "*Mais sa politique n'est pas laïque et le droit international est désormais exclusivement laïque*" (loc.cit., p. 133). Brusa accepted the conclusion of the Court of Appeals to the effect that "*le pape a perdu toute espèce de souveraineté*" (*ibid.,* p. 116). If 1877 marked a political turning point in the Roman question, 1883 marked a juridical one.

in the three decades and more before the First World War is now abandoned. The question to ask is why the thesis was ever maintained at all? Customary law should have told the legal writers of that period that the papacy remained a subject of international law after 1870, for the simple reason that the states continued to recognize his right of legation and other attributes of sovereignty. All during that period of debate, as we have noted, the facts of international practice were giving the lie to the theories. Curiously enough, even Ernest Nys of Brussels at one time acknowledged this, although he did not draw the conclusions therefrom that he should have.

Writing in 1878 in the review already cited (of which he was secretary) Professor Nys alluded to the contradictions evident in the diplomatic situation of the papacy at that time. It was only too obvious that the states were ignoring the theory by continuing to have diplomatic relations with the Holy See. "From the theoretical point of view [*he wrote*] there is here a flagrant anomaly. The only persons in international law are the states. Outside of the states nothing has capacity for rights or is subject to responsibilities." The facts, however, he added, do not conform to the principle: "One of the chief prerogatives of sovereignty, the right of embassy and negotiation, has been exercised and is still being exercised. Where is the mistake? Is it on the side of theory? Or is it on the side of practice?"[9] The question was clear, but the author's answer was ambiguous. In later years he chose to consider that the theory was right. In the end, the "principle," which was in reality only a working hypothesis, yielded to the genuine needs of the international community, capitulated, that is, to the constant practice of the nations. The doctrinaire attitude of the learned Brussels scholar, who incidentally had made special research into the institution of diplomatic representation and was perhaps a prisoner of his own theories, was only too common in his time. It explains a great deal of the unrealism that marks the legal writing on this subject at that period.

Across the Channel the less emotionally involved English writers showed a more realistic attitude toward the meaning

[9] *Rev. de dr. int. et de lég. comp.*, x (1878), pp. 501-38. Contrast this with the same author's treatise, *Droit international*, II, pp. 317-18.

of this contradiction between theory and practice around the Pope. T. L. Lawrence wrote before the First World War: "It is quite true that most of the privileges and immunities he possesses are conferred by the Law of Guarantees. It is equally true that, if these were withdrawn, many states would be likely to interfere and some perhaps by force of arms. An Italian statute cannot confer international personality; but the tacit consent of a large number of states to treat a given prelate as if he possesses some of the attributes of an international person puts him in a very different position from that of an ordinary individual. The position in question is indefinable. . . ." The author added this observation, "The insuperable difficulties connected with it is a testimony of the strength of moral and spiritual influences in a sphere where we are sometimes told only brute force counts in the last resort."[10]

Rapprochement between the old theories and the manifest practice of the nations was well advanced on the eve of the Lateran settlement of 1929. It is significant that in a treatise appearing just before the 1929 pacts a leading international lawyer, Professor Dionisio Anzilotti, who had been president of the Permanent Court of International Justice, lightly dismissed the Esperson thesis that had so long ruled the roost, especially in Italy, with this comment: "The dogma which a priori limits to states the character of subjects of international law, necessarily considers as purely gratis, voluntary and revocable, the recognition of diplomatic character to envoys of the Supreme Pontiff on the part of the different states. This was the sole means of interpreting current practice in harmony with such a premise. But one may wonder whether, in this way, instead of interpreting practice for what it is, one interprets practice for what one would like it to be."[11]

Legal theory has come full circle since 1876. If we compare present-day opinions in international law on the status of the Holy See we find that they are closer to that originally expounded by the Cavourians who authored the Law of Guarantees of May 13, 1871 than to the conception of Esperson, Man-

10 Lawrence, *Principles* (ed. Boston, 1910), p. 83.

11 Anzilotti, *Corso*, 3 ed., p. 139; 4 ed., p. 135. On subjects of international law other than states, see Siotto-Pintor, *Recueil des cours*, 1932.

cini, and the anti-clericals of the late 19th century. Having recognized once again the spiritual sovereignty of the papacy, the law of nations has rejected the "concession" theory that had so much vogue at the turn of the century. The fact that the Holy See is a non-territorial institution is no longer regarded as a reason for denying it international personality. The papacy can act in its own name in the international community. It can enter into legally binding conventions known as concordats. In the world of diplomacy the Pope enjoys the right of active and passive legation. He can send and receive representatives who are public ministers in the sense of international law. But this is not new or original. This was the view of the very men who in 1870 stripped Pope Pius IX of his temporal domains by armed invasion.

For a full understanding of the verdict reached after the many decades of controversy, it is important to grasp the precise juridical point at issue. The issue was not whether the Pope was still temporal ruler of the papal states. It did not turn upon whether a dispossessed prince retained his right of legation. The question was rather this: whether, *despite* the assumed loss of the temporal sovereignty, the Pope continued to enjoy international personality at least as head of the Catholic Church, as a "spiritual sovereign." Some papal writers did attempt to argue that the Pope remained at least a *de jure* temporal prince. They adduced various reasons to establish this, such as the injustice of the annexation or the refusal of the Pope to acquiesce in the status quo. These arguments, however, were hardly convincing from a juridical point of view. They served rather the purpose of demonstrating that the Roman question was not as dead as the Italian government would like to have it believed. The intense debate reflected in the post-1870 literature on the subject was not given over to the temporal sovereignty of the Pope, but to his spiritual sovereignty.

It is necessary to stress this point because it is a common error to suppose that the Lateran Treaty of 1929 finally reestablished the papacy as a subject of international law. This misapprehension ignores the evolution of legal thinking during the preceding decades. By the time the situation was politically ripe for the Lateran accord, legal opinion was already prepared to concede the Pope's legal status. Had the Vatican State never come into being in 1929, international law would have increasingly recognized the non-territorial sovereignty of the papacy. Yet it must be conceded that the long years of the Roman question tended to confuse the two different issues: the political and the spiritual sovereignty. Theoretically distinct and separable, they were linked politically and emotionally in the rupture between the papacy and Italy. Many pro-papal writers were themselves responsible for this confusion of thought. They wrote as though only the temporal power was the issue. They played down the spiritual sovereignty on the grounds that it was a purely imaginary, extra-legal invention of the Italians, tailor-made to suit the political purpose of usurping the papal states. They refused to be misled from the chase by what they considered the will-o'-the-wisp of spiritual sovereignty. For this reason they tended to pour scorn upon any sovereignty not based on territory. The Marquis de Olivart, one of the ablest of these writers, exclaimed, "As for those more or less fanciful distinctions of titular, or honorary, or such-like sovereignty, these are encountered only in books and cannot exist in the world of reality."[12] They would settle for nothing but the restoration of territorial sovereignty. For them, spiritual sovereignty was not enough.

Even the language of official papal spokesmen was less than clear on this point. On many occasions the Vatican curia seems to say that there was no sovereignty that was not based on territory. Papal spokesmen rarely expatiated upon papal sovereignty without linking it with temporal power. What they meant to imply, of course, was that spiritual sovereignty was not in itself sufficient for the full independence that the Pope needed. They did not wish to say that the Pope was not also a spiritual sovereign in international law. In the end, the satisfactory guarantees were achieved by the creation of the Vatican State. In the meantime, however, minds had become confused over the real issue of the legal debate.[13]

12 de Olivart, *Le Pape*, p. 12.

13 Maritain, for instance, exemplified the effect of this one-time stress on the civil sovereignty when he wrote, "The pope, as a temporal sovereign, has a diplomatic service as formerly he had an army" (*Things That Are Not Caesar's*, p. 42). More exact and precise is Delos: "*Ce n'est pas parce qu'il constitue un*

In 1870, before the protracted polemics had obscured issues, the distinction was clear. The men who brought about the unity of Italy by the downfall of the Pope-King did not contemplate expelling the Pontiff from Rome. They were compelled to reckon with the continuing presence of the head of the Catholic Church in the Eternal City. They hoped that the Holy See would reconcile itself to the new situation. To this end, they needed a formula which would answer their problem. In the European community it was commonly agreed that the Pope needed to enjoy independence from any political power. The Cavourians thought they had found a solution by dividing the Pope's prerogatives into two categories. In the first they placed those rights which he exercised as the civil ruler of the papal states. These rights in united Italy would go over to the House of Savoy. Under the second category they placed those rights which accrued to the sovereign Pontiff as supreme head of the Catholic Church. These rights they were fully prepared to recognize and preserve, guaranteeing them, if necessary, by treaty with the other states. The Law of Guarantees tells us what these spiritual rights were conceived to be. They included the right of immunity, of inviolability and of extra-territoriality, the right to have violations of these rights punished, and the right to exchange diplomatic representatives.

The Law of Guarantees did not, and was not intended to, "confer" any international rights upon the Holy See. What the lawmakers did was to enact legislation which constituted *recognition* of preexisting rights. The law merely conformed domestic legislation to a juridical situation that Italian law could neither create nor abolish. That this was the intent of the legislators emerges clearly from the declarations and acts of the government spokesmen. Their statements before the September 20, 1870 march upon Rome, their formal defense of the draft legislation in the parliament, along with the explanations and assurances given the foreign governments, are consistent and unambiguous on this point. Contrary to what was often claimed at a later date, the government of Italy had a perfectly clear

---

Etat, que le Saint-Siège est souverain, c'est au contraire, la création de l'Etat pontifical qui constitue une conséquence de la souveraineté inhérente à la nature de l'Eglise" (in *Rev. gén. de dr. int. pub.*, 1929, p. 429).

and coherent conception of the international non-territorial personality of the Holy See. The policy of Lanza and his cabinet was based on the validity of the distinction and separability in international law of the temporal and spiritual sovereignty. The success of their invasion of papal territories while the French, traditional defenders of the temporal power, were powerless to intervene, depended upon their ability to convince the foreign governments, even the non-Catholic ones, that the Pope would not become a tool of the regime which now held him in its political power. The new masters of Rome were sincere in their belief that the Pope remained a sovereign, stripped though he was of his temporal rule. The spiritual prerogatives of the papacy, in their view, need not be affected by such a political change. They recognized that, on the contrary, it was now Italy's special responsibility to modify its own laws so as to guarantee the Pope's free exercise of the spiritual sovereignty.

Rising in the Chamber of Deputies on January 30, 1871 to defend his government's conception of the new status of the Pope in relation to Italy, Foreign Minister Emilio Visconti-Venosta declared that the Pontiff did not become a subject of Italy by the fact of the annexation of the papal states. On the contrary, the Pope retained his right of free action and unimpeded communication with foreign governments. "But," argued the foreign minister, "do you think we would grant this privilege to a bishop, an Italian subject, whose jurisdiction does not extend beyond the limits of his own diocese? Or do you think the governments would accredit ministers and ambassadors to a subject of the King of Italy? To recognize the right of diplomatic representation is to recognize at the same time this juridically sovereign situation of the Pontiff. . . . This will be a spiritual sovereignty, a sovereignty *sui generis*, insofar as it does not have territory and cannot be juridically determined by frontiers, since these do not exist, but which is endowed with those privileges, such as that of inviolability, which though not conferring civil jurisdiction, nevertheless makes it immune from the jurisdiction of others."

Earlier, before the same body, Visconti-Venosta had insisted upon the correctness of the spiritual sovereignty concept. "The

Pontiff," he declared on December 21, 1870, "is not merely the spiritual head of Italian Catholics. He represents the supreme religious authority, exercising jurisdiction over the Catholic communities which form part of the public law of other states and, as an ecclesiastical authority, he has with these states concordats and agreements of international form which regulate and also recognize this jurisdiction." The speaker went on: "To recognize the Pontiff's right of diplomatic representation and to deny an international character to the juridical position of the Papacy as a religious institution, seems to me an evident contradiction."

The viewpoint expressed in the two parliamentary speeches cited above was common in the course of the debates on the Law of Guarantees. The Italians wished to leave entirely unchanged the purely ecclesiastical prerogatives of the Pope in the international field. They wanted only to assume political control of the Italian peninsula. Their strategy to disarm opposition abroad was to recognize ungrudgingly the status of the papacy in international law as a purely religious institution. Need it be said that, from the Vatican's standpoint, this was equivalent to a thief breaking into a house and giving to the despoiled owner some of his own valuables as a "gift" before making off with the rest. But the Italians saw that the spiritual sovereignty could be isolated. They made the most of it.

One more citation may be introduced at this point, this time from Visconti-Venosta's Senate address of April 22, 1871. This contribution at the close of the long debate shows how consistent and clear was the conception of the authors of the law. Said the foreign minister: "All the governments maintain a diplomatic mission to the Pontiff. This mission has been accredited both to the temporal sovereign of Rome and to the Pontiff. But certainly the character of Pontiff took precedence over that of the sovereign. And in the future the governments will have representatives accredited to the Pontiff, under one form or another, for the purpose of treating religious matters; for, independently of the territorial sovereignty over Rome, Catholics recognize in the Pontiff the high spiritual sovereignty. I do not need to add that the governments believe it is to their interest that the Pontiff, who exercises jurisdiction over such a large percentage of their people, should not on his part be subject to the jurisdiction of any particular state." A more concise statement of the position of the Lanza government, which sponsored the Law of Guarantees, could hardly be expressed.

It might be argued that the words of a foreign minister defending his government's bill before a national legislature are of purely domestic significance. As such, they do not concern the international community. The Law of Guarantees was, in itself, an instance of unilateral internal legislation. It was never sanctioned by the other states, much less by the Pope. The expression of the Italian viewpoint was not limited, however, to the national assembly. It was also expounded in the international forum. What Visconti-Venosta told the deputies and senators before the enactment of the Law of Guarantees he repeated for international purposes after the law went into force on May 13, 1871. A week after that event the foreign minister addressed a circular to all the governments abroad to report the action and to interpret for their benefit the significance of the act. As before the march on Rome the foreign ministry had assured the governments that the Pope's religious independence would remain intact through a special statute, so it was only a natural development when the foreign governments were formally notified of the passage of the law fulfilling those promises.

The circular, dated May 20, 1871, announced that the Italian parliament had just enacted measures aimed at guaranteeing the position of the sovereign Pontiff. The Law of Guarantees, said Visconti-Venosta, was a proof of the good faith of the new rulers of Rome. Accompanying the text of the law was a running commentary, article by article. The comments of the foreign minister on Article 11, which deals with the envoys accredited to the Holy See and those sent by the Pope, are a clear recognition that the law only recognized, and did not pretend to create, these rights. In the copy received at Paris, Visconti-Venosta declared: "The law of May 13, in recognizing the existence of a diplomatic corps accredited to the Holy Father as well as the right to continue to dispatch nuncios to the heads of other governments, leaves untouched the eminent position that the public law of Europe has recognized in the Pope, as far as the exercise of his lofty spiritual mission is concerned."

After pointing out how the law provided penalties for those violating the immunities of the Pope and of the diplomats sent and received by him, the circular continued: "Our duty is therefore to make it known to Europe that nothing has been changed in the position of the papacy, from the viewpoint of public law, as far as his spiritual authority is concerned. It is with this aim that we bring to the attention of the French cabinet the law that has just been promulgated. This law is nothing else, in its first part, than a formal and explicit recognition of the prerogatives and honors that international law accords to the papacy."[14]

The "first part" of the Law of Guarantees, referred to in the preceding quotation, deals with the prerogatives of the sovereign Pontiff and of the Holy See. The statement of the Italian foreign minister could hardly be more unambiguous, especially when read in the light of the declarations already made during the parliamentary debates. There is no trace here of the "concession" theory.

The foreign governments took the Italian government at its word. They expected that their acquired right to send envoys with diplomatic immunities to the seat of Roman Catholicism would be unchallenged. During the succeeding years, even the anti-clerical government of the Left never dared alter the diplomatic situation. The most it did was to elaborate new interpretations of the status quo and of the law which covered it. The message sent by the Austro-Hungarian foreign minister to his two representatives on the Italian peninsula illustrates concisely enough the attitude of the governments. Alluding to inspired rumors suggesting that Vienna might, for the sake of good relations with Italy, consolidate its double diplomatic mission— that is to say, suppress the embassy accredited to the Vatican— Count von Beust instructed the respective heads of the two missions: "Our right to maintain a mission to the Holy See is perfectly established and we have not the slightest reason to

[14] Original French text from Paris archives cited in present author's *Rise of the Double Diplomatic Corps in Rome*, pp. 17n, 18n. Excerpts from Italian parliamentary debates, *ibid.*, pp. 87-92.

abdicate the exercise of a right which serves very important interests. This mission should enjoy the immunities granted everywhere to the diplomatic corps and its competence extends to all questions which concern the Catholic interests of Austria-Hungary in their relationship to the Holy See." The Austrian foreign minister added: "Regardless, therefore, of the editorials in the semi-official newspapers on the status of the diplomatic corps at Rome, we cannot today think of changing what presently exists and we cannot suppose that it is the intention of the Italian government to ask for such a change. Make this known to all about you on every possible occasion." These instructions were issued under date of September 22, 1871, after the Law of Guarantees had had some months to operate, and a full year after the invasion of Rome.[15] The presence of a separate foreign mission in the Eternal City was a constant annoyance to the Italian government, but, as the message of Count von Beust shows, they were dealing here with an established right that the foreign governments did not want to surrender and which Italy itself had pledged to respect.

During all the years from 1870 to 1929, the Kingdom of Italy sought to avoid any conflict with the foreign governments on the subject of the Pope's right of active and passive legation. There was no desire to give states abroad the opportunity of intervening in the Roman question. Even the most bitterly anti-clerical cabinets did not interfere with the foreign missions accredited to the Holy See. They scrupulously respected the customary privileges and immunities, even though at the same time they sought to convey the idea that this was a pure courtesy on their part and not the consequence of any obligation. As a result, the diplomatic clauses of the Law of Guarantees never got a real test on the international plane, at least until the First World War.

A significant trial of the conception underlying the Law of Guarantees, as seen by its authors, was nevertheless experienced within a few years. It was occasioned by the Kulturkampf in Germany and arose out of the vigorous opposition raised by Pius IX against Bismarck's anti-Church legislation. As this historic conflict developed in intensity, the resistance put up by the

[15] Original text from Vienna archives, *ibid.*, p. 59n.

Pontiff became more and more enraging to the Iron Chancellor. Bismarck's anger reached a new high when, on February 7, 1875, Pius IX issued an encyclical declaring the May Laws invalid. He cast about him for means of retaliation. His wrath fell upon Italy, which he blamed for being legally responsible for the actions of the Pope.

Bismarck's complaint never took official form, but the lesson of the episode is no less pointed. The first thing that the Italians knew of the Chancellor's irritation was on the occasion of an official reception in Berlin. Bismarck said to Count Launay, the Italian minister, that he did not consider Italy very friendly to Germany. To the Italian diplomat's surprised query as to the reason, Bismarck replied that the way Italy permitted the Pope to attack Germany was no friendly act. Formerly, said Bismarck, had the Pope written such things about the German government, it would have been possible to send a fleet to blockade Civitavecchia until proper amends were made. But now that the Pope had no territory of his own, argued the Chancellor, it was Italy's responsibility to see that friendly powers were not insulted in this way by the Pope.

Visconti-Venosta's representative in Berlin reported this incident to his chief on March 13, after Bismarck's aide in the foreign office had again broached the matter. An answer had to be made, wrote Launay, in which Italy rejected any responsibility for the papal utterances or actions. The Italian foreign ministry replied on March 21 with a long and spirited defense of the "spiritual sovereignty" of the Pope under the new order of things on the peninsula. Italy, stated Visconti-Venosta, could not assume responsibility for what the Holy See did without by that very fact infringing on the immunity that was inherent in sovereignty. It was not in the interests of either Italy or Germany, or any other country for that matter, that the royal government in the Quirinal should be made watchman over the Holy See.

On the general principles of spiritual sovereignty the foreign minister denied Italy's responsibility for the attacks by Pius IX upon the German Empire's laws and policies. The question of diplomatic representation also came into the answer of March 21. As a spiritual sovereign the Pope already enjoyed a special status in the international community. Italy could not suppress the diplomatic missions which the governments considered to be their right to maintain at the papal court. Visconti-Venosta expostulated: "Even supposing that we had had the intention of doing so, would it have been in our power, or is it now in our power, to abolish the public law character of the papacy? Would one of our laws have been sufficient to forbid him to receive ambassadors or ministers, or to dispatch nuncios to foreign courts? Long after the publication of the Law of Guarantees His Highness Prince Bismarck kept in the budget of the German ministry of foreign affairs an allocation for the embassy at the Holy See. It is only recently that this item was eliminated, with the right to restore it if circumstances should so advise. It is evident that the Pope, who receives and sends ambassadors, cannot be at the same time subject to the Italian law. Inviolability the most complete is the only guarantee, the very essence of sovereignty without territory."[16]

These arguments were impressive and entirely consistent with the previous Italian policy. The matter went no further. In later years, as we have seen, many anti-papal writers claimed that the Pope was a private person, merely an Italian citizen. But they were as prompt as they were inconsistent in disclaiming Italy's responsibility for the acts of the Pontiff.

The spokesmen for the Kingdom of Italy under the Rightist anti-clerical government, 1870-1876, may seem to have at times gone out of their way to extol the "spiritual sovereignty" enjoyed by the Pope under international law. The Bismarck episode helps to explain why. Their solicitude was not derived from any affection for the Pope, whose domains they usurped in the face of excommunication. To the extent that they exalted the Pope's international personality as a religious authority, they diminished by that fact his status as temporal sovereign. Their advantage lay in developing the distinction between the two sovereignties. It mattered little to them that they enhanced thereby the papacy's status in international law. Their object was, in fact, to quiet apprehensions and to deprive their foes and critics, at home and abroad, of one of the Pope's most ef-

---

[16] The full text of this letter is published in Salata, *Per la storia diplomatica*, pp. 273-82. For other details of this incident, see Graham, *op.cit.*, pp. 93-96.

fective arguments. As the Roman curia argued that the temporal sovereignty was necessary for the independence of the sovereign Pontiff, so Italy's answer was that this independence was satisfactorily guaranteed through his sovereign immunity. But the position of the papacy was then, and never ceased to be, that papal sovereignty required, for its completeness, the possession of territorial sovereignty. Thus, while the new masters of Rome made a point of separating the two sovereignties, the Vatican made a point of linking them.

The Holy See was closer in agreement with the Cavourian conception than it was ever willing to admit. Too wholehearted accord on the issue of spiritual sovereignty would have been interpreted, in the controversial atmosphere of those post-1870 decades, as surrender on the temporal power. Nevertheless, every once in a while the Vatican had to take a formal position on the papacy's spiritual sovereignty. This was particularly true with the rise to power after 1876 of the Leftist governments, beginning with that of Depretis.

Some of these occasions were provoked by disputes over diplomatic precedence abroad. It was inevitable for the question to arise whether, with the loss of the papal states, the Pope's diplomats continued to enjoy the deanship of the diplomatic corps. One of the earliest tests occurred in Peru in 1877, where the precedence of Mario Mocenni was challenged. Archbishop Mocenni in that year came to Lima with the title of apostolic delegate and envoy extraordinary (not as internuncio). A dispatch of the secretary of state on December 2, 1877 insisted that the question of the papal states was irrelevant as far as the delegate's diplomatic status was concerned: "It was not the territory possessed by the Pontiff that made the difference in his nuncios, but the dignity of the Supreme Head of the Church." The 1877 episode was smoothed over, but the question popped up on numerous occasions in Latin America and elsewhere. It came to life again in the same Peruvian capital of Lima in 1891. The minister plenipotentiary of Venezuela argued that not merely was the deanship not a right enjoyed by the apostolic delegate but that the papal representative did not even have diplomatic standing. The end of the papal states, he said, also ended the status of the Holy See as a subject of the law of nations. As a consequence, the agents of the Pope were accredited principally to settle questions relative to the internal discipline of the Church and not to treat of those affairs having a diplomatic and political character. The concordats, he went on to argue, could not be considered international treaties and the papal agents abroad did not possess in their own right a true diplomatic status. In sum, the apostolic delegate had no right to be a member of the diplomatic corps, let alone be its dean.

We recognize the line of argumentation characteristic of the anti-papal jurists of the Esperson school. According to Pinchetti-Sanmarchi, from whom these details are drawn,[17] the papal envoy replied by declaring that the position of the Venezuelan minister contained four unacceptable propositions: (1) that the Pope enjoyed the right of active and passive legation only as a temporal king; (2) that the Pope had no international personality as the head of the Catholic Church; (3) that the object of the mission of the pontifical envoys was limited to questions relative to the internal discipline of the Church; (4) that whatever diplomatic position the Pope enjoyed was due to the Law of Guarantees.

The reply of the apostolic delegate in Lima, Msgr. Macchi, is of special interest in its denial that the juridical position of the Pope rested upon temporal sovereignty. There is, however, an even more authoritative statement of the Vatican position, in the form of general instructions on precedence issued by the secretariat of state to its representatives abroad in April 1900. Referring expressly to the Lima incident of 1891 the Vatican directive declares:

"Such an assertion of the Venezuelan minister does not need refutation. For it is evident that the usurpation of the temporal power of which the sovereign Pontiff has been the victim, did not alter in the slightest either *de jure* or *de facto*, the position of the papal diplomats accredited to the governments of Europe and America. Not *de jure*, because even prior to 1870 the representatives of the Holy See had, as they do today, neither more nor less, for principal scope to promote and defend the spiritual and religious interests of peoples at the seats of the various governments. They were representatives of the Pope, as pastor

17 Pinchetti-Sanmarchi, *Guida diplomatica*, I, pp. 221-23, 294.

of souls much more than as temporal king. And as such they had and still have a true and real, if special, diplomatic status, a status *sui generis* but superior to that of the lay diplomats. The events of 1870 have not changed anything in that respect."

The instruction then alluded to the dispatch to Mocenni, already cited, and explained: "Nor *de facto*. For, as we read in the dispatch of the secretary of state of January 21, 1891 to the internuncio of Brazil, 'all the governments continue to keep their respective ambassadors and ministers accredited to the Holy See, with their full diplomatic status, recognizing thereby the sovereignty of the Pontiff, notwithstanding the *fait accompli*, which they do not wish to seem to approve, directly or indirectly.' "[18]

The clarity of this Vatican stand is somewhat in contrast with the language employed by the pro-papal writers in the press of that day. It frankly declares the papacy's independence of the temporal power for its legal status.

Another case not directly concerning the right of legation but of greater significance because it goes to the heart of sovereignty was the famous Martinucci litigation. This can be said to have marked the open declaration of war by the governments of the Left in Italy. It brought a significant change in the official interpretation of the Law of Guarantees. In 1882 a decision of the Italian Court of Appeals contradicted one of the major underpinnings of that law as envisaged by Lanza, Minghetti, Visconti-Venosta, and its other sponsors. An architect named Vincenzo Martinucci had brought suit against the Vatican for non-payment of professional services. He sued in the Italian court. Instead of declaring themselves incompetent because of the Pope's inviolability recognized by the Law of Guarantees, the court accepted jurisdiction. Although Martinucci did not win his case, even upon appeal, the assumption of jurisdiction at two levels was in open conflict with the presumed guarantees of the law of May 13, 1871.[19]

The significance of even the procedural decision of the royal Italian courts was not lost upon the Vatican. It pounced upon the incident as proof of the inadequacy of the law as a supposed

[18] *Segreteria di stato. Istruzione.*
[19] Soderini, *Pontificato di Leone XIII*, II, pp. 90-100; Brusa, in *Revue de dr. int. et de lég. comp.*, 1883.

guarantee of papal independence. If every succeeding government or even court could interpret or nullify or repeal or violate the law at will, of what value was it? The Martinucci case proved, in the Vatican's eyes, that spiritual sovereignty without territory was in itself a very unstable foundation of papal independence. This conviction grew in succeeding years as similar court decisions in analogous cases in other countries followed the lead of the Italian courts.

The denial of papal inviolability called forth a defense of spiritual sovereignty on the part of the papal spokesman. In a protest addressed to the foreign envoys at the Vatican, Secretary of State Cardinal Jacobini said on September 11, 1882: "It would be a great mistake to compare the political status of the Pope with that of a dispossessed prince. The Holy Father has remained a sovereign not only *de jure* but also *de facto*, by reason of his divine mission and in virtue of his Apostolic Office which he exercises with supreme authority in the entire world, even after the loss of the temporal power. This status of real sovereignty is recognized by all the powers which have accredited to him extraordinary legations and permanent embassies, endowed with diplomatic privileges, which publicly render to him those acts of respect and homage which are accorded only to reigning princes."[20]

This affirmation of the spiritual sovereignty which is the foundation of the papal status in international law was not subsequently openly pressed by Vatican spokesmen after the Martinucci case, for the reasons already stated. Yet there is no doubt that it represents the papal view of the Holy See's sovereignty in international law. The position stated by Jacobini parallels not only the ideas of the Cavourians but also the contemporary dominant theory of international law.

[20] Bastgen, *Römische Frage*, III, p. 191.

CHAPTER 8

PAPAL SOVEREIGNTY IN CANONICAL
PUBLIC LAW

THEORETICAL FOUNDATIONS OF
PAPAL DIPLOMACY

IT IS IMPOSSIBLE to talk about the spiritual sovereignty of the Holy See without relating it to the nature of the Catholic Church as seen by its own canonists. We have been discussing the Pope's right of external legation or embassy without being specific about the authority he wields as the supreme head of the Catholic Church. By this time, however, it should be evident that it is neither the fortuitous chance of human history nor the possession of temporal power that has provided the basis of papal authority or of papal diplomacy. The Pope's role in history has been what it is because of what he is in the Catholic Church. Ultimately, his authority is merely a function of the Church's own authority.

The past century has witnessed a considerable clarification of two questions: the scope of the papal authority within the Church and the juridical nature of the Church. "What is the Pope?" was the title of a celebrated controversial pamphlet that appeared when Pope Pius VI visited Joseph II in 1782 in Vienna. That question is no longer in dispute so far as Catholic doctrine is concerned. The Vatican Council of 1870 spelled out the prerogatives of the Roman Pontiff in terms beyond cavil, thereby dealing a death blow to various opinions which had tended to minimize the authority of the papacy in the Universal Church. The Pope is the highest authority in

Bibliographical Note: Public ecclesiastical law has developed greatly in the past half-century as a separate discipline of canon law. Most of the existing treatises, however, devote major attention to the juridical problems arising out of the concordats. They seem to regard diplomatic relations with the states as an auxiliary institution without great interest. Frequently the difference between the internal legation and the external legation of the Pope is insufficiently stressed. Much yet remains to be done by the canonists to develop the concept of the perfect society in its diplomatic connotations. In addition to the authors cited in the footnotes of the present chapters, the following writers mentioned in the Bibliography may be consulted: Bettanini, Casoria, Conci, Jannacone, de Luise, and Perugini.

the Catholic Church. Even the decrees of ecumenical councils require his sanction. In virtue of his succession to the See of Peter, the Roman Pontiff exercises a primacy of jurisdiction over the bishops and over the faithful. He is not therefore merely *primus inter pares* (first among equals), a presiding chairman without authority over his fellow bishops. Furthermore, his jurisdiction extends not only to matters affecting faith and morals but also to all those matters which appertain to the discipline and the law of the Church throughout the world. He has the power not merely to alter individual canons but even to codify and reform the whole of canon law. When pronouncing *ex cathedra*, or from the plenitude of his apostolic powers, on matters of faith and morals, the judgment of the Pope is infallible.

These prerogatives are far-reaching, but they are based upon the nature of the Church herself. Pontifical diplomacy, like other prerogatives of the Popes, has its roots in the constitution and mission of the Catholic Church. The Popes are but organs of an institution founded by Christ. For an understanding of the theoretical basis of papal diplomacy we must now turn to an examination of the juridical nature of the Church in canon law.

It cannot be the purpose of the present work to present a systematic and complete study of the Catholic Church as a society. It is sufficient to lay down certain points of Catholic doctrine which bear upon papal diplomacy. These may serve to throw this unique phenomenon into correct perspective even for those who cannot be expected to accept that doctrine as their own. Doubtless the conception that the Catholic Church holds of its own constitution is not shared, at least not wholly, by those who are not Catholics. For centuries theological controversy has raged between Catholics and Protestants on this theme. Many Protestants do not share the Catholic view that Christ instituted His Church as a visible society placed under the jurisdiction of the Apostles and their successors, the bishops. They reject the closely knit juridical organization to be found in the Catholic Church as they reject the notions of authority and jurisdiction held by Catholics. In this they are joined to some extent by the dissident Churches of the East. There are some Protestant sects which not only reject the idea of the Church as a visible society, but object to religion's having anything to do with the civil power. For such sects, if the Church should have nothing to do with the State even on the national scene, how much more should this be avoided on the international scene, and above all in the diplomatic world? Papal diplomacy would come off very badly indeed if it were judged on Protestant premises.

The modern State does not claim to pass judgment upon the correctness of either the Catholic or the Protestant views of the nature of Christ's Church. It cannot therefore criticize or evaluate papal diplomacy by Protestant criteria. Of the Catholic Church the most it can demand is that it be consistent with its own principles. This attitude is likewise the only possible one for those who wish to prescind, as we do in this book, from purely theological argumentation. In the following paragraphs on the juridical nature of the Catholic Church we wish only to delineate what that doctrine is, particularly as it applies to papal diplomacy, without evaluating the theological considerations supporting that doctrine.

The terms "diplomacy" and "sovereignty" are so intimately linked that one implies the other. Diplomatic representation is one of the touchstones of sovereignty. This is because it has been surrounded by so much protocol and identified with so many political situations directly related to the existence and independence of states. Traditionally it is the characteristic instrument by which, in time of peace, the sovereign states carry on their business with each other precisely as sovereign states. It is the visible symbol of the independence and equality that states claim in the international political community. Semi-sovereign states look forward to full, reciprocal, and unrestricted diplomatic representation as the beginning and sign of their emancipation. This institution took its rise with the beginning of the national states, flourished in the heyday of absolute sovereignty, and, it may not be too much to say, will pass out with the end of the system of national sovereignties upon which our present world political community is based. Although itself an extra-legal institution, diplomatic representation has become inseparably associated with the juridical concepts of sovereignty.[1]

For this reason, when the Catholic Church systematically engages in diplomatic activity it by that very fact manifests that it shares in some way the independence and autonomy symbolized by this prerogative. When the states for their part exchange representatives with the Holy See they necessarily indicate in this manner their recognition of the special independence of the Church. This independence is assimilated to that which one state acknowledges in another state with which it has diplomatic relations. Or, to put this in another way, as the states claim a territorial sovereignty, the universal Church claims its own kind of sovereignty, of a spiritual nature, it is true, but one possessing the same essential characteristics as the civil sovereignty of the states.

In the eyes of the canonists the universal Church is, in fact, very much like a state. It is sovereignly independent of any other juridical entity, including the State. In its own domain its authority is unshared and total. The power which it exercises over its members is jurisdiction in the proper sense and not merely moral influence or persuasion. The Church enacts legislation in its own name in the fields within its spiritual jurisdiction. It claims and exercises the right to pass judgment upon transgressors and to assign sanctions. To use the language of the canonists, the universal Church is a *perfect society*, supreme and independent in its own sphere, like that other perfect society which is the State.

The best-known formulation of the Church as a perfect society was given by Pope Leo XIII in his encyclical letter *Immortale Dei* of November 1, 1886, a long treatment of the nature of civil and religious society and their reciprocal relations. The Church, said the Pope, is a society just as the State is, but differing in its end, which is religious. He goes on:

"Although this society is made up of men, just as the civil community is, yet it is supernatural and spiritual, on account of the end for which it was founded, and of the means by which

---

[1] La Fontaine expressed this association with sovereignty in his own way (*Fables*, I, 3): "*Tout petit prince a des ambassadeurs, tout marquis veut avoir des pages.*" The same link of diplomacy with sovereignty was expressed more juridically by Genêt, *Traité*, II, n. 561, p. 6.

it aims at attaining that end. Hence it is distinguished from and differs from civil society and, what is of great importance, it is a society perfect in its nature and in its title since it possesses in itself and by itself, through the will and loving kindness of its Founder, all needful provision for its well being and its operation. And just as the end at which the church aims is by far the noblest of ends, so is its authority the most exalted of all authority, nor can it be looked upon as inferior to the civil power or in any manner dependent upon it."

In short, the Church claims, in respect to its spiritual mission, the same authority claimed by the State in its own temporal mission. The states themselves, as Leo XIII pointed out, implicitly recognize this when they deal with the Church as they deal with other sovereign powers. He specifically mentioned the exchange of diplomatic representatives. Said the Pope a little further on:

"Princes and all those invested with the power to rule have themselves acknowledged this, in theory as well as in practice. In the making of treaties, in the transaction of business matters, in sending and receiving ambassadors and in the conduct of other kinds of official dealings, they have been wont to treat with the Church as with a supreme and legitimate power."

The theory of the sovereignty of the Church thus formulated by Leo XIII is not necessarily generally accepted by the states themselves. A few Catholic states in recent concordats have formally recognized the Church as a perfect society in the sense described above by Leo XIII. For example, art. 2 of the Spanish concordat of August 27, 1953 declares: "The Spanish state recognizes in the Catholic Church the character of perfect society and guarantees it the free and full exercise of its spiritual power and of its jurisdiction. . . ." A similar article is found in the concordat of the Dominican Republic signed shortly after, on June 16, 1954. Such a declaration is a recent innovation in concordats. For, in most cases the states do not feel compelled to interpret their diplomatic relations in the same terms as those used by Leo XIII. What is relevant here is what the Church herself considers to be its juridical nature as a society.

Properly speaking, the study of the Church as a perfect society belongs not so much to the realm of theology as of canon law, specifically to public ecclesiastical law. This is the branch defined as "the system of laws on the constitution and rights of the Church considered as a perfect society ordained to a supernatural end," to quote Cardinal Ottaviani.[2] As the name indicates, it is the public law of the Church, as distinguished from private law, which concerns individuals and not the Church as a society. As usually divided by the canonists there are two sections, *internal* public law and *external* public law. The former deals with the nature of the Church and its authority considered in itself. This would therefore correspond in a sense to civil constitutional law. The second considers the relation of the Church as an independent society toward the State. This corresponds to international law, in the sense that it considers the mutual relations of two sovereign entities each of whom recognizes the autonomy and independence of the other in the respective spheres.

Cardinal Ottaviani, whose definition is cited above, has indicated the relationship that exists between papal diplomacy and public ecclesiastical law. In his treatise the writer says that the relationship is reciprocal, each discipline assisting the other. "Public law," he writes, "precedes diplomatic law and provides it with the principles by which in practice, along with the principles of the law of nations, the rights of the Church and of the state are brought into harmony; and contrariwise, through diplomatic law are clarified and strengthened the requirements of public law and particularly in propounding the art of finding the means for removing the obstacles which may stand in the way of the external exercise of the rights of the church."[3] In sum, for the Church as for the State, diplomacy and sovereignty go hand in hand.

The term "perfect society" which forms the key phrase of contemporary treatises on public ecclesiastical law had not been widely used, if used at all, in canonical writings up to a hundred years ago.[4] Even today it remains an expression useful primarily

[2] Ottaviani, *Institutiones*, I, n. 6.

[3] *Ibid.*, n. 13.

[4] The canonists were much more tardy than the Roman curia in adopting the term. In a protest against the Caesaropapist claims of the Czarist regime, Cardinal Consalvi wrote to the Russian minister Italinsky under date of June

in this branch of canon law and is hardly known outside of ecclesiastical science generally. Prior to that a more significant word was used. The Church was not "like" a state; it *was* a state.

As late as 1863 the Roman canonist Guglielmo Audisio wrote in his treatise on public Church law, "We affirm, therefore, that the church should be defined a government and a state, for it is a true society, subsisting by itself and ordained to one end, by means of laws and shepherds proper to it whence it draws its essence and its form."[5] In 1840 the canonist Giovanni Soglia wrote in like manner, "We affirm that the church is a state and there are many arguments to prove it."[6] Much earlier, similar language had been used. Giovanni Devoti, a Roman canonist whose textbook was widely used (published in 1803), described the Church variously as a "state" or "republic." (. . . *Non collegii sed reipublicae rationem habeat a civili distinctae et ideo proprio, eoque summo regatur imperio.*)[7] Zallinger zum Thurm, even earlier, termed the Church in the same connection variously as a "sacred state" (*status sacer*), an "ecclesiastical state," and a "hierarchical state."[8] Obviously the canonists were groping for terminology, but for lack of a better one they did not hesitate even to apply the word *state* to the universal Church. What they were driving at, however, was clear. The Church was organized on juridical principles like a state, enjoyed the same rights to its independent existence, and was not subject to any civil authority in the execution of its mission.

The reason for the lack of precise language which made itself evident when the canonical writers, still in search of the right word, termed the Church a "state," is the simple fact that public ecclesiastical law was yet in its infancy as a separate canonical discipline. The Church was very slow in adopting a technique that was early picked up by the Protestants and by the canonists of Catholic monarchs in conflict with the Holy See. It was

---

22, 1817: *"L'Eglise est une famille bien réglée et une société parfaite; elle doit donc nécessairement entretenir une libre et continuelle communication entre les chefs et les membres, les fils et le Père"* (Boudou, I, p. 88).

[5] Audisio, *Diritto pubblico*, I, p. 25.

[6] Soglia, *Institutiones Juris Publici*, Pars II, pp. 149, 151.

[7] Devoti, *Institutionum Canonicarum*, Prol., par. vi.

[8] Zallinger zum Thurm, *Institutionum Juris Naturalis et Ecclesiastici Publici*, lib. v, c. vi.

not until 1824 that this new science achieved a recognized place in the curriculum of sacred studies. In that year Pope Leo XII instituted chairs of public ecclesiastical law at Rome and Bologna on the occasion of a reorganization of university studies in the papal states. In the meantime a running battle had been going on involving the juridical nature of the Church. One of the most important controversies in this connection arose out of what is known as Febronianism.

Febronianism derives its name from the pseudonym adopted by the author of a book that first appeared at Frankfurt-on-Main in 1763 with the title *Justini Febronii Jurisconsulti de statu ecclesiae deque legitima potestate Romani Pontificis ad uniendos acatholicos liber singularis.* The work aroused immediate controversy. Before long it became known that the real name of its author was Johannes Nikolaus von Hontheim (1701-1790), auxiliary bishop of Trier, a learned man but educated in the school of the Jansenist canonists of Louvain. The ostensible purpose of the book (which was dedicated to the reigning Pontiff, Pope Clement XIV) was to advance the cause of Catholic-Protestant reconciliation. But the author's means to this praiseworthy end was to expand the authority of the national churches, while diminishing at the same time the primacy of the papacy. Theoretically, the book was a treatise on the nature and the constitution of the Catholic Church. In practice it envisaged an entirely new politico-ecclesiastical system for Germany. In this system the Church was subordinated to the civil power. The work was promptly condemned in Rome and its author ultimately issued a retractation, though some doubt remains as to his sincerity in doing so. The thesis had been launched at an explosive moment in the political as well as ecclesiastical atmosphere in Germany. Numerous editions followed in the next few years; these were matched by polemical literature from the other side refuting the Febronian theses.

Febronius denied the monarchical nature of the papal power. He also denied that the Church could be compared in any way, even in a purely religious sense, to a state. For him, the Church was but a college, a corporation or voluntary society. As such, it was subject, like any other such body, to the control and regulation of the prince who was entitled for this reason to issue the Placet on all papal decrees, and in other ways to supervise the Church.

This thought was not original with Febronius. The collegial system had already been introduced in some Protestant parts of Germany, but this applied only to the Protestants. Febronius was the first Catholic to apply it seriously to the Catholic Church. He frankly acknowledged his indebtedness to the Protestant natural-law philosopher Pufendorf, who had propounded it as a system of Church-State relations. Inasmuch as Febronius himself cites long passages from Pufendorf on this subject, in full agreement, it is useful to read just what precise line of argument had been advanced. Pufendorf's theory was propounded in a short work published in 1687 bearing the title *De habitu religionis ad vitam civilem.*

Pufendorf used the principle of state sovereignty, as so many others were to do later, as the instrument for bringing the Church (he was thinking primarily of the Protestants, but his argument could apply to Catholics, too, as Febronius was aware) under the subjection of the civil power. His line of thinking was clearly indicated in the answer he gave to his own question, whether there was in the Church any need for judges to resolve controversies. The answer was negative, on the grounds of divided sovereignty within the state. Wrote the German philosopher:

"In this way two supreme authorities would be introduced into the one state. For the citizens could be held to the decisions of this judge as much as by decisions in civil cases. For since such a religious authority does not emanate from the end of organized states it must be something special and separate from the civil authority. Hence if it exists in the person of the one who also has the supreme civil power in the state, then he will be the lord of conscience as well as of life. And if that power resides in someone else then such a one will also have the power of executing the sentence passed by himself, or at least he will consider it sufficient to hand over its enforcement to the civil rulers, after having passed sentence. In the former case the two supreme authorities in one state would generate great inconveniences and difficulties; in the other case the civil rulers only carry out the bidding of the sacred judges as mere bailiffs."[9]

Pufendorf concluded that, divided sovereignty being ruled out, there is thus no justification for further dispute over a question that once preoccupied both Catholics and Protestants, namely, whether the Church had a monarchical, aristocratic, or democratic form of government. Such arguments supposed that the Church was a "state" and enjoyed a "supreme power," or sovereignty. The writer said, "In organizing churches, there is no need for any provisions concerning the forms of government; the question whether the monarchical, aristocratic or democratic form appertains to the church is absurd. For all this applies to a state (*status*) or a *civitas*. But the church is not a state."[10]

Febronius explicitly accepted this position and the argumentation of Pufendorf. It should be noted that he must have known that when Pufendorf denied the Church was a state he did not mean to say that the Church was not a *civil* state. Pufendorf meant that the Church did not enjoy any sovereign independence vis-à-vis the State upon whose territory it existed. For he defined clearly the meaning of "state" by saying, "We take the word *status* in the popular meaning, to signify an independent society of men which is held together and ruled by a supreme authority."[11] Such a *status*, in the Latin of the 17th century, corresponds to the "perfect society" of the present-day canonists. Pufendorf and, after him, Febronius for the Catholics denied that the Church was or could be what is now termed a perfect society.

Febronianism was an effort to subject the spiritual power to the secular power. As Pastor has said, Febronius handed the Church over to the secular arm. This was not entirely new in the history of the Holy Roman Empire, but the weapon was new: the theory of the undivided sovereignty of the state. If

[9] Pufendorf, *op.cit.*, par. 36. Febronius, *op.cit.* I, c. i, par. 5; c. ii, par. 12, n. 6. Pastor, *History*, XXXVI, pp. 250-75; XXXVIII, pp. 407-16; XL, pp. 1-28.

[10] Pufendorf, *op.cit.*, par. 32: "*In ecclesiis formandis non opus est decreto super certa regiminis forma introducenda; absurdaeque sunt quaestiones, monarchica, aristocratica, an democratica forma competat ecclesiae. Hae quippe formae cadunt in statum aliquem, seu civitatem. Ecclesia autem status non est.*"

[11] *Ibid.*, par. 30. "*Accipimus heic vocabulum status populari modo, pro societate hominum independente, quae summo Imperio continetur et regitur.*"

sovereignty meant exclusive, unshared domination over all institutions, religious and secular, in the realm, then there could not be two sovereignties and the Catholic Church was not supreme and independent in its own sphere. The anti-Febronius polemicists drew the logical consequences of his doctrine.

The Dominican Thomas Mamachi exclaimed in his *Epistolae ad Justinum Febronium* (1776): "You call it a college! You will soon call it merely a college; for as you know the college has no authority in the state except that which it derives from the prince or the nobility or the people." Furthermore (argued Mamachi) the college or corporation can have no intercourse or dealings with foreigners without the consent of the civil rulers. The Church therefore is cut off from free intercourse with the highest superiors, the Pope in Rome. In addition, a Church which has no more legal existence than that of a *collegium* can be dissolved by decree of the prince. More, since no kingdom is dependent upon another, then neither can one Church be linked with another in another realm, since any authority of the corporations proceeds from the civil power. Thus also the universality and unity of the Church is destroyed. Such consequences are inadmissible for the Church of Christ. The Roman controversialist concluded: "The Church is not therefore just a corporation, but a republic, as has already been abundantly shown, a state or a *civitas*."[12]

The argument employed by Mamachi is a negative one. The Church cannot be subject to the civil power and therefore is not a *collegium* or corporation. Therefore the Church itself is a state. Other polemicists developed the positive doctrine of the constitution of the Church. In his *Anti-Febronius Vindicatus* (1771) Francesco Maria Zaccaria, another Roman canonist, took this line: "The Church is a society, 1°, external and visible; 2°, endowed with supreme power, in a way that in it not all are equal but there are those who rule and others who must obey or be punished if they rebel; 3°, and is not subject to any other power however great, in those things which are within its domain. The Church is therefore a state."[13]

[12] Mamachi, *Epistolarum*, lib. II, par. 26, pp. 351-52.
[13] *Op.cit., pars I, diss. ii, c. i.*

Today this doctrine seems elementary to Catholic writers, but it was not so elementary in the time of Febronius. The canonists had not up to that time been seriously challenged on the score of divided sovereignty. The idea of the division of the two powers, temporal and spiritual, was of course an old one. Men were expected to render to Caesar what was Caesar's and to God what was God's. But up to the development of the idea of state sovereignty in the 17th and 18th centuries, the issue had never turned squarely on the nature of the Church as a juridical entity in itself, and apart from maxims of Roman law. The canonists had in consequence never developed any systematic doctrine on the constitution of the Church as a perfect society or "state." Such questions as dealt with this subject were treated at random, as occasion presented itself, throughout the Decretals, which provided the text for canon law instruction.

The Roman canonist Devoti, whom we have cited already as attributing to the Church the nature of a republic or state, addressed himself to the objection that if the Church enjoyed supreme power, or sovereignty, it would enter into conflict with the state. He argued that Church and State had distinctive spheres of competence and therefore there could be no legitimate conflict between the two. His argument made it clear that he was challenging the Protestant (and Febronian) conception that sovereignty was indivisible even in relation to the Church. The words of Devoti were echoed later by Leo XIII in the encyclical *Immortale Dei* and are worth citing for their contribution to an understanding of the real issue at stake. On the alleged contradiction expressed in the idea of a "state within a state," Devoti said:

"But the competence of the civil power is one thing and that of the ecclesiastical power is another, each having its own certain and definite kind, in which it is supreme. The one looks after the advantage of the citizens and the civil authority, the other concerns itself with things sacred and divine. There is no contradiction and no confusion and there is no *status in statu*, as the Protestants say, but each is a state of a distinct kind and each has its own province, which it may not transgress. And in this lies the true and precise distinction between the ecclesiastical and the civil power: one belongs to the natural order while the other belongs to the supernatural; one is ordained to civil matters and the temporal happiness of men while the other presides over things sacred and divine and has the charge of those things which appertain to eternal happiness."[14]

It is clear that here Devoti is not merely proclaiming the general difference between things temporal and things spiritual, a distinction that Febronius and the German princes with their canonists did not dream of denying. The distinction, he holds, is deep and complete, to the extent that the Church is so supreme in its own domain that not even the much-valued civil sovereignty of the 18th century princes was superior to it. There was no contradiction, not because the Church was not a state, but because it was a state of a different nature.

The controversy over Febronianism provides one historical reason why the Catholic Church today assumes the position of a "perfect society" existing alongside the civil society. Its independence, as conceived by itself, would otherwise be threatened. Though it originated with an ecclesiastic, Febronianism was welcomed by the princes as a doctrinal instrument by which they could bring the Church to a position of dependence. The weapon used in this attack upon the freedom of the Church was a new one, the argument of sovereignty, drawn from the domain of public law. The Church replied by developing its own theories of public law, by which the juridical nature of the Church, especially in relation to the modern state, was systematically laid down. As one of the earliest Catholic writers on ecclesiastical public law wrote, "When the kind of warfare changes the means of defense must also be changed."[15] This was Zallinger zum Thurm, who in a canon law treatise published in 1792 admitted that he felt compelled, much against his own impulses, to treat the subject of public law apart. One convincing argument that decided him, he told his readers, was that this new science was being used as a weapon against the Church and it was necessary to reply with the same weapon.

The "new science," however, took a long time to reach its

[14] Devoti, *op.cit.*, Prol., par. vii.

[15] Zallinger zum Thurm, *Institutiones Juris Ecclesiastici Maxime Privati Ordine Decretalium*, Prol., c. I.

maturity. The first Catholic canonist to bring it into its own and provide it with its permanent form was Camillo Tarquini, professor at the Roman College, now known as the Gregorian University, who published his *Juris Publici Ecclesiastici Institutiones* in 1862. The author was rewarded with the red hat for his services to the Church though he did not long survive this recognition. The text is a thin volume but it had gone through fifteen editions by 1892 and its influence upon succeeding manuals is acknowledged and manifest. It was the right book at the right time, further aided by the publication of the encyclical *Immortale Dei* of Leo XIII already cited in which the Pope set forth the nature of the Church and its relation to the civil society. Cardinal Tarquini was the first canonist to base his whole system upon the concept of the perfect society.

In the introduction to his treatise Tarquini argued that the Church needed public ecclesiastical law as a weapon against attacks upon the Church's authority. In former times, he wrote, if the faithful had made no special studies in the field of public law, there was an explanation for that. No one questioned the Church's authority and whenever difficulties arose between the *sacerdotium* and the *imperium* there was a simple formula that dispensed them from further difficulty or learned arguments. Whatever came under the heading of sin *(ratione peccati)* came under the jurisdiction of the Church. "But today," admitted Tarquini, "the light of this simple formula is too strong for the contemporary world."[16] That is the reason, he went on to say, why the Protestants welcomed the introduction of public Church law. It provided them with a new source of law, independent of the Decretals. The Catholic absolutists, too, especially in Austria, found public law a convenient vehicle for their purposes.

Against this kind of attack, based upon a complete legal system, the only full answer (argued Tarquini) was to reply with yet another system of public Church law, equally well if not better organized. For from false principles (e.g., the principle of the subjection of the Church to the State, or denial of the full sovereignty of the Church, or the denial that the Church's enactments possess the force of real jurisdiction), the foes of the

16 Tarquini, *Juris Publici,* p. ix, x.

Church drew logical conclusions. From the principles of public law as developed by themselves, the Febronians, Josephinists, and other regalists deduced their right to carry on their repressive actions against the Church, such as the right of the Placet and the prohibition of untrammeled communication with the Holy See. It would be "very harmful and dangerous," the Roman canonist held, to leave this field unchallenged to the competition. A false system, he said, could be refuted only by a true one. If the enemies of the Church wished to argue *ex natura rerum*, or from the nature of law and sovereignty, so could he, but upon more solid and orthodox foundations. The essential feature of his system was to establish that the Church is a perfect society and, as such, on a par with the civil power.

Tarquini defines the perfect society abstractly as that which is "complete in itself and therefore has within itself sufficient means for carrying out its purpose." This is a definition applicable in the first instance to the state or civil society. But the author has so framed his definition that it also applies to the Catholic Church. As the State carries within itself all the necessary powers to achieve its own end by the enacting of laws, by judging and punishing violations of these laws, and is not a part of a higher society to which it is subordinate, so also the Catholic Church, by divine foundation, is a society with the same ultimate powers. It enjoys as much independence and autonomy as the State itself.

As can be judged from what has gone before, this is by no means an idea original with Tarquini. The polemicists at the time of Febronius showed that they had grasped the essentials of this definition. Tarquini not only based his whole treatise on the concept but he refined the concept in a way that his predecessors had never done. The author was in fact perhaps more original than he was willing to admit as he made his bold plunge, basing an entire branch of canon law upon the natural-law concept of the perfect society.

Aristotle had indeed spoken very clearly, at the beginning of his *Politics*, of the "perfect community," by which he meant the civil power or the state, as against the "imperfect community," by which he meant the family. The imperfect community was part of a large community and its authority was exercised by precepts rather than by laws. The family was imperfect also in that it needed the State to assist it to achieve its end. But Aristotle's ideas are not fully developed and he merely says that the family is not perfect because it is part of a whole, that is to say, a part of the State and dependent upon the State. He did not cite religion as constituting a "perfect community." St. Thomas Aquinas did not carry Aristotle much farther in this connection. Although the Angelic Doctor commented upon the idea of the *communitas perfecta* (he did not use the term *societas perfecta*), he did not in his writings use it in reference to the Church. Tarquini does not claim that St. Thomas ever referred to the Church as a perfect society, although it would have helped him had he been able to say so. The future Cardinal does no more than imply that St. Thomas had his idea in mind, stating that his own definition of the *societas perfecta* comes back to, is reducible (*recidunt*), to what St. Thomas implied (*innuit*) when he said that a perfect society (community) is not part of another society.[17]

But the Angelic Doctor at the point cited (*Summa Theologica, 1,2, q.90, a.3, ad 3*) did not add that the society was "complete in itself," or had the "means within itself sufficient" for the prosecution of its end. St. Thomas did not say either that such a perfect society is not subordinated to another, a detail that Tarquini judged necessary to add to his own con-

---

[17] The *societas perfecta*, said Tarquini, "*ea dici debet, quae est in se completa, adeoque media ad suum finem obtinendum sufficientia in semetipsa habet.*" In a footnote he adds: "*Huc recidunt quae de notione societatis per ectae habet St. Thomas 1, 2, q. 90, a. 3, ubi innuit societatem perfectam eam esse, quae non sit alteri pars, quaeque finem non habeat ad alterius finem (in eodem scilicet, genere) ordinatum; adeoque sit in suo genere independens et in se completa; unde consequitur, quod media ad sui conservationem, propriique finis assecutionem necessaria in semetipsa habere debet*" (*op.cit.*, pp. 3, 4, 4n). The theologians of the preparatory commission *De Ecclesia* preceding the Vatican Council discussed the Church as a perfect society. They did not, however, choose to adopt the refined formula elaborated by Tarquini. In their explanatory comment on a draft canon they made it plain that they were concerned primarily with refuting the collegialism of Pufendorf, whom they cited as the leading adversary: "*Novatores . . . negant: II, Ecclesiam esse societatem perfectam, quae uti pars sive membrum nulli alii insit vel subsit societati propriamque habeat et a societate civili distinctam ac independentem potestatem; sed affirmant, III, Ecclesiam esse instar collegii, quod libera hominum coitione et sociis jure aequalibus constat, et cujus constitutio a libera confoederatione proficiscitur; unde dicunt, IV, Ecclesiam subesse veluti partem vel membrum civili societati. . . .*" (*Collectio Lacensis*, VII, coll. 580-84, *Adnotationes, Schema de Ecclesia.*)

ception. In short, if St. Thomas and other medieval writers had any conception of the *communitas perfecta* as applied to the universal Church it was not a clear one and served no purpose for the controversialists of the 18th and 19th centuries. Some canonists have been so misled by Tarquini's vague allusions to St. Thomas that they have attributed the whole definition to the latter.[18]

Having once defined the nature of the perfect society considered abstractly, Tarquini then proceeded to demonstrate that the Catholic Church fulfills that definition. He based his arguments upon Scriptural sources, the practice of the Church, the practice of governments and the consequences that would logically ensue if the Church's independence were menaced by denying to it a full juridical existence. Almost a century had passed since Febronius launched his attack upon the Church by undermining its juridical foundations. Febronianism was by now a dead issue. Josephinism, with which it had so much in common, had worn itself out. But the modern State, with its claims upon the social life of man, continued to grow in power. Disputes with the Church over marriage and education and other issues where both Church and State had a common interest dotted the course of the 19th century. The so-called "mixed questions" were, in the eyes of the State and its theorists, often enough not "mixed" at all, but belonged exclusively to the sphere of the State. The Church, for its part, alleged that no changes could be effected in these institutions, at least within a "Catholic State," without the consultation and consent

---

18 It is easy to fall into the supposition that the idea of the perfect society is necessarily implied in the words of Christ on God and Caesar, or at least in Pope Gelasius' 5th century admonition to the emperor on the "two powers." In reality, as Lecler has recalled, until at least the Middle Ages the two powers were not thought of as residing in two separate and autonomous societies or organisms. Until the 12th century, the priesthood and the royalty were considered as parts of one and the same organism termed the "Ecclesia." The famous quarrels were between parts of one and the same body: *"Mais ces conflits apparaissent surtout comme des querelles personnelles entre deux autorités d'une même Eglise, ils ne sont pas le choc de deux organismes distincts de deux sociétés rivales, comme seraient de nos jours l'Eglise et l'Etat"* (Lecler, *Etudes*, 1930, p. 669). Even after the 13th century, the idea of two separate societies was very slow in developing. As the history of canon law proves, Tarquini owes as much to the developments of the 17th and 18th centuries as to the political theories of the Middle Ages. For another development of the origins of the idea of the Church as a society distinct from the civil society, see Figgis, *Churches*, Appendix I.

of the religious authorities. The State, on the other hand, declared that it alone was competent to pass upon such subjects which already formed an important part of the civil legislation. The issue was joined. The Church's basic theoretical answer could only be that the Church, too, was a perfect society and shared jurisdiction with the State in the "mixed questions."

Two separate incidents which occurred some years before the appearance of Tarquini's treatise may illustrate the significance of the new development of public ecclesiastical law. One of these was the dispute between the Holy See and the Kingdom of Sardinia in 1850. The other was a dispute with the Grand Duchy of Baden ten years later. Under date of March 27, 1841 Gregory XVI had entered into an agreement with Charles Albert of Sardinia which regulated in formal terms the condition of the Church in that nominally Catholic kingdom. But in 1850 the government thought itself obliged, in order to carry out promises exacted from it during the revolution of 1848, to repudiate this agreement. At issue in particular were the provisions affecting ecclesiastical immunities. A law, known from the name of its sponsor as the Siccardi law, but authored by Cavour himself, was therefore enacted in this sense, despite the objections of the Holy See.

Cardinal Antonelli, as papal secretary of state, protested that the Siccardi law was a violation of a solemn treaty. "The undersigned Cardinal," he wrote on May 14, 1850, "must refer to the concordats solemnly entered upon by the Holy See and the governments of His Majesty, the King of Sardinia. He could not pass over in silence these solemn treaties in which, on the one side, certain points of ecclesiastical discipline have been modified and, on the other side, there were established, with reference to the exercise of certain rights, norms for the observance of which the two supreme powers in the territory of His Majesty the King of Sardinia, the ecclesiastical authority and the civil authority, had respectively obligated themselves in those matters which concerned them." The Cardinal argued that these agreements ("these treaties"), even though their content-matter affected ecclesiastical discipline, retained for all that an international character.

In the reply to these remonstrances, the Sardinian government, through the then prime minister and foreign minister, Massimo d'Azeglio, challenged the papal claim that the concordats had the character or essence of treaties. The position taken by the cardinal secretary of state, said d'Azeglio on June 3, amounted to making an international question out of what was, "in reality, a question of ecclesiastical discipline, of political expediency or necessity, a question of the independence and autonomy of the state." In other words, the Kingdom of Sardinia was fully within its rights in enacting legislation that openly conflicted with the agreement of March 27, 1841. That agreement manifestly, in the eyes of Premier d'Azeglio and his government, had no legally binding force.

The Sardinian reply thus brought to a point the basic question at issue. A further reply by Antonelli presented a formal statement of the papal position on its juridical relations with the State. On July 19 the secretary of state was explicit in his declaration of the juridical nature of the Church and the consequent binding effect of agreements which it entered into with the secular governments under the form of concordats:

"Is it permissible for a state, especially a Catholic state, when changing its political organization, to prejudice the disciplinary rights of the Church, without the consent of the Holy See? For those who do not wish to deny to the Church the character of true and perfect society, independent of the civil power, which belongs to it by Divine institution, the answer must be in the negative. The Church alone, which has no territorial limits, is and should be the arbiter of its own discipline."[19]

A few years later the Grand Duchy of Baden strove to repudiate in its turn an agreement it had negotiated with the Holy See. A law of October 9, 1860 rendered null and void the concordat of June 28, 1859. In his allocution *Multis gravibusque* delivered before the cardinals in consistory on December 17, 1860, Pius IX challenged the right of the government to repudiate its agreements in this unilateral fashion. The Church, he argued, was a true and perfect society and had the right to

---

[19] *Acta Pii IX. Prima Pars*, ɪɪ: Antonelli to Sardinian chargé d'affaires on May 14, p. 145; d'Azeglio to Antonelli on June 3, pp. 157-58; rejection by Antonelli, July 19, pp. 165-66; d'Azeglio reply on July 24, pp. 163, 169.

enter into agreements with governments and to expect their observation, not a unilateral arbitrary disavowal of them. He complained that the governments treated the Church on the Protestant principle that the Church is a *collegium*, without any inherent independence.

The Pontiff returned to the same theme less than two years later in his allocution *Maxima quidem* of June 9, 1862. He condemned the theory that "the church is not a true and perfect society entirely free and does not possess its own proper and permanent rights given to it by its Divine Founder, but that it belongs to the civil authority to decide what are the rights of the church and the limits within which it can exercise those rights." From this false premise, the Pontiff went on, it is contended that the civil authority can interfere in those things which appertain to religion, morals, and spiritual discipline. The false doctrine, said the Pope, leads its proponents so far that they even prevent the bishops and faithful from communicating freely with their spiritual head, thus shattering the unity that should exist between the members of the Mystical Body and their Head.

The last complaint of Pius IX was an allusion to the state of affairs in Russia. Here, contrary to the situation in Sardinia and Baden, there was no concordat. In this case the Holy See did not have to defend its right to enter into legally binding bilateral treaties, its *jus foederis*. But it did have the need of defending its diplomatic status, its *jus legationis*, in the Czarist domains. In a series of communications the papal spokesmen developed the nature of the Church as a perfect society in order to confute the restrictive claims of the Czarist government over Catholic affairs in Russia.

We have already seen that no permanent nuncio was ever received at St. Petersburg. There were not lacking, however, times when negotiations to this end seemed on the verge of reaching a positive conclusion. In 1862 the situation had reached a point where Foreign Minister Gortchakoff had indicated his government's readiness at least to allow a papal nuncio to take up residence in the imperial capital, who would balance off the imperial minister in Rome. But the Russian government laid down one important reservation: the nuncio could not have any direct relations with the local clergy and faithful. Since the nuncio was the representative of a foreigner, argued Gortcha-koff, he would have to limit his contacts exclusively to government channels. In justification of this restriction the Russian foreign minister adduced the example of states in Western Europe where the nuncio was assimilated to a diplomat.

In his rejection of this condition, which reflected a European practice now already a dead letter in other capitals, as we have seen in the previous two chapters, Cardinal Antonelli stated that the nature of the Catholic Church as a perfect society put the papal diplomat in a position different from that of any ordinary envoy. His reply is dated May 11, 1862:

"Everyone knows the difference that exists between an apostolic nuncio and the representative of any civil power. The Sovereign Pontiff, supreme head of the Church, which was established by God as a true and perfect society and therefore independent, has the duty of extending his apostolic solicitude to all the faithful scattered in the various parts of the Catholic world. It is in consequence of this ministry that he sends his legates everywhere in order through them to succor the spiritual needs of the faithful at close hand, to remedy the more urgent needs of the Church and to be more accurately informed on the true state of religious affairs so as to adopt appropriate measures."[20]

This activity of the nuncio, the papal secretary of state took pains to add, was not something apart from his relations with the government. It served to foster good relations with the civil power which, in concert with the Church, should have at heart the religious welfare of the people.

The Piedmontese and Baden controversies are characteristic of the Church-State conflicts in the decades immediately preceding the appearance of Tarquini's trail-blazing treatise. The middle of the 19th century was a time of great changes in the constitutional thinking of Europe. For a while after the elimination of Napoleon, the old monarchies on the continent under the leadership of Prince Metternich, the Austrian chancellor, had attempted to return to the past. This try at restoration failed under the pressure of resistance, and within two decades

[20] *Segreteria di stato. Expositio,* pp. 132-33.

the spirit of revolution was again on the march. It was inevitable that, in the general review of the political institutions of Europe, the question of Church-State relations should also be prominent. New legislation was drafted and enacted that was often in conflict with canon law. Even in Catholic states the view gained ground that the state was exclusively competent in many of the "mixed questions" in which both Church and State had formerly shared responsibility.

As we have seen in the case of at least two states, one Catholic and the other Protestant, the existence of formal agreements with the Holy See did not constitute any bar to unilateral action. Both Piedmont and Baden considered their accords with the Holy See not as international agreements binding on both parties but acts of internal legislation. In other words two new questions had come to the fore: (1) the juridical nature of the concordats and, (2) the legal capacity of the Holy See to enter into agreements with the states.

Strange to say, although the language of the concordats was couched in formulae customarily used in bilateral international agreements, their juridical nature was not clear. There was a time when neither the State nor the Church wished to recognize the concordat as binding on both sides. For the State, the concordat was an act of internal legislation concerning its own affairs and therefore revocable for any reasons it considered sufficient. For the Catholic Church, the concordat was a concession or privilege accorded to a State. That meant the Church, too, could annul its terms for reasons it considered sufficient.

It is now generally agreed, as we have already seen, that the concordat is an international agreement in the sense of international law and that its provisions are binding upon both parties. The canonists tend to favor the theory that the concordat is not a unilateral grant or privilege accorded by the Church through the Holy See but a bilateral contract of binding force. The civil lawyers, for their part, generally hold today that the concordat is an agreement to be honored in the same way as all other agreements with sovereign powers and is not to be treated as if it were a piece of internal legislation.

We are concerned with the concordat only in its relation to papal diplomacy. The Church-State controversies in the past century brought into the open questions that had long remained implicit. Prior to the last century there was no occasion to force a decision on the issue of the legal nature of the concordat. A point was eventually reached, however, when the question had to be answered. In arguing for the bilateral nature of the concordat, the Catholic Church logically had to develop, in its own mind as well as for the benefit of the states, the conception of the Church as a perfect society, juridically capable of entering into legal agreements with the civil power.

In the present century the number of concordats has multiplied. The rise of the "succession states" after World War I, resulting from the disintegration of the Austro-Hungarian and the Czarist empires, led to formal agreements with almost all of the new-born Central and Eastern European states. In Western Europe, the signing of the Lateran Accords of February 11, 1929 was an important event in the history of the public law of the Church. The accords were two: a *treaty* concerning the State of Vatican City and a *concordat* regulating Church-State questions in Italy itself. Speaking of the concordat, Pope Pius XI himself indicated that the Church considered itself equally sovereign and independent with the State, the religious nature of the Church giving it priority, however, over the State. In a formal letter of May 30, 1929, addressed to Secretary of State Cardinal Pietro Gasparri, the Pope declared: "In the concordat there are present, if not two states, most certainly at least two sovereignties in the fullest sense, that is to say, fully perfect, each one in its own sphere, a sphere necessarily determined by their respective ends, whence it is hardly necessary to add that the objective dignity of the ends, determines no less objectively and necessarily the absolute superiority of the church." The doctrine of the perfect society has been imbedded into the contemporary structure of Church-State relations on the international plane.

We are now in a position to put into proper perspective some observations or critical commentaries voiced at times on the Vatican's diplomacy. The Catholic Church, through the Holy See, is the only religious institution which carries on this form of official relations with the states of the international community. It thus differs from the various Protestant denominations or any non-Christian religion. From these quarters there naturally tends to arise the reproach that the Roman Catholic Church demands a situation in world affairs that bears too close a resemblance to the position of the political powers. They see papal diplomacy as an abuse, a misguided effort to clothe an essentially religious institution with the trappings of civil power which ill become it. They see it as an illegitimate exploiting of prerogatives belonging to states in the interests of a religious institution.

This viewpoint, proclaimed in Protestant circles, finds additional material for argument in the temporal power of the papacy. This (it is argued) has served as the base of departure for the adventures of the Roman See into world politics. The Roman Pontiff has managed over the centuries to capitalize on the fact that he was once lord and ruler of large areas in central Italy and even in what is now the southern part of France. The Popes used the diplomatic channels open to them by reason of their temporal power as instruments as well of their religious affairs, thus usurping for the Pope as Pontiff the rights he was entitled to only as king. The long struggle waged by the papacy between 1870-1929 is sufficient proof, according to these critics, that the Catholic Church regards the temporal power as the veritable foundation of the international position of the Church vis-à-vis the states. With the restoration of at least the token sovereignty embodied in the tiny State of Vatican City, the anomalous position of the Holy See in the diplomatic world was in this respect regularized. By this means the Pope became once more a crowned ruler with a corresponding place in the society of nations. From this he proceeds to act in the interests of the Catholic Church, in a way denied to the leaders of other religions. Thus runs what we might style the "usurpation theory."

There is yet another hypothesis, which may be termed the "survival theory." This attempts to rationalize papal diplomacy as a mere relic of the medieval ages which has managed to linger on thanks to the strong element of tradition in diplomatic matters, especially where mere protocol is concerned. If even great modern states, such as Great Britain, like to preserve old forms long after the substance has gone out of them, it would not be extraordinary that the papacy—an age-old institution, after all—should maintain even in this day some of its former protocol and even get it tolerated by the governments. This would not be the only anachronism to be found among us. If the Popes insist upon retaining some of the outward symbols of bygone days there is no real harm in that.

The "usurpation" theory is based upon a particular (and Protestant) idea of what the Church of Christ should be like. It is not based upon the Catholic Church's own conception of its rights and duties toward the civil authorities. The fact that the Catholic Church is the only religious institution to engage in diplomatic activity throughout the world should at most suggest only that the Catholic Church has its own, non-Protestant, doctrine of the nature and powers of the Church founded by Christ. The position of the Catholic Church may or may not be accepted, and it is certainly rejected by Protestants, but one can hardly allege abuse or usurpation on the sole basis of a conception of the Church which the Catholic Church itself does not accept.

It is therefore begging the question when diplomatic activity by any religious body is judged on purely theological presuppositions to be unjustified. Diplomatic representation is not per se a wholly political act. When the Catholic Church enters into official relations with a State this does not necessarily constitute the use of political instruments for political ends. If the Catholic Church is a perfect society, as its theologians and canonists claim, then it must act like one. It must retain internally the legal structure of laws, authority, and sanctions which is proper to a perfect society. Toward institutions external to it, particularly the State, it must maintain its independence and liberty. In cases of dispute with the civil power negotiations are necessary in which the sovereign rights of both Church and State are given their just consideration. These disputes have been constant, just as they are chronic among even friendly states. There is no inherent hostility between the Church and the civil power. But their respective spheres do touch and even overlap, and it is in the nature of things that the two institutions, both conscientiously jealous of their respective prerogatives and sovereignty, one in the temporal field and the other in the religious, shall have need of constant communication. In some instances, the ordinary diplomatic channels are sufficient when the matters to be discussed or adjusted do not present a fundamental high-policy decision. In other instances the situation may require the conclusion of formal agreements in legal form. In both cases the State and the Church confront each other on terms of mutual respect, with each remaining on its own terrain.

In short, never are the domains of religion and politics more sharply defined and therefore separate than in diplomatic interchanges or in concordats. Through the development of the concept of the perfect society, the Church has been enabled to deal unambiguously with the State precisely as a religious sovereignty.

"Separation of Church and State" has by no means made ecclesiastical diplomacy less legitimate or necessary. As long as the two powers were closely linked in a traditional alliance expressing itself in the national legislations, the individuality of Church and State was obscured. Separation has brought out that individuality, but it has not ended the need for mutual cooperation. On the contrary, separation has contributed directly, as experience has shown, to making diplomatic relations with the Holy See all the more necessary.

A lay anti-clerical canonist has pointed out the logical consequences of separation in this connection. In a book published at Paris in 1906, shortly after the Law of Separation of 1905, André Mater, who was professor of the New University in Brussels, wrote, "The separation will have for principal effect to restore to the church the character of perfect society."[21] He emphasized the word "restore" for, in his view, the Church had suffered diminution of its juridical completeness through the interference of the State, especially in France. To the extent that the states separated from the Church, he wrote, the Church itself recommenced functioning as an independent juridical society. Professor Mater was one of a group of anti-clerical intellectuals who gave public support and approval to the Separation Law in France. Yet he found no contradiction between this

[21] Mater, *Eglise catholique*, p. 4.

law and his own thesis. On the contrary, in the separation he found confirmation of his thesis.

Mater's book, entitled *L'Eglise catholique. Sa constitution. Son administration,* envisaged the Church as organized and operating on the same basis as a state, that is to say, as a perfect society. "If the church thus shares the aspect of a state, why not describe it as one describes states?" asked the author, not illogically. In his work, therefore, he portrays the Church as a society with territory divided into administrative divisions (provinces, dioceses, and parishes), with subjects (the laity), an aristocracy (bishops and prelates), a form of government (monarchy), officials (the priests and religious), governmental ministries (the Roman Congregations), an expansion movement abroad (the foreign missions), public domains (Church property and assets), public income (Peter's Pence, diocesan taxes, the offerings and tithes of the parishes), a judicial organization (tribunals and sanctions), and so on.

Professor Mater argued that if the Church is a perfect society, canon law itself should be divided along this basis. In reality, as he pointed out, the idea that the Church is a perfect society appears only at the beginning of canon law textbooks, in an introductory section on general principles. In the body of canon law itself, no further account is taken of this fact. What the writer commented upon in reference to the Decretals has remained true even after the codification of canon law in 1917. The new code does not follow the plan Professor Mater suggests as the only logical one for an institution whose juridical basis is the concept of the perfect society.

The ingenious plan worked out by the Brussels scholar is not so logical as its author thought to make it. He did not complete the analogy by pointing out that a perfect society should also have a ministry of foreign affairs (secretariat of state of His Holiness) and a foreign service (nuncios and internuncios). The reason for this omission is perhaps obvious. France had ruptured diplomatic relations with the Holy See the year before the Separation Law, this move having long been regarded as a preparation for the separation. But the logic of events made up for the lack of logic in Mater's treatise. After World War I France renewed diplomatic relations with the Vatican, without restoring the concordat it had repudiated. Church and State remained separated but two perfect societies now faced each other across well-defined common frontiers, and neither chose to ignore the other.

The experience of France shows that to identify separation with the absence of diplomatic relations is to misunderstand the real direction taken by the complex forces in play. Separation almost necessarily leads governments to have diplomatic relations, for the simple reason that having renounced their own control over Church affairs in their country they must betake themselves to Rome to ask as a favor what they formerly took as their right. The modern State can, short of outright persecution, have three possible attitudes toward the Catholic Church: (1) It can ignore the existence of the Church, sincerely and completely; (2) it can interfere in the life of the Church, wilfully or not, by arbitrary unilateral action in the legislative, administrative, or other field; (3) it can negotiate on a friendly and bilateral basis with the Holy See in the solution of problems to which an answer cannot be otherwise found. These three categories apply both for international and domestic problems, for foreign policy or internal policy.

The application of the above division to the case of the United States is developed in Chapter 12. In general, it can be said at this point that it is not easy for the State to ignore entirely the existence of the Catholic Church. Pure separation of Church and State is very close to an abstraction. Whether it acknowledges the fact or not, the modern State is necessarily concerned with many issues in which religion as well as the State has a legitimate concern. On the other hand, a State applying unilateral action to the solution of religious problems is only inviting controversy with the Holy See. The third course is therefore the one followed today by most states. Through diplomatic representation the states are able to take up, with a minimum of embarrassment and a maximum of results, the problems that arise from the coexistence of religion and the civil power in the era of religious freedom.

The French journalist, Maurice Pernot, an acute observer of the papacy, has described succinctly three of the principal motives that induce modern governments to have official relations with the Holy See. In the first place, they recognize that the papacy is a great moral, political, and social force in the world and they want to make sure that this influence will be favorable to them, or at least not hostile. Secondly, they consider it useful to be familiar, through direct and continuing observation, with the movements, plans, and tendencies of the Roman authorities to the extent that these elements touch world affairs. And, finally, to use Pernot's own words, "compelled to recognize the rights of the spiritual authority, they seek at least to control its exercise strictly and they negotiate with Rome for the purpose of remaining masters in their own house." It will be noted that these considerations are valid even for a state that professes separation of Church and State at home. As the author cited goes on to remark, the question of internal regime (separation or concordat) is independent from that of diplomatic relations. But since states must at one time or another enact legislation concerning ecclesiastical matters, many governments today as in the past find it useful, without departing from the principle of separation, to consult with the Holy See so as to avoid later difficulties. Writes Pernot: "Since the Catholic Church is the most highly organized of all the churches and the one whose juridical principles and administrative traditions are most solidly established, the civil governments have found it advantageous to achieve, through a prior exchange of views, the most complete accord possible between their legislation and the discipline of the church, and to obtain for the regime which they intend to set up for their Catholic communities, either the approval or at least the toleration of the Holy See."[22]

The consideration instanced by Pernot as one powerful factor inducing even "separation" governments to negotiate with the Holy See bears further development. Implicitly, the civil governments who recognize the Holy See diplomatically realize they are dealing with a permanent institution exercising supreme authority in an independent legal system. It is commonly said that governments recognize the Holy See because the Pope is a great "moral authority." Sometimes that phrase is employed for the purpose of glossing over the fact that he is primarily the head of the Catholic Church. But governments do not have

[22] Pernot, *Saint-Siège*, pp. 59-62.

official relations with a mere "moral leader," such as a philosopher or a prophet. A religious leader whose leadership is but honorary and who exercises upon his adherents mere moral suasion but no real jurisdiction cannot interest a government because negotiations with him can lead to no abiding and definite results. The governments, it is safe to say, are not interested in the Roman Pontiff merely because of his moral prestige in the affairs of men, however important that may be, but basically because he is the supreme head of a perfect society. For the peace of the nation, the governments strive to achieve the most complete accord possible between their own legislation and the discipline of the Catholic Church. As Pernot pointed out, the governments find it advantageous to do this, even in a regime of separation of Church and State.

Thus there is paradox, but no contradiction, in the fact that our modern age, which prides itself upon the secularization of its national and international legal systems, has worked itself to a point where most governments entertain diplomatic relations with the head of the Catholic Church. In separating the two legal systems, they have made all the more challenging the problem of coordinating them. By disengaging Church law from the structure of the State's own law, the governments have given stimulus to the Church to develop its own juridical organization more systematically. As a result, the divorce of the canonical from the civil law has only multiplied occasions for negotiations between the temporal and the spiritual power. Doubtless this outcome was not foreseen by those governments which thought to end discussion by passing a law. But having voluntarily broken with the past alliance of throne and altar at home, the governments find themselves confronted with the Holy See, a sovereign authority, external to themselves, with whom they have to come to some kind of terms.

The "usurpation" theory is therefore valid only insofar as one supposes that the Catholic Church is not and cannot be a perfect society. For those who conceive the Church founded by Christ to be a simple community of the faithful not subject to any hierarchical authority exercised by one's fellow humans, manifestly the diplomatic relations of the papacy with the governments is uncalled for and scandalous as well. But the Catholic Church cannot be judged exclusively, or at all, by the theological opinions of those who do not share the Catholic viewpoint. The important thing is whether the pontifical diplomacy has genuine and profound roots in the religious mission of the Church as conceived by its own theologians and canonists. The new science of public ecclesiastical law developed in the past century to cope with the phenomenon of the sovereignty of the modern state is warrant that the diplomacy of the papacy does, in reality, spring from these spiritual sources and not from any unconscious confusion between temporal ends and spiritual ends, much less from any willful ambition to use religion for material power and advantage.

Enough has been said to show that the "survival" theory is also very questionable. There is no disposition on the part of the Church's canonists to base the papal role in world affairs today on medieval concepts of Church-State relations. It may have taken the canonists a long time to elaborate a new legal system, but by now this has been largely accomplished. Public ecclesiastical law, hardly known or recognized a century and a half ago, was forged in the conflict of modern political theories with the age-old canons. It is a response to today's needs and does not carry on medieval institutions that have long since been emptied of content. Mere force of tradition cannot explain the present-day vigor of pontifical diplomacy. The papacy has indeed come down from the Middle Ages and earlier times. But the modern states, too, have their roots in past European civilization. The papacy has evolved with them.

This chapter upon the theoretical basis of papal diplomacy might suitably close with a reference to a Pope of our own day who was saluted in his lifetime and welcomed to the See of Peter as a "religious" Pope. This was Pope St. Pius X, who reigned from 1903 until 1914, dying in the first month of World War I. He was canonized in 1954. This holy man demonstrated in his brief pontificate why the Roman Pontiff must necessarily command the attention of the civil governments. It was not that St. Pius X interfered or concerned himself with politics but rather that he cared nothing for politics and proceeded in the execution of his religious mission "to restore all things in

Christ" with a very undiplomatic disregard of the political consequences of his decisions.

St. Pius X, for all his asceticism, or because of it, was conscious
that he was the head of a perfect society and as such was bound
to enter into negotiations with the civil governments for the
good of souls. In the first days of his pontificate he declared his
intention in this regard. For the benefit of those who imagined
that the "religious" Pope, succeeding to the "political" Pope,
which Leo XIII was held to be, would take the Church out of
"politics," Pius X declared in his first consistorial allocution to
the cardinals on November 9, 1903 that these might be deceived.
"We know," he said, "that We will displease some persons in
saying that We intend to occupy Ourselves with political affairs. However, anyone who takes a serene view of reality will
concede that the Sovereign Pontiff cannot separate politics from
the authority which he exercises in faith and in morals. In addition, since he is the head and director of a perfect society,
the Church, the Pope must wish to maintain good relations
with the rulers of states and the moderators of public affairs,
for if he does not he will not be in a position to assure for
Catholics, always and everywhere, their security and liberty."

CHAPTER 9

PAPAL SOVEREIGNTY IN COMPARATIVE
CONSTITUTIONAL LAW (1)

CONCURRENCE OF THE TWO JURISDICTIONS

IN THEIR EFFORTS to disprove the international law status of Vatican diplomacy, some 19th century writers pointed among other things to the domestic nature of Church affairs. All situations existing on the State's territory and involving its own citizens, they argued, are essentially internal and as such within the exclusive jurisdiction of the State. Church matters, therefore, could not be the proper object of "international" negotiations by either the nuncios or the so-called ambassadors at the Holy See.

This objection has already been dealt with and answered in part in a preceding chapter. The full answer is best sought in the domain not of international law but of constitutional law. On this matter, national legislation has evolved significantly in the past hundred years. The State does not hold that Church affairs are of its exclusive jurisdiction. It recognizes another concurrent sovereignty, that of the Church itself. With this sovereignty it is prepared to negotiate.

Most textbooks in international law fail to note that the relationship between the Holy See and the several states is not identical in pattern with that existing between State and State. State-to-State relations might be termed *horizontal*, or geograph-

Bibliographical Note: Much of the material contained in this and the following chapter is treated by other writers under the heading of "toleration," "religious liberty," or "separation of Church and State." For reasons indicated in the text we present the problem in terms of the divisibility of sovereignty. Gierke, in his *Natural Law and the Theory of Society* touches on this. For a theoretical analysis of the problems of the concurrent political and spiritual sovereignty, the best treatment is found in Professor Louis Le Fur's *Le Saint-Siège et le droit des gens*. A recent background study is in the Bampton lectures of Thomas Parker, *Christianity and the State in the Light of History*.

For a convenient discussion of the various systems of regalism (jurisdictionalism), such as Gallicanism, Febronianism, and Josephinism, see Don Luigi Sturzo's *Church and State* (Longmans, New York, 1939). Studies on the concordats contain some pertinent material, but many of these treatments are not relevant to non-concordat states. Among writers cited in the Bibliography these may be consulted, for one or another aspect of the problem: Balladore-Pallieri, Del Pozzo, Jannacone, La Brière, Ollivier.

ical, in the sense that they involve jurisdictions mutually exclusive and clearly marked out by territorial borders. The relations between the State and the Holy See, on the other hand, can be described as *vertical*, or coterminous, in the sense that both the temporal and the religious sovereignty are exercised on the same territory and over the same subjects, even though at different levels of human activity. The State deals with a religious authority located outside its territory, concerning institutions and persons who, civilly, are within its own jurisdiction. This is a feature not encountered in the pure State-to-State relationship. It is for this reason that the concept of spiritual sovereignty must be looked at not merely as a problem of international law but also as a problem of constitutional law.

The present chapter and the next endeavor to describe the present state of papal sovereignty in domestic law and to show, at the same time, how relevant this is to the broader question of the Pope's standing in international law and diplomacy. The best way of describing contemporary doctrine and practice is to study the remarkable transition that constitutional law has undergone in the past several centuries. To learn where papal sovereignty has arrived today, it is useful to know the point from which it departed in former times. As the following pages will show, the evolutions in legal theory have been substantial. From a system that held to the possibility of only one sovereignty within the nation's boundaries, the civil society has come to acknowledge, with good or bad grace, the concurrent sovereignty and independence of the Roman Pontiffs in that same territory and over the same individuals. In no clearer way is this reflected than in the evolution of the State's attitude toward papal diplomacy.

In the latter half of the 19th century, as we found in Chapter 7, the foes of the papacy sought to establish that the nuncios were not real diplomats. They were willing to allow the Pope to exercise his ecclesiastical jurisdiction without hindrance, but they challenged the legal status of his nuncios. In other words, they acknowledged his right of internal legation while they denied his right of external legation. Their purpose in assuming this position was to undermine papal authority by depriving

it of an important institutional basis. If the Pope were successfully stripped of the guarantees afforded him by international
law, it would be that much easier to deprive him of his influence generally in human affairs. But, a century earlier, by one
of those inversions not uncommon in history, the Pope's foes
took an exactly opposite line. They recognized his external
legation while combatting his internal legation. That is to say,
in the latter half of the 18th century the papal foes stressed the
diplomatic status of the nuncio just as those who came after
them minimized it.

The explanation for this reversal of attitudes is quite simple.
The earlier line of argument, although tending to the same
ultimate effect, started from a different set of reasoning and from
different circumstances. The 18th century was a time of rigorous
domination and control of religious matters (both Catholic
and Protestant) by the civil power. The State looked with hostility upon any religious authority independent of itself. It
sought at every turn to subject Church affairs to its supervision
and direction. The Holy See was a special object of jealousy.
The State used every possible legal device to prevent the free
exercise of papal religious jurisdiction or at least to circumscribe that jurisdiction by safeguards of its own. In order the
better to accomplish this end, the absolutist princes of that
century found it both useful and necessary to play up the status
of the Roman Pontiff as a "foreign ruler." This conception they
applied to the Pope not merely as a temporal ruler but also
as a religious authority. Indeed, in their eyes the relevant thing
was not that the Pope was an "outside prince" so much as that
he was an "outside bishop." It was no problem for them to
eliminate papal civil jurisdiction in their domains. What the
state wanted was to see that the papal authority was circum-
scribed in its domains even in ecclesiastical matters. Hence they
elaborated the analogy of the "foreign ruler." Within such a
basic hypothesis they constructed a series of techniques intended
to limit the exercise of the papal religious jurisdiction. It was
against this conception that the Count de Maistre was protesting when he wrote (*Du pape*, ii, 9): "No doubt the Pope as
a temporal prince is, just as all the others, a foreigner outside
his own domains; but, as sovereign pontiff, he is a foreigner

nowhere in the Catholic Church any more than the King of France is an alien in Lyons or Bordeaux."

One of the direct consequences of placing the Pope in the category of a foreign ruler was that the apostolic nuncio was thereby interdicted from exercising any ecclesiastical jurisdiction in the nation. As the Pope was a foreigner, so his nuncio was treated as the envoy of a foreign sovereign. The nuncio was indeed accorded great honors at the Court. He enjoyed precedence over the other diplomats. But the distinctions served only to emphasize what the crown wished clearly understood, that the nuncio was nothing if he was not an ambassador. As an ambassador he had to limit his official relations to the government. He could not, in accordance with diplomatic protocol, have any official relations with any member of the clergy or with the laity. He could exercise no direct jurisdiction over Church matters of the country where he was stationed.

The conception of the Pope as a "foreigner" opened yet other possibilities of subjecting the papal authority to the State. In the system developed widely throughout Europe, in the spirit of the 18th century, Church business with the Holy See had to be conducted through governmental channels. The bishops or laity having matters of importance to transact with Rome were obliged to proceed as though they were dealing with a neighboring civil ruler on purely temporal and political matters. Their communication had first to go to the Ministry of Worship for examination. It was then passed to the Foreign Ministry for further examination, after which it was passed on by government courier to the ambassador in Rome. That official delivered the missive to the appropriate papal office. The reply in the form of letter or rescript came back via the same circuitous route. If the State so chose, the rescript was not delivered; or the original letter was pigeonholed before it even left for Rome. There was no recourse, for such was the sovereign will of the State. Penalties were provided for those who sought to "smuggle" papal documents through other channels, and without the knowledge and consent of the government. As for papal decrees of a general nature, even purely dogmatic ones, these could not be promulgated in the country until they had received the royal *Placet* or seal of approval. Should any such decrees come to be common knowledge, despite all the precautions, they were held to be invalid until the State's approval was forthcoming. Those who attempted to enforce such unsanctioned decrees were liable to punishment. In matters spiritual the Pope's writ did not run without the king's counter-signature. For the Pope was an outsider, a "foreigner," *un étranger, ein fremder Mann.*

By a similar line of reasoning the bishops were forbidden to leave the country, that is, go to Rome, without the government's permission. This was in the age of free movement in every other respect, before passports came into use. There were other regulations whose purpose was the same: to obstruct in any way possible the exercise of Roman jurisdiction. Is it any wonder why, in the 18th century, the princes exalted the Pope's diplomatic status?

The key to this strange system of Church-State relations can be found in the doctrine of sovereignty current in the 17th and 18th century. This was not an age in which the idea of the "two powers" was popular. On the contrary, political theory at that time insisted upon the indivisibility of sovereignty. There could be only one power, one sovereignty, in the State—the civil, not the ecclesiastical, power. Everything, including Church matters, by one heading or another, fell under civil jurisdiction. By various titles the State intruded itself into the internal functioning of both the Catholic and Protestant churches. But the most sweeping of these titles of authority was the argument of indivisibility. Rousseau was only reflecting the spirit of his age when in the *Social Contract* (IV, 8) he hailed Hobbes' theory (*De cive*, VI, 18) of the unity of power and proclaimed the need to reunite the "two heads of the eagle." It was clearly bad, wrote the philosopher of Geneva, to give man "two codes of legislation, two rulers, and two countries." This, in his view, destroys social unity and makes good government impossible. Rousseau's counsel merely formalized a practice that had already taken root in the absolutist courts of Europe. In that age of Enlightenment, the prince wanted to be more than ever *maître chez soi* (master in his own house). He would permit the exercise of papal jurisdiction only under whatever controls he thought necessary to assure his ultimate domination. It would be, in his eyes, to share sovereignty with another were he to permit the Pope to act in his realms without supervision.

Today we have developed a less sweeping doctrine of State sovereignty. Experience has taught us that it is neither necessary nor desirable for the civil power to interfere in Church administrative matters, much less in purely doctrinal questions. Today we no longer seek, in the name of sovereignty, to put shackles upon the religious jurisdiction of the Holy See. We realize that civil sovereignty is not merely divisible between several political authorities, as happens in the case of a federal State, but that another sovereignty, the religious one, can coexist with it. Without perhaps ever formally saying so, the State has recognized the real independence of the Church within the State. What is more significant is that it has conceded this autonomy of operation to a religious pontiff who lives outside the national boundaries. In contemporary constitutional law it is not regarded any longer as a derogation of national rights when the Pope freely carries on his mission, whether by written decrees or through his own envoys permanently stationed abroad. In modern law the Pope is no longer a "foreigner."

The implications of this legal evolution have not been generally appreciated at their full significance. The State has indeed voluntarily conceded a zone of autonomy to the papal authority. But that is only half the story. The State remains concerned with the impact of papal jurisdiction in the country. It cannot be entirely indifferent to the political implications of many Church decisions. Barred by a self-denying ordinance from the high-handed police-state techniques of a past century, the State has only one choice: to negotiate with the Holy See in those matters in which some understanding and settlement is necessary. Hence, today the State unashamedly uses diplomatic channels and the traditional instruments of international relations, not as devices to block papal authority, but as a means of resolving points of difference by amicable negotiations. For the unilateral action of the past the State has substituted bilateral action. The Placet has given way to the Concordat. If the Pope is still a "foreigner" it is only in the sense that he is recognized as having a sovereignty of his own, a spiritual sovereignty. If at times the conflicts of interest go to the point of rupture and reversion to unilateral action, the controversy usually ends, as history shows, by a mutual, agreed settlement in which the respective independence of the two parties is implicitly or explicitly recognized.

The system described in the introduction to this chapter naturally took various forms in different parts of Europe. The actual practice did not always correspond to the theory. But if there was any coherent doctrine that was the one. It was prevalent in the Catholic countries and the Protestant ones as well. In fact, the Catholic monarchs were the most zealous promoters of this political principle and they had more opportunity than the Protestant princes to perfect the system. The views of the Bourbon kings of France, Spain, Portugal, and the Two Sicilies did not differ much from those of the Hapsburg rulers of Austria, Bohemia, Hungary, Northern Italy, or Flanders. In the Protestant states of Prussia and the Netherlands, analogous laws were created, with England exercising its own form. Orthodox Russia adopted the European system as it found it. The small princes imitated the great ones, while the republics followed suit after the monarchies.

In the present chapter and in the following, an analysis of concrete instances will show how these political principles were applied in specific countries, only to be abandoned by the middle of the 19th century. We can begin by selecting the case of France. This sample is particularly instructive because France's jurisprudence in respect to the papacy was the most clearly defined in all Europe and also because the example of France influenced most other countries.

The first coherent outlines of the now repudiated system were already apparent in Gallicanism, particularly in the classic formulation of its political aspects by Pithou. In his famous *Libertés de l'eglise Gallicane*, published in 1651, Pierre Pithou laid down in 83 propositions the limitations that the papal power was subject to in the kingdom of France. For, in the Gallican theory, France enjoyed a special privileged status within the Catholic Church, under the Pope. According to this theory, the Roman supremacy was, in France, conditioned by ancient customs. Said Pithou (art. v): ". . . Although the Pope's suzerainty in spiritual matters is recognized, nevertheless in

France his absolute and unlimited power does not have full effect but is checked and limited by the canons and rules of the ancient councils of the Church received in this kingdom. *Et in his maxime consistit libertas ecclesiae Gallicanae. . . ."*[1] Through such a formula Pithou recognized in theory the authority of the Roman See, while at the same time he effectively put limits to its exercise.

The corollaries to these and similar "liberties" were exploited with great diligence in the century that followed. The defense of the rights of the French Church lay in the hands of the king (not of the bishops). Hence, the Pope could not send an envoy armed with special jurisdiction, such as a *legatus a latere*, without the royal request or permission. The Roman curia could not levy a tax on Church properties without royal consent. The Pope or his legate could not take cognizance of ecclesiastical causes in the first instance. With such a start, the French political theorists were destined to construct a more complete Church-State system based not so much on the "privileges" of the French Church as on the general principles of political sovereignty. From the claim to supervise the exercise of papal authority in France in the name of the Gallican Church, it was but a short step to assert that the king had such power in things ecclesiastical not because he was the Eldest Son and Protector of the Church but also, more simply, because he was king.

There are two forms of Gallicanism, one theological the other political. The first deals primarily with the relations of the Pope to the ecumenical councils; the other concerns the relation of the royal power to the Holy See. The impact of political Gallicanism upon diplomatic institutions is of chief interest here. Pithou noted (art. LXXVI) that it was naturally necessary to adopt various ways by which these "liberties" or privileges could be safeguarded and preserved against papal encroachment. First of all, he said, this could be done by direct negotiations with the Holy See ("through friendly negotiations with the Holy Father, either in person or through ambassadors"). The method of friendly negotiation was only the first step to be employed. The Gallicans were prepared to go farther

[1] Mirbt, *Quellen*, n. 505, p. 363.

in defense of the Liberties. A second means cited by Pithou was to check all papal bulls and rescripts sent into France, in order to ascertain if they contained anything in conflict with the prerogatives claimed by the Gallicans. Another instrument was the *appel comme d'abus*. This is a judicial action whose effect is to remove an ecclesiastical issue from the canonical to the civil forum. Another way of circumventing or at least delaying papal action was the appeal to a future ecumenical council. But at least this had the merit of being within an ecclesiastical framework, whereas the *appel comme d'abus* and the inspection of papal bulls was a direct intrusion of the civil power into the domain of canonical jurisdiction.

In general, the backers of the royal power against the papacy did not think that they were in any way departing from conduct proper to good Catholics. On the contrary, Pithou argued that the kings of France had earned these sweeping prerogatives in virtue of their great services to the Church. The kings of France, in his mind, richly deserved the titles of "Most Christian King" and "First-born Protector of the Church." Louis XIV did not himself subscribe to the tenets of the extreme Gallicans. But his lifelong policy evidenced the determination of princes to control Church operations in their realm. Though professing filial attachment to the Holy See, the *Roi Soleil* showed no hesitation in interposing his own authority between the Pope and the faithful in France.

The memoirs of the Duc de Saint-Simon provide numerous instances of the policy of Louis XIV to keep a tight rein over papal administrative machinery in France. This ambitious courtier kept a voluminous diary which is today a mine of information on events and procedures at Versailles in that era of absolutism. In his notation for 1707 Saint-Simon remarks that the Court had long forbidden the bishops to have direct communication with Rome. In all things except fiscal matters, such as those concerning benefices, says the diarist, they were obliged to get the king's permission and to act through the secretary of foreign affairs: "To write directly to the Pope, or to his ministers, or to persons located at the papal court, or to receive letters from these sources, without the knowledge and permission of the king and of his secretary of state, was a state crime which was not tolerated but punished, so much so that the practice of such communication has ceased entirely."[2] Saint-Simon had personal knowledge of these regulations, as he himself ruefully admitted. He had been a party to negotiations on behalf of the Archbishop of Arles involving the relics of a saint. But the secret of this rather prolonged correspondence with Rome came to light. The prelate was severely reprimanded by Louis. In our own time one might think that the efforts to exchange relics of saints would hardly concern the civil power. Louis XIV, however, took a different view. And so did the political thinkers who were beginning to perfect their theories of sovereignty in religious matters.

It is true that, at the end of his long rule, Louis XIV somewhat relaxed his prohibition against direct communication with the Pope. He permitted a few selected high prelates to bypass the customary channels. A limited number of other churchmen, five or six of lesser rank, says Saint-Simon, were allowed limited contact with the nuncio in Paris. But these exceptions only brought out the general rule. Contact with the Holy See or its representative was still illegal in principle. "As regards the nuncios," wrote Saint-Simon in his diary in 1715: "There was no contact or visits. Any bishop or simple priest or even a monk would have been severely reprimanded for seeing the nuncios (no matter how circumspectly), without the knowledge of the minister of foreign affairs who in turn would inform the king. Even this contact was never permitted beyond the degree of strict necessity."[3]

According to the court diarist, the king was "very particular" about the observance of this "salutary practice."[4] Even the purely fiscal matters concerning benefices had to be expedited by the royal officials, the *banquiers expéditionnaires*, who were specially licensed to carry on such business with Rome.

The successors of Louis XIV carried on the Gallican premises with loyal logic. One writer, the Marquis du Marsais, who died in 1756, expressed the attitude toward the nuncio in these words: "We do not acknowledge the power or jurisdiction of the nuncios whom the Pope sends to France. We consider them

---

[2] Saint-Simon, *Mémoires*, XIII, p. 113.

[3] *Ibid.*, XXVII, pp. 29-30.

[4] *Ibid.*, XXXVII, pp. 57-58.

only as ambassadors or envoys of foreign princes." The same writer goes on to say: "The legates commonly called nuncios are not cardinals but simple priests of the Church of Rome. We do not tolerate their exercising any act of jurisdiction, even though the Pope gives them such power and though they have often attempted to exercise it."[5]

If the system was simple in its basic construction it was not easy to maintain it integrally. Louis XIV, as we have seen, at the end of his long reign found it useful to close his eyes to departures from the rule or even formally to approve direct communication of his subjects with the Roman Pontiff. His successors had their own difficulties. Complaints increased about papal documents, even bulls and briefs, being sent clandestinely to France through various means not approved, for example, via Germany or Avignon. The instructions issued to the French ambassadors in the last fifty years of the old regime reflect the concern felt about these evasions of the established safeguards. Each new ambassador was reminded that papal bulls should be passed through official channels. Only matters concerning individual persons were exempt from the general rule. Even these cases should at least be transmitted through the *banquiers expéditionnaires*. In such terms, for instance, did France instruct the Marquis d'Aubeterre sent to Rome as ambassador in October 1763.[6] It is hardly necessary to say that the government's system was not simply a postal service for the convenience of French Catholics. These were not sealed communications. Their contents were inspected by the royal authorities, who approved or rejected them as they saw fit. This was a strange procedure for the kings of France to adopt toward the Roman Pontiff whom they professed to reverence filially but whom they treated as a foreigner when it came to the practical exercise of the papal jurisdiction.

The Bourbons were not alone in their effort to interpose the civil power between the Pope and the faithful. If they had their Gallicanism, the Hapsburgs had their Josephinism. As perfected under Joseph II (d. 1790), this politico-ecclesiastical system extended to the extreme the principle of State domina-

[5] du Marsais, *Exposition*, p. 194.
[6] Hanotaux, *Rome*, xx, pp. 440-44.

tion in religious matters. Within the hereditary estates of the Hapsburgs the imperial and royal power effectively substituted itself for the Church authority. "I myself intend to be, in my own realm, Pope, Archbishop, Bishop, Archdeacon, and Deacon," was the statement attributed to Duke Rudolf IV of Austria, in the early rise of the dynasty.[7] This did not necessarily signify something harmful to the Church. The Hapsburgs once performed, like the Bourbons, great services to the Church. So long as the papacy was strong, their role in Church matters did not present any danger to the papal authority. But it was inevitable that in time the line of demarcation between what the Emperor could do as a civil ruler, and what he could do in his role of protector, became quite obscured. The abuses grew with the weakening of the papal authority in the 18th century and the rise of the spirit of the Enlightenment. Under Joseph II the Church paid a heavy price for the "protection" afforded by the imperial crown. The unprecedented visit that Pope Pius VI made to Vienna in 1782 to salvage what he could from the Josephinists was a token of the desperate straits to which the papacy had been reduced.

The domination of the Church was duplicated in the other Hapsburg possessions, such as those in North Italy, where Joseph's brother and eventual successor, Leopold II, ruled as Grand Duke of Tuscany. In Hapsburg-ruled Flanders the Jansenist canonist, Bernhard Van Espen, had years before formulated a canonical position ready-made for the doctrine which put the Placet in a place of respectability. In his study *On the Promulgation of Laws*, Van Espen argued that laws required the assent of the king before they could have any validity, even canonically, let alone in civil law. In this way the State claimed the right to subject to its good pleasure the promulgation of Church laws and, in general, of all the acts of jurisdiction of the Church authorities. "This happy device," wrote Charles of Lorraine, governor general of the Austrian Netherlands to Maria-Theresa in July 1763, "has put a stop to many abuses." He warmly urged his Empress to make good

---

[7] Maass, *Josephinismus*, I, p. 14: The perfect Josephinist doctrine was formulated by Chancellor Kaunitz in a letter to the nuncio Garampi on Dec. 19, 1781 (*ibid.*, II, n. 114, pp. 291-94).

use of this legal arm in her own realm.[8] In Vienna, however, such encouragement was hardly needed.

The same assumption of jurisdiction in religious matters existed in Protestant states, particularly in Germany. Historically, the princes played a dominant role in the Protestant Churches from the first days of the Reformation. It was inevitable that their extraneous role in the religious questions of that time came to be regarded by them as inherent in their sovereign rights as rulers. Various politico-ecclesiastical theories were developed over the years to justify this control and domination. But no matter how much they varied, they all came down to the principle of the power of the civil ruler to be sole master in his own house.

Historians distinguish three main theories. After the Confession of Augsburg the Protestant princes assumed all the power that had previously been exercised by the bishops, without distinguishing whether that power had been political or religious. They acted *in loco episcoporum*. This assumption of quasi-episcopal authority was, theoretically, only provisional. It was considered to last only as long as the religious conflict remained unsettled. Under this system, known as the Episcopal System, the civil rulers acted as religious rulers. The prince was also the "bishop" of his subjects.

This theory labored under inherent contradictions and was soon supplanted in favor by another. The impropriety of a civil ruler claiming to be the depository of episcopal authority was too evident. A new basis was found in what came to be known as the Territorial System, because it was based on the concept of territorial sovereignty. One of the best exponents of this system was Hugo Grotius who presented his ideas in a small study *De Imperio Summarum Potestatum Circa Sacra,* which has been described as a "perfect handbook of regalism."[9] Grotius based the prince's rights in religious affairs not upon any canonical principles but upon the principles of government. According to him, the prince should not be considered as a sort of vice-bishop, or as the heir of the rights and jurisdiction of the former bishops now suppressed in the Protestant

---

[8] LeFèvre, *Analecta Vaticano-Belgica, Nonciature de Flandre,* IX, p. xvii.
[9] Lecler, *Tolérance,* II, p. 269.

countries. Instead he possessed a certain competence over religious matters in his own right as a prince. His was a case then not of *devolution* of the bishops' rights but *restitution* of his own rights. *Imperii jus quoad sacra non minus quoad profana extendi.* That is to say, the prince, being supreme ruler of the country, enjoyed a sort of eminent domain over religious questions. To use the expression employed by Grotius himself in his book, the prince did not have *jus in sacra* but rather *jus circa sacra.* Translated, this meant that the civil ruler had power or jurisdiction not in religious matters as such but rather in their external effect upon the community. In the Territorial System it was an essential adjunct of territorial sovereignty to have at least indirect power over Church matters.

Grotius' theory got a benevolent reception from the princes, Protestant or Catholic, who in that age of princely absolutism did not care particularly how their authority over Church matters was explained, so long as it was not challenged or diminished. But in time the Territorial System itself underwent modifications. For if the Episcopal System could be criticized for confusing the office of bishop and prince, the Territorial System could be criticized for failing to recognize the evangelical freedom of the Christian religion. Consequently a new theory was developed by Pufendorf and others which took the name of Collegial System. In this conception the Church was conceived as an independent community, a corporation, a *collegium,* within the State. As such it could enjoy a certain amount of autonomy in purely Church questions. In the final analysis, however, the Collegial System, like those which had preceded it, left the final say in the hands of the sovereign civil power. To sum up, the princes were building up a jurisprudence that established firmly their own right to interfere in ecclesiastical matters, regardless of legal and canonical theorizing. When, in the middle of the 18th century, as a result of wars and treaties, the Protestant princes first began to rule over Catholic areas, they naturally attempted to apply the prevailing practice to this new situation. At this point conflict with the Holy See was inevitable.

What were these "sovereign rights in Church matters," these *jura majestatica circa sacra,* which take up such a large place in the canonico-civil literature of the Holy Roman Empire in the 17th and 18th centuries? Two categories of rights can be distinguished, one negative and the other positive. One was designed to protect the State against intrusion into the civil jurisdiction on the part of the religious authority; the other opened the way to the royal initiative in religious jurisdiction. The first was the *Aufsichtsrecht*, the *jus cavendi*, also known as the *jus defensionis et praecautionis*. This was the power of the State to see to it that the State was not injured by any abuse of Church authority, or under any religious pretext. The second was the *Schutz- und Vögtei Recht* or *jus protectionis siu advocatiae*. It was not merely the right but even the duty of the civil ruler to protect the Church. This was a ready formula, in the age of absolutism, for wholesale interference in ecclesiastical matters. The excesses of the Josephinists suffice to show how far this principle could be interpreted by any ruler who had a mind to it.

To these two basic "rights" in Church matters, there can be added a third, called *jus supremae inspectionis*. This expresses the general principle of the right of the prince to keep himself informed about Church matters. This too was a very broad prerogative. It afforded rich opportunities for political interference in purely internal Church matters. Another right asserted in the earlier days of the Reformation and Counter-Reformation was the *jus reformationis*. This was the right of the princes to supervise ecclesiastical reform in their own domains.

It can be seen that the domination of the civil power over the spiritual power at the close of the 18th century was the fruit of several centuries of historical development. To the tradition of interference in religious matters there naturally was added a theoretical juridical system whose essential effect was to provide a framework for existing jurisprudence. The theory of the uniqueness of public power, of the indivisibility of sovereignty, was only a doctrinal foundation for an existing situation. The princes or magistrates were already accustomed to see in their religious power the simple consequence of their political sovereignty. "It only remained," as Lecler points out, "for the theoreticians of law and of political sovereignty to put into formulas what had already become a reality in practice." This same writer notes that the princes asserted their *jura circa sacra* at the same time that they themselves felt detached from any religious confession: "The Protestant state secularizes itself without for that fact abandoning its hold over religion."[10]

A controversy over the papal nunciatures that resounded in Germany on the eve of the French Revolution throws much light on the position of the nuncio in the prevailing Church-State relationship. The kings of France made a point of treating the nuncio as an ambassador because this served to bring Church matters under more direct royal supervision and control. Implicit in this attitude was the priority of the civil over the religious power. But the Gallicans generally did not go to the extreme of denying that the Pope had any right at all to be represented abroad by his own legates. They simply prevented this right from being operative, in the name of a sweeping privilege valid for France but not for the rest of Christendom.

In Germany, some of the leading prince-bishops went farther than this and made a frontal attack upon the papal primacy. They denied that the Holy See had any inherent right—quite aside from any external restrictions from the civil power—to exercise direct jurisdiction in the territory of the local hierarchy. The nuncios, they argued, were only ambassadors; they could not exercise any powers in canonical matters independently (that is, over the heads) of the diocesan authority. The Pope, according to this contention, could send his envoys on a mission to the civil powers (*ad extra*); he could not send envoys armed with jurisdiction over the local bishops and faithful (*ad intra*).

Though bitter, the German controversy was short-lived, for its instigators were soon swept away in the revolutionary tide that engulfed Europe. The debate had the result, nonetheless, of stressing the twofold role of the nuncio.

For several centuries up to 1785 there had been three nunciatures for Germany and Switzerland, those of Vienna, Lucerne, and Cologne. The Vienna nunciature's responsibility included part of Bavaria; that of Lucerne included the rest of Bavaria;

---

[10] *Ibid.*, II, pp. 266, 271.

the Cologne nunciature took in what remained of the empire. This embraced the Palatinate and the two dukedoms of Berg and Juliers. Consequently when in 1777 the Elector of the Palatinate, who was Duke of Berg and Juliers, became also Elector of Bavaria, he found he had to deal with not one but three different nuncios, all of whom lived outside his domains. It was not surprising that Charles-Theodore petitioned Pius VI for a nuncio whose seat would be in Munich and whose jurisdiction would cover the whole territory of the Elector. The Pope acceded to this request and in February 1785 named Giulio Cesare Zoglio as first nuncio. Thus, where there had been three nunciatures before, there would now be four. This purely administrative reorganization, however, raised a storm elsewhere in Germany.

Four powerful prince-bishops took the position that the apostolic nuncios could have no jurisdiction, alleging that the presence of a papal representative armed with Church power —at least on a permanent and stable basis, outside of special cause—was in violation of the rights and privileges of the Catholic Church in Germany. These prelates were the Archbishops of Salzburg, Mainz, Trier, and Cologne. When their expostulations to the Holy See failed to stop the new appointment, they appealed to Joseph II as emperor. They got partial satisfaction from Vienna, for on October 12, 1785 an imperial rescript addressed to the prince-bishop of Mainz declared, among other things: "I therefore recognize the papal nuncios only as papal emissaries competent to deal with political matters and those with which the pope is directly concerned as supreme head of the Church. I cannot, however, allow these nuncios to exercise jurisdiction in spiritual affairs nor allow them a judicature which is not within the competence of, and cannot be conceded to, the papal nuncio in Cologne, nor the one here in Vienna, nor any other that may come in the future into the territory of the German empire."[11] The four prince-bishops took this as a vindication of their position and they carried the fight farther. Nevertheless, the rescript had no effect on the establishment of the Munich nunciature, nor did it prevent the Holy See from naming a new nuncio in Cologne

[11] Pastor, *History*, XL, p. 38. The nunciature dispute is treated *ibid.*, pp. 28-65.

with the same Church powers as before, the famous Cardinal Bartolomeo Pacca, who in his memoirs on his nunciature points out that the emperor's rescript was ambiguous and contradictory, probably deliberately so, in order to leave each local ruler free to interpret it as he wished.[12] At this stage of the moribund Holy Roman Empire it was very questionable what force the imperial rescript had in any case.

The next phase in the nunciature dispute was the conference that met at Ems in July 1786 in which the same four prince-bishops were represented. From this emerged a declaration in 23 articles, known as the Punctation of Ems, in which the papal authority in various ecclesiastical matters was challenged and limited. While admitting that the "Pope of Rome is and remains the supreme head and the primate over the universal Church, and is the center of unity, holding jurisdiction from God Himself," they asserted they would not recognize those prerogatives and privileges which, in their view, were not based on that source. One of these was the right to send legates with canonical jurisdiction, the nuncios being merely ambassadors. Article 4 declared: ". . . The nunciatures shall cease completely in the future. The nuncios can be nothing but papal envoys and may not—according to the Imperial declaration of October 12, 1785, which is based upon ecclesiastical law as well as on the fundamental law of the Empire—any more exercise acts of voluntary or contentious jurisdiction."[13]

These and other theses of the Ems Punctation were far-reaching and contradicted the manifest practice and doctrine of the Church. Where did such ideas come from? It must be remembered that the important sees, or prince-bishoprics, of Germany were open only to the nobility and too often were given to persons who might have been suited to be princes but not to be bishops. The Archbishop Elector of Cologne was the brother of Joseph II. Germany at that time was strongly under the influence of the Enlightenment. But most of all, for present purposes, these prelates were all Febronians.

We have elsewhere described the work of Bishop Hontheim, alias Febronius, and the revolution in Church organization he

---

12 Pacca, *Oeuvres*, II, p. 188.
13 Mirbt, *Quellen*, n. 553, pp. 414-15.

attempted to launch. We need here only note his stand on the nuncios, that is, on the Pope's right to exercise his jurisdiction through envoys. In his treatment (II, x) of the Roman Primacy (which he acknowledged, after his own way), Febronius argued that the papal envoys had a purely diplomatic mission. "In the beginning the pontifical legates did not exercise the slightest degree of jurisdiction but were merely *Apocrisarii* and *Responsales*. When the Church began to prosper under the Christian emperors the Popes had their legates at the imperial court who would present important matters to the emperors and report back on these to the pontiff, after the manner of the legates of the other princes." In France, Belgium, and Sicily, he said, the nuncios had no jurisdiction. It was only in Germany that they had a wider power. It was time for Germany, implied Febronius, to put the papal nuncios back into their exclusively diplomatic role as envoys accredited to the sovereigns.

Febronius did not originate the distinction between the papal envoys as intermediaries between the Pope and sovereign and as delegated ecclesiastical authorities. Much earlier Marco Antonio de Dominis in his *De Republica Ecclesiastica* (1617) had enunciated an analogous idea in these words: "In our time, however, the nuncios of the pope to the Emperors, kings and Christian potentates are in the same position as the envoys of kings stationed at the courts of secular princes for treating and furthering chiefly secular matters. Indeed, to best describe them, they are suppliants (*oratores*) and not spies (*exploratores*)."[14]

This work was condemned by the Holy See but we find the idea revived by Febronius and the four prince-bishops of Germany. Rome's reaction to the Punctation of Ems and the imperial rescript took the form of a brief entitled *Responsio ad Metropolitanos Moguntinum, Trevirensem, Coloniensem et Salisburgensem super Nuntiaturis Apostolicis*, dated November 14, 1789. This "brief" belies its name, for it is a quarto of at least 350 pages in some editions. It is a detailed refutation of the arguments raised against the papal authority in Germany not only at Ems but also in the innumerable polemical pam-

---

[14] *"Nuncii vero Papae nunc dierum ad Imperatores, Reges, Potentates Christianos eodem pariter loco sunt, quo Regum legati in curiis principum saecularibus pro negotiis potissimum saecularibus tractandis et indagandis commorantes. Et certe si optimo eos nomine insigniamus, sunt oratores, sin vero exploratores."*

phlets that flooded Germany in connection with the dispute. The eighth part of this learned study is devoted to the Pope's right to dispatch ordinary as well as special nuncios, armed with permanent jurisdiction. The purpose of that section, which traces the history of the papal legates back to the 5th century, is to demonstrate that it was not unusual for the Roman Pontiff to send his own representatives wherever he thought necessary. These representatives went not simply as diplomats accredited to Emperors or other princes but as agents empowered to intervene in ecclesiastical matters in the Pope's own name and with his authority. The papal legates, it was argued, were necessary adjuncts to the universal primacy of the See of Peter. As the *Responsio* (viii, 24) expresses the principle:

"The Roman Pontiff has the right to have persons who, especially in distant places, represent his absent person, who exercise his jurisdiction and authority by a regularly established commission and who, in short, take his place. This is deduced from the essential force and nature of the primacy, from the rights and privileges connected with the primacy, and from the constant practice of the Church from the first centuries. . . ."

The famous nunciature dispute came to an abrupt end when the French troops of the First Republic crossed the Rhine and thereby put an entirely new face upon the political and ecclesiastical situation. Joseph II himself died in 1790. He had never been fully sympathetic with the four metropolitans. The suffragans, for their part, resented the claims of the archbishops and failed to support them. The thesis stated by the Holy See in the *Responsio* has been succinctly expressed in Canon n. 265 in these words: "The Roman Pontiff has the right, independently of the civil power, to send envoys to any part of the world, with or without ecclesiastical jurisdiction."

In essence the dispute turned upon a strictly canonical point, namely, the extent of the papal power to delegate authority to legates. This aspect of the problem does not concern us directly. What is important is the understanding why, in the 18th century, the anti-papal forces exalted the Pope's diplomatic prerogatives. It should be noted that when the Gallicans,

Josephinists, Febronians, and others of similar tendencies insisted that the nuncio was only an ambassador, they did not mean that he represented the Pope only in political matters. This was asserted by Marco Antonio de Dominis in the citation given above, but it is factually erroneous. The nuncios represented the Pope as head of the Church as well as ruler of the papal domains. Even Joseph II acknowledged that in his rescript. What he and those of his style of thinking would not admit was that the Pope should, as a regular thing, exercise that authority through the nuncio directly upon the clergy and faithful of the country. To adapt the terms of de Dominis, the civil rulers of the 18th century did not object to the *oratores* of the head of the Catholic Church, but they were jealous about his *exploratores*.

Gabriel Hanotaux has written that, in theory at least, Gallicanism should have gone out with the *ancien régime*. In his essay on Gallicanism which introduces the collection of instructions to the Bourbon ambassadors at Rome he shows the special link there was between the royal power and the claims asserted by it over the Church of France. The First Republic or the Empire could not make the same claims to privilege that were made by the Most Christian King of France. Yet, as it turned out, Gallicanism did survive the French Revolution. Indeed, it reappeared in a more refined and systematic form, but with the same import, namely, as a theory designed to assert the dominance of the State power over the Church.

Peace came to the Church of France with the concordat of 1801, which Napoleon as emperor signed with Pius VII. But, alongside this bilateral instrument, Napoleon saw fit to sanction a unilateral enactment which in many ways nullified the concordat. Such were the Organic Articles of the 18 Germinal (April 8, 1802). Their chief architect was J.-E.-M. Portalis (1745-1807), a gifted jurist and minister of worship, whose objective was to bring to life again the old Gallican principles. His achievement was to codify in the Organic Articles a neo-Gallicanism based essentially upon general principles of government and not upon any claim that the emperor was a sort of post-Bourbon Eldest Son of the Church.

The Organic Articles were never recognized by the Holy See, and their promulgation was vigorously protested by the pro-Nuncio Cardinal Caprara, who protested that they "set up in France an ecclesiastical code without the participation of the Holy See."[15] This new code, said the Pope's representative in the name of Pius VII, protesting to Talleyrand, "concerns the doctrines, morals and discipline of the clergy, the rights and duties of the bishops as well as those of their subordinate ministers, their relations with the Holy See and their manner of exercising their jurisdiction." The Articles were an unwarranted invasion of the imprescriptible prerogatives of the Church, he protested. The Catholics were not alone in having grounds for complaint. Analogous articles, 44 in number, were issued at the same time for the regulation of Protestant (Lutheran and Calvinist) worship. But to the protests that went up, Portalis answered that such control was necessary and proper for good government. The State, in his mind, could not refrain from asserting the wide control envisioned in the Organic Articles. It had the right, independently of any negotiations or agreement of the Holy See, to exercise vigilance over all things, including Church matters, that transpired on the soil of France. If any implicit assent was to be sought in the concordat he could point to the first article of the concordat. This allowed the State to establish any *police regulation* which it should judge necessary "for public tranquillity." But Portalis had his own theory of Church-State relations and did not need to invoke Article 1 of the Concordat to justify the seventy-seven Organic Articles.

The first of the Organic Articles strikes a familiar note. It shows how little had Gallicanism vanished with the Bourbons. As before, the government wished to interpose itself between the Pope and the Church of France: "No bull, brief, rescript, decree, order, provision or signature in lieu of provision, nor any other documents emanating from the court of Rome, even those concerning individual persons, can be received, published, printed or otherwise put into force, without the authorization of the government."

[15] Ollivier, *Nouvel manuel*, p. 135. Text of Organic Articles in Mirbt, *Quellen*, n. 559, pp. 420-22.

A second article expressly prohibited the nuncio from exercising any religious jurisdiction on the soil of France without like authorization: "No individual calling himself nuncio, legate, vicar or apostolic commissioner, or claiming any other such title, can without . . . authorization, exercise, whether on the soil of France or elsewhere, any function relating to the affairs of the Gallican Church."

A parallel declaration in the same Article 2 applying to the Protestants stated: "The Protestant churches or their ministers cannot have relations with any foreign power or authority."

Portalis' defense[16] of his Organic Articles was based essentially upon the unity of authority or the indivisibility of sovereignty that should exist within the state. The Church had no real sovereignty except that which the State wished to recognize, in the name of its own authority. "No doubt," he wrote, in a reply dated September 22, 1803, "there is an authority which is proper to the Church. But this authority does not resemble in any respect that authority which is wielded in every state under the name of public power" (p. 129). This power, he argued from Scripture, "has nothing in common with the power to rule which belongs to human governments." This sovereignty is inherent in the nature of political power; it is not related to the existence of any official religion. "It is correct to say that a government or a sovereign can legitimately and freely exercise all the rights inherent to sovereignty in a state, regardless of the religion professed by this government or by this sovereign." These rights claimed by Portalis were, therefore, not dependent upon whether the king was a Catholic or

---

[16] Portalis, *Discours*. Hereafter we cite his papers. For the convenience of the reader we cite the page at its proper place immediately following the text quoted. Ollivier makes the striking contrast between Consalvi, who wanted to accept the Revolution, and the lay jurist Portalis, who wanted to return to the old system: "*Le principal rédacteur des lois et décrets organiques est Portalis, jurisconsulte et canoniste éminent, mais à la façon des Pithou et des Guy Coquille, et qui, n'ayant pas compris la grandeur et la nouveauté de la Révolution Française, n'y avait vu qu'une bourrasque passagère, après laquelle il suffisait de réparer l'ancien édifice endommagé. Le Concordat, oeuvre du prêtre, consacre les résultats de la Révolution de '89 et accepte la séparation qu'elle avait établie entre les deux pouvoirs, en laïcisant le gouvernement et la législation. Les lois et décrets organiques, oeuvre du jurisconsulte gallican, impliquent la négation fondamentale du principe de la Révolution et rétablissent dans une large mesure l'union entre le trône et l'autel, défaite en '89*" (*Nouveau man., vii*).

a Protestant but accrued to the ruler or regime in virtue of the principle of right order in government.

The papacy has been charged in the past with extending its spiritual power far into fields not relating to religion, on the grounds of seeing there moral issues, and in the name of religion. Here the reverse is taking place. Portalis argues on behalf of the State that the temporal power, by reason of sovereignty, extends even to purely religious matters. Where there is conflict, he leaves no doubt where the decision should fall. The civil power must prevail; otherwise anarchy ensues. "It is necessary that there be a superior and preeminent power which reigns in this domain which is, in some respects, common [*to both Church and State*]. This is the power which has the right to weigh the respective interests involved and which is responsible for general and public order. Only this power can be termed a power in the proper sense." For Portalis, the concluding and fundamental argument is the indivisibility of sovereignty, an argument, he points out, so valid that the ultramontanists dare not deny it but apply it rather to their own cause. "The unity of public power is a principle so necessary and evident that the ultramontanists do not deny it but try to invoke it on behalf of the spiritual authority." The protagonists of this new Gallicanism even contended that the sovereign status of the ruler even puts him above excommunication by the Church. ("The principle of the unity and independence of the public power is so strong that it exempts from any censures those who exercise this authority," pp. 163, 143-44).

Portalis leaves no doubt that he makes his claims not in the name of the old "Liberties of the Gallican Church" but on the basis of the general principles of government. He conceived his Organic Articles as simply an expression of a general rule applicable to all governments and to all religions. "We conclude," said he, "that the principle of the state's independence in temporal matters is the supreme law of all empires. It cannot be considered as a right peculiar to France or to any other privileged nations but belongs to the human race" (p. 129). This statement appears reasonable enough on the face of it but, for Portalis, "temporal matters" included the whole scope of public matters, including Church affairs.

One last corollary can be drawn from the argument of indivisibility. If the power of the State is supreme and cannot be shared, then it follows that the Catholic Church's own authority in religious matters cannot be termed "sovereignty" properly so-called. An additional argument to the same effect is that the Church does not possess the means to enforce its authority by coercive measures: "The Church has therefore no capacity for coercion. Consequently, as far as the principle of the unity of public authority is concerned, this axiom cannot be applied to the power of the keys which is not a power in the proper sense. The principle of the unity of public authority suffices to solve the great question of mixed matters" (pp. 143-44).

Such are the rules, the maxims of public law, and, "so to speak, of the kind of law of nations that exists and which has always existed between the Priesthood and the Empire" (p. 163), concluded the distinguished jurist who was the author of the Organic Articles.

Although Portalis insisted that the general principles of political science sufficed to establish the rights of the State over religious matters, he was not reluctant to appeal to yet another title of interference. He referred, in his defense of the Articles, to the role of the temporal sovereign as the "protector" of religion. In this role the State had, as under the old regime, a permanent pretext for wholesale intrusion into Church matters. Portalis himself in the course of his tenure of office repeatedly used his authority in a way reminiscent of the Josephinists. He wanted preeminence not merely in "mixed matters" (those in which, like marriage, both the State and the Church had joint and overlapping claims) but also in matters which could be called "mixed" only upon the broadest interpretation. On the occasion of the papal jubilee of 1803, for instance, Portalis took elaborate moves in the execution of his duties, as he saw them, as minister of worship. Even the simplest prayers and indulgences, he decided, had to be investigated by the civil authorities. The sovereign did not, admittedly, "as a political magistrate" have the right to take cognizance of purely spiritual matters, but this right belonged to him under another heading, as the "protector" of religion. And even in this extension of the domination of the civil power over the religious power, Portalis found another proof of his thesis on the indivisibility of sovereignty. He argued (p. 137):

"But the right of protection of which we speak, which is acknowledged in all sovereigns, is not this a new proof of the great principle of the unity of the public power, that principle which excludes the interference of the pontiffs and which subjects both persons and things to the supervision and material control of the state? We have said enough to demonstrate that, in mixed questions, the sovereign has the right to make laws and, when reasons of state so counsel, need not approve the ecclesiastical regulations which might be suggested relative to these same matters."

We are quoting from the spirited defense which the author of the Organic Articles made of his own creation. In practice the positions taken by Portalis were considerably modified. Napoleon himself ignored them when he chose to do so. But the theories expressed to justify the Articles reflected the prevailing outlook of the civil power at that time not only in France but elsewhere in Europe. The State was extremely jealous of its control of Church matters within its territory, and it regarded this as a normal requirement of the integrity of its sovereignty. It assumed effective surveillance of religious matters at home. And, in particular, it laid great stress upon its right to circumscribe the authority of the Holy See over its citizens. The distrust the French jurists felt in the authority of Rome was given a practical expression in Article 207 of the Penal Code of 1810. This declared that any ecclesiastic who should entertain correspondence "with a foreign court or power" upon religious matters or questions, without having previously informed the minister of worship and without having received permission, should be punished by a fine of from 100 to 500 francs and of imprisonment of from one month to two years. Gallicanism was not dead.

Some of the language in the citations from Portalis' defense of the Organic Articles may appear, at first view, to indicate that their author was confusing the temporal sovereignty of the Roman Pontiffs with the papal spiritual jurisdiction. But the distinction between the two was perfectly clear to Portalis. There was no reason for him to make a special effort to prove that the Pope had no jurisdiction in France as a temporal prince. The weight of his argumentation was rather to prove that the Pope had no uncontrolled *spiritual* authority in France. Wrote Portalis:

"The Pope is at once the visible head of the universal Church and the temporal sovereign of a particular state. As visible head of the universal Church he cannot exercise any authority save that regulated by the canons. He cannot prejudice the rights, privileges and liberties of the national churches. As the temporal sovereign of a particular state, he cannot have any interests contrary to those of another state."

Portalis added that Article I was only an essential safeguard, "founded on the law of nations and upon the general practice of all peoples."

This is perhaps the place to mention an episode that occurred over sixty years after the issuance of the Organic Articles but that closely parallels the thinking and mentality revealed by the above citations from Portalis. At the time this episode took place the doctrine preached by Napoleon's Minister of Worship had already fallen into desuetude. Its attempted revival by his would-be followers at least demonstrates the tenacity of neo-Gallicanism. The resurrecting of the old theories was occasioned by the 1864 encyclical *Quanta Cura*. In this document, with the attached oft-quoted Syllabus of Errors, Pius IX condemned various errors and dangerous tendencies of the day. To put it more accurately he brought together condemnations he had made on previous occasions. The Minister of Justice, to whom copies had been communicated, admonished the bishops individually to publish only that part of the encyclical which treated of the jubilee, whose purpose it was to announce. They were not to publish the Syllabus (which, as a matter of fact, was not destined per se for publication but was meant originally to serve as a guide to the bishops in their own pastorals and sermons).[17]

The government's intimations were widely disregarded by the bishops. The Syllabus condemned the very system of which Portalis had been the chief protagonist in France. Among other things, Proposition 29 denounced the principle that indults

[17] For text of Syllabus, cf. Moody, *Church and Society*, pp. 232-34.

conceded by the Roman Pontiffs should be considered invalid unless they had been solicited through the State. But in particular, its proclamation from cathedral pulpits was a direct challenge to the Organic Articles. The government of Napoleon III took counsel and issued a condemnation of two bishops who had dared to promulgate both the encyclical and the Syllabus. The government's condemnation merely denied that the Syllabus had any legal effect in France. But whereas it was alleged that the motive of the condemnation was merely the "political" nature of the Syllabus, the decree of condemnation adduced the Organic Articles in defense of the action.

The idea that the simple promulgation of a decree at Rome, or at least its reading from the pulpit in a cathedral, sufficed for promulgation was utterly contrary to all principles of good government, it was contended. The State's position was argued with considerable indignation by Maître Victor-Charles Chaix d'Est-Ange, a member of the Council of State, who published a lengthy brief in the official journal of the Empire, *Le Moniteur universel*, on February 23, 1865. The idea that papal decrees took official effect independently of the State's consent was counter to all principles of government, exclaimed the writer:

"[*This theory*] is too contrary to the rights of sovereigns, to the independence of the state, and to the most elementary principles concerning the promulgation of laws and other public acts, to stand in need of any refutation. How can one be obliged to obey a law known only indirectly and put in circulation without legal promulgation? How can subjects be obligated in matters concerning the temporal order without a decree of the temporal power that rules over them? Is the pope master everywhere? Is Rome the capital of all the states? Are there no longer any frontiers between empires? Do the governments no longer prescribe the laws of their country? Is the pope the legislator and the law-giver of the people? Does everything, temporal as well as spiritual, wait upon his decrees? Such fantastic ideas are an insult to common sense. It is enough to mention them in order to show how wild they are! ! !"[*Exclamation marks in text*]

Despite the high reputation of Chaix d'Est-Ange as a jurist, the emotion of the honorable councillor of state was as little shared by the majority of his contemporaries as his point of view. Although the Syllabus of Errors was widely criticized in the Europe of the 1860's, on this point it was Imperial France that went against the spirit of the times. Chaix d'Est-Ange was defending a legal system that had already become obsolete. The modern State had begun to concede that the Pope's religious authority should be allowed to function without interference from the civil government. By the 1860's the Placet was already on the way out, and with it the notion that, to safeguard its sovereignty, the civil power had to exercise strict supervision over Church matters. The old slogan of the indivisibility of sovereignty had lost its validity. The strong language of the councillor of state was in significant contrast to the feeble and purely formal gesture of protest against the two bishops who had dared to publish the encyclical of Pius IX without so much as a nod to the civil power.

We owe to Chaix d'Est-Ange, however, a final formulation of the principles upon which the old system was based. Its clarity is all the greater in that it ignores the developments of the previous half-century and more:

"The power to rule belongs to human governments. The spiritual authority of the Holy See is exercised only in the things of religion and the Faith. The State should therefore establish whether the decisions coming from abroad trespass upon its rights, regardless how high and venerable the authority from which they emanate. Master in its own house, it does not share the temporal power with anyone else. It is its honor, its right and its duty not to tolerate any foreign intrusions which would be for the state a diminution of its authority and, for its subjects, a source of disturbance. No one rules in France but France alone. Rome cannot therefore interfere. It is an outside power whose decisions have no validity until they have been shown to treat only matters concerning the faith and until they have been accorded the exequatur. To allow any different course would be to share sovereignty, to divide the public power."

In that formula, already outmoded when it was composed in 1865, the ghosts of Portalis and of Pithou walked again, or rather, were conjured up momentarily, to dissolve again into the mists of the past.

CHAPTER 10

PAPAL SOVEREIGNTY IN COMPARATIVE
CONSTITUTIONAL LAW (2)

FREE CHURCH IN A FREE SOCIETY

THE system of Church-State relations which had its vogue in the 18th century is not easy to describe, so completely has it vanished from governmental practices. Today it does not seem at all strange that the Pope of Rome is able to administer the affairs of the universal Church without being under the necessity of clearing first with the government whose citizens are concerned. If the various countries—Catholic or Protestant or other—have some special prerogatives in this regard, this comes to them in consequence of a specific agreement arrived at by common consent. They do not arbitrarily assert unilateral control simply in the name of sovereignty. By the same token, the diplomats accredited to the Vatican no longer serve as the clearing agency for all the business transacted by the clergy and faithful at home with the Holy See. Their function no longer is to serve as an intermediary, or screen, between the Pope and his religious subjects throughout the world. The nuncio and the internuncio entertain direct and constant contact with the clergy and faithful of the country where they are stationed, and this by no leave of the civil power. With the passing of that system, papal diplomacy entered a new phase. The sovereignty in spiritual matters is now generally acknowledged by the laws of the states.

Bibliographical Note: The non-participation of the civil governments at the Vatican Council in 1870 is perhaps the most striking monument of the new status of public law in the mid-19th century. The states neither sought nor were invited to be represented. On this matter see Ollivier, *l'Eglise et l'Etat au Concile du Vatican*. Bismarck's failure in 1872 to rally support among the governments for his ideas on controlling future papal elections was another sign of the tacit new entente between Church and State.

The British parliamentary debates in 1851 occasioned a Blue Book on the existing systems of Church-State relations, in the various countries of Europe. This was the British Paper, "Correspondence respecting the Relations existing between Foreign Governments and the Court of Rome." The reports, contributed by English envoys in the different countries, are as a whole extremely informative, although of uneven quality.

The evolution of Church-State relations, particularly in Germany, is outlined by Stutz-Feine.

It is not necessary to take up each and every European country in order to demonstrate the workings of the old system. There was a consensus on the role of the State in religious affairs. The particulars of State control varied from country to country, but the pattern was a consistent one. After the example of France, the laws were built to impede the free operation of papal authority. Typical was the case of the Prussian basic law of February 5, 1794 which applied to both Protestants and Catholics. Paragraph 117 stated that no bishop might make any new decrees or receive any from any foreign ecclesiastical superiors without the permission of the State. Paragraph 118, in the manner of the first of the Organic Articles, stated that all papal bulls, briefs, and other rescripts of alien religious superiors must be submitted for approval before publication. Paragraph 135 prohibited any alien bishop or other ecclesiastical superior from exercising any jurisdictional power in church matters.[1]

An interesting document from the archives of the Prussian ministry of worship describes in detail what the Prussian system meant in practice in regard to the Catholic Church, particularly where the Holy See itself was involved. In 1821 the Hanoverian government inquired officially what Berlin's practice was in its relation to the papacy. The reply was drawn up by Privy Councillor Johann Heinrich von Schmedding, a Catholic from Muenster and long an advisor in the department of religious affairs. In a reply of August 1821 Schmedding gave first the general theory, based upon the collegial system (described in earlier pages), and then the machinery of its application:[2]

"The general law of the land proceeds from the principle that the king is the source of all law, including church law, Catholic as well as Protestant. This fundamental rule is the soul of Prussian legislation and the norm of all administration. Catholicism, on the principle of the Divine foundation of the Church, holds for a duality of the supreme power, whose boundaries can be adjusted through peaceful agreement. But the general law of the country is in direct conflict with this conception. The resolution of this contradiction is found in the Collegial System.

1 Mirbt, *Quellen*, n. 557, pp. 417-19.
2 Meier, *Römisch-Deutschen Frage*, I, pp. 425-27.

This leaves the state a free hand to permit the church a kind of autonomy, without any prejudice to its own sovereignty. Prussia has employed this remedy with great indulgence. Purely spiritual matters are entirely free. Only new constitutive decrees and new foundations need the approval of the state. Recourse to the papal See is permitted only in spiritual matters and under the supervision of the state, through the legation as intermediary. The Placet is necessary for indults of foreign spiritual superiors."

The Prussians were proud of their system, which had a marked influence upon the other Protestant states of Germany. The Catholic states of Southern Germany naturally tended to follow the example of both Austria and France. In Bavaria the domination of the civil power was particularly strong during the ascendancy (1799-1817) of Count Maximilian Montgelas, a man thoroughly imbued with the spirit of the Enlightenment. Montgelas once wrote, "The Dukes of Bavaria from the beginning exercised upon the persons and the goods of their clergy all the rights which sovereignty by its very nature guarantees to the leaders of civil society and which the Author of Christianity never thought of denying them." When the Church comes into conflict with the State, in his opinion, it is the State that must act to assert its superiority. There can be only one master in the State. "The doctrine of the two powers," held Montgelas, "is a monstrosity of priestly ambition. The church is in the state and not the state in the church."[3]

Such statements seemed to offer little promise that the governments of a later time would take a more tolerant, much less detached view of the untrammeled exercise of Church jurisdiction by a foreign pontiff in their domains. Yet forces were at work in the first half of the 19th century that were to reverse completely the dominant theories of the 18th century. The spirit of the times was manifest in the revolution of 1848, but the trend was already in motion. Let us try to pin down some details of the great changeover which terminated in the State's abdication of its quondam claims in religious matters and in its implicit simultaneous recognition of the papal sovereignty.

The first perceptible break in the old tradition may perhaps

[3] Doeberl, *Montgelas*, pp. 123-24.

be traced to the revolutions of 1830 in both France and the Low Countries. The constitutions of the Monarchy of July and of the new Belgian State each reflected revulsion against the 18th-century *polizei-staat*. A regime that claimed to respect the liberties of all its citizens and which, moreover, affected an official neutrality in religious matters could hardly justify high-handed interference in Church matters. This is not to say that in France the authorities did not attempt to carry over the former practices. But they encountered increasingly effective resistance when they did so. Little by little it was borne in upon the governments of the mid-19th century that the liberal state owed it to itself to repudiate the regalism of the preceding century.

The logical implications of a constitutional provision are not always evident at once. In France, despite the Constitution of 1830, the ministry of worship claimed the right to exercise surveillance of the correspondence of the bishops with the Holy See. The government protested to Archbishop de Quélen of Paris, in the name of the first of the Organic Articles, when that prelate published in 1834 the letter of Pope Gregory XVI condemning de Lamennais' *Paroles d'un croyant*. The minister of worship also reprimanded the bishop of Clermont for having refused ecclesiastical burial to a certain individual in 1838. He claimed the right, in a circular of 1841, to order the bishops not to leave their dioceses without the king's permission. The Gallican liberties and the Declaration of the Clergy of 1682 were mentioned in the Chamber and in the official correspondence of the ministry of worship with all seriousness.[4]

The anachronism of invoking the old Organic Articles in the new state of the "Bourgeois King" of the House of Orleans exploded into public attention in 1845. That year featured the publication of a canonico-legal treatise by André Dupin, under the title *Manuel du droit ecclésiastique français*, which was based unashamedly upon the classic Gallican principles. The Archbishop of Lyons, Cardinal de Bonald, denounced it roundly. In a scathing pastoral decree of February 4, 1845 he alluded to the Organic Articles, with their provisions subjecting papal directives to censorship. The Cardinal commented caustically

---

[4] Martin, Jacques-Paul, *Nonciature de Paris*, p. 277.

on the contradiction the Placet was to freedom of opinion and of the press in the new constitutional State:

"This is the form of control which the lawyers call the *droit d'annexe [French legal term equivalent to Placet]*. It is an essential right of the government, they say. It is even a 'liberty' of the Gallican Church, according to Pithou's 44th article. It is one of the glories of the clergy. And so it happens that the most frivolous writer can every morning launch his serial stories and his *novelles* into the public domain, dispatching them to the most remote places. But the Vicar of Jesus Christ cannot, without the approval of the temporal power, write to his brethren condemning error, teaching submission to the established authorities, explaining the holy teachings of religion! We, like the Catholics of the rest of the world, have the right and the need to develop likemindedness among us by a free and holy intercourse which brings to our children the mind and teaching of our common father and which strengthens unity and good order in discipline."[5]

The rights claimed by the state, protested the Cardinal, were by no means inherent in the nature of civil power.

The government took the condemnation of Dupin's *Manuel* as an attack against the authority of the State. The cardinal's condemnation was itself condemned on March 9 by the Council of State, which declared the act of the Archbishop of Lyons to be without validity. But, when sixty bishops rallied to the defense of the cardinal by spoken or written protests and when public opinion evidenced appreciation of his logic, the government withdrew into discreet silence and inaction. Even after the book had been condemned in Rome itself and put on the Index of Prohibited Books, the government refrained from rising to check this challenge to the Organic Articles.

If the lawyers of the Monarchy of July still lived with the law books of the old regime, the politicians were more alive to the spirit of the times. The new regime of liberty of expression and of worship required the government to employ new means to

[5] *Ibid.*, 279; Ollivier, *Nouveau manuel*, p. 361. The chargé d'affaires of the Holy See, Msgr. Garibaldi, had earlier commented in a report of August, 1834: "*Dans un pays où chacun peut imprimer ce qu'il veut, c'est un peu singulier de vouloir assujettir à une censure les publications qui regardent la religion*" (Martin, *op.cit.*, pp. 277-78).

accomplish what it had once achieved by direct interference. Deprived of the weapon of police action, the State was now obliged to rely more and more upon the argument of persuasion. It would have to solve its problems not by invoking its *jura circa sacra* but by the more indirect and conciliatory channels of diplomacy. Whether or not this was realized at the time, the road was opening to the recognition of the spiritual sovereignty of the Holy See.

The curious case of the special diplomatic mission to Rome of Pellegrino Rossi in 1844 was characteristic of the new trend in the relations of the civil governments to the papacy on the diplomatic level. The particulars of this episode deserve more than a passing reference. In 1844 the question of the universities became a hotly debated political issue. The government of Guizot was violently attacked by the opposition which availed itself of the popular anti-Jesuit legends to strengthen its cause. It became imperative for the government to dispose of the Jesuit question somehow. Louis Philippe's prime minister was unwilling to have recourse to the old method. He wanted to avoid expelling the Jesuits. The thought came of adopting the expedient of asking the Pope himself to order the Jesuits to disperse themselves. In so doing the government would not sacrifice the possibility of taking more direct measures later if this should prove necessary. On the other hand, if the strategy succeeded and the Jesuits were withdrawn by an order from Rome, an immense lot of trouble and embarrassment would be spared the monarchy of July. It was the old story of the contest between the Sun and the Wind as to which could sooner make the traveler take off his cloak. Guizot preferred the method of the Sun. He relates his plan of action in these words:

"I proposed to the King and to the Council not to drop the laws in force against the non-authorized religious congregations but to delay their enforcement and to present the question of the dissolution of the Society of Jesus in France to its supreme and unchallenged head, to the Pope himself. France would not thereby abdicate any of its legal weapons but, for the sake of religious peace in France, it would urge the spiritual authority of the Catholic Church to make it unnecessary for us to use these measures. The King and the Council adopted my plan."[6]

The man selected to accomplish by diplomacy what could not be done by law or administrative action, was Pellegrino Rossi. Since the delicate task envisaged appeared beyond the capacities of the then ambassador to the Holy See, Count de Latour-Maubourg, who was ailing, this diplomat was given a leave of absence. In his place in March 1845 went Rossi with the title of envoy extraordinary and minister plenipotentiary ad interim.

Guizot's instructions to Rossi, outlining the procedure he was to follow in approaching the Holy See, were filled with high-sounding language: "In adopting this course of action the Court of Rome will never have made a more timely or more prudent use of the high papal authority, or one more in harmony with the high supervisory mission by which the successor of St. Peter is charged to solve by the intervention of his wisdom, or eliminate by the use of his supreme spiritual authority, those problems which could become serious dangers to the Church in times of crisis or emergency."[7] In such language, under veiled threats, the French government asked the Pope to do for the king what the king was himself politically unable to do.

We are not concerned with the details of the negotiations conducted by this extraordinary personality thus called to perform a diplomatic mission at Rome in the "new style." Italian-born, Pellegrino Rossi was a specialist in constitutional law. He had become a citizen of Geneva, where his public services are still remembered with gratitude. Later, he had gone to Paris to become professor at the College of France and, in time, to become a peer of France. With the end of the monarchy of July he was to be welcomed back to Rome by Pius IX, who made him virtually premier with the mission of reorganizing the papal states on the model of contemporary constitutions. His career was cut short by the dagger of a Roman revolutionist, a loss that may well be considered a catastrophe for the papal states, in view of later events.

Suffice it to say that Rossi's mission was successful. That is, through him, the vexing problem of the Jesuits was brought to a satisfactory conclusion. If the Pope did not issue formal

[6] Guizot, *Mémoires*, VII, p. 352.
[7] *Ibid.*, VII, pp. 397-98.

orders to the General of the Jesuits, sufficient gestures of appeasement were made by the closing of a few of the Jesuit residences in Paris. Thus the issue that at one time had assumed proportions threatening the Guizot cabinet petered out. When the test arose in the Chamber, Guizot was able to achieve a resounding vindication. In the end, if the Jesuits were not suppressed, at least the "problem" of the Jesuits was.

Guizot, who was of Huguenot extraction, himself bears witness to the special significance of the Rossi mission and of the spirit that lay behind it. It was one of the actions which gave him the most satisfaction in his long political life, not only because of its success, but also and especially because it seemed to point out how in the future the Catholic Church and the constitutional liberal state could cooperate with each other. He wrote in later years:

"The outcome of the Jesuit affair was one of the things that gave me, in the course of my political life, the most profound satisfaction, not merely because of the passing parliamentary success it was but above all because it showed that an understanding and alliance was possible between the Catholic Church and the constitutional state and that the right policy could make itself understood and accepted. The task will be difficult and long, but it has at last begun."[8]

The Rossi special mission, though important, was not the first one in which a French government solicited the intervention of the papacy to resolve its political problems by the exercise of the Roman authority. In 1828, under the Restoration, an analogous mission had been dispatched to Rome. Commenting on these two acts, the historian of the monarchy of July points out that it is no surprise that ultramontanism was on the rise in the middle of the 19th century. Wrote Thureau-Dangin: "When one sees all the cabinets one after the other invite the papacy on their own initiative to dictate the conduct of the clergy and the Catholics in the affairs of France can we believe they have any right to complain of what they call the advance of ultramontanism?"[9]

It should also be noted that Guizot himself was not entirely

---

[8] Thureau-Dangin, *Histoire*, v, p. 569.
[9] *Ibid.*, v, pp. 555-56.

consistent. He, too, found occasion to defend Article 2 of the Organic Articles. When the nuncio in Paris sent directly to the French bishops the Apostolic Letter of Pius IX instituting a Jubilee, Guizot instructed Rossi, in a letter under date of December 31, 1846, to protest this as a trespass of his function: "The nuncio is only an ambassador, and as such he can entertain official contact only with the government of His Majesty."[10]

At the time that France was making faltering and erratic steps away from the Organic Articles, in Belgium the issue was crystal-clear. From the start the new State repudiated the old political control of Church matters. Following their successful revolt (a few months after the July Revolution) against the Kingdom of the Netherlands, the southern provinces established a Kingdom of Belgium. The constitution of 1831 reflected the trends of the times as well as the lessons of the past. The Kingdom of the Netherlands, under Protestant rulers, had adopted the Church policies of Prussia. The handling of the predominantly Catholic provinces exasperated the feelings of the populace. But, whereas the Hohenzollerns' Catholic provinces never revolted, those of the House of Orange did. Their chief points of grievance were mirrored in the constitution. This envisaged a hitherto unknown system of "separation." The State was not to interfere in the appointment or installation of ministers of religion. The citizens of the new Belgium could correspond with their religious prelates without interference. They could publish their proceedings without seeking the permission of the State, except insofar as the ordinary laws regulating publications were in question. By these provisions some of the essential principles of the old system were formally excluded.[11]

The Belgian constitution did not profess "separation of Church and State" in so many words. Its provisions served nonetheless to establish in Belgium a regime of separation as it was understood in those times, that is, a free Church in a free State. The question of whether the separation was com-

---

[10] Martin, *op.cit.*, p. 278.

[11] Pertinent paragraphs of the 1831 Constitution in Moody (ed.), *Church and Society*, p. 322. Encyclical *Mirari Vos, ibid.*, p. 230. It is not commonly stressed that although the Belgian Constitution was based on the idea of separation of Church and State, the Encyclical *Mirari Vos* of August 15, 1832 did not affect the Belgian situation.

patible with diplomatic relations with the Holy See came up almost immediately. By the Treaty of November 15, 1831 the powers had recognized the independence of Belgium and established its international status of neutrality. As soon as the ratifications had been exchanged, the young State hastened to send missions abroad charged with the duty of announcing in as formal a manner as possible the foundation of this new member of the European concert of states. This action was all the more necessary since the Netherlands itself had not yet reconciled itself to the course of recent events. Even the major powers who had signed the birth certificate of the infant State were not too enthusiastic about their godchild. For this reason prudence dictated an act of diplomatic presence in all the capitals of Europe. Among others, a mission was sent to Rome.

The special envoy sent to Rome was Vicomte Vilain XIIII, who arrived in the Eternal City in November 1832. A liberal Catholic of the de Lamennais school, the envoy did not conceal his opposition to the maintenance of permanent relations with the Holy See. To him, diplomatic relations recalled too vividly the former system of State domination which had used the diplomatic channels as an instrument. In a long dispatch dated February 10, 1833 the Vicomte recommended the suppression of his own post. Such a legation in Rome, he said, was "useless," especially insofar as the Concordat of 1827 (entered into with the Netherlands) no longer had a practical application. As another argument against diplomatic relations he adduced the reciprocity that would be involved. A minister plenipotentiary in Rome implied a nuncio in Brussels. But, as he argued, such a papal representative would inevitably fall under the influence of Austria and consequently be ill-disposed toward the new constitutional government. The king, too, would inevitably tend to use the legation in Rome, as well as the nunciature (or internunciature) in Brussels, to interfere in the internal affairs of the Church.[12]

The views of Vicomte Vilain XIIII on the inadvisability of having diplomatic relations with the Holy See were shared by many Catholics in Belgium. As they saw it, such direct relations by the king could jeopardize the free correspondence with

[12] Van Zuylen, in *Revue générale*, 1930, p. 32.

Rome that had been guaranteed in the constitution. It is not unnatural that the leaders of the revolution of 1830 looked upon diplomatic relations as a step backward likely to endanger the achievements of the revolution.

The government attempted to quiet these apprehensions. On January 28, 1836, when the bill to establish a permanent legation in Rome came before the Chamber, Foreign Minister de Muelenaere protested that the government had "only acted for political reasons and in view of the political influence exercised by the Court of Rome in Europe." He denied that the legation was a violation of what was described by opponents as "the constitutional separation of Church and State." He rejected the allegation that the right of Catholics to correspond directly and without interference with the Sovereign Pontiff would be jeopardized by such diplomatic relations: "Some uneasiness has been manifested about the existence of a legation in Rome. The fear is expressed that this may perhaps prejudice the rights guaranteed by our constitution in religious matters. I cannot repeat enough that these fears are entirely groundless. This legation has been created with quite another purpose in view. Despite the presence of an internuncio in Brussels, the bishops are not deprived of their right to communicate directly with the Holy See in religious matters. This is a fact that should by itself answer all objections."[13]

This apparently candid statement did not portray the full state of affairs. Leopold I, a Lutheran of the German house of Saxe-Coburg, was convinced that even in the new regime of liberty a strong politico-religious policy was necessary for peace and stability in the young state. He did not intend to interfere with the communication of the Belgian bishops with the Holy See. But he planned to employ his own diplomatic representative in Rome to counter their actions, and to further his own ideas. What is more, the king wanted a nuncio or internuncio in Brussels. Through this papal official accredited to him he hoped to be able to exercise influence over the national hierarchy. What Vilain XIIII had feared was exactly the aim of Leopold. As early as September 1832 the king had expressed

---

[13] Banning, *La Belgique et le Vatican*, i, p. x. For details on Leopold's use of his diplomatic relations with the Holy See, see Simon, *Politique religieuse*, pp. 63-73.

his desires for a nuncio in a letter to Metternich asking the Austrian Chancellor's support. It is true that Leopold hoped to strengthen Belgium's political prestige by diplomatic action at all the European courts. But the royal minister in Rome was to have an additional function as the instrument of the king's politico-religious policy. The envoy received direct instructions from the sovereign, apart from those he got from the foreign ministry.

Under these circumstances it can be understood why the bishops reacted with great coolness to the presence of a papal envoy in Brussels. The nuncio was the "king's man." His instructions, in fact, had been drafted in Rome on the basis of recommendations made by Leopold. It took several decades marked by tensions and controversy before an equitable balance could be reached in the new relationship that now existed among the bishops, the nunciature, the king, and the Holy See. Centuries of regalism could not be wiped out in a day.

The wary attitude of Belgian Catholics toward diplomatic relations with the Holy See during this period was prompted by their unhappy experiences under the Dutch. As time went on, however, it was perceived that such relations were not necessarily a threat to the liberties guaranteed to the Catholics of Belgium or a symbol of government interference. The State itself came to realize the necessity of concerting with the Holy See not in the old spirit of unilateral action but on the basis of equality, on the pattern of its relations with other outside authorities whose sovereign independence it recognized. As Baron van Zuylen has written in his 1930 account of the first mission of Vicomte Vilain XIIII, the State now had just as much need as before for such diplomatic contacts. Having lost its police power over the Church, it had to compensate by the method of diplomacy: "Deprived by the constitution of the rights of supervision and control that the preceding concordats had given it over the Church in Belgium, the state had an even greater reason for maintaining close contact with Rome for the purpose of informing the papal authorities and also in order to anticipate or resolve the conflicts which might arise in Belgium between the Church and the state."[14]

[14] Van Zuylen, *loc.cit.* Years before, Professor Nys had called attention to the fact that even the Liberal cabinets might find it useful and even necessary to

It is fair to say that today, though the constitution has remained unchanged, diplomatic relations with the Holy See are no longer regarded by the Catholics as a threat to their freedom from governmental interference.

Unlike the Belgian Catholics, who had the benefit not only of a new constitution but of a new state, the Catholics of Prussia had to wage a bitter and long struggle before they too were able to throw off governmental restrictions. On January 1, 1841 a decree of the young King Frederick William IV abolished the Placet. Unimpeded intercourse with the Roman Pontiff was thereafter to be permitted, according to this rescript. The government, however, admonished the bishops to be prudent in their use of this new faculty. A few days later, on January 11, an administrative order established a Catholic section within the ministry of worship. Prussia's revised constitution of January 31, 1850 formalized this trend, especially in Article 16, which reaffirmed freedom of communication of the religious communities in Prussia with their "religious heads" outside the country. The promulgation of ecclesiastical decrees was, in the same article, made subject only to the general limitations affecting all publications.[15]

After 1841 the Prussian legation at Rome went into a phase of relative unimportance. Although it was never suppressed it was often without a titular, as though it had lost its reason to exist. In 1867, however, the mission entered a new phase when Bismarck sent Count Harry von Arnim.

That quarter-century of diplomatic eclipse was in sharp contrast to the era of controversy that culminated in the king's 1840 decree. The dispute which came to an end in that year with the accession of Frederick William IV is known in Church

---

be able to negotiate at Rome through diplomatic channels. *"C'est à Rome même que, profitant de la centralisation du Catholicisme, les gouvernements devraient agir; au lieu de se borner à défendre leurs droits de souveraineté dans leur territoire, ils devraient essayer d'amener la Papauté à des idées qui soient moins en contradiction avec l'esprit de progrès et de liberté. Et à ce point de vue une représentation des puissances auprès du Saint-Siège peut représenter une grande utilité"* (Nys, in *Rev. de dr. int. et de lég. comp.*, 1878, p. 533). In 1878 the Liberals, newly arrived to power, were contemplating negotiations with Leo XIII on the school question. Nys, a Liberal, did not at this time believe he was jeopardizing the sovereignty of the state by negotiating at Rome on internal matters.

15 Mirbt, *Quellen*, n. 592, pp. 444-45.

history as the *Kölner Wirren,* or the Cologne Troubles. The controversy stemmed from the efforts of the Prussian government to impose on Catholics legislation governing marriages between Catholics and Protestants. We are chiefly concerned with the role played by the Prussian legation at Rome (there was no papal envoy in Berlin or Cologne).

Niebuhr's influence as Prussian minister in Rome (1816-1823) had, by the standards of that day, been a liberal one. According to the testimony of Bunsen, his successor in office, Niebuhr did not believe in the system of direct government interference in religious affairs. He did not believe, contrary to the prevailing political theory of his time, that the "highest wisdom of a government consists in exercising a sort of minute and centralized police surveillance and administrative control over the Roman Catholic Church." In Niebuhr's mind this surveillance of the Roman Catholic Church should be limited to the preservation of the State's independence and the indispensable vigilance of the government against the encroachments of the ecclesiastical power. Niebuhr opposed even more strongly the idea at one time entertained in Berlin of trying to reorganize the Catholic Church in Prussia on royal authority alone and without negotiations with the Holy See. His viewpoint prevailed, for the reorganization was accomplished by the Bull of Circumscription drafted after negotiations conducted at Rome.

Niebuhr succeeded to some extent, according to Bunsen, in diminishing the severity of the existing requirements governing the routing of papal documents:

"Among others the well-known fact may be referred to, that upon his proposals made from Rome, the government immediately consented to the direct transmission of the Roman Catholic requests for dispensations of marriages from the bishops to the embassy charged with their presentation or advocacy, and to the immediate transmission of the papal rescripts to the bishops—a measure which produced a most desireable simplification of nine-tenths of the current business between Prussia and Rome."[16] As can be gauged from this statement, marriage questions were vital.

[16] Niebuhr, *Life and Letters,* p. 599. Bunsen's contribution was dated from London, February 28, 1838. He had just left Rome.

One serious conflict had to take its course before the liberalism of Niebuhr reached its full fruit. The Prussian constitution of 1794 had required that in the case of mixed marriages the sons were to follow the religion of the father and the daughters that of the mother.

At least, the offspring were to be so raised until their fourteenth year. This was superseded, in the eastern provinces, by a royal decree of 1803 which declared that *all* the children were to be raised in the religion of the father. The purpose of this law was to avoid the dissensions that the original legislation had produced. The decree also prohibited the parents from entering into any agreement between themselves contrary to the intent of the law.

This decree was, in 1825, extended to the western provinces. But this time it met with determined resistance. Partially successful negotiations with the Holy See did terminate in a brief of Pius VIII of March 25, 1830, but no settlement was reached on the question of the religion of the children of mixed marriages. For this reason the papal brief which was transmitted, according to custom, through the Prussian legation was held up by Berlin and did not come officially to the knowledge of the bishops in West Prussia. Finally, on June 19, 1834 the Prussian Minister at Rome, whom we have just cited, Chevalier Bunsen, met Count Ferdinand Spiegel, Archbishop of Cologne, in Berlin. Between them a new instruction was drawn up concerning the practical treatment of mixed marriages that would be followed in the Cologne archdiocese. In this agreement there was no insistence upon the necessity for the non-Catholic party to promise to raise the children in the Catholic religion. Archbishop Spiegel prevailed upon his suffragans, the bishops of Muenster, Trier, and Paderborn, to accept this agreement. Knowledge of this pact and its implementation was kept from the Holy See. But a year later (August 1835) Archbishop Spiegel died. Shortly thereafter, Cardinal Lambruschini, the papal secretary of state, wrote to Bunsen inquiring about some rumors that had filtered back to Rome. It was reported, said the cardinal, that the late prelate, Count Spiegel, had issued instructions to his clergy that distorted the express intent of the Holy See, and that in concert with the Prussian government.

Bunsen chose to deny that any document or agreement of such a nature existed. Matters remained at that point until in November 1836 Bishop Hommer of Trier, on his own death-bed, signed a letter to the Pope in which he revealed the existence of the agreement, declaring that he now saw that the principles and precepts of the Church had been violated by its terms. He attached to his recantation a copy of the instruction that had been sent out to the clergy in his name.

Clemens August von Droste zu Vischering, the new head of the Cologne archdiocese, was a man of quite different character from Count Spiegel who has been described as an "ecclesiastical *grand-seigneur* in the style of the prince-bishops of the Enlightenment." The successor was a strong personality whose views were known to be opposed to the government's policy. His acceptance by Prussia, for reasons judged good at that time, astounded everyone. Berlin soon had cause to regret its momentary lapse. Droste zu Vischering repudiated the "non-existent" agreement as soon as he learned of it, and his example stiffened the courage of his suffragans, who also annulled it. Berlin reacted by jailing the archbishop on November 20, 1837.

But the government had gone too far. It had miscalculated the strength of the Catholic opposition and had not reckoned on the fiery leadership of this new Athanasius. Worst of all, from its own point of view, its illiberal course was disapproved by many non-Catholics. The arrest of the Archbishop of Cologne was the culmination of a bankrupt policy. His release in 1839 signaled the "utter defeat" (to use Mirbt's expression) of the government. Then in 1840 King Frederick William III died after a long reign that had begun in 1797. His son and successor, long convinced of the error of Prussia's approach to the religious problem, lost no time in pacifying his Catholic subjects. His first step was to bring about an entente with the Holy See. A special mission to Rome headed by Count Frederick William Brühl in 1840-1841 (Bunsen had had to leave Rome as persona non grata) liquidated the outstanding issues. We have already noted the legislative changes introduced in 1841. As a sign of the new era of religious peace and the new winds that blew in Berlin, Frederick William IV undertook to resume construction of the Cathedral of Cologne, on which work had been stopped for a century.[17]

Such radical shifts in policy in the leading Protestant State of Germany were bound to have their effect elsewhere. Bavaria on March 25, 1841 finally permitted free communication with the Holy See. The Netherlands abolished the Placet from the penal code in 1847, confirming this the year following in a constitutional amendment authorizing unimpeded communication with religious authorities. The revolutions of 1848 speeded up the process of disintegration of the old doctrine that a state owed it to itself to keep tight and jealous reins upon the exercise of the papal authority within its boundaries. This change was especially noticeable in Austria, hard-hit by the revolutionary forces. An imperial decree of April 18, 1850, in its first article declared: "It is permitted as well to the Bishops as to the faithful under them, to address themselves on ecclesiastical affairs to the Pope, and to receive the ordinances of the Pope without previous consent of the temporal authorities." This provision was incorporated in the concordat of August 18, 1855. Article 2 of this death-knell to Josephinism declared: "The Roman Pontiff having by divine right throughout the entire Church the primacy both of honor and of jurisdiction, the mutual communication of the bishops, clergy, and faithful with the Holy See in spiritual things and ecclesiastical matters will not be subjected to the necessity of securing the Royal Placet but will be entirely free."[18]

We have an authoritative explanation of the meaning of the new Austrian policy in which the young Emperor Francis Joseph turned his back upon Joseph II. The report of Count Thun, the Minister of Public Worship and Instruction, dated April 7, 1850 and preceding the decree of April 18 already cited, is a frank admission that the old system had had its day. We give the translation appearing in a contemporary British Parliamentary Paper [LIX *(1851)*]:

"The communication with the Apostolic See has hitherto been guarded by the law with very great precautions. Every

---

[17] In addition to Mirbt's *Quellen* on this episode, see same author on Droste-Vischering in Schaff-Herzog, IV, pp. 6f.

[18] Mirbt, *Quellen*, n. 598, pp. 447-48.

papal edict—with the sole exception of dispensations by the Penitentiary Courts—was subjected to the Placet of the Sovereign. This Placet was granted to those edicts only which were issued through the mediation of the Imperial Agency established in Rome; and the latter was only allowed to act in matters conveyed to it through or with the permission of, the authorities of the State. . . . The continuation of the limitations which have hitherto existed is, in fact, in the opinion of the faithful and obedient Council of Ministers, no longer possible. They constitute portions of a legislation which is explicable in the circumstances of the period in which it was developed, but which is incompatible with the essentially altered position of things now existing."

Württemberg entered into an agreement with the Holy See in 1857. Article 6 of the agreement signed by the plenipotentiaries on April 8, 1857 declared that intercourse by the bishops, clergy, and laity with the Holy See on ecclesiastical matters was *völlig frei* (entirely free). Decrees could be published without prior inspection by the State.

The meaning of the new trends in constitutional law throughout Europe was not immediately recognized in Spain. There the *pase regio* remained on the books, although its real force was a matter of opinion. When in 1854 Pius IX proclaimed the dogma of the Immaculate Conception, the government prosecuted a Church organ for having published the papal decree of December 8 before the royal Placet had been given. The bishops in protesting this action did not fail to point out the anachronism. Here was a purely dogmatic decree which even in Austria was exempt from the imperial Placet. It was absurd, they argued, for the government to try to censor the publication of a pontifical decree that had already been amply reported by every political newspaper in Spain, against which no action was or could be taken.

A similar situation was repeated on the occasion of the encyclical *Quanta Cura* in 1864 and its attached Syllabus. The government found itself in the same predicament. How could it punish the Church authorities for having printed in their own organs without official permission a papal document that had already been completely reported and commented on in every newspaper in the land? On the other hand, how could the *pase regio* be safeguarded if no action were taken? The government settled on a *pase regio a posteriori* as a means of getting around the difficulties and thereby saving both face and the principle of the Placet. This was done by a decree of March 6, 1865. But in Spain as elsewhere officialdom was slow in giving up a long-standing prerogative, even long after it had become outmoded. As late as 1883, the future Cardinal Rampolla, then nuncio in Madrid, found it necessary to protest against the State's claim to pass upon papal decrees in the virtue of the *pase regio,* "abolished," said the nuncio, "in most of the European states."[19] He could have added that the Vatican Council of 1870 had formally condemned the doctrine that the decisions or decrees of the Holy See lacked force and validity until they had been confirmed by the Placet of the secular power.

Czarist Russia held to the Placet to the end of its days. In Chapter 3 we have shown how imperial Russia had taken over the Prussian system and applied it with rigorous consistency. The same sort of control was set up through the instrumentality of the Russian legation in the Eternal City. But whereas, in the course of time, these controls were relaxed by those who

---

[19] Becker, *Relaciones diplomáticas,* pp. 218-23. The Madrid nunciature, unlike that of Paris, exercised a certain jurisdiction. It had its own tribunal with competence in litigation involving Spanish ecclesiastics. Taking its cue from the concordat negotiations with Napoleon, Spain came forward at the end of 1801 with some proposals to eliminate this manifestation of direct papal authority. The Spanish envoy at Rome proposed that the papal representative should limit himself to the functions of an ambassador of the Pope as a temporal prince, or at least to the ceremonial role of symbolizing the communion of the Church in Spain with the center of Catholicity in Rome. In either case the nuncio would cease to exercise any canonical jurisdiction. Consalvi rejected this proposal in a letter dated January 9, 1802. The Pope's representative was primarily a spiritual vicar, he said, and only secondarily the representative of a temporal prince. Moreover, as a religious envoy, he had a real and not a merely symbolic mission to perform. *"La souveraineté temporelle de sa Sainteté n'est que secondaire, à côté de son apostolat suprême. Sa Sainteté ne peut avoir que des nonces. Ce titre appartient à ses ambassadeurs. C'est ce caractère qui leur fait obtenir le premier rang. Les papes ont toujours envoyés des légats ou des nonces, avec l'objet réel de veiller aux intérêts des catholiques éloignés, et n'ont jamais eu l'idée de croire par là, montrer parité de communion entre l'église Romaine et les autres églises"* (Artaud de Montor, *Pie VII,* ed. 1836, i, pp. 229-32). A somewhat similar theory, limiting the nuncio's role in domestic affairs, was advanced in the same country by the editor of the Carlist newspaper, *El Siglo Futuro,* in the time of Leo XIII. It was rejected by Cardinal Jacobini, the secretary of state, in a letter of April 13, 1885.

originated the system, Czarist Russia never reconciled itself to the change of the times. In 1847, after lengthy and painful negotiations, a quasi-concordat was reached between the Holy See and Russia. It is noteworthy that among the items upon which the negotiators "agreed to disagree" was precisely the issue of free communication between the Catholics of Poland and the Church administration in Rome otherwise than through the imperial legation.[20]

This system existed on the eve of the First World War. We find a dispatch in the *London Times* of January 11, 1911, relating to a dispute turning on this point. In 1909 Pope St. Pius X had inaugurated a new official organ called the *Acta Apostolicae Sedis* which was to serve as the means for promulgation of papal decrees and other acts of the Holy See. Items published in the *Acta* were considered to go into effect after ninety days, without any further formalities such as official

[20] Boudou, *Russie et le Saint-Siège*, I, p. 567. It is probable that, had the Czarist regime emerged intact from the World War, the situation of the Catholic Church would have been radically improved. Following the manifesto of April 17, 1905, which promised religious liberty, preparations were made to transform this pledge into law. A high-level commission, comprising the ministers of the departments concerned, was established shortly before the war for the purpose of revising the existing laws in regard to the Catholic Church. This little-known story of "what might have been" has been told by Nicholas Bock, one-time chargé d'affaires of the imperial legation at the Vatican. This diplomat later became a Catholic and subsequently a priest in the Jesuit order. His testimony appeared in the ecumenical review *Unitas*, organ of the Unitas Association of Rome:

"Almost all the ministers and the Czar himself declared themselves in favor of a complete revision of existing laws and dispositions concerning the Catholic Church in the spirit of the imperial manifesto. The greater part of the Duma and of public opinion were in complete accord with this attitude, and preparations were at once begun for this revision and for discussions with the Holy See. At the Vatican, negotiations with the Russian government were in the hands of an extremely gifted young diplomat, Monsignor Pacelli. Everything seemed to point to a great success, but at the last moment these diplomatic efforts ran aground first of all by reason of the outbreak of the World War and then because of the ensuing revolution.

"I had been summoned from Rome and at the beginning of 1914 was working in St. Petersburg for the subsidiary commission of Foreign Affairs. My discouragement was great, indeed, when Mr. Sazonow, then Minister of Foreign Affairs, declared to me one day his deep regret that the Commission for Catholic Affairs would have to adjourn in view of the fact that the menacing clouds on the political horizon compelled the ministers to concentrate all their attention on another extraordinary commission, that of National Defense. In consequence of this, he proposed that I should return to Rome and promised that he would recall me to St. Petersburg as soon as the situation cleared. A few months later the World War was well under way." (*Loc.cit.* Oct.-Dec. 1952, p. 201.)

notification to governments or the local hierarchy. This innovation caused no difficulty in countries where the Placet had ceased to exist. But it conflicted with Russian practice. Copies of the official organ which had been shipped to the bishops in Russian Poland and Russia proper arrived scissored and bluepencilled. To protests from Rome over these mutilations the reply was given that the imperial government recognized as valid only those portions of the *Acta Apostolicae Sedis* which it itself had transmitted to the hierarchy. It did not concede that mere publication of such decrees in Rome sufficed for validity in the domains of the czar. The policy, adopted from 18th century absolutism in Western Europe, was formally reaffirmed in Article 17 of the "Code for Ecclesiastical Affairs Respecting Foreign Religions."

On the Italian peninsula, the termination of the Placet (or Exequatur) was tardy and reluctant. Cavour made a great deal of the slogan "a free Church in a free State," which he had borrowed from Montalembert. But as late as 1863 the newly declared Kingdom of Italy put into force a decree stating that any Church provision "emanating from an authority not residing in the Kingdom" could not be published or executed until it had received the royal Exequatur. Even in Italy, however, the trend of the times was recognized. Article 16 of the 1871 Law of Guarantees abolished, except for some categories, state interference in papal decrees. The concordat of 1929 finally wiped out the last traces of the Exequatur.

Thus by 1871 the constitutional law of the European states had evolved to a point where it made some sense to talk, as Visconti-Venosta did in the Italian Parliament, of a "spiritual sovereignty." By that time the State no longer generally speaking argued that sovereignty, by its very nature, had to extend to purely religious matters. In abdicating the old *jus circa sacra* in favor of the Holy See, the State abandoned the arguments drawn from the alleged indivisibility of sovereignty. The State willingly left a place for the exercise of papal authority within the country, independently of the civil power. It no longer served any purpose to describe the Pope as a "foreigner."

The new pattern of Church-State relations which now ensued was by no means one of harmony between the two sovereignties.

On the contrary, as we know from the history of the last decades of the 19th century and the first of the 20th, conflict was often bitter. The whole 19th century is frequently pictured as a period of almost unrelieved misfortune for the Catholic Church. It is not sufficiently recognized, however, that this was also the century of the triumph of ultramontanism. The very "state of siege" in which the Church lived contributed to strengthening the authority of the Roman Pontiffs. The condition of the Church was so grave that only the strong hand of centralized leadership could cope with the challenge. In France, the alienation of the clergy from the government upon which it had traditionally relied led, after 1830, even the most Gallican of the bishops to look to Rome for direction. In Germany the disintegration of the old medieval ecclesiastical structure raised problems whose solutions could be found only in Rome. In England and Ireland the Church suffered under the penal laws, the traces of which did not immediately disappear with the Emancipation Act of 1829. In Russian Poland, where Russification meant schism, the situation of the faithful was desperate. Spain, in the turmoil of several revolutions, ruptured with Rome on each occasion. Outside of Europe organizational problems evoked far-reaching exercise of the papal authority. In the New World the revolt of the Spanish colonies from the mother country called for reorganization of the Church in a politically divided hemisphere. It was at mid-century, too, that the Catholic Church in the United States developed through frequent provincial councils the basis of its present organization and orientation. At the same time missionary opportunities were opened to the Church, under pontifical direction, as they had not been since the flowering of the missions to the Indies in the 17th century.

Faced with despotic autocracy in Eastern Europe, the revolution in Western Europe, and unprecedented opportunities outside of Europe, Rome reacted with a strong hand in both discipline and doctrine. Its condemnations of de Lamennais in France and of Hermes in Germany earned for it the charge of being a fountain-head of reaction and the foe of liberty and of science. Later, this charge took on classic dimensions when the Syllabus of 1864 appeared. There was some foundation for these reproaches, for Rome could not easily forget what it had suffered in the name of liberty or ignore the doom openly prepared for it by unbelievers into whose hands the governments of many states were falling. In the middle of the 19th century such strong and uncompromising policy in Rome was accepted by the majority of Catholics, who welcomed the papal assertion of authority in the midst of political disorder and the growth of unbelief.

The governments themselves contributed to the triumph of ultramontanism by abolishing, of their own volition, the shackles and hindrances that had formerly kept the papal power in check in the name of regalism. More, the governments at mid-century had found it to their advantage to make use of the papal authority in their own behalf. A contemporary diplomatic dispatch paints for us in particularly sharp outline the attitude inspiring the European governments toward the papacy. On December 8, 1854 Pope Pius IX solemnly proclaimed the Immaculate Conception of the Blessed Virgin Mary as a dogma of the Catholic Faith. This event was to have its parallel (and sequel) almost a century later when on November 1, 1950 Pope Pius XII defined the dogma of the Assumption. The Rome of Pius IX witnessed such a concourse of bishops and faithful that could only strike the onlooker as a sign of the high state of papal prestige. Diplomatic observers, more concerned with the political aspect of the scene than with the purely religious nature of the occasion, could not refrain from reflecting on the remarkable change in papal fortunes in the recent years. In the first place, this prestige of the Pope as a spiritual leader was in sharp contrast to the low estate into which the Pope's temporal power had fallen. But, in the second place, this indication of the magnetic attraction of the Roman see as the guide of all Catholicity was a new thing. Thirty years earlier such a spectacle in Rome would have been inconceivable. The governments would not have allowed their bishops to go in such numbers (if at all) for such an occasion; Gallicans, Febronians, and Josephinists would hardly have presented themselves of their own desire. A political dispatch of the English semi-official agent a few days after the solemn event interpreted it against the background of the new status of Church-State relations.

This report merits quotation *in extenso*. It was sent from Rome by R. B. Lyons to Foreign Secretary Henry Lytton Bulwer, under date of December 11, 1854.

After commenting upon the decline of the papacy as a temporal sovereignty, the British semi-official agent resident in the Eternal City points out that this eclipse on the political plane had been counter-balanced by the rising prestige of the papacy in the eyes of the faithful. He pointed out that the governments themselves contributed to this development by seeking in Rome a solution to their domestic problems. The dispatch continues:

"It cannot however be denied that the power of the Pope over the Church at large is on the increase; a disposition is nearly everywhere manifested to appeal on all important questions to his authority, and absolute and implicit obedience to his decisions seems to be almost universally professed. The course of political events has, of late years, in a very remarkable manner favoured the tendency of the Roman Catholic Church toward centralization. In several countries the restrictions on ecclesiastical intercourse with Rome were swept away on ultra-liberal principles, during the troubles which followed the French Revolution of 1848. In some absolute states, and especially Austria, the governments have, with entirely different views, deliberately abandoned all control over the communications between the clergy and the Pope. Alarmed at the spread of socialist and revolutionary principles, these governments desired to oppose to them the influence of religion; they say that the Roman Catholic Church had lost its hold upon the people, by having come to be looked upon as a department of the State, and hoping that it might be more useful to them as an ally than as a dependent, they voluntarily abdicated the greater part of their sovereignty over it. They trusted to the natural bias of the Court of Rome and to their own influence there, to ensure them the support of the Pope, in their endeavor to maintain obedience among their subjects. And indeed, as long as the Pope is the absolute sovereign of a disaffected and discontented people, the Papal Court will always be likely to give aid and sympathy to governments in a similar situation. Moreover, the increasing difficulty in the present state of public feeling, of controlling the clergy in religious, or quasi-religious matters, by legislative enactments and penalties, appears to have produced an opinion among many statesmen, even in non-Catholic countries, that the most practical mode of checking violence on the part of the Roman Catholic clergy, is to come to an understanding on ecclesiastical matters with the Court of Rome.

"Rome seems to have adapted her policy with her usual tact and prudence to the actual state of things. She has abstained from attempting to mix directly in purely political affairs, and has apparently concentrated her ambitions on the two cardinal points, of rendering the Roman Catholic clergy in every country, as independent as possible of the State, and as dependent as possible upon herself. She has been on the watch to make herself the arbiter of disputes between the clergy and their governments. While she presents herself to the clergy as the inflexible maintainer of their influence and independence, she holds herself out to the Governments as full of moderation in the practical application of her principles, as anxious to compose strife, as free from local passions and prejudices, and as a calm and conciliating umpire."[21]

21 *Public Record Office. General Political Correspondence. Italy. Mr. Lyons. F. O. 43-58.* This report is apparently as yet unpublished. Its evidence of the change that had ensued in the middle of the 19th century in Church-State relations was duplicated a few months later in Prussia. In a report on the possibility of a papal nunciature in Berlin, Heinrich Abeken, Prussian privy councillor, submitted a memorandum reviewing the past policy of the Prussian rulers in their relations with Rome. The old system of using the Roman legation as a means of exerting control over the Catholic Church was passé, he wrote, and the new form of diplomatic relations had a different role, that of defending strictly political interests of the state in matters affecting the Catholic Church: "*Die Gesandtschaft in Rom ist nicht mehr eine Generalagenzie für die geistlichen Angelegenheiten, sondern eine wirkliche Gesandtschaft, welche allerdings auch die Interessen des Souveräns in Beziehung zur katholische Kirche, aber nicht als kirchliche, sondern als Staatsinteressen vertritt und wahrnimmt.*" This is from a *pro-memoria* dated Berlin, November 4, 1854 (cited by Bastgen, *Forschungen*, p. 670). Lord Lyons' viewpoint should also be read in the light of the controversy that had shortly before arisen when Pius IX, in a brief of September 29, 1850, reestablished the Catholic hierarchy in England. Commons reacted by passing an ecclesiastical titles act which, however, as Phillimore complains, was not enforced and indeed backfired. In denouncing the brief, Sir Travers Twiss alludes to the (up to then) general practice of requiring the consent of the civil authorities before establishing new sees. The decree of Pius IX, he argued, was not only a violation of English law but also contrary to the public law of Europe (*Letters Apostolic*, p. iv, pp. 67-69. See also Phillimore, *Commentaries*, II, p. 506). The viewpoint of Sir Travers Twiss, as well as the legislation enacted in the aftermath of the brief, did not long prevail. The act was not enforced and was finally repealed in 1871.

This analysis by the non-Catholic envoy of a non-Catholic government, couched in the terse and precise language of a professional diplomatic report, seizes the central points of the developments affecting the papacy at mid-century. The latter portion of the dispatch, incidentally, can usefully be read in the light of British policy in Ireland at that time.

The contrasting destinies shrewdly anticipated by Lord Lyons reached their climax at virtually the same time. On July 18, 1870 the Vatican Council solemnly defined the dogma of papal infallibility; and on September 20, a few weeks later, the white flag of capitulation run up on Castel Sant' Angelo meant the end of the papal states. Whereas the states who had intervened in 1815 and 1849 to save the temporal power did not in 1870 make a move to help the Pope, so those governments which in times past had subjected papal dogmatic decrees to the Placet did not in 1870 move to block an event that marked the final victory of the papacy over the Gallicans and other foes of the papal power. There were exceptions, but these only proved the rule. Catholic Bavaria raised the shield of the Placet, whether out of habit or under the impulsion of the Old Catholics who refused to submit to the decree. In Hungary and Croatia, under the Dual Monarchy, and in Württemberg and Baden the Placet was also applied. But not even Bismarck's Prussia thought of applying such a measure, either to approve or to block the decree. In Austria itself, though the government adduced the decree as a justification for abrogating the concordat of 1855 it did not revive the Placet. Stremayer, the minister of worship and education, in a report of July 25, 1870 declared that the Placet was an act of State interference that belonged to the *Polizeistaat* of the past two centuries and was out of place in the *Rechtstaat* of modern times.[22] For that reason no recognition was taken of the decree either to approve it or censor it.

Europe after 1870 was a new world for the spiritual leadership. If regalism was dead, laicism soon emerged as the chief antagonist of the papacy. The State was all the more ready to yield jurisdiction in purely Church matters in order to claim undisputed sway in everything else. It was glad to consign the Church to the sacristy while it strove to secularize every

[22] *Collectio Lacensis*, VII, col. 1718.

institution of the State, especially education. Once it was established that sovereignty was indeed divisible, the next question
was at what point the line of demarcation had to be drawn. In
1877 the French voters returned an anti-clerical majority to
the Chamber. This was the first stage in the long battle ultimately culminating in the rupture of diplomatic relations in
1904, and the repudiation, in the year following, of the Concordat of 1801. Anti-clericalism was potent for decades throughout Europe. Nevertheless the basic constitutional framework
had changed. Time was to prove the possibility, as Guizot had
once fondly hoped, of an understanding between Church and
State on terms of mutual respect. There were many ruptures
of diplomatic relations in the course of the history of Church-
State conflicts of the pre-World War I decades. But these did
not necessarily signify a rejection of papal spiritual sovereignty
any more than a diplomatic break between states at war implies
a denial of the respective sovereignties. On the contrary, the
resolution of the conflict invariably signaled the restoration of
diplomatic relations on a basis of even clearer recognition of
the inherent sovereignty of the Holy See. Today, in times of
normal relations, the states do not feel any longer that, in
negotiating through diplomatic channels with the Holy See
over domestic issues, they prejudice either the sovereign rights
or the national honor of the nation. They are reconciled to
the concurrent sovereignty of the Holy See over their own
citizens.

PART FOUR

TESTS AND CHALLENGES

CHAPTER 11

PAPAL DIPLOMATIC RELATIONS
IN TIME OF WAR

1915-1918 to 1940-1945

THE general European war in 1914 brought with it the first real test that the Italian Law of Guarantees had yet faced. Ever since this law had gone into effect in 1871 it had been the object of constant attacks by the Holy See, which never recognized its validity. The Vatican lost no occasion to point out its shortcomings as a law supposedly designed to guarantee the freedom of the Holy See. For its part the Italian government never let an opportunity go by to insist that the law was basically sound and that it gave no legitimate grounds for complaint. Among their arguments was the apparently satisfactory situation of the foreign diplomats living in Rome and accredited to the Vatican.

It is true that, up to the war, the foreign diplomats and their governments had relatively little to complain about regarding the operations of the Law of Guarantees or the attitude of the Italian government. Until Italy entered the First World War, incidents involving the members of the diplomatic corps or their personnel were few, or at least not publicized. Italy had no reason for creating difficulties with the home governments. The Law of Guarantees authorized all the privileges and immunities customarily enjoyed by diplomatic agents. As long as such prerogatives were respected, the foreign diplomats had no cause to inquire whether this treatment was given them in virtue of international law or in virtue of an act of the Italian parliament. Why should Italy provide a pretext for foreign intervention in the Roman question by imposing limitations on the official relations with the Holy See, when the

Bibliographical Note: The situation arising from the state of war as it affected the Vatican diplomatic corps must be pieced together out of memoirs or newspaper accounts. One valuable recent synthesis is to be found in Paul Duclos' study on the Vatican in the Second World War. Other possible sources cited only in the Bibliography are Boggiano-Pico, H. Johnson, Ireland, Salandra, and Wright.

Law of Guarantees itself did not require such limitations? On the contrary, the government found it useful to concern itself ostentatiously with the situation of the envoys, since this served to heighten the idea that these foreign representatives were guests, highly privileged though they were, of the Italian State.

Italy did not at once enter the war in 1914, and the problem of the diplomatic agents at the Vatican did not therefore arise automatically with the outbreak of hostilities. But in the spring of 1915 Italy began to take the road toward belligerency against the Central Powers. The question that had for so many decades remained untested now came to the fore. What should be the status of those Vatican envoys whose countries were in a state of war with Italy?

The Law of Guarantees was silent on this question. In the pre-1870 proposals for a settlement of the Roman question between the Pope and Italy, Cavour had favored, at least for the nuncios, a situation that would remain unchanged "even in time of war." This recommendation was not incorporated into the Law of May 13, 1871, and the records of debate show that the omission was deliberate. An amendment proposed by Deputy Corte on February 15, 1871 would have suspended all privileges and immunities not only of the ambassadors of the Holy See but even of the Pope himself, in the case of war between Italy and any other power. The same would hold in the case of a war in which Italy remained neutral, or in any other case which made such action necessary for the internal or external security of the state.[1]

Such a far-reaching proposal virtually made the operation of the Law of Guarantees contingent upon the discretion of the government at any time. This was much farther than any of the Italian leaders were willing to go. Rapporteur Bonghi asked Corte to withdraw his amendment. "I know the amendment that the honorable Deputy Corte has proposed," he said in the Chamber in reply, "but I beg of him to withdraw it because

---

[1] The Corte amendment as proposed in the Chamber of Deputies: "*Tutti i privilegi accordati al Papa, e che si riferiscono agli ambasciatori presso alla Sede Pontificia ed all'invio di telegrammi e di corrispondenza postali, saranno sospesi in caso di guerra tra l'Italia ed altre Potenze, in caso di guerra in cui l'Italia rimanga neutra, ed in qualunque altro caso che sembre necessario per la sicurezza interna ed esterna dello Stato.*"

it seems to me that it will only serve to raise difficulties that we cannot now provide for in this law."

Writing in 1921, Victor Emmanuel Orlando argued that the silence of the law was deliberately designed to leave to the Italian government of any future time a broad liberty of action. That law, he said, was the product of the golden age of the Italian parliament. "If this law, the result of the collaboration of so many great men, fails to consider and regulate the case of war, this was certainly not through negligence or lack of foresight. On the contrary, the parliamentary sources clearly show that the omission was noted and, in a certain sense, deliberately intended, on account of the difficulties of adequately formulating a general rule for such a case. These difficulties were, and are, almost insurmountable."[2]

The silence of the law was all the more reason to disturb partisans of the papal cause. The time of war was, for Filippo Crispolti, writing in 1905, the *ponte dell'asino* of the new system established unilaterally by Italy after the annexation of the papal states. At a time of particular tension between France and Italy in 1892, during which war seemed impending, papal circles expressed their fear that the Pope might find it necessary to leave Rome in order to safeguard his independence. In its issue of August 20, 1892 the *Civiltà Cattolica* published an article entitled, *"Della condizione del Papa in caso de guerra,"* in which the preoccupations of the Vatican were plainly reflected. Writing on the same hypothesis, the professor at the papal college for diplomats, Msgr. Alfredo Giobbio, pointed out that the Pope could not be said to "correspond freely" with the whole Catholic world if he could not maintain at the papal Court the spokesmen of the governments with which he was in diplomatic relations. The state of war anywhere, far from being a reason for interrupting or diminishing this contact, was rather a time for intensified diplomatic activity. The envoys accredited to the Holy See should, therefore, argued Giobbio, continue to enjoy the same status even though Italy was at war with their countries.[3]

---

[2] Orlando, *Miei Rapporti*, 2 ed., pp. 36-37.

[3] Giobbio, *Lezioni*, I, p. 355. The author took pains to warn his readers that in his discussion of the effect of the Law of Guarantees he was not to be interpreted as recognizing its validity.

The crisis with France in 1892 passed, and it was therefore only in 1915 that the problem came to plague everyone concerned. According to Orlando, it was Germany which took the first step. As war neared, the German ambassador to the Quirinal asked the Italian foreign minister on May 7 what intentions his government had in regard to the imperial minister to the Holy See. On the same day, Bavaria put the same question in the form of a *pro-memoria*. But certain sections of the Italian public had already brought the issue into open discussion.

Some Italians called for the suspension of Article 11 of the Law of Guarantees, which is the one guaranteeing diplomatic privileges and immunities of foreign diplomats. Writing for the *Corriere della Sera* of May 3, in an article entitled, *"I rappresentanti esteri presso il Vaticano et l'articolo 11 de la Legge delle Guarentigie di fronte ad un caso di guerra,"* Francesco Scaduto recalled the Corte amendment of 1871 and declared that the time had come to apply the principle therein expressed. The same authority, writing in the preface of a book published at this time, said: "It is not therefore merely a supposition that the envoys of the belligerent powers to the Holy See could avail themselves of their diplomatic immunities to plot more conveniently against us. Hence the necessity of suspending these immunities in the case that we should take the field." It was a secondary question, he said, whether the Corte amendment itself or some equivalent should come into force as a new law or by royal decree. The essential was that the immunities should be suspended in case of war, at least in respect to those governments with which Italy was in fact at war. Scaduto claimed that the government would show that it was motivated exclusively by security considerations if it extended the suspension only to these and not to the diplomatic corps as a whole or to the Pope himself.

The above views of Scaduto, a man then in retirement but qualified in the matter, were presented in a work on the same theme, *Il Papa, l'Italia et la guerra*, by Guglielmo Quadrotta. It would be idle, argued Quadrotta, to expect the diplomatic representatives of the enemy belligerents to leave Rome of their own free will and thus spare Italy the embarrassment of expelling them. What reason, he asked, would they have for leaving the Eternal City spontaneously? "Why should they wish to remove difficulties for the Italian government in the very moment of going to war with Italy?" It would be rather childish to expect a solution of this kind, he claimed. The possibility that the Vatican would take the step of solving the problem by itself asking these diplomats to go on "vacation" was also ruled out by the writer.[4]

Strange to relate, the possibility that Quadrotta excluded as the least likely was precisely the one which actually transpired. The diplomats of the Central Powers withdrew of their own accord. There was no need either for Italy to expel them or for the Vatican to ask them to leave. On the day that Italy entered World War I, the representatives of Prussia, Bavaria, and of Austria-Hungary accredited to the Holy See left for home. The Holy See for the rest of the war was without direct diplomatic contact in the Vatican itself with the Central Powers. Its passive legation in respect to them was inoperative.

While the departure of these diplomats was voluntary it was a consequence of the policy that the Italian government had decided to adopt. This is not to say that Italy sought to adopt a restrictive interpretation of the Law of Guarantees, as urged by Scaduto, Quadrotta, and others. On the contrary, the government policy was in general what it frankly considered a generous one. According to Orlando, who was minister of worship at that time, the Holy See would not only keep all the prerogatives expressly granted by the law for the time of peace; others not conceded expressly in the law but arising out of the circumstances of war would also be granted. Among these new facilities were the following: (1) the provisions concerning enemy aliens would not be applied in the case of officials in the service of the Holy See; (2) the higher ecclesiastical officers (cardinals, bishops, heads of religious orders) coming from enemy countries would be allowed free access to Rome.[5]

Consequently, when the German query arrived at the offices of the foreign minister on May 7, 1915 and was examined together by Premier Salandra, Sonnino, and Orlando, there was no hesitation. The government decided against the suspension

[4] Quadrotta, op.cit., p. 73.
[5] Orlando, op.cit., p. 38.

of Article 11. As far as they were concerned, since the law did not mention the case of war, they were at liberty to adopt a policy in wide freedom, as they saw fit in the circumstances.[6]

The three ministers were in agreement that the reply would have to be transmitted directly to the Pope. In the official viewpoint of Italy this was an internal matter to be discussed only between the Quirinal and the Vatican, "whose special sovereignty, guaranteed by our law, the Italian government was firmly decided to assure in every case, conformably to that law." To reply directly to the German ambassador to Italy in a question concerning his colleague accredited to the Holy See could be interpreted by some as conceding that there was an international question involved, an interpretation that Italy could not admit. The *pro-memoria* was therefore addressed to the Pope, who received it on May 10. In the accompanying letter the government stated that in consequence of its desire, according to the Law of Guarantees, to guarantee the Pope's "special sovereignty" it was ready to permit the envoys of the powers with which Italy was at war to remain in function at the papal Court. The note stipulated three conditions, however. The most significant of these for present purposes was the following: in the communication of the enemy diplomats with their home governments such correspondence was to be carried on through the Pope as intermediary. The Holy See would assume responsibility that no abuse of this facility occurred.

No reply, comment, or objection is known to have been received officially from the Vatican. On May 24 war was declared. On that evening special trains left Rome carrying the diplomats of the Central Powers, including those accredited to the Holy See. The next morning that carrying the ambassador of Austria-Hungary passed through Lugano, Switzerland. A later train carrying von Mühlberg, the minister of Prussia, stopped at the same city, where the diplomat got off. A still

---

[6] This is the question submitted in the German ambassador's note of May 7: "*Il Governo Reale è disposto a garantire la sicurezza della persona dei Ministri accreditati presso la Santa Sede, del loro personale, del loro domicilio, nonchè la libertà dei loro movimenti, che è la base indispensabile del libero esercizio delle loro funzioni diplomatiche? Inoltre saremmo grati se ci fossero fatte note le intenzioni del Governo Reale per ciò che riguarda l'attuazione pratica dei provvedimenti necessari a tale effetto*" (*Ibid.,* p. 68).

later train carrying Ritter von Grünstein, minister of Bavaria, arrived at Lugano, where he also got off. The representatives of the two countries prepared to set up their headquarters in Switzerland. The envoy of Austria-Hungary continued on to Vienna.

According to Orlando, there had been no further discussion of the situation of the diplomats prior to their departure. The exodus of the representatives of the Central Powers took place silently and without any declaration or communication. It was not until May 30, a week later, that the *Osservatore Romano* lifted the curtain somewhat upon the reasons that had motivated this departure. In what was obviously a semi-official declaration, it declared that reports alleging that the departure had been requested by the Pontiff were erroneous. It said that these diplomats had been obliged to leave Rome "because their remaining in our city, in the present circumstances, had become impossible." It was impossible, said the *Osservatore Romano,* not because their personal safety was in danger but because their position would have become "morally intolerable and unacceptable." The same newspaper amplified this explanation some months later when it declared on December 7, 1915, " We are informed that the Italian government did not guarantee the right of free, reciprocal, independent and coded correspondence between the ambassadors and their governments, but that it sought to subject this correspondence to a certain supervision, perhaps that of the Holy See itself." The reason why this clarification was offered to the public at that late date was that on the previous day a communiqué of the Stefani news agency had declared that the envoys of the Central Powers had of their own free accord decided to leave Rome in spite of the most formal assurances of the government that their personal safety and the privileges to which they had a right, according to the law, would be respected. The Stefani communiqué was confirmed in the Chamber on December 7, when Orlando insisted, "I repeat to the Chamber, in the most formal and definite fashion, that they left of their own and perfect free will."

There is no doubt that the envoys did leave of their own free will, but only because the conditions under which they could remain were unsatisfactory. An inkling of their point of view can be gathered from a dispatch published in the neutral Catholic press from Lugano, shortly after the arrival there of the German and Bavarian representatives. It was a matter of prestige. The envoys of Austria-Hungary, Prussia, and Bavaria, according to this account, took the view that their dignity prevented them from accepting the protection of a state which by the fact of war had become their enemy. It was not that the good faith of the Italian government was doubted for an instant. The representatives of the Central Powers thought that the proposal to utilize the papal diplomatic courier for their own diplomatic dispatches was inappropriate. It would have been unusual procedure, these diplomatic sources said, for envoys to send dispatches to their home governments through the medium of the very government to which they were accredited. In addition, considering the circumstances of war, episodes were bound to arise out of such a situation. Why should the Holy See take responsibility in the eyes of the Italian public for whatever these diplomats should write?

These reasons were substantial ones and together justify the decision to leave Rome. The tenor of the note of May 10 amounted to a declaration that Italy, which officially held that it was doing a favor to the Holy See anyway, was willing to extend a like favor to the diplomats of the countries upon whom it was just about to declare war. This would have indeed been an anomalous situation for the representatives of the Central Powers to find themselves in. Added to this abnormal relationship, the idea of using the Pope's own diplomatic courier for their own dispatches home was also bizarre, as presumably the correspondence would sometimes include matters then in the process of negotiation with the Holy See. Finally, as the coming months were to show, the relations that the Vatican continued to have with the Central Powers, even through far-off Lugano, were an occasion of suspicion and accusations by various Italian critics. What would have been the case if the Holy See had formally assumed responsibility for the avoidance of abuses?

Though the representatives of the Central Powers left Rome without comment, the opportunity to embarrass Italy was too good to be neglected. All during the war political capital was made out of the fact that the Law of Guarantees had not, in reality, served to guarantee the full independence of the Pope at the very time of war, when he needed his independence the most. In Germany and Austria wide discussion, encouraged by the governments, took place on the issue of the Roman question. Erzberger took an active interest in projects being elaborated for a settlement of the long-standing dispute between Italy and the Vatican. While the Allies sought to minimize, when they could not ignore, the handicaps suffered by the Pope under the existing system, the Central Powers ostentatiously expressed solicitude for the Holy Father, cut off from direct official contacts with one of the belligerent blocs. Catholic writing of this period also reflected the political currents. French and Belgian literature was discreetly reserved on the subject, while German and Austrian Catholic studies abounded.

For instance, Ulrich Lampert, a Catholic writing in 1916, charged that the withdrawal of the diplomatic missions from the Vatican was a substantial diminution of the Pope's right of legation. He charged that even the communication of the Pope's own nuncios abroad was not free and safe, despite Italy's protestations that it was. He said, in addition, that even the Vatican's diplomatic pouch destined for the envoys at Lugano had been tampered with. This, he said, was a consequence of accusations already made by anti-clericals and others in France and Italy that the Pope was serving as a spy in the interests of the Allies' enemies.[7]

The accusation that the Vatican was being used as a spy center was fed by the sensational trial of a German ecclesiastic belonging to the papal secretariat of state. This prelate, Msgr. Rudolf von Gerlach, was accused of having used the papal diplomatic pouch for espionage purposes. The correspondent of *Le Temps*, Jean Carrère, writing at the opening of the trial in Rome in the issue of April 14, 1917, stated without qualification that Monsignor von Gerlach had conducted his (alleged) espionage through the means of the Vatican's diplomatic pouch, slipping his information therein and receiving through the

[7] Lampert, *Völkerrechtliche Stellung*, p. 56. On Erzberger's plans for a solution of the Roman question, see Epstein, *Matthias Erzberger*, pp. 144-48.

same channel both information and money. However, the Italian military tribunal in its verdict of June 23 absolved the Holy See from any connection with the case, while finding the accused and his accomplices guilty. The tribunal particularly emphasized that the Vatican's diplomatic correspondence had not been employed for such purposes. The text of the decision published in *Le Temps* of June 26, 1917, as far as it concerned the Vatican, is as follows: "The tribunal does not even pause to discuss the defense's allegation that immunity and extraterritoriality are involved in the case. It has been clearly proved that Gerlach had disobeyed the formal and severest orders of the Holy See, just as it has been proved that, for the transmittal of the information, the use of the Vatican's own diplomatic pouch must be absolutely ruled out and that Gerlach used his own and special means. The Holy See is therefore absolutely not involved in the criminal acts. On the other hand, these acts did not transpire in the Vatican: Gerlach performed his criminal acts not as a prelate but as a simple individual." The *London Times* of August 8, 1917 assigned a minor role to this controversial and curious personality. Gerlach abandoned orders after the war. In 1940 the Nazis reported he had fled to Canada and charged him with consorting with British agents before the war.

The Gerlach case was only the most sensational instance in which the foes of the papacy in Italy and France sought to link the Vatican with the espionage of the Central Powers. These latter, for their part, adduced the same episodes and rumors as illustrating the essentially impossible position forced upon the Pope by depriving him of his own territorial sovereignty.

Orlando acknowledges in his memoirs of this period that the propaganda based on the withdrawal of the envoys compelled a formal reply by the government. On June 1, 1915 the official declaration was made in the Chamber of Deputies that the Law of Guarantees had not been suspended in respect to those diplomats. On the contrary, said the government, when this question was brought to the attention of the Consulta by the German embassy the reply was that the special sovereignty of the supreme Pontiff was guaranteed by the law and that the

Italian government was determined to maintain it in every case, in conformity with that law. "There was added," said the statement, "the assurance that the envoys of the foreign Powers to the Holy See could in every eventuality reside freely in Rome, and that the Italian government would take every possible measure to guarantee their security."[8] The statement did not mention, however, the restrictions that Italy had stipulated to the Vatican in its note of May 10.

What was the reaction of the Holy See to this situation? As already seen, the Consulta of the Italian government, comprising Premier Salandra, Foreign Minister Sonnino, and Minister of Justice and of Worship Orlando, was unanimous that the issue of the envoys called for direct contact with the Vatican alone. It was stated explicitly in the note of May 10 that "there is question here not of relations between the Italian state and foreign states, but of a question of relations between the Italian state and the Supreme Pontiff. . . ." In short, this action implied that the status of the diplomats was not a matter of international law but of internal Italian law.

This approach could not be accepted at the Vatican, which had never recognized the Law of Guarantees. The papal secretariat of state of His Holiness refused to reply to this note for the same reasons that the Consulta refused to reply to the original *pro-memoria* of the Germans. There were no official relations, of course, between the Quirinal and the Vatican and it can be supposed that the note of May 10 was transmitted through Orlando's own subordinate and friend, Baron Monti, director general of the *Fondo per il Culto,* who enjoyed personal friendship with Benedict XV and whom Orlando confessed he employed on more than one occasion for similar missions.

The question of form and principle aside, on which both the Quirinal and the Vatican understood each other perfectly, it was natural that the Pope should take the first occasion offered him after the envoys' departure to allude to the practical effects of the Law of Guarantees therein manifested. His first public allusion was made in a consistorial allocution of December 6, 1915, *Nobis Profecto.* He declared that the absence of the diplomatic representatives of one of the belligerent

---

[8] Orlando, *op.cit.,* p. 73.

groups in the war was a serious limitation of his independence and could be attributed directly to the status quo against which he and his predecessors had protested since 1870.

The Pontiff continued: "But who can deny that this is now even more evident today? No doubt the good will of the rulers of Italy was not lacking to remove the handicaps. But this fact alone shows clearly that the position of the Roman pontiff depends on the civil power and that this position, with the change of times and of men, can itself change and even become worse. No man of judgment can say that this situation of the pontiff, uncertain and subject to the arbitrary will of others, is such as becomes the Apostolic See. In any case, many serious difficulties would remain. To omit others, it is enough to note today that some of the envoys of foreign governments have been obliged to depart for the sake of safeguarding their mission and their dignity. As a consequence we witness how the ordinary and peculiarly apt instrument which the Apostolic See is accustomed to employ in dealing with foreign governments has been both diminished and eliminated. It is especially regrettable in this matter that the situation has gone so far that among the belligerents of the other side the suspicion can arise that, in affairs concerning the belligerents, We almost necessarily are judging and acting on the basis of those viewpoints which alone come to our attention."

In sum, the Pontiff complained that the Law of Guarantees left too much to the discretion of the Italian government, in time of war particularly. While paying full tribute to the good faith of that government, Benedict XV pointed out that it was not compatible with the dignity of the Holy See to be dependent in such wise upon the good will of any government at any time. The Italians themselves, by their interpretations of the Law of Guarantees, had created the impression abroad that they were obligated in nothing to the Holy See and that what they did for the Pope and for his envoys were free concessions without commitments for the future. The absence of all the Central Powers' representatives from the papal Court strengthened the fear that the aims and policies of one of the belligerents were not adequately presented to the supreme head of the Catholic Church who enjoyed such a penetrating moral influence on vast numbers of Europeans.

The protest of the Pope on December 7 had no other effect than to add new arguments to an old debate. Later on in the war, by a decree of August 25, 1916, Italy seized the former Austrian embassy to the Vatican on the Piazza Venezia. The protests raised on this occasion by the Vatican had likewise no other effect than to manifest the inability of the papacy to protect the rights of the diplomatic missions accredited to it and, by the same token, add still another item to the long list of grievances which the Holy See had against the status quo.

The outbreak of World War II found the papacy reconciled with Italy and, what is more, in possession of a tiny bit of territory in the center of Rome over which it exercised unchallenged sovereignty. Basically, therefore, the situation of the envoys accredited to the Vatican was quite different from that which had faced their forerunners in 1915. Their position was in theory the same as that of their colleagues living in any neutral country, such as Switzerland, surrounded on all sides by states at war. But the neutrality of the Vatican was anything but the "armed neutrality" of Switzerland. Could the symbolic acres in the center of the Eternal City avoid being engulfed in the events that the surge of war was to bring to the Italian capital?

The area surrounding the State of Vatican City was controlled successively by three political forces whose respective attitudes toward the papacy were different. The Italy of Mussolini was party to the Lateran accord and therefore had a formal reason for respecting the neutrality of the Vatican. When the German military authorities took over Rome after Badoglio's armistice with the Allies in 1943, they followed suit in respecting that neutrality. No change ensued when the Allies, driving up from the south, entered the city in June 1944. No doubt there must have been moments in the course of those years when the independence of the Vatican territory and even the inviolability of the Pontiff himself hung in the balance. It is believed that Hitler contemplated seizing the Pope and was only awaiting a favorable moment, a change for the better in his military and political fortunes, to bring this about. Rumors were constant during the war that the Pope might find it necessary to leave Rome for the sake of freedom from political pressure or physical violence. The Lateran treaty held firm, however, and the respect that the successive masters of Rome maintained for the neutrality of Vatican territory was a kind of international sanction of what was, in its origins, a bilateral treaty between Italy and the Holy See.

The war, then, brought a particular confirmation and sanction of Article 24 of the Lateran Treaty, according to which the Vatican City would be "always and in every case considered neutral and inviolable territory." But what was the fate of Article 12, which deals with the active and passive legation of the Holy See, that is to say, with the status of the nuncios and other diplomatic agents dispatched by the Holy See and those other diplomats of states accredited at the Vatican?

The provisions of this article are vague concerning wartime. When the active legation of the Holy See is treated there is no obscurity. Even in time of war, the diplomatic agents *sent* by the Holy See, as well as the papal messengers, continue to enjoy on Italian soil the same privileges and immunities, according to international law, given to such agents and couriers on the territory of third states. At the same time the Holy See is guaranteed, "always and in every case," freedom of correspondence with all states, including belligerents.

The above provisions, as noted, regard the exercise of active legation by the Vatican. As concerns the passive legation, or the status of the diplomats of foreign powers received by the Vatican, the second paragraph of Article 12 is less clear. It states that "the envoys of the foreign governments to the Holy See continue to enjoy in the Kingdom all the privileges and immunities applying to diplomatic agents according to international law and their residences can continue to remain on Italian territory enjoying the immunities due them according to the norms of international law, *even if their states do not have diplomatic relations with Italy*" (italics added).

When the shadows of war began to lengthen over Europe, this last clause preoccupied the diplomats of the Vatican in Rome. The Lateran Treaty was hardly less reticent than the old Law of Guarantees on the subject of belligerency. Considering the earlier experiences during the First World War, this omission can only have been deliberate. One of the most authentic published accounts of this phase of Vatican diplomatic history is that of François Charles-Roux, the French ambassador to the Vatican at that time.

In his book *Huit ans au Vatican*, the French ambassador writes that as war seemed more and more imminent he pressed the papal secretary of state, Cardinal Maglione, to clarify in advance the position that the Italian government was likely to assume in regard to the diplomats of the countries against which Italy was contemplating a declaration of war. Would these diplomats continue to enjoy the same privileges and immunities on Italian soil? Or would they be required to withdraw, as the diplomats of the Central Powers had withdrawn in 1915?

Discussions between Cardinal Maglione and the Italian foreign ministry produced the information that in the Italian view the crucial paragraph of Article 12 did *not* apply to those envoys in time of war. The Italian government remained unmoved in this restrictive interpretation despite representations by the papal nuncio at the Quirinal. As a consequence, in May 1940, when Italy seemed on the verge of war with France, the papal secretariat of state circulated a memorandum to the missions accredited to the Vatican, stating that, since the Italian government could give no guarantees for the missions on Italian soil of those countries with whom she was at war, these delegations would be received within Vatican territory, should they wish to retire to this refuge. (Normally, all diplomatic missions are located, not in the Vatican City but in Rome). The memorandum added that on account of the shortage of space, it would be possible to accommodate only the ambassador and his family, with a secretary. In the aftermath, when Italy declared war on France and Great Britain the respective French and British envoys withdrew into the Vatican precincts. Their countrymen belonging to the sister diplomatic mission accredited to Italy naturally were repatriated.[9]

---

[9] Charles-Roux, *op.cit.*, pp. 380-82.

As the fortunes of war changed and the city of Rome came to be occupied by the Allies, those diplomats who had lived in the Vatican since 1940 were able to resume their former place of residence. It was then the turn of the Axis diplomats to take up their domicile in the Vatican. These included the representatives of Germany, Hungary, Finland, and Japan. At this point, however, it appears that the Holy See renewed its contention that the provisions of the Lateran Treaty guaranteed to the diplomats the right of immunity on Italian territory even during war. If this viewpoint were accepted by the new military masters of Rome, the Axis diplomats would not have to take refuge in the Vatican. An article published in the Catholic paper, *Il Quotidiano*, on June 13, 1944 recalled the thesis upheld by the Vatican in 1940 with the Italian foreign ministry to the effect that Article 12 of the Lateran Treaty should be interpreted as guaranteeing the security of the envoys on Italian territory even in time of war. This thesis was apparently argued anew before the Allied authorities, this time for the benefit of the Axis diplomats. The statement of the newspaper implied that the Allied authorities had ordered the Axis diplomats to leave Rome within forty-eight hours, that is to say, to withdraw to the Vatican. Unable to make its contention prevail on this second occasion, the Vatican was at least able to secure a lengthening of the period within which those diplomats were to leave the area occupied by the Allies. The pretext for this delay was the inconvenience and hardship that would be caused the Allied diplomats, some of whom had lived in the Vatican since 1940, but who would have to be displaced if the order were carried out as planned.

In his memoirs the German ambassador, Ernst von Weiszacker, reports that when the Allied armies entered Rome he withdrew to the ambassador's residence at Villa Bonaparte, bringing with him all his staff. They were obliged to remain there, presumably while the Vatican secretariat of state and the Allies were arguing the interpretation of Article 12. Some weeks later the German embassy was ordered to go to the Vatican, where, however, only half of the staff could be accommodated.[10]

---

[10] Weiszacker, *Erinnerungen*, p. 367.

The secretary of the Yugoslav legation and the United States chargé d'affaires, Harold Tittmann, Jr., moved into the Vatican with their families in 1941. The representatives of all the Latin American republics having diplomatic relations with the Vatican, and at war with Germany, soon did likewise. The minister of China and his secretary took up residence there in 1943.[11]

The situation of Poland and Belgium was rather exceptional. The Polish ambassador, Papée, never took up residence in the Vatican. Poland having already been invaded by the Nazis and liquidated politically before Italy entered the war on the side of the Axis, a state of war between the two countries was impossible, according to the Italian viewpoint. Italy did not declare war on Belgium in 1940 and when subsequently the Belgian government in exile declared it considered itself at war with Fascist Italy, that government refused to acknowledge the existence of a state of war. As long as the Mussolini government controlled Rome, the Belgian embassy was not interfered with. For the sake of form the Belgian representative did withdraw to Vatican City for about four months but soon afterward returned to his usual residence and offices. A slight change transpired when the Nazis took over Rome, at which time the Belgian ambassador was informed, not too peremptorily, that he should leave Italian territory. After lengthy postponements the envoy did go to the Vatican a few days prior to the arrival of the Allied forces. The archives of the embassy were sealed by the nuncio to Italy, Archbishop Borgongini-Duca, who acted as protector of the enemy diplomatic missions in the Italian capital.

Mention has already been made of Harold Tittmann, Jr., Myron Taylor's assistant in Rome, who retired to the Vatican after Pearl Harbor. What was the status of the Taylor mission in the eyes of Italy and the Vatican? Mr. Taylor was absent from Rome when Italy declared war on the United States. He was permitted to cross Italian territory on only one occasion

---

[11] Anon., in *Tablet*, 1943-1944. The Yugoslav envoy, Mirosevic Serge Niko, was at first allowed to remain in the Italian capital but later encountered the suspicion of the fascist government. Despite vigorous Vatican protests he was in mid-July 1941 ordered out of the country and prevented from taking refuge in the Vatican. The rest of the Yugoslav staff, however, was allowed to go to papal territory. Cf. Roberto Ago, in *Istituto di diritto internazionale*, 1946, p. 135n.

while the Mussolini government was in control of Rome. On September 17, 1942 Secretary of State Cordell Hull announced at a press conference that Mr. Taylor would return to Rome for "a brief stay" and added that it would be "fair to assume" that arrangements for his safe-conduct through Italy had been made. The personal representative of the president landed at an Italian military airport outside of Rome and on September 28, his business completed, he returned to the United States by the same route. The official Italian press ignored his presence. Permission to pass through Italy was not again granted and Mr. Taylor was able to revisit the Pope only after the occupation of Rome by the Allies in June 1944. But in the interval, Mr. Tittmann was in residence in the Vatican, in company with the diplomats of the Allied powers.

It is now known that the Italian foreign office refused to recognize that Tittmann had any diplomatic standing entitling him to withdraw into the Vatican under the same circumstances as those of representatives formally accredited to the Holy See. Tittmann's official position, according to the *Annuario Pontificio*, was simply that of "Assistant to the Personal Representative of the President of the United States to His Holiness." This is not a diplomatic title. In that case, two consequences logically followed. If Tittmann wished to remain in Rome, his status could be only that of an enemy alien. If he chose to return to the United States, he would have to depart as a private citizen and not with the diplomatic train carrying the members of the American embassy to Italy.

The solution to that difficulty was obvious and simple. Washington named Tittmann chargé d'affaires of the United States to the Holy See. This is the lowest rank of diplomatic agent recognized in international law, but it was sufficient to enable the American representative to perform his functions in the Vatican until 1944. (The nature and circumstances of the Tittmann appointment as chargé are discussed in the next chapter.)

A foreign representative is of little use if he is not able to communicate with his own government. It would have served no purpose for the diplomats of the various belligerent powers to take residence in the Vatican if they were unable to send or receive official dispatches. As a matter of fact the Vatican authorities could theoretically admit any person they so desired upon the sovereign territory of Vatican City. During the war this prerogative, inherent in territorial sovereignty, was employed to give sanctuary to numerous political refugees from the Fascist and Nazi police. The crux of the problem was not the question of residence but rather that of correspondence. The freedom and immunity of diplomatic correspondence depended not on the Holy See alone but also upon Italy, across whose territory such dispatches had to be carried.

Article 12 of the Lateran Treaty guarantees the freedom of correspondence of the Holy See with all states, including belligerents, at all times. This could legitimately be interpreted as including as well the right of the diplomats accredited to the Holy See to enter into direct contact with their own governments. Reciprocal diplomatic representation is one of the means of this correspondence which in turn implies unimpeded communication in both directions. A dispatch telephoned to *Le Temps* of Paris by its Roman correspondent on May 31, 1940, a few hours before Italy declared war, shows that the issue of correspondence was very much in the minds of the French embassy to the Holy See at that fatal moment. The correspondent pointed out that there was no point for the French or any other Allied envoy to remain in the Vatican if he was to be isolated from his government. The freedom of correspondence is guaranteed to the Holy See, he recalled, but the question is how that correspondence is to be transmitted. Then there was also the question of the changes of diplomatic personnel that might periodically become necessary. "It remains to be found out," he concluded, "how the transmittal of the correspondence and the diplomatic journeys will be guaranteed."

Just what arrangements were entered into between Italy and the Holy See concerning the facilities to be enjoyed by the diplomats in the matter of official dispatches has never been published. Some system satisfactory to all concerned was arrived at, as might be judged from the lack of protests during the war from any of the parties who might have had cause for grievance. It does not seem likely that, normally, the diplomats enjoyed the use of their own diplomatic pouch or courier.

Such a facility is not guaranteed them in the Lateran Treaty. On the other hand, the Vatican's own right to continue to send couriers with diplomatic dispatches is explicitly stated in Article 12.

It is not improbable that Italy revived its offer of 1915 by which the diplomats of the Central Powers would retain their right to correspond with the home government, provided the Holy See assumed responsibility that no abuses occurred. In the Italian proposal the diplomatic dispatches of Austria-Hungary, Prussia, and Bavaria would not be in code and would be transmitted by the Vatican's own messengers. Although this offer was turned down in 1915 as impractical and foreign to diplomatic usage, some such system must have been in operation during World War II, by the mutual agreement of all concerned. Such a supposition is supported by a document published after the war but stated to have been drafted July 6, 1943 and discussed at a meeting that took place at an undisclosed place in France under the German occupation. The paper's author was François Charles-Roux, ambassador at the Vatican in 1940, who became a high officer in the French foreign ministry after leaving Rome. According to this paper the Fascist government in 1940 was not at first willing for the French and other Allied diplomats to withdraw into the Vatican, much less remain in Rome proper. One of the difficulties was that of communication. On this subject the qualified reporter states: "Our own embassy after June 10, 1940 could not communicate with us except by means of the diplomatic pouch of the Holy See between the Vatican and the Apostolic Nunciature in Berne. The nuncio delivered to our ambassador in Switzerland the letters destined for our foreign ministry. The answers went by the same route." The writer professed ignorance of the means by which other governments received the reports of their envoys immured in Vatican City: "Could the minister of England, for instance, or the ambassador of Brazil, or the chargé d'affaires of the United States, communicate with their governments or use the Vatican's radio to send or to receive coded telegrams? I have no positive information on this point." He said he would be surprised if the Holy See would allow these diplomats to use coded messages over Radio Vatican: "I should rather believe that communication, an essential requirement for diplomatic action, was possible for those countries accredited to the Vatican, but at war with Italy, only after delays, through the Holy See's own facilities and under its responsibility (*au ralenti, sous le couvert du Saint-Siège et sous sa responsabilité*).[12] Guariglia, a fascist official who had reason to be well informed on this matter, seems to imply that the arrangement included coded telegrams which the British, American, and other envoys in Vatican City sent and received at various times during the war.[13]

The lack of direct information even today on the problem of communication during World War II is no doubt the result of the discretion that had to be observed at that time. The method of communication that seems to have been employed was a dangerous one for the Holy See. It exposed the Pope to charges that Vatican diplomatic facilities were used to transmit military information. Even if the diplomats put themselves on their word of honor not to use the pouch for security matters, opinions could easily differ as to what constituted military information. In any case, the relative absence of publicized complaints or protests during the war, by contrast to 1915-1918, was a tribute to the prudence exercised by all parties.

If the First World War showed the serious limitations of the papacy's international diplomatic position, the second global conflict, coming after the Pope had become sovereign of at least the few acres of Vatican City, showed that the passive legation could survive and be of effective use to the governments. It also showed that the Holy See could guarantee and defend the prerogatives of the foreign agents accredited to it. This was accomplished not by the use or threat of arms, but by moral and legal means that proved just as effective.

[12] Charles-Roux, in *Monde français*, 1946.
[13] Guariglia, *Ricordi*, p. 586.

CHAPTER 12

UNITED STATES-VATICAN RELATIONS

AN INTERPRETATION OF
THE MISSION OF MYRON C. TAYLOR

A FTER the departure of Rufus King from Rome as United States minister-resident in 1868, under the circumstances described in a previous chapter, the occasions of official relations between the two parties were few and far between. Unless one includes the representation of President Franklin Delano Roosevelt by Joseph B. Kennedy, then American ambassador at London, at the enthronement of Pius XII, there were no direct relations between the United States and the Vatican that could be called diplomatic in any strict sense until the outbreak of the Second World War.

On December 23, 1939 on the approach of the first Christmas of the war, announcement was made at the White House that President Roosevelt intended to send Myron C. Taylor as his "personal representative" to the Pope, with the rank of ambassador. The purpose of the mission of Mr. Taylor, who was not a Catholic and who was not in politics, would be to endeavor to further the parallel peace efforts of the president and the Holy Father. At the same time, it was announced, Mr. Roosevelt had addressed letters to certain prominent Protestant and Jewish leaders in the United States inviting their cooperation with him in his efforts to advance the cause of peace throughout the world.

In due time, Mr. Taylor arrived at the Vatican, where on February 27, 1940 he was received by the Pope with full diplo-

Bibliographical Note: The memoirs and correspondence of Cordell Hull and Myron C. Taylor, as well as the life of Harry Hopkins by Robert Sherwood and the study of William S. Langer and S. Everett Gleason, are first-class sources, if essentially fragmentary. On the Taft mission see also Farrell and Goss. Some considerations on U.S.-Vatican relations were published in *America* by the present author in 1951 and 1953. Perhaps the most complete survey to date of all episodes involving U.S.-Vatican relations, from 1779 until the 1951 appointment of Gen. Mark Clark by President Truman, is that prepared by Martin F. Hasting, S.J. This doctoral thesis (Univ. of California) deals mainly with the problems of recognition and representation, but it provides a generous bibliography and presents hitherto unpublished State Department and other archival material.

matic honors. He did not take up permanent residence in Rome but made frequent visits, including one while Italy and the United States were in a state of hostilities. An assistant, however, Harold Tittmann, Jr. (mentioned in Chapter 11) remained on the spot and, after Italy's declaration of war upon the United States, moved with his family into the Vatican City precincts for the duration of the war. After the death of Roosevelt, President Truman sent Taylor again to Rome on May 3, 1946, according him the same title of "personal representative" and the rank of ambassador. This phase of American-Vatican relations came to an end after ten years when Mr. Taylor, who was then 76, resigned on January 18, 1950, after having taken part with the diplomatic corps in the ceremonies opening the Holy Year. Shortly afterward, the assistant and secretary constituting the Vatican office in Rome were reassigned elsewhere. But although this unique decade of diplomatic history had come to such a complete termination it had left behind it precedents and experience that inevitably would influence in great measure the pattern of future relations between the United States and the sovereign Pontiff. An analysis of some of the characteristic problems posed by the mission of Mr. Taylor is therefore in order.

A question pertinent to the object of the present study is whether and to what extent this mission constituted diplomatic relations between the United States and the Holy See. Various aspects and formalities of the case tend to obscure the exact character of Mr. Taylor as a representative of the United States. On the one hand, it is certain that he was not an ambassador appointed in the usual way. According to the United States Constitution, such appointments must normally be confirmed by the Senate. At no time was Mr. Taylor's status as the president's personal representative with rank of ambassador submitted to the Senate for such action. On the contrary, in what was meant to be a clarification issued on December 27, 1939 by the White House spokesman, it was stated that "the President has the right under the Constitution to send a personal representative to any place, at any time, or on any occasion. There is no reason why it [*the newly announced mission*] should lead to any assumption that it is a diplomatic move."

Somewhat later, in a letter addressed to Dr. George A. Buttrick, president of the Federal Council of the Churches of Christ in America, on March 14, 1940, Mr. Roosevelt wrote: "Mr. Taylor is in Rome as my personal representative. This appointment does not constitute the inauguration of formal diplomatic relations with the Vatican. The President may determine the rank for social purposes of any special representative he may send; in this case the rank corresponding to ambassador was obviously appropriate."[1] In addition, no funds were ever appropriated by Congress or were ever asked for. A White House special contingency fund was called on to meet the expenses of the mission. Mr. Taylor himself served without recompense.

But in face of declarations coming from the White House that Mr. Taylor's mission did not constitute formal diplomatic relations with the Vatican, in Rome a different interpretation was taken. The president's "personal representative" was received by the Pope with the honors usually accorded to diplomatic representatives. For his part Mr. Taylor took no step which authorized the Vatican to conclude he was not a diplomatic representative. He took his place with the other envoys accredited to the Holy See and was accepted by them as one of themselves. He was furnished by the president with a letter which in substance, though not in form, amounted to letters of credence. He was listed from the start in the *Annuario Pontificio* as a member of the diplomatic corps, with the date of presentation of his "Letters of Credence." Neither President Roosevelt nor his representative communicated to the Vatican, certainly not publicly, any of the denials communicated to the American public concerning the diplomatic status of the mission. Abroad it was generally recognized that the newly invented formula of "personal representative" with the rank of ambassador was only one more device employed by the young Republic in the New World to get around constitutional difficulties that the Old World had difficulty understanding. Outside the United States, Mr. Taylor was regarded for all practical intents and purposes as the diplomatic representative of the United States.[2]

[1] Cited in Stokes, *Church and State*, ii, p. 104. Abundant documentation can be found in this balanced treatment (ii, pp. 85-112).

[2] See, for instance, Nava, *Sistema*, p. 75.

Having given the form he did to the Taylor mission, President Roosevelt could not at his will declare that this did not constitute diplomatic relations. The forms of international intercourse are not subject to arbitrary interpretations made by only one party in question. This is especially true when as in the present case the interpretations had their origins in purely internal constitutional and political considerations. Of such matters, neither the Vatican nor the international community were obliged to take cognizance. As far as the Pope and the general world public were concerned, it was clear from the circumstances that it was the desire of President Roosevelt that Mr. Taylor be and act as a diplomatic representative.

The title of "personal representative" carried by the presidential envoy, far from weakening his diplomatic standing, only strengthened it. Every ambassador is theoretically a personal representative, as the historical origins of embassies attest. When one considers that according to the United States Constitution the president is charged with the determination and conduct of foreign policy and was in fact at that critical moment of world conflict exercising this prerogative personally, it might be conceded that the title of president's personal representative only enhanced the diplomatic standing of Mr. Taylor in the eyes of the Vatican and of the international community. It goes without saying that the title "personal representative" was not intended to mean that Mr. Roosevelt's private business was in question.

It remains, however, that Mr. Taylor was not accredited to the Holy See in the manner customary in established diplomatic practice. Under the circumstances the Holy See was justified in treating him as a diplomatic agent as at least a gesture of courtesy, in the interests of cooperation for peace, a gesture which is, just the same, not without meaning for international law. But it was conceivable that the Holy See wished to reserve its right not to extend the same consideration to any other person whom the president might wish to send under the same formula at a future date. The fight that the papacy waged after 1870 for the integrity and unambiguity of its right of active and passive legation, described in previous chapters, suggested that it might disapprove as a permanent practice the dispatch of envoys whose exact diplomatic status was not crystal-clear.

The desire that the "personal representative" phase of U.S.-Vatican relations come to an end was expressed by Pius XII in a letter sent to President Truman under date of July 10, 1952. In that letter the Pontiff said that the status of Myron Taylor had been a provisional one and that it should be regularized. We learned about this letter in a comment published in the *Osservatore Romano* of February 12, 1953. The danger was, of course, that the other countries might seek to imitate the United States. The Holy See does not wish to see a repetition of the Rooseveltian formula of a "personal representative." Today, said the newspaper, it is evident that there could be "no question of anything but an official and stable diplomatic representation."

Did President Roosevelt and the State Department realize in 1939 that the United States was treading a well-beaten path when they adopted this formula? Earlier chapters have shown how Prussia, Russia, and Great Britain found themselves obliged to transact business with the Pope but unable or unwilling for domestic legal or political reasons to give these relations regular diplomatic form. They avoided as long as they could sending diplomatic missions to the Holy See. In their place were conceived various formulae which had this common feature that they were refusals to face realities and served in the end only to the disadvantage of the states which persevered in them. What the United States contributed in 1939, was simply a new formula to evade the same reality. In this respect, the mission of Myron C. Taylor, "personal representative of the President of the United States, with rank of ambassador," presents little that is essentially new in diplomatic history.

If the position of Mr. Taylor was exceptional and therefore open to various interpretations, there is no ambiguity over the standing of his assistant, Mr. Harold H. Tittmann, Jr., whose appointment as chargé d'affaires was officially communicated to the Holy See within a few days after Italy's declaration of war upon the United States on December 11, 1954. Mr. Tittmann retained this title for the two and a half years that he resided in Vatican City, that is, until the liberation of Rome by the Allied troops. Chargés d'affaires, as we are told by Green Hackworth in his *Digest of International Law*, are "diplomatic representatives of the third class, commissioned by the President and accredited by the Secretary of State to the Minister for Foreign Affairs of the country to which they are sent."[3] The term, he adds, is used to denote the officer in charge of a diplomatic mission to which an ambassador or minister has not been appointed or from which an ambassador or minister has been withdrawn. Though this kind of officer is of the lowest rank of diplomatic agent, his rank is nevertheless clearly diplomatic. In the person of Mr. Tittmann, therefore, the United States maintained diplomatic relations with the Vatican during the first years of war after Pearl Harbor.

The circumstances of this appointment are characteristic and revelatory of U.S.-Vatican relations in the recent past and perhaps for the future as well. When Italy declared war upon the United States, arrangements were naturally made for the repatriation of their respective diplomatic missions from Rome and Washington. Mr. Taylor was not in Rome at that time. Mr. Tittmann, according to newspaper reports, withdrew into the Vatican precincts and there joined company with the British, French, Polish, and Yugoslav diplomats who had already been in residence for some months. We know now that the Italian government raised difficulties at this point. Mr. Tittmann had been recognized up to then only as "Assistant to the Honorable Mr. Taylor." This was not a rank entitling him to take up residence within Vatican City under the same conditions as diplomats of the Allied powers. The solution was an obvious one. If the Italian authorities objected that Mr. Tittmann was not a formally accredited diplomatic agent and, on that score, might have to leave the Vatican and Italy, then it would be sufficient for the Department of State to formally appoint him chargé d'affaires.

A statement published in the already cited issue of the February 12, 1953 *Osservatore Romano* is quite clear and positive on the step taken by the United States at this time. "The United States of America itself had a chargé d'affaires at the Vatican beginning from December, 1941," it said, in a manner that plainly indicated it spoke with authority, "in the person of Harold H. Tittmann, whose appointment was officially com-

[3] Hackworth, *op.cit.,* IV, par. 371.

municated to the Holy See. Mr. Tittmann remained in the territory of the Vatican State in his diplomatic status until 1944."

This was a revelation at the time it was published in the *Osservatore Romano*. During the war Tittmann had been referred to in the dispatches of various correspondents as the "American chargé d'affaires." Until the Vatican organ made the revelation, however, it was not known that the State Department had formally named him to that position. It had been widely supposed that the title of chargé was simply an informal way of describing Tittmann's position in the Vatican City in the absence of Taylor. The *Osservatore Romano* statement, however, shows that Tittmann's rank as a full diplomat began in December 1941, that is to say, not on his arrival in Rome but after Italy's declaration of war.

A document in the Roosevelt archives supports the Vatican's revelation. This is a memorandum sent to President Roosevelt by Under-Secretary of State Sumner Welles under date of December 17, 1941. In this letter he calls the president's attention to the fact that the Italian government might raise strong objection to the continued residence of Taylor's assistant in Vatican City unless he received some official diplomatic status such as a chargé d'affaires. This problem had been brought to his attention by the Apostolic Delegate in Washington, Archbishop Cicognani, in a letter dated December 13. Welles went on: "The Secretary [*Cordell Hull*] agrees with me that it is of very great importance that Tittmann remain in the Vatican City so that we may continue contact through him with the Holy See. If we ascertain that the Vatican will have to give in to Italian pressure and agree to have Tittmann leave, it seems to me that you will wish to consider favorably Tittmann's designation as chargé d'affaires in order to avoid this result." The papers in the Roosevelt library indicate that Mr. Roosevelt authorized the appointment should it become absolutely necessary in order to avoid Tittmann's departure.[4]

There is therefore no room for doubt. The objection of the Italian government was that Tittmann, as "assistant to Mr. Taylor," had no regular diplomatic standing. For that reason

[4] Graham, in *America*, 1953, pp. 591-92.

he had no title to take up residence in the Vatican with the privileges of the regularly accredited diplomats. The answer of the United States, which was accepted by the Italian government, was to make up that deficiency and formally name Tittmann chargé d'affaires. It was not very creditable on the part of the United States, however, that this appointment was never officially and publicly acknowledged. The only indication of Mr. Tittmann's promotion is an ambiguous note appearing in the Foreign Service List of January 1, 1944 describing Mr. Tittmann as on "special and temporary detail" in Vatican City, with December 24, 1941 as the date of his appointment. In a preceding list, Tittmann's appointment in Vatican City is given as April 1941. This is the sole hint in any published State Department source that Tittmann became American chargé d'affaires in the Vatican after Pearl Harbor.

This phase of U.S.-Vatican relations came to an end in 1944 when the arrival of the Allied troops in Rome permitted the American chargé to leave Vatican territory. Tittmann resumed his former title upon the return of Taylor. The incident throws light upon the real nature of the mission of Myron C. Taylor, whose work Tittmann carried on. It exemplifies circumstances which can easily arise to compel a country to set up formal diplomatic relations with the Holy See. Up to Pearl Harbor this country had been able successfully to skirt the issue by the formula of a "personal representative." Faced squarely in December 1941 with the choice either of naming Tittmann in the normal way, or seeing itself deprived of the useful presence of an American representative in the Vatican, the State Department did not hesitate. Overriding both the fears of adverse public opinion and possible constitutional objections, it made the bold step and entered into formal diplomatic relations with the papacy for the first time since 1868. The Tittmann episode may perhaps be dismissed as a formal gesture of no importance, initiated under the pressure of events. Yet any diplomatic relations with the Vatican in the past or future constitute a "formal gesture" done under the pressure of circumstances. It was not a purely formal matter when the difference between a chargé d'affaires and a "special assistant" meant the difference whether Mr. Tittmann remained at the strategic Vatican listening post or not.

Myron Taylor was at the least an official representative of the United States. He was dispatched on a public mission on public business by the highest official charged by the Constitution with the conduct of foreign policy. This decade of relations with the Holy See, if they were not diplomatic, were certainly official. For a government organized from the commencement upon non-intervention in ecclesiastical matters, the Taylor decade raises vital questions concerning the character of relations that can legitimately and normally exist with the Holy See.

There is probably no state in the world where governmental functions are separated from ecclesiastical functions with such rigor and completeness as in the United States. Many governments officially profess separation of Church and State while exercising in reality a role that by American standards is incompatible with such separation. From this point of view it is comprehensible that a state officially Muslim, such as the United Arab Republic, has better grounds for official relations with the Roman Pontiff than the United States, which while avowedly Christian has enacted a self-denying ordinance of non-intervention in Church matters, whether these pertain to Catholics, Protestants, or Jews. As a consequence, any sort of official relations with the Pope would seem on the face of it to be an unwarranted innovation. It is this question, rather than pure anti-Catholic prejudice, which lay most profoundly at the base of objections raised by responsible Protestants against the Taylor mission. In a statement issued on January 26, 1940 by the Executive Committee of the Federal Council of the Churches of Christ in America, this issue is clearly outlined: "If the appointment should unfortunately prove a stepping-stone to a permanent diplomatic relationship, we should feel obliged in good conscience to oppose it as a violation of the principle of separation of government functions and religious functions, which is a basic American policy and which both history and conscience approve, and as an ultimate injury to all faiths."[5]

[5] Stokes, *op.cit.*, II, p. 102.

It is not necessary in a work of this scope to discuss at length the origins and meaning of the "basic American policy" concerning the relations of State to Church. The First Amendment of the Federal Constitution prohibits Congress from enacting any law in respect to the establishment of religion. This amendment was adopted at a time when some of the states forming the federal union officially recognized the denominations which in fact were identified with their origins in the colonial days. In the course of time, by reason of the multiplicity of sects, a complete and unambiguous hands-off policy became a permanent feature for the states as well as for the federal government. The system of "separation" proclaimed by many European and Latin-American countries is in practice too often only a mask for interference in the Church's essential mission.

It is useful and instructive, however, to touch upon some of the few events in United States diplomatic history which have a bearing on the relations of the United States with the head of the Roman Catholic religion in Rome. The hands-off policy in regard to Church affairs antedates even the present Constitution, as can be learned from a resolution taken by the Second Continental Congress in 1784. In a letter dated July 28, 1783 the papal nuncio in Paris had written to Benjamin Franklin stating that Rome wished to reorganize the ecclesiastical administration in the American colonies as a consequence of their political separation from England. Hitherto the clergy and faithful had depended upon a vicar apostolic residing in London, an undesirable situation whose political consequences disquieted Franklin. The authorities in Rome, declared the nuncio, had come to the determination to establish in some city of the United States an American citizen with the powers of vicar apostolic with the episcopal character, or a prefect apostolic who would not be a bishop. In the event that no United States citizen could be found, Congress was asked to consent that "the choice be made" among the subjects of a foreign nation the most friendly to the United States, an obvious allusion to France.[6]

6 Baisnée, *France*, pp. 49-51; Hunt, *Journals*, XXVII, p. 369. The text of the nuncio's letter is also found in Wharton, *Revolutionary Diplomatic Correspondence*, VI, p. 614. On page 615, *ibid.*, is a note reporting the related fact that, after the purchase of Louisiana, Bishop Carroll consulted with the government on the choice of a bishop for New Orleans. Washington declined to intervene

After due deliberation on the communication transmitted to it by Franklin, the Continental Congress declared itself incompetent in the matter. In its session of May 11, 1784 it pointed out that such questions were reserved to the several states and that it could not pronounce one way or the other. It resolved: "That Doctor Franklin be desired to notify to the Apostolical Nuncio at Versailles that Congress will always be pleased to testify their respect to his sovereign and State; but that the subject of his application to Doctor Franklin, being purely spiritual, is without the jurisdiction and powers of Congress, who have no authority to permit or refuse it, these powers being reserved to the several states individually."[7]

The Federal Constitution which soon after came into force changed nothing in this respect. The instructions sent by Secretary of State Buchanan to the first chargé d'affaires in Rome in 1848 have already been cited *in extenso* in Chapter 3. Here the United States disclaimed any desire or capacity to enter into discussion upon purely ecclesiastical matters. The American representative was to confine himself to economic and political matters, the protection of United States citizens as needed, and any other purely political questions arising from the Pope's position as ruler of the papal states. If the mission had not already been closed in 1868, it is almost certain that the events of 1870 would have brought it to an end. Considering the world position of each of the two parties at that period, a diplomatic mission to the Pope after 1870 would have been virtually without object.

The voluntary renunciation of any right of veto or previous notice thus expressed by the young American Confederation in 1784 must have come as a surprise to the Court of Rome. The letter of the nuncio, acting upon instructions from the Eternal City, of course, shows it was taken for granted there that such approval or notification would be required by the Congress. Almost every other country with which Rome had experience

---

in any way but let Carroll know it appreciated his tact in going about the appointment in such a manner. Bishop Dubourg was named to the New Orleans See.

7 Baisnée, *op.cit.*, p. 66.

up to that time, including Sweden and Norway, where very few Catholics lived, required at least notification of major ecclesiastical appointments. The history of the diplomatic relations of non-Catholic countries with the Holy See, as sketched elsewhere, demonstrates that the primary if not the sole motive and foundation of such relations was the regulation of ecclesiastical matters. Frederick the Great pretended to recognize in the Pope only a temporal sovereign like himself, but in reality the compelling reason why he and his successors maintained their representation in Rome was because the Pope exercised significant authority in religious matters within their domains. The czars entertained a similar attitude and recognized in the Pope only the Bishop of Rome and the sovereign of the pontifical states. But they in their turn had for primary motive the adjustment of Church affairs in Poland and in Russia proper. The lesser Protestant states during and after the Napoleonic era negotiated with the Holy See on almost exclusively religious questions. In other countries, at a later state of Church-State theories where the laws left a certain amount of freedom of action to Rome, the temptation was strong to appeal to the authority of the Roman Pontiffs in order to resolve chronic internal political difficulties. Thus, as already seen, England sought to use the papal authority as a means of making British rule in Ireland easier. In Belgium, although the constitution of 1830 proclaimed separation of Church and State, the Liberal and the Catholic governments found themselves in turn recurring to Rome to ease their internal difficulties. France at the same period was doing likewise, as the Rossi mission evidences.

From this order of things the new Republic in the New World kept itself conspicuously aloof. The first encounter of the apostolic nuncio with the United States did not reflect a momentary impulse on the part of the Continental Congress but was the forerunner of a consistent policy. Though surprised by this unique abdication of power which stood so much in contrast to its experiences with almost every other government, Rome naturally made use of the freedom of action which the young Republic willingly accorded the Church. The history of the Catholic Church in the United States features practically no consultation on ecclesiastical matters.[8]

All this might seem to lead to the conclusion that there is no legitimate basis for diplomatic relations between the government of the United States and the Holy See. A state which by its own laws, traditions, and desires remains consistently abstentionist in ecclesiastical affairs affecting its own citizens, even when the supreme authority of one significant group is found outside the national territory, seems to have no matters to transact or to negotiate with the sovereign Pontiff. Yet, the ten years' service of Myron C. Taylor at Rome proves that, to the contrary, occasions can arise when such official relations are both useful and necessary, even to the point of commanding the assent of patriotic Protestant clergymen.

There is not very much mystery in this apparent contradiction if the present international positions of the United States and of the Holy See, respectively, are taken into account. As long as one remains on the narrow basis of purely internal Church matters affecting exclusively United States citizens and the Holy See, there is a serious contradiction. In this sphere, the question of relations seems excluded. But does this hypothesis adequately portray the full range of possible ways in which the papacy can impinge upon the United States at the second half of the 20th century? Since the advent of Leo XIII to the See of Peter in 1878, because of the rivalries among the European powers which culminated in the First World War, international diplomacy tended to become more than ever before multilateral rather than bilateral. The Vatican no less than any other diplomatic center entered into the calculations of European rivals whether they wanted it so or not. Governments had an interest in the Holy See not only for internal reasons but also because of its relationship with third countries and to the international community in general. The moral

---

8 The bizarre activity of the Bellamy Storer couple related by Stokes (II, pp. 401-05) is the exception that proves the rule. In mid-century, Pope Gregory XVI was able to reorganize the American Church without the least interference from the U.S. government. This experience, so much in contrast with what he experienced in Europe, once prompted the Pope to testify gratefully, *"In nessuna parte del mondo mi sento tanto papa, quanto negli Stati Uniti!"*

authority of the papacy became a factor that could not be ignored by governments engaged in close rivalry with each other. The First World War brought this trend to the point. It was this factor that led Great Britain in 1914 to dispatch Sir Henry Howard to the Vatican. It was the same factor of international influence that led France in 1920 along the road to restoration of relations with the Holy See.

The outbreak of the Second World War found the United States in a situation analogous to that of Great Britain in 1914 just as the end of the war found it in a position similar to that of France in 1920. The relations of the United States to the Holy See had nothing to do with the religious condition of Catholics in America but very much to do with the Pope's world role and his relations with other countries in which America had a pressing interest. It was, for instance, the special relationship of Pope Pius XII to Italy and the Pontiff's strenuous efforts to keep Italy out of the war in 1939-1940 that alone would have justified the presence of an American representative at the Vatican. President Roosevelt was pursuing an identical objective and it was important for his peace efforts that such action should be coordinated if possible. This case typifies the situations in which the United States constantly found itself in respect to the Holy See. What was true of attempts to keep Italy out of the war was true also in the broader sphere of world peace and international order generally. These are not ecclesiastical questions, properly speaking but they fall, nevertheless, under the legitimate functions of a world spiritual authority. The viewpoint of such a world authority cannot be ignored by many governments, least of all by those playing a major role in world politics.

Up until 1939 the United States and the papacy had seldom crossed paths. Their contacts in World War I were indirect. The outbreak of a second world conflict in which the two were leading neutral forces working for a just and durable peace inevitably brought them together as long as the crisis should last. The close of hostilities appears to have lessened the importance of the Vatican post for the United States, but in view of the worldwide responsibilities assumed by the United States it may be doubted that in its own interests it will long find it advisable to be absent diplomatically from the Vatican. One of the striking facts of the history of diplomatic relations with the Holy See has been that no major power conducting a far-reaching foreign policy has long been able to remain absent from the Vatican. Lutheran Prussia, Orthodox Czarist Russia, the England of "no Popery," lay and anti-clerical France have successively presented themselves at the Holy See, after having reckoned up the cost of their past absence. Of the major powers only the Soviet Union and the United States remain unrepresented at the Vatican. Historical precedents suggest that the latter, at least, having become the leader of the Western powers, will not long continue to be an exception to the general rule.

The experiment of the Myron Taylor mission established that, in the present state of world affairs and the ambitious scope of United States foreign policy, there exist certain areas of common interest which are neither purely political on the one hand nor purely religious and ecclesiastical on the other. The two parties can enter into formal relations with each other without jeopardy either to the purely temporal mission of the first or the purely spiritual mission of the second. The broad question of peace has already been cited as the classical case in point. Under this heading alone are included a large range of questions which do not oblige the Pope, on the one hand, to enter into purely political questions having no relation to his spiritual and moral mission, nor oblige the United States, on the other, to enter purely ecclesiastical matters, at least as these concern the domestic scene. The status of the holy places in Palestine is an international problem in which the political and religious authorities are both legitimately concerned and upon which it is conceivable joint action or consultation may be necessary. There are other cases less well defined but nevertheless of the same nature.

In addition to questions broadly falling under the heading of international peace and world order, in which according to the language of Article 24 of the Lateran Treaty the Holy See reserved its right to exercise its moral and spiritual mission, is it certain that purely ecclesiastical questions can always be excluded from range of consultations between the United States and the Vatican? The international responsibilities assumed by the United States all over the world suggest that it might not always find it possible to exercise the hands-off policy that it has been generally able to exercise within the fifty states of the Union.

Anti-clerical France found that it was not wise or useful to apply its laicizing policies outside the metropolitan area. In the words of Gambetta, anti-clericalism was not an article of export. Will the United States find that the American conception of Church-State relations is an exportable concept? This is very doubtful. In many countries of the world in which the United States has a direct interest, religion and politics are almost inextricably mixed. This is especially true of Muslim and Orthodox countries. But it is also true of Catholic and Protestant countries where politico-ecclesiastical matters are tightly woven into the basic legal structure. To such a situation so alien to American traditions the United States can conceivably become the political or the legal heir, whether it likes it or not.

America's own history illustrates that international treaties may sometimes compel a departure from the usual path. The Taft mission to the Pope in 1902 is an illustration of what is likely to happen when the United States takes over responsibilities in foreign soil under a different legal and political system. In that year, William Howard Taft, then civil governor of the Philippines, newly acquired from Spain, was sent by President Theodore Roosevelt to Rome in connection with a problem which had plagued the United States in the islands and to which there had appeared no solution short of violating treaty engagements. In the course of the centuries of Spanish possession, the Friars had come into possession of large landed estates which the native population now demanded should be redistributed. It was at length suggested at Washington that the key to the solution of the problem lay in Rome. And so it turned out.

It developed in the course of the negotiations at Rome that the United States wished the Holy Father not only to order the Friars to dispose of their lands according to the desires of the United States but to order them recalled to their native

Spain. Although the American authorities naturally tended to represent to the public that the Taft mission was a negotiation in real estate, it was in its nature an appeal to the Pope to use his authority to relieve the United States of an inconvenience that could be disposed of otherwise only by a violation of an international juridical obligation. In the language of a contemporary knowledgeable reporter, "the question which the situation in the Philippines called upon us to face was one as to which an expression of the Pope's pleasure would be likely to be final, as regards any interests opposed to those of the United States."[9] The "Pope's pleasure" was nothing less than his ecclesiastical authority which President Theodore Roosevelt was right in expecting to be final.

It is true that the commission headed by Governor Taft did not have a diplomatic character. The secretary of war, under whose jurisdiction the islands existed at that time, declared in his instructions that the errand would "not in any sense or degree be diplomatic in nature" but rather "purely a business matter of negotiation." But it is clear that the United States in 1902 found itself obliged to enter into official negotiations with the head of the Catholic Church and to invoke his ecclesiastical authority in its interests. The lesson of the episode is that in its very first years as a power with primary responsibilities overseas, the government of the United States realized how difficult it is to export the American conception of separation of Church and State. The history of the American military occupation of Germany and Japan after the Second World War, if studied from this point of view, would probably confirm that the earlier experience was repeated.

The success of the temporary mission of Governor Taft to the Vatican in 1902 naturally invites the question why President Franklin Delano Roosevelt in 1939 chose to give a more formal character to the mission of Myron C. Taylor. Could he not have sent a representative who would be "incognito" or placed in some less official category than the president's personal representative with the rank of ambassador? And why did he not formally instruct Mr. Taylor to avoid anything

[9] Baldwin, in *Yale Law Journal*, 1902, p. 3.

which might be construed abroad as indicating he enjoyed diplomatic standing, after the manner of the instructions of the secretary of war in 1902? If in the future questions arise concerning which the United States and the Holy See need to negotiate or to concert their action, is it necessary that such contacts take place through diplomatic or quasi-diplomatic channels?

We are not told in documents published up to the present why the President and Department of State seem not even to have considered sending an unofficial agent to Rome. In 1902 one reason that did not exist in 1939 was that the United States wished to avoid complications with Italy in seeming to treat with the Pope as with a sovereign. President Franklin D. Roosevelt was right when he told Dr. Buttrick, in the March 14, 1940 letter already cited, that under the circumstances the rank of ambassador was the only one appropriate. Since the Holy See has the right of active and passive legation, the question why the United States did not treat with the Pope through less formal agents could be just as well posed in regard to any state in the international community. The Holy See has the well-established right to carry on its relations with governments on the same basis as governments deal with one another. It would be perfectly justified in paying small consideration to an envoy who represented minor authorities or none at all. For the president to send to the Pope an emissary with lesser credentials than those given Mr. Taylor would have been little short of a discourtesy and to that extent self-defeating. No really important business can be transacted by agents lacking the proper standing for such purposes. An emissary of this type might be received with all courtesy at the Vatican but he would not get much farther than the Pope's antechamber for the purposes he had in mind, as the Dutch government spokesman said in 1915, replying to a similar question. In the nature of things this is not surprising. Other countries which have taken the pains to recognize the sovereign independence of the Pope by accrediting formal diplomatic envoys officially representing their government would certainly have grounds for complaint were it otherwise. For the success of the mission Mr. Taylor had to accomplish it was essential that he possess at least the formal character accorded him by Mr. Roosevelt. It is not improbable, for the same reasons, that his work at the Vatican might have been more to the interests of the United States if his residence had been permanent. The very institution of permanent diplomatic missions is a witness to the inadequacy of temporary missions on the part of governments having broad and continuing world interests. The necessary mutual comprehension and confidence can be built up only by continued residence and constant personal contact.

As a means of resolving one of the difficulties posed by official U.S.-Vatican relations, it has been suggested that the president's representative was sent to the Holy Father in his capacity of sovereign of the State of Vatican City and not as the head of the Roman Catholic Church. In this interpretation of the Taylor episode the problem of Church-State relations appear to some to be eliminated. In fact, in 1848 the American chargé d'affaires was told in so many words that the United States wished to deal with the Pope exclusively in his capacity as sovereign of the papal states. After the Lateran Treaty of 1929 a natural inclination manifested itself among international lawyers, diplomats, and laymen to interpret the diplomatic standing of the Pope as the function and consequence of his position as head of the tiny state of Vatican City. This manner of envisaging the Pope's international capacity became particularly common in the United States for the reasons already indicated.

Even so qualified a source as Archbishop John McNicholas, of Cincinnati, in a letter written as chairman of the administrative board of the National Catholic Welfare Conference, and released on January 28, 1948, seems to have taken that viewpoint: "The Vatican is a tiny state recognized as the stronghold of the world for the defense of human rights and for the exposition of moral principles. President Roosevelt and President Truman have sent a personal representative with the rank of Ambassador to the Pope, who is at the same time the ruler of a sovereign state. We send an ambassador to England, where the king is the head of the Established Church. The ambassador's mission is not to the Church or England, but to the British government. Forty governments throughout the world have found it to their advantage and to that of peace among nations to have representatives at the State of the Vatican."

Is it necessary or even correct to adopt such a formula to interpret American relations with the Pope? The objective of Archbishop McNicholas was to demonstrate that, in his words, "Catholics have never considered this mission a religious affair." The presidential mission, he added, "is not a channel for church affairs." It is certain from the history of the origins of the Taylor mission that ecclesiastical matters affecting the position of Catholics in the United States were excluded. But will this formula resist examination when applied to the field of foreign policy and international diplomatic practice? Several considerations, on the contrary, tend to show rather that Mr. Taylor could not have been sent to the Holy Father in his sole capacity of temporal sovereign.

In the first place, the State of Vatican City has no foreign service specifically its own and no foreign ministry distinct from that of the Holy See. In virtue of Article 3 of its Fundamental Law this international entity carries on its international intercourse, such as it has, through the secretariat of state of His Holiness. A state wishing for some reason to enter into official relations only with the Vatican State would have in any case first to deal with the Holy See. Secondly, there is at present no diplomatic mission accredited to the Pope uniquely, if at all, in his capacity of temporal sovereign. Considering the existing practice, it is unlikely that the Holy See would make an exception in favor of a state which wished to send an envoy to the Pope exclusively as a temporal sovereign. There is no indication in the correspondence between President Roosevelt and Pius XII that the former sought to make any distinction between the two capacities of the Pontiff.[10]

The nature of the business transacted during 1940-1950 would in any case have belied at every moment the effort to picture this mission as one to a purely temporal ruler. The

[10] The letters of credence presented by the envoys accredited to the Pope generally carry no mention of the "Vatican" or "State of Vatican City." Prior to the occupation of the papal states in 1870 the letters of credence made no mention of the Pope as sovereign of the papal states. Hence after 1870, happily for the governments, no issue arose over the proper form of credentials. These remained unaffected by the change in the Pope's situation.

United States, as indeed the rest of the countries, has little interest in the Vatican City. Most states are concerned with the Pope precisely in his role as head of the Catholic Church, at least in his aspect of world moral authority. Only Italy has any substantial grounds, for obvious geographical reasons, to negotiate on purely temporal matters with the Pope and his agencies.[11]

In sum, it would appear better founded in principle and more to the honor of the Holy See and of the United States to interpret the Taylor mission as one sent to the Holy Father not indeed for the treatment of ecclesiastical matters of the Catholic Church in America but for the purpose of concerting with him in his capacity of a world moral leader on the objectives of peace and order proclaimed by the United States. The Roman Pontiff certainly has no desire to see his "moral and spiritual mission" translated into terms of pure politics among temporal states. The Pope's international position is not a manifestation of political status or ambitions but the outcome of his sublime religious mission in the world. Those not of his communion need not be expected to regard the Roman Pontiff as the Vicar of Jesus Christ but they will at least wish to pay him the honor of expecting him to live up to his own declared

[11] The distinction between the Holy See and the State of Vatican City as international personalities, while subtle and sometimes difficult to apply in practice, is nevertheless clear in concept. But an ambiguity in terminology tends to bedevil discussions on this subject. The word "Vatican," so often employed, can refer to two objects. It can mean the *Stato della Città del Vaticano*, that tiny geographical entity situated within the City of Rome. Or it can mean the *Palazzo Vaticano*, where the Pope lives and where is located, in addition, the secretariat of state of His Holiness. In informal diplomatic correspondence and in journalism it is customary to identify a government by the name of the street, locality, or building associated with the foreign ministry. Hence the use, for convenience purposes, of the terms "Whitehall," "Quai d'Orsay," "Wilhelmstrasse," "Ballhausplatz," and so forth. The term "Vatican" was in use to signify the Holy See especially after 1870 and hence long before the Vatican State was heard of. At the present time, only the context can indicate in which of these two senses this diplomatic abbreviation is employed.

After 1957, in order to eliminate a source of recurring perplexity to itself, the United Nations in agreement with the Holy See discontinued the use of the term "Vatican City." Thenceforth, the nomenclature "Holy See" would be used at all UN-sponsored international conferences to which the papal authorities were invited, regardless of whether the conference touched on strictly territorial or on humanitarian issues. Thus, in May 1958, the papal delegation to the Conference on International Commercial Arbitration was designated as that of the "Holy See."

character. To see in the Pope only the political ruler of the Vatican State falsifies the real position of the papacy on the international scene and sets the stage for charges sometimes made that the Vatican is engaged in diplomacy for purely material interests.

The question of U.S.-Vatican relations poses constitutional and other problems whose solution will be clear only after a sustained period of study and experience not only in Washington but also in Rome. Among those concerned in the issue are not only the White House and the Vatican, along with non-Catholic Americans, but also the Catholics in the United States. For both clergy and laity, the existence of U.S. relations with the Holy See presents some risks. The presence of a representative of the White House at the Vatican, with direct access to the Holy Father, is almost a direct invitation to interference in internal American Church affairs. It would be a simple matter for the President of the United States to indicate, however discreetly, his preferences when there is question of the choice to be made for the head of a major U.S. see. Franklin D. Roosevelt is known to have been solicited by his advisors, such as Harold Ickes, to let his ideas be known in Rome when the see of Chicago became vacant with the death of Cardinal Mundelein in 1939. He appears to have refrained from taking any overt step in that direction. The story might have been different had regular diplomatic relations existed at that time.

In addition to the danger of White House interference in domestic ecclesiastical affairs, there is also the danger that the government might seek to influence Catholic opinion on internal legislation. This fear is not an academic one. It is known from Robert Sherwood's life of Harry Hopkins and Langer-Gleason that President Roosevelt asked Pope Pius XII to refrain, at least temporarily, from making any statement which might jeopardize passing of the bill to extend Lend-Lease to Russia. There was concern that, should the Vatican take any action that could be interpreted as unfavorable to aid to Russia, the opponents of the extension bill would seize upon this to defeat it. It is safe to say that the many Catholics who at that crucial moment of history opposed Lend-Lease and particularly its extension to the Soviets, would have been bitterly indignant at the President's move, had they known of it at the time. And they would have had natural grounds for complaint, for this was to use Catholic consciences and the official contact with Rome in order to influence controversial domestic legislation. It matters not that the request made to the Pope was to refrain from saying something, and not a request to do something. The effect was the same.

These are hazards against which both the Vatican and Washington must learn in time to protect themselves, if their relations are to offer promise. In the meantime, the immediate problem for the United States arises not from relations but from the lack of relations. What should be the relations between the two sovereignties which have no relations?

The Vatican is fated to be a continual object of United States interest. International life is no respecter of national susceptibilities or customs. In the coming years, as in the past, occasions for the exchange of formal greetings will not be lacking. These are courtesies that betoken and beget good will. At times some individual problem of coordination may arise and be satisfactorily handled by informal and indirect contacts. But, even supposing the best of good will on both sides, the experience of other countries and the canons of diplomacy itself teach this lesson: it is unrealistic to expect that really important issues can be solved short of direct and avowed diplomatic relations. There is no substitute for the orderly procedures established by international custom. By backdoor methods the State which declines to have diplomatic relations with the Holy See implicitly asks the Vatican to engage its own spiritual sovereignty without a corresponding engagement of the sovereignty of the petitioning power. The United States, having freely made its decision not to entertain formal relations with the Holy See, should not embarrass both itself and the Vatican by attempting to carry on sustained or major negotiations in the Eternal City by indirect methods. Yet the temptation to do just that will always assail a great power such as the United States. Out of such circumstances diplomatic relations are at length born.

CHAPTER 13

THE HOLY SEE AND THE SOVIET UNION

CATHOLIC CHURCH
AND COMMUNIST STATE

ARLIER chapters on Prussia, Great Britain, imperial Russia, and other non-Catholic states showed how religious differences, though once a bar to diplomatic relations between them and the Holy See, are no longer a decisive factor. Both parties to the exchange have, perhaps without ever saying so, recognized that such relations do not perforce carry theological or doctrinal implications. This pragmatic disregard of otherwise important questions of principle is characteristic of diplomacy generally. When one State recognizes a new regime it does not always intend to signify thereby approval of the form of government or to pass judgment on the means by which the government in question came to power. International life would be seriously handicapped if the states could have official intercourse only with those regimes which they approved.

The papacy does not therefore draw the line, diplomatically, at heretics, schismatics, infidels, and pagans. Is there any reason why it should balk at having relations with an officially atheistic government, such as the Soviet Union?

At first sight it may seem pointless to take up the question of diplomatic relations between the Vatican and the Kremlin.

Bibliographical Note: For the purposes of diplomatic history, authentic information on Vatican-Kremlin relations is extremely limited. Official documentation from either source is sparse. This scarcity of direct information has led to more than the usual proportion of speculation and fancy in newspapers and popular books. Newspaper allegations of imminent negotiations are not infrequently inspired by Soviet sources for immediate propaganda or political purposes, without any basis in fact. On the other hand, denials issued by Vatican spokesmen also complicate the problem of the historian. These denials are sometimes diplomatic in nature, designed to put the brake on premature speculation. Their real force needs close scrutiny in each case.

Partial reviews of Soviet-Vatican relations in the interwar period are found in Salvatorelli, Pernot, and von Lama. For a partial study of wartime based on documents, see Duclos. The diplomatic memoirs of those in a position to say something give only fragmentary pictures of these relations. Some clues to Vatican policy can be found in the reports of Myron C. Taylor and in Robert Sherwood's life of Harry Hopkins.

The struggle between these world forces has developed such dramatic quality that it requires great effort of the imagination to envisage the day when the two will ever have "normal" relations. The Soviet Union, in its domestic as well as its foreign policy, has come so squarely in conflict with the Catholic Church that no useful armistice—as distinguished from temporary relaxation on tactical grounds—seems possible for the foreseeable future.

The source of the conflict is, of course, ideological. On the one side there stands the Soviet Union, which, to its missionary program of worldwide revolution, joins doctrinal and practical atheism as a fundamental of its expanding political system. Opposite, there stands a worldwide religious organization two thousand years old which has the tenacity that only religious faith can give to human beings and which, confident in its destiny, does not reckon in terms of years but of centuries. The effect of this tension is felt in almost every domain and in almost every country. Rarely in history have ideas spilled over into world politics so markedly as in this duel.

To the extent that the conflict is ideological, the Church's stand appears to be, and is, intransigent. The oft-quoted statement of Pius XI on the incompatibility of Christianity and Communism is a monument to this doctrinal stand. In the 1937 encyclical "On Atheistic Communism," the Pope declared: "Communism is intrinsically wrong and no one who would save Christian civilization may collaborate with it in any field whatsoever." A similar theme was sounded by Pius XII in his 1956 Christmas message in which he warned against coexistence and the tendency of some Catholics to seek to engage in "dialogue" with the Communists. The Pope warned: "Out of respect for the name of Christian, compliance with such tactics should cease, for, as the Apostle warns, it is inconsistent to wish to sit at the table of God and at that of His enemies."

This is strong language. Yet, if such statements stress the doctrinal source of the Holy See's attitude toward the Soviet Union, there are other pronouncements which sound a more conciliatory note, on the practical plane. The same Pius XI who in 1937 spoke so strongly against collaboration in 1929 uttered other sentiments equally significant in any analysis of

Vatican policy toward totalitarian governments. At the time of a dispute on education with Mussolini, the Pope enunciated yet another principle of action, itself also oft-cited. To the students of the Mondragone college on May 14, 1929 Pius XI said: "When there is question of saving souls, or preventing greater harm to souls, We feel the courage to treat with the devil in person." And his successor, Pius XII, in the same 1956 address already mentioned, made it clear that his words were directed primarily at individuals who, on their own personal authority, undertook to involve the cause of religion in "negotiations" with the Communists. The Pope in that Christmas discourse left room for the action of "responsible governmental and political leaders" as well as for what "competent ecclesiastical authority" decides it should do for the peace of the world and the good of the Church. Pius XII thereby introduced a distinction which his predecessor had not made, at least explicitly, twenty years earlier.

In short, the Vatican's reputation for absolute intransigence toward the Soviet Union requires some qualification. If doctrinal firmness is commendable in an institution which regards itself as the custodian of Christian revelation, there is still room for an attitude of generosity and conciliation toward those in error. The intransigence which the popular mind attributes to the Vatican, while no doubt flattering to the principles on which the Holy See moves, is hardly a tribute to its prudence and its spirit of conciliation to all men, including the sinner. To suppose that the sole fact of atheism of the Bolsheviks excluded the possibility of compromise with the new regime in Russia is to imply that the Holy See jeopardized, that is, abandoned, without demonstrated necessity, hundreds of thousands of its own adherents living under Bolshevism,[1] while foregoing chances of possible favorable developments in the future by an

---

[1] After the treaty of Riga of March 18, 1921, establishing the Polish-Russian border, there remained in Russia more than 1,500,000 Catholics. These were grouped in five Latin rite dioceses and one exarchate for the Catholics of the Slav-Byzantine rite. (Galter, *Red Book*, pp. 39-40.) They included an estimated 950,000 Poles, 400,000 White Ruthenians, 48,000 Armenians, 35,000 Georgians, and 200,000 others, mostly of German origin, descendants of colonists settled along the Volga or in the Ukraine during the 18th century. There were only a few thousand Catholics of the Slav-Byzantine rite, placed under the Exarch Feodorov.

extreme policy at the outset. Looked at from this point of view, the "intransigence" of the Vatican would not be a virtue but a lack of the discretion that a shepherd must exercise for the good of the flock committed to him. Indeed, some critics of the Church have found in the fight on Communism not an indication of zeal for God's truth but rather bigoted and unreasonable opposition to a rival.

The history of papal diplomacy belies the image of rigidity which many minds seem to attach to its relations with the Soviet Union. Where inflexibility seems to exist this is due to practical, not theoretical, obstacles. To phrase the issue in diplomatic terms, a state of war exists with the USSR. It is this war and not the atheism of the regime which is the immediate obstacle to normal relations. Moreover, it is a war which was declared by the Bolsheviks and not one which the Vatican itself sought. In the practice of Vatican diplomacy it is not the official ideology of a regime (heretical or godless) which is the crucial point so much as the regime's policy of toleration. Such a toleration was granted to the Catholics of Prussia and other Protestant countries. In the case of imperial Russia, despite many stormy interludes, the Pope sought to maintain relations with the czars. Both Rome and St. Petersburg had an abiding interest in maintaining these relations. A certain degree of toleration existed in the old Russian empire, with a reasonable hope of greater toleration in the future. The Soviet regime, however, demonstrated more clearly with each passing year that the death or enslavement of religion was its objective. If Communist atheism is an obstacle to diplomatic relations with the Vatican it is because it is an intolerant and persecuting atheism. As the price for peace, the Holy See may not perhaps demand the abandonment of official atheism, but it legitimately may ask for a certain toleration in Russia and an end to religious subversion abroad.

In the rest of the present chapter we shall pass in review the broad outline of Vatican-Kremlin relations since 1917, concluding with some speculation on the future of these relations. In sum, it was not until 1930 that the policy of the Vatican took the form of hardened opposition which so many observers of a later day have assumed to be inherent in the papal system. Although Vatican spokesmen castigated the doctrines of Bolshe-

vism and denounced the terrorism of the Reds from the beginning, relations with the Leninists were not so cold and reserved
as to be non-existent. In fact, while in our time many voices
are heard reproaching the Vatican for its rejection of the Soviets,
the contrary complaint was aired in the first decade of the Revolution. White Russian exiles roundly denounced the Pope for
temporizing with the new rulers of Russia. They pointed out
that, while Rome was strong in condemning the doctrine of
Communism and in expressing its sympathies for the famine
victims, it still kept open the door to negotiations. That door
was unequivocably slammed shut only in 1930.

The fall of the autocratic regime of the Romanovs in 1917
appeared to Catholics to presage the dawn of a bright new day.
Even the Bolshevik revolution of eight months later did not
quench optimism about the future of the Church in Russia.
In the Vatican itself, conflicting reactions were reflected in official reserve. But many observers of the chaos and disorder
could not believe that the Lenin regime would last or in any
case that it would persist in its anti-religious attitude. To those
who lived under the restrictions of the old regime, the future
could only be better.

Religious freedom was felt immediately after the abdication
of Czar Nicholas II. In response to popular sentiment, the Provisional Government in April 1917 repealed all the existing
laws which discriminated against Russian citizens on religious,
racial, or nationality grounds. The Holy See did not delay
making use of its new liberty of action. It appointed a new
archbishop of Mohilev, in the person of Edward de Ropp, formerly bishop of Vilna, a member of the first Duma, and signer
of the Viborg Manifesto, who had been banished from his see
by the Czarist regime. Mohilev, with its see at St. Petersburg,
was the largest (Latin rite) diocese in the world. In theory, it
reached from the Baltic to Siberia; in reality, for many years
it had been impossible for the bishop to make pastoral visitations to distant parts of his diocese. A bishop was named to the
see of Kamenetz, which years before had been suppressed by
the czars and arbitrarily annexed to that of Luck-Zhitomir. The
man who had long ago been named bishop of Minsk but whose
appointment had not been confirmed by the government was

at length able to take possession of his see. Most significantly, perhaps, with the sanction of the Provisional Government the Catholics of the Byzantine rite—a mere handful—were allowed to have their own spiritual leader. This prelate was the heroic Leonidas Feodorov, who became exarch of the Russian Catholics of the Byzantine rite. In view of the history of the Czarist policy which carried on forced schism among non Latin-rite Catholics loyal to Rome this legalization of the status of Byzantine Catholics in Russia was a startling innovation.

In the summer of 1917 a special commission presided over by Prince Lvov, head of the Provisional Government, met with Archbishop de Ropp and other Church officials to draft formal legislation regulating the definitive status of the Catholic Church. The partial results of these negotiations as approved by the government were published in the official acts of the Provisional Government on August 25, 1917. The November Revolution interrupted this development.

The Bolsheviks, upon gaining power, did not immediately alter the existing situation except to eliminate provisions for financial assistance. In a short time, however, a decree of January 23, 1918 proclaimed "separation" of Church and State and declared all Church property the "patrimony of the people." Legal personality was denied to Church bodies. Despite this law the Catholics and other religious groups were able to continue to use Church buildings which now legally belonged to the State. Religious life was therefore able to go on.

Toward the Catholics, in fact, the Bolsheviks paid at first only secondary attention. Their chief fury was vented upon the representatives of the former official Church. Denied a patriarch since the time of Peter the Great, the Orthodox Church in Russia had long been completely at the service of the regime. Yet the blow was to strike the Catholics nonetheless, chiefly in the form of arrest and harassment of the bishops. Archbishop de Ropp was arrested at the end of 1918, and sentenced to death as a common criminal. In December 1919, however, he was exchanged for Karl Radek, then in a Polish prison. Bishop Joseph Kessler of Tiraspol was driven from his see, as well as Bishop Peter Mankowski of Kamenetz and Bishop Lodzinski of

Minsk. For the moment the Bolsheviks contented themselves with depriving the dioceses of their regular heads.[2]

These vexations took place at a time of virtual chaos in the former Russian Empire. Archbishop de Ropp was one of those who put on the record his belief that the Bolshevik regime would not last. For this reason, evidently, he did not protest (in the few months that he was free) against the nationalization of Church property. He even complied with regulations by allowing the appointment of lay persons who, according to the new law, were authorized to administer the Church property which was absolutely necessary for divine services. Even in exile, de Ropp did not cease his conciliatory efforts. In the fall of 1920 an important meeting took place in Berlin at which both Catholics and representatives of the dissident faiths participated. As one result of this conference, the Archbishop of Mohilev sent to Moscow proposals for a basis of religious peace with the State. These contained three points: freedom of conscience and of worship, freedom of education, restitution of the churches and of the goods belonging to the Church.[3] Nothing came of these proposals, but they do demonstrate that at that time the Catholic Church leaders had not abandoned hope of entering into some kind of agreement with the new regime, atheistic though it professed itself to be. The 1920 proposal was later repeated by the Vatican itself in the course of the Genoa conference of 1922, to which we can now turn.

Pope Benedict XV had been active in arousing concern for the victims of the food shortages induced by the postwar confusion in Russia. The famine had progressed so far that the Bolsheviks themselves were constrained to seek help abroad. Among appeals sent with the regime's approval was a letter

---

[2] *Documentation Catholique,* t. 14 (1925), cols. 751-767. In those corners of the former Russian empire not yet under Bolshevik control, new units were created. A vicariate apostolic of Siberia was created as late as December 1921, as well as an apostolic administration for the Armenian Catholics and a vicariate apostolic for Caucasus-Crimea. A new diocese of Vladivostok was created in February 1923. Their existence was shortlived.

[3] Pernot, *Saint-Siège,* p. 164. Archbishop Signori told a Milan correspondent that Chicherin, at the supper in Genoa, had made allusions to such efforts at an agreement: "[*Cicerin*] *aggiunse che un vescovo cattolico, a Mosca, l'aveva sollecitato a stabilire un concordato con la Santa Sede, ma che egli aveva riposto declinando l'invito, precisamente in omaggio al principio di libertà professata in rapporti ai vari culti*" (*Corriere della Sera,* April 30, 1922).

dated July 13, 1921 addressed by Maxim Gorky to the American people. On August 5, Benedict himself issued a worldwide call for relief and himself contributed to Protestant organizations active in that work. By an agreement reached at Riga on August 20, 1921 the Soviet government, represented by Maxim Litvinov, granted the right to distribute relief, under safeguards, to an American relief mission headed by Herbert Hoover. The Vatican, in continuance of its efforts in this field, sought to dispatch a mission of its own. In the last days of Benedict, who died in January 1922, negotiations to this end were still going on in Rome with the Soviet commercial representative in Italy, Vaclav Vorowski. An agreement had already been concluded when, on April 10, the international conference opened at Genoa.

The Genoa conference had been called by the powers of the Allied Supreme Council with a view to settle some of the issues, principally economic, that remained unresolved in Eastern and Central Europe in the aftermath of the war. This was the first international meeting to which the Lenin regime was admitted. Moscow was still not recognized *de jure* by most of the participating governments. These were withholding full recognition pending settlement of such questions as Soviet assumption of responsibility for wartime and prewar Czarist debts. The Bolsheviks' repudiation of the public debts of the previous regime was regarded as a breach of international law.

On April 7, a few days before the conference opened, the new Pontiff, Pius XI, addressed a letter to Archbishop Signori of Genoa in which he praised that prelate for asking his people to pray for the success of the conference. The Pope did not allude even indirectly to the Russian problem. His words were interpreted at that time by some French circles as pro-German because they seemed to call in question the Versailles settlements, especially those relating to reparations.

Events soon focussed attention on Vatican-Kremlin relations. An episode that took place in the course of the conference started a flood of rumors concerning a future entente between the two. On the occasion of an official supper held on board the Italian battleship *Dante Alighieri*, in the presence of the king in the harbor of Genoa on April 22, Archbishop Signori and the Soviet Foreign Minister Chicherin found themselves by the accident of alphabetical arrangements face to face at the same table. The story was too good to be lost. Newspapers described alleged amiable conversations, mutual toasts, and the exchange of autographed menus between the representative of Rome and the Bolshevik minister.

Although the fact of the meeting of the two personalities was correct, the details of the nature of their relationship were quite distorted. The incident was enough to set in motion a series of rumors in the press. On the following day, for instance, the *Daily Mail* reported that a treaty had been signed. The Jesuits would be allowed to go to Russia to establish schools while the Franciscans would be admitted to evangelize the country. This story was picked up and recirculated in the continental press. In the atmosphere that had been shaken by the Russo-German Rapallo pact just a week earlier, a similar pact involving the Vatican did not seem too fantastic to be put on the wires.

As the conference of Genoa proceeded, running into increasingly rough weather, new developments inspired another Vatican move. This consisted in a second papal letter, this time addressed to Cardinal Gasparri, the papal secretary of state, and dated April 29. It, too, expressed hope for the success of the conference. But in contrast to the previous letter, the Pope alluded pointedly to the grave predicament of the peoples of Russia and their need for peace and order.

The letter of April 29 was read with interest in Genoa and even with gratification. Lloyd George considered it an aid in his efforts to keep the conference going. But it was followed within a few days by a surprising initiative. From Rome on May 5 the Vatican sent a special emissary and official of the Vatican secretariat of state, Msgr. (later Cardinal) Giuseppe Pizzardo. He was the bearer of a memorandum to the conference on behalf of religious freedom in Russia. Pizzardo presented copies of the Pope's letter to Gasparri, together with another note explaining that the memorandum was being communicated in person at Genoa because of the lack of sufficient time to send it through diplomatic channels. By one way and another Pizzardo managed to communicate the memorandum not only to those countries with which the Vatican had normal relations but also to such countries as Italy and the Soviet Union with which it had no relations.

The memorandum restated the principles of religious freedom which had already been presented in vain by Archbishop de Ropp. Stated the papal memorandum: "At the historic moment when the readmission of Russia to the community of civilized nations was being treated, the Holy See wished that religious interests, which are the basis of every real civilization, should be safeguarded." The message went on to ask that, in the agreement among the powers envisaged at Genoa, these three clauses, or their equivalent, should be expressly included (as "an essential element"):

"1. Full freedom of conscience for all Russian citizens or foreigners is guaranteed in Russia;

"2. The public and private practice of religion and worship is also guaranteed. ('This,' added the papal memorandum, 'is in conformity with the declarations made by Chicherin at Genoa' —a reference perhaps to the publicized conversations with Archbishop Signori on board the *Dante Alighieri*.)

"3. The real property which belonged or still belongs to any religious denomination whatever will be restored to it and respected."[4]

By this time the conference was already foundering. On May 10 the papal memorandum was considered by the five inviting powers. Although France's Barthou favored discussion of the proposal, Lloyd George's opposition prevailed. For the British prime minister the conference was already on too shaky a footing to be further endangered by the introduction of such a theme. Religious freedom and religious education, he said, were very controversial even among the five powers. Besides, he argued, exacting such a pledge would be an unjustifiable interference in the internal affairs of Russia. In the end it was decided to refer the memorandum to the subcommittee on political affairs to be read and noted, that is, to be tabled.[5]

[4] Walsh, *Last Stand*, p. 214; Fauchille-Bonfils, *Traité*, I, 1ère partie, pp. 754-56. It should be recalled that the convening powers had themselves set their own conditions for recognition of the Bolsheviks ("Cannes Resolutions"). The religious clause was, therefore, not a novel type of proposal.

[5] Mills, *Genoa Conference*, p. 210.

The reaction of Chicherin was equally negative. On May 12, a press communiqué from the Soviet delegation stated that the three points were based on what it called an insufficient understanding of Soviet legislation. The matters raised, said the statement, were already taken care of adequately in the decree of separation of January 23, 1918. "This decree," it went on, "fully guarantees freedom of conscience and the free exercise of religion as well as the use of buildings and objects necessary for worship." Officially, therefore, the issue of religious freedom got no farther than to be incorporated in the minutes of an international conference. On May 19 the conference adjourned in failure.

What was the meaning of this surprise move by the Vatican? It bore the marks of a sudden decision, if not of a reversal of policy. One clue was offered in *Figaro* of May 10. A dispatch in this as well as other papers stated that the Vatican had been negotiating with the Russians earlier, prior to the conference (in reference to the relief mission), and had been at first impressed by their promises and explanations. But it soon found out that their professions of official respect for religious freedom did not correspond with the facts. At this point, said *Figaro*, the Vatican decided to put the issue before the world powers in a formal and public way.

A circumstantial two-column account of the Pizzardo mission appearing in the May 15-16 *Osservatore Romano* supports the interpretation already expressed in the public press. Hardly had the letter of April 29 been published (*appena pubblicato*) in the press, said the report, than from Russia there arrived new and detailed information on the sad state not only of the Catholic Church but also of all religious denominations. Despite the much-cited decree of January 23, 1918, said the Vatican newspaper, reliable information had been received from various provinces that the law bore no relation to the real state of affairs.[6] The Holy Father, concluded the report, wished that this situation should be presented to conference before the Russian

---

[6] Walsh had arrived in Rome on May 4 from his advance survey in Russia. The firsthand information he brought no doubt had a bearing on the Vatican's decision to send Pizzardo to Genoa in haste. The clauses concerning religious freedom in the treaty of Riga were interpreted in the same way as the corresponding clauses in the Soviet constitution.

question ("which seemed on the point of solution") was settled.

Whatever the interpretation of the papal démarche it was not meant to signify a rupture with the Soviets. At this very time, it has been noted, preparations were going forward on the dispatch of a relief mission to Russia. Msgr. Pizzardo on May 9 visited the Soviet Foreign Minister Chicherin at the latter's headquarters in Santa Margherita, near Genoa and there personally handed him the papal letter with the memorandum. The occasion or perhaps pretext of this visit was to discuss final details of the projected visas for the Vatican relief agents. The memorandum was therefore not viewed by the Vatican as an attack which the Soviets would necessarily have to regard as a diplomatic affront.

For a fuller understanding of the significance of the rumors circulating in the European press at this time concerning Vatican-Kremlin relations, it is necessary to describe at this point the attitude of the legitimist Russians in exile. The highly-colored reports of the "cordial" conversations of Archbishop Signori and Chicherin on the royal vessel on April 22, followed soon after by the papal letter of April 29, were profoundly disturbing to emigré circles. They were interpreted as sure proof of an alliance between Rome and Moscow, at the expense of Orthodoxy. The White Russians generally were opposed to any kind of dealings with the Reds. They criticized, for instance, the United States project for famine relief in Russia on the grounds that it would only help the revolutionists. In the case of the Orthodox clergy particularly, with their centuries-long tradition of hostility to the bishop of Rome, the Pope's concern with Russian affairs stirred suspicion. Some of them were convinced that the Holy See wished to use the distress of their coreligionists in Russia and the collapse of the old regime to advance the cause of Roman Catholicism. In their eyes, the papacy would not shrink from compromising itself with the Bolsheviks in order to accomplish its long dream of winning the Russian Church to union with Rome. Out of such feelings emerged violent protests when reports multiplied in the European press of good relations between the Soviets and the papacy, an even of an imminent "concordat." As the brunt of persecution was at that very moment falling heavily upon the Orthodox

(Patriarch Tikhon had been arrested in April), they saw in this tête-à-tête at Genoa an unholy conspiracy to exterminate Orthodoxy.

On May 5 the Russian emigrés' Comité National of Paris published an open letter to the Pope denouncing the Pontiff for "negotiating" with the Bolsheviks. The mere fact that the Pope had any contacts whatever with the Bolsheviks, regardless of object, they found reprehensible.[7] Several leading Paris newspapers published on May 7 a letter of flaming indignation written by Dmitry Merezhkovsky, a Russian writer and leader in exile circles in the French capital. He charged that if the (supposed) "concordat" were signed, the conscience of all Christians would be revolted and the papacy cursed forever in the soul of every true Russian. He decried what he pictured as the spectacle of "the priests of the Western Church, with hands which have touched the Sacred Host, shaking the bloodied hands of these murderers."[8]

Grotesque stories were repeated in these circles during and after the Genoa conference. The visit which King Albert of Belgium had paid to the Pope shortly before was described in a Berlin sermon with all its details, but transformed into a visit of Chicherin himself. In vain was it pointed out that, contrary to newspaper predictions, Chicherin had not gone to the Vatican and that the "concordat" was nothing but an agreement on a relief mission, while the memorandum presented by Pizzardo was as much in the interests of the Orthodox as it was of the Catholics. A morbid dislike of any gestures of settlement with the Bolsheviks (of which the Vatican was not the sole target) kept alive for some years the stories of an alleged Vatican-Kremlin "concordat."[9] The failure of the Vatican to burn its

[7] Cardinal Mercier's diplomatic but firm rejection of the protests sent him by the exiles in Paris is cited by d'Herbigny, *Tyrannie soviétique*, pp. 246-52.

[8] Vaclav Vorowski, a Pole, the Soviet commercial agent in Italy, with whom the negotiations were carried on by Msgr. Pizzardo, was assassinated in Lausanne a year later by an anti-Bolshevist Russian of Swiss citizenship.

[9] McCullagh, *Bolshevik Persecution*, pp. 100-05. The Great Soviet Encyclopedia, fundamentally a guide to the party line, does not yield much original or serviceable information on Vatican-Kremlin relations. In its article on Cardinal Gasparri, however (x, 261), it fixes March 12, 1922 as the date on which the cardinal secretary signed, with the Soviet representative, the agreement concerning the admission of a Vatican relief mission during the famine. Walsh, it charged, was later obliged to leave Russia on account of his espionage activities.

bridges with the Bolsheviks was alone sufficient proof in emigré circles that Rome had ulterior motives.

It is no doubt true that, as already mentioned, the fall of the Russian empire had given Catholics great hopes for the future. A religious revival in Russia even in those disturbed times opened, momentarily, great new perspectives. It was also true that the Holy See earnestly wished the Russian Church to unite with Rome. But the Vatican's critics did an injustice to its intelligence in imputing to it a hostility to Orthodoxy so great that it would compromise itself with the Bolshevik regime to gain this end. Rome in fact was by no means indifferent to the plight of the Orthodox. On various occasions it interceded for the Orthodox leaders, at some risk of ridicule. On March 12, 1919 Cardinal Gasparri, Secretary of State for Benedict XV, sent a telegram to Chicherin asking for an end of the persecutions and confiscations then carried on against the Orthodox Church. His reward was a long reply in which the Soviet foreign minister noted with irony the Pope's "special concern" for "a religion regarded by Rome as schismatic and heretical." According to Chicherin, the Pope would do better to exercise his concern for humanity on behalf of the friends of the Bolsheviks who were fighting for humanity and were enduring harsh treatment at the hands of the "Whites."[10] This gesture of the Pope was acknowledged with thanks by the Patriarch Tikhon in a letter to Archbishop de Ropp dated July 22, 1919.[11]

Despite this tart reply from the Kremlin, another appeal was sent by the Vatican on behalf of the patriarch. On May 14, Msgr. Pizzardo wrote an appeal for Tikhon. The letter also alluded to reports that the Soviets insisted on the sale of valuable objects of worship on the grounds that the money was needed for famine relief. The Pope was declared ready to buy these objects. On May 17 Chicherin acknowledged receipt of this communication and said it would be forwarded to Moscow. No answer was forthcoming to this proposal; nor was an answer given to another telegram sent directly by Gasparri to Lenin on June 7. The alleged "indifference" of the Vatican toward the plight of the Orthodox victims of Bolshevism is therefore

10 *Documentation Catholique*, t. 7 (1922), cols. 1278-80.
11 *Osservatore Romano*, August 5, 1923.

a figment of the exiles' distraught minds, as well as a wrong to the Pope. The incident has its value, however, in showing that in the first years of the revolution the Vatican was charged not with being hardened to the Bolsheviks but, on the contrary, of seeking to acquire a privileged position in the country by following what the Paris Comité National on May 5 termed the "crooked paths of the base politics of our time."

Whatever the outcome of the Vatican's demands for a pledge of religious freedom in Russia, the project for the errand of charity did not fail. At the end of July a team consisting of eight priests and three lay brothers of various nationalities left Bari, en route to a Black Sea Russian port. The Pope himself said mass in their presence in his chapel as a sign of his personal bond with them and their work.

The Vatican relief mission was under the direction of an American Jesuit priest, Edmund A. Walsh, of Georgetown University, who had already arrived in Russia in March. He was later joined by another Jesuit, Rev. Louis J. Gallagher, of Boston. The rest of the Catholic team was recruited from Italy, Germany, Spain, Yugoslavia, and Czechoslovakia, as a result of the special direct Vatican agreement with the Soviets. The Vatican mission was, from the procurement point of view, affiliated with the American Relief Administration headed by Herbert Hoover.[12] It got its supplies through the transportation and purchasing facilities of the ARA, but at its own expense. In the field it operated as an independent unit. Its work was exclusively relief—the feeding and clothing of destitute people, especially children, regardless of their religion or politics. It had no diplomatic status, although the mission shared the privileges and immunities of the ARA in regard to freedom of communication and in other ways. It did no proselytizing. Yet the needs of the Catholics of Russia were great and the presence of Father Walsh on the scene—plus the means of

---

[12] According to Bishop d'Herbigny, Father Walsh brought a personal letter from Pius XI to President Harding in which he requested United States support for the mission. The writer paid tribute to both the President and to Mr. Hoover (*Tyrannie*, p. 98). On the Vatican relief mission, consult the obituary notice, *Father Edmund A. Walsh*, by Rev. Louis J. Gallagher, S.J., Georgetown University (privately printed, 1957).

direct communication with Rome—made it possible for him to make timely representations with the Bolshevik officials. But the tide of persecution was mounting and a new wave was to engulf the Church. On March 21, 1923 the trial of fifteen leading Catholic prelates and priests opened. They were charged with resisting the government law requisitioning Church property. Among these was Archbishop John Baptist Cieplak, apostolic administrator of Mohilev, with headquarters in Leningrad. Along with his vicar general, Constantine Budkiewicz, he and 13 other priests and one seminarian were found guilty. Archbishop Cieplak, though sentenced to death, was allowed to go into exile in April of 1924, reportedly at the intervention of the British. He died in February 1926 in Passaic, N.J. Msgr. Budkiewicz, however, was executed immediately.

In the course of time the 1923 Moscow trial was to establish itself as symbolic of Communism's war upon the Catholic Church and upon religion itself. The immediate reaction of the Vatican, however, was surprisingly restrained. Once again Rome indicated its willingness to go to extreme lengths to salvage something from the bitter situation. The words of Pius XI at the consistory of May 23, two months later, rang with a note of moderation. While he saluted the sixteen victims by name, he reaffirmed his wish to carry on the relief work that he had already launched, determined, as he said, with St. Paul, not to return "evil for evil." The continuation of the Vatican relief mission was in his eyes more than simply a work of alleviating human suffering; it was a token of the papacy's hope of finding some settlement if such could be had without sacrificing fundamental principles. The Pope's words amount to an enunciation of Vatican policy:

"And this, too, will be a means of showing how We long for peace with all, preserving all rights due in justice to the little ones, the weak and the suffering, especially those who suffer for justice and truth; safeguarding above all things and before all things (to the advantage also of the supreme interests of the civil society), the rights of the Catholic Church established by Divine disposition as the one and only custodian and teacher of justice and truth, because the one and only guardian of the incorruptible teaching and Blood of the Divine Redeemer.

"The inviolability of these rights will always be for Us a line over which it is not possible to pass, desirous as We ever are to be in peace with all and to cooperate in the universal pacification; willing as We are, where it is permissible, to make all concessions which may be necessary to attain less troubled conditions of life for the Church, and pacification of minds everywhere."

In such words the Pope seems not merely to announce his desire to seek settlement with the Soviets despite the Moscow trial, but he seemed to find it necessary—perhaps as an answer to criticisms from his own cardinals—to stress that he would not sacrifice principle for this end.

With the failure of the Genoa Conference, those powers which had not yet recognized Russia *de jure* naturally postponed that action indefinitely. In 1924 the Soviets began at last to make progress in their campaign to win general diplomatic recognition. Britain took the step of announcing *de jure* recognition on February 1, followed in the next weeks by Italy, Austria, Norway, Greece, Sweden, and other countries. France recognized the USSR on October 28. The question naturally arose at this time as to the Vatican's intentions. A press dispatch to the *Corriere della Sera* of February 24 stated that, contrary to reports, the Holy See had no intention of recognizing the Soviet Russian government either *de jure* or *de facto*. There is some evidence that efforts were in fact made at this time to search for a practical solution of current difficulties. In Berlin, on July 4 of that same year, according to an AP dispatch of that day, the papal nuncio, Archbishop Pacelli, met with Maxim Litvinov, described as "chief of the Soviet Russian legations abroad." But this conference of diplomats, which took place on "neutral" ground (i.e., neither in the Russian embassy nor in the nunciature), appears to have had no positive results, beyond indicating the mutual desire of the two parties at least to meet. On the contrary, the meeting was followed shortly afterward by the definitive closing of the relief mission.

The fate of the operation headed by Father Walsh needs

recounting at this point. This mission did not possess any official character, from the standpoint either of the Kremlin or of the Vatican. Its presence in Russia did not, therefore, constitute any sort of official recognition of the Soviet regime. Indeed, as far as the ARA itself was officially concerned, the mission was only one of a number of American groups, directed and financed by voluntary organizations. Technically speaking, Father Walsh represented the National Catholic Welfare Council. At this time (1922) it would have been a boon for the new regime had the Vatican given the mission a more official status. According to Francis McCullagh, the Soviets pretended that it was the Vatican which sought by this means to force recognition of its mission, whereas the contrary was the case.[13]

The American Relief Administration, declaring its purpose fulfilled, wound up its operations on June 20, 1923. In his final report of June 19, Father Walsh stated that the Catholic mission had daily fed an average of 158,000 children, in five separate regions (Crimea, Orenburg, Moscow, Rostov on the Don, and Krasnodar). This report did not, however, mark the immediate end of the Vatican mission. Under a separate agreement with the Soviets, the work continued for a while. In November, the director left Russia for "consultation" in Rome but did not return. The mission itself continued on a reduced scale for a year longer but finally closed for good in September 1924.

At the year's-end consistory of December 18, 1924 Pius XI marked the end of that stage of Vatican-Kremlin relations. While stating his hope to continue to aid the stricken popula-

---

[13] McCullagh, *op.cit.*, p. 332n, 100. According to the same foreign correspondent, in a Warsaw dispatch to the New York *Herald* of December 30, 1923, the termination of relief work was hastened by petty impositions designed to oblige the Vatican to transform its mission into a nunciature or at least to recognize the regime *de facto*. For instance, the officials insisted on quartering one of their own agents in the house occupied by the mission, despite a long-term lease guaranteeing exclusive occupation. At the same time Chicherin informed the director that the privilege of sending letters to the Vatican by special courier was to cease: "The Bolsheviks themselves intimated clearly that the instant this recognition were accorded all difficulties would disappear, the mission would be allowed to use a papal courier, to enjoy extraterritoriality, to possess all the diplomatic privileges of an embassy, to fly the papal flag, to do anything that the German minister or the English commercial agent could do." McCullagh noted that by *de jure* recognition of the Bolsheviks the Vatican would acquire an "impregnable stronghold" for its religious action in Russia.

tion of Russia, his words by their sharpness registered the Vatican's decision that diplomatic restraint was no longer called for:

"Certainly no one has thought that with the aid We have been giving to the Russian people We have ever helped in any way a kind of regime which We are so far from approving that We indeed think it Our duty—after having for so long, with all Our heart and all Our strength, tried to alleviate the terrible sufferings of that people by right of the universal Fatherhood given us by Almighty God—to warn and earnestly exhort all in the Lord, especially the civil leaders, that . . . they may use every effort to keep far from themselves and their fellow citizens the most serious dangers and the quite certain harm of Socialism and Communism. . . ."

The closing of the relief mission was in itself a measure of the deteriorating religious situation in the Soviet Union. The time had passed for the regime to harbor even a humanitarian mission, let alone one which represented the Pope, concerning whose religious adherents the Bolsheviks had plans of their own. At the end of 1924 ecclesiastical organization, never strong under the Czars, was on the verge of paralysis. The heads of the five Latin rite sees were in prison or in exile. A special fate was reserved for the exarch of the Catholics of the Byzantine rite, Msgr. Leonidas Feodorov. He was dragged from prison to prison until he died in 1935.

As prospects grew more and more somber during 1925 it became evident in Rome that extraordinary measures would be necessary to preserve the apostolic succession in Russia. In view of the impossibility of restoring the regular bishops, the decision was taken by the Holy See to provide emergency leadership in the person of apostolic administrators. Some would be titular bishops, others not. Both classes of prelates, however, would have the authority of bishops and would exercise special powers until the return of normal times. The area of jurisdiction would not correspond to the former diocesan boundaries.

As it was dangerous as well as useless to ask the permission of the Soviets for this step, it was decided that these new prelates would be installed in secret. Since the Bolsheviks professed "separation" of Church and State, the Vatican was only taking them at their word in regarding the contemplated ecclesiastical reorganization as nothing of which the Soviets could legitimately complain. Those who were to be made bishops would, therefore, be consecrated in secret.

The man selected for carrying out this measure of desperation was the rector of the Oriental Institute in Rome, the French Jesuit Michel d'Herbigny. This scholar went to the Soviet Union for a brief tour in October 1925. Since he was a French citizen, his travel permits were obtained for him by France, for the purpose of reporting on the ecclesiastical and other related institutions sponsored for decades by France in imperial Russia. A few months later he reentered Russia to perform his dramatic mission.

En route to Russia in the spring, Father d'Herbigny stopped in Berlin where, on March 29, 1926, he was himself secretly consecrated a bishop in the chapel of the Apostolic Nunciature. The consecrating bishop was the nuncio himself, Archbishop Pacelli, the future Pius XII. On Holy Thursday, three days later, the new bishop was already in Moscow. In the course of a six weeks' stay in Russia he consecrated several bishops and formally communicated to them and to the others their designation as apostolic administrators. The names and titles of these men were not officially published until it became certain, years later, that the Soviet authorities knew all about them.

It is likely that the Soviets were early aware of the real role of the French visitor. They betrayed no surprise and even affected indifference when, a few months later, Bishop d'Herbigny applied for a visa for a third (and last) visit to the Soviet Union. The French officials, in presenting his application, made no secret of the fact (up to then unannounced even to d'Herbigny's associates) that he was a bishop. They stated that the applicant had received episcopal consecration. The Soviets replied that the passport of the applicant already stated that he was an ecclesiastic and that, since in any case the state was "indifferent" to religion, it made no difference what the particular rank or title of the churchman happened to be. They granted a visa valid for only a few weeks.[14]

14 d'Herbigny in *Etudes*, 3 (5 mai) 1927.

The papal emissary arrived in the Soviet Union on August 1. In Moscow on August 15, to the surprise and consolation of the faithful, he celebrated an unheralded pontifical mass in the church of St. Louis of the French. In the short time of his visit he confirmed many hundreds of persons. On September 5, on the eve of his departure, there even took place an outdoor procession, in the course of a pontifical mass. It is probable that Bishop d'Herbigny also consecrated one or more bishops and installed other apostolic administrators. His visa was not extended and he left the country after six weeks.

Bishop d'Herbigny had no direct relations or contact with the Soviet officials on his trips. On every occasion he stressed that he had "no diplomatic or political mission." This was necessary in order to forestall Bolshevik distortion of his mission. It was necessary to make this clear also to quiet the apprehensions of emigré Russians who even at this late date remained abnormally susceptible to any signs of Vatican-Kremlin conversations. The White Russians speculated that the Vatican emissary had gone to negotiate a diplomatic entente with the Soviets and a religious entente with the Orthodox in Russia. In reality, the Soviets simplified d'Herbigny's problem in this regard by themselves refusing to have anything to do with him. It was through the French diplomatic representatives that the minimum necessary contact was maintained. On his part, d'Herbigny made no effort to seek contact with the Narkomindel, or foreign office. He had no contact, either, with the dissident clergy.

The anxieties of the emigrés were quite unrealistic. The situation was already too desperate for any contact with the Soviets, or with the Orthodox, who were by now firmly under Bolshevik control. On his return, Bishop d'Herbigny stressed his pessimism over the state of religion in the country. If he was aloof from the Bolsheviks, he said, this was not because of any political reason but because of the religious persecution. In an interview appearing in the Paris *Figaro* of September 25, 1926, a few weeks after his return and following his report to the Pope, he repeated that in all his trips he had no diplomatic mission whatever. He stated that the Soviets had many times betrayed the desire to have the Pope recognize the regime officially. These efforts had remained vain, he said, "for how could the Holy See recognize an atheistic government based on hatred of religion, all religions and especially the Catholic Church?" The refusal of recognition was therefore not politically motivated, he pointed out, but was based on the Bolsheviks' own war on religion.

The spectacular, last-ditch effort to preserve the minimum elements of Church organization was doomed to end in disappointment. Three of the four bishops secretly consecrated, as well as all the other apostolic administrators not raised to episcopal rank, were within a few years imprisoned at one time or another.[15]

As long as the d'Herbigny mission was not a known failure, the Vatican continued to nourish hope for the future, deriving some encouragement from the relative personal tranquility enjoyed by the faithful. In 1929, however, anti-religious action was taken up on a broad front. In that year Stalin was able at last to consolidate his power by triumphing over his rivals.

15 On this historic effort see *Tablet*, July 23, 1946 reporting a series of broadcasts on Russia by Vatican Radio in June 1946. The authoritative *Red Book of the Persecuted Church*, edited by Galter (pp. 46-50), enables us to bridge over the sparse data available on the d'Herbigny mission. Ten apostolic administrators were appointed in the fateful year of 1926. On his second visit d'Herbigny appears to have consecrated three bishops: the administrator of Moscow, the French Assumptionist, Pius Eugene Neveu; the administrator of Odessa, Alexander Frizon; the administrator of Mohilev and Minsk, Boleslas Sloskans. A fourth person is listed in the *Annuario Pontificio* as having been consecrated August 13, 1926 and therefore during Bishop d'Herbigny's third trip. He was the apostolic administrator of Leningrad, Anthony Malecki.

Bishop Sloskans was arrested in September 1927 and, after a term in Siberia, was exchanged for some Polish Communists. After the Second World War he became apostolic visitor to the Byzantine rite Catholics in Western Europe. Bishop Frizon, after many terms in prison, was arrested a last time in 1937 and shot. Bishop Malecki was arrested in 1930. After several years in Siberian prison camps he was deported in 1935 to Poland, where he died the following year. Bishop Neveu long enjoyed relative immunity because of his French nationality. But when he returned to France in 1936 for medical treatment he was unable to get a reentry visa.

To complete the picture of papal efforts to continue some vestiges of Church hierarchy in Russia, it should be added that in 1935 a French Dominican, John Baptist Amoudru, was secretly consecrated a bishop. He was soon expelled from the Soviet Union. Another known case is that of Theophilus Matulionis, one of those sentenced at the famous 1923 Moscow trials, who was consecrated in 1929. He later became bishop of Kaisedorys in his native Lithuania. Arrested in 1944, he was repatriated from Siberia in 1956. In 1957 he was reported as being confined to a hospital for the aged in Mordovia (*Red Book*, p. 79). It can only be surmised that the consecrating bishop in both cases was Bishop Neveu.

The first Five Year Plan, while economic in purpose, coincided with a new anti-religious policy. On April 8 the existing laws concerning religion were revised and tightened so as to leave virtually no room for any Church activity.

Rome was all too aware of the darkening prospects. On February 2, 1930 Pius XI in a letter to Cardinal Pamphili, Vicar of Rome, recalled the efforts of the Holy See for the people of Russia. He set March 19 as a day of prayer and expiation. This day was widely observed throughout the world and effectively drew world attention to the rising tide of persecution. A month later the Pope transformed the Pontifical Commission for Russia into an independent organ reporting directly to himself. The establishment of an autonomous body for Russia indicated the entirely exceptional, in other words, catastrophic, status of the Church in Russia. The lines of battle were forming sharply and clearly. The Vatican joined the "bourgeois states" as a target of Moscow's ire. At the 16th Congress of the Communist Party of the Soviet Union on June 27, 1930 Stalin mentioned the "clerical 'crusade' headed by the Pope against the USSR" as one of the factors "menacing the international position of the USSR." On March 8, 1931 V. M. Molotov, as chairman of the Council of Peoples' Commissars, reporting at length on the foreign scene to the 6th All-Union Congress of Soviets, attacked the Vatican and charged that the Roman Catholic priests were "spies serving on the anti-Soviet general staffs." The Vatican, he said, "has in the past few years been trying to intervene actively in international affairs—to intervene, of course, in defense of the capitalists and landlords, the imperialists, the incendiarists of war."

As the Communist danger grew worldwide in scope with the advancing world economic crisis, Pius XI on March 19, 1937 delivered his strongest indictment against the Soviet Union, with the encyclical "On Atheistic Communism" (*Divini Redemptoris*). The beginning of the Second World War found the Soviet Union and the Vatican still locked in grim ideological conflict. The Catholic Church in Russia was virtually non-existent as an organized society. At the time of Hitler's June 1941 attack on the USSR there were only about twenty Latin-rite priests still living in Russia, with about fifteen Armenian priests. Of the first group only two were at work in their parishes, while the rest were deported; of the second group almost all had been arrested for such illegal activities as teaching religion to youth under eighteen years of age.

In mid-1941, accordingly, as the Nazi attack was sweeping everything before it, the Axis governments attempted to make whatever capital they could from the Communist war on religion. The propagandists of Germany and Italy presented the assault upon the Soviet Union as a benefit to religion and to the Church. In particular, they tried to get the Pope to express his approval of the Russian campaign and even to declare it a holy war or crusade.

The Vatican did not fall into such a trap. The first (June 29) major address of the Pope following the June 22 zero hour passed without any allusion to the event. This omission was as deliberate as it was conspicuous. The papal silence was a disappointment to the Axis and was perhaps a surprise to some in the West. Prior to the war, many persons, particularly political exiles from Italy and Germany, thought they saw an identity of views between the Holy See and the Axis. But while there were some prominent clergymen, such as Cardinal Baudrillart of the Catholic Institute of Paris, who did put their influence behind the idea of an anti-Communist crusade, the Vatican itself maintained a rigorous silence, even when it seemed that the city of Moscow—and the whole USSR—was surely within Hitler's grasp.

After the war, Pius XII alluded several times to this significant silence. On February 25, 1946, for instance, addressing the diplomatic corps, in the presence of the College of Cardinals, he recalled this phase of wartime politics. Said the Pope: "We took special care, notwithstanding certain tendentious pressures, not to let fall from Our lips or from Our pen one single word, one single sign of approval or encouragement of the war against Russia in 1941."

The Pope returned more formally to this subject six years later in his encyclical *Sacro Vergente Anno* of July 7, 1952. This was a message addressed to the peoples of Russia. He recalled that, while he had not hesitated to attack the errors

of atheistic Communism, he had not rejected the errant individuals, hoping they would return to the truth:

"When the last long and terrible conflict broke out, We did
all that was within Our power, with words, with exhortations
and with action, that discords might be healed with an equitable
and just peace, and that all peoples, without difference of origin,
might unite in friendly and fraternal concord and work together for the attaining of a great prosperity. Never, even at
that time, did there come from Our lips a word that could
have seemed to any of the belligerents to be unjust or harsh.
We certainly reproached, as was our duty, every iniquity and
every violation of rights, but We did this in such a way as to
avoid with all diligence whatever might become even unjustly,
an occasion for the greater affliction of oppressed peoples. And
when pressure was brought to bear upon us to give Our approval in some way, either verbally or in writing, to the war
undertaken against Russia in 1941, We never consented to do
so, as We stated clearly on February 25, 1946, in Our allocution
to the Sacred College of Cardinals and all diplomatic representatives accredited to the Holy See."

A new era of hope, recalling the optimism after the fall of
the Czarist regime, was born again with the involvement of
Russia in the war. The Kremlin had all it could do to keep up
the morale of the people. It needed also to remedy the distrust
engendered in world opinion by its years of religious persecution. Stalin's awareness that his anti-religious policy was a lia-
bility began to show itself in several significant ways. Some
restrictive measures were gradually relaxed; the godless maga-
zines went out of existence "for lack of paper." On September
8, 1943 took place, with Stalin's permission, the election of a
patriarch, the first since the death in 1925 of Tikhon. On May
22 of that year *Pravda* had already announced the dissolution
of the Comintern, another obvious concession to Allied distrust. Faced with the possibility that these changes might, after
all, be irreversible, Catholics entertained hopes that the long
darkness might soon end in Russia. In any case, even if these
moves were tactical and forced upon the Communists by the
gravity of their military defeats, they were at least reluctant
proof of the tenacity of the religious problem. In spite of all the

years of contrary indoctrination, religion still remained a vital force which the regime had to appeal to in its hour of peril.

Although the Vatican was officially aloof from the Nazi-Soviet conflict and avoided being a tool of Nazi propaganda, it was not entirely inactive before the new situation. For all the bitter disappointments of former times, Rome could not forget the spiritual needs of the faithful who had survived the long years of isolation from the center of unity in Rome. Nor could it overlook the possibility that perhaps the time had at last come for the union of the dissident Churches with the Holy See. Missionaries who had long prepared themselves for the apostolate of Russia availed themselves of the opportunities offered them by the military operations. Priests conscripted as common soldiers into the Wehrmacht and official chaplains with Italian units on the Russian front sought contact with the local population. One authenticated case is that of the Italian Jesuit, Pietro Leoni, who entered the Soviet Union with a Fascist division for the express purpose of carrying on his apostolate for which he had prepared himself at the Russicum in Rome. He established himself in Odessa, once a thriving center of Catholic life. Conformably to his original design, he remained there even after the retreat of the Axis forces. For a year he was able to carry on his ministry in freedom and with Soviet permission. He was finally arrested and sent to the mining city of Vorkuta, near the Arctic Circle. He was repatriated in May 1955.[16] Leoni's work was duplicated by others of whom few details are known. Like him, most wound up in Siberian labor camps.

The Nazi attack of June 1941 naturally completely changed the policy of the Western powers toward the Soviet Union. The Allies lost no time in extending assistance to the Soviets. Inevitably, the attitude of the Vatican toward allied military and political aid to the beleaguered Soviets became a matter of importance. From that time on, the press began to talk more of Vatican-Kremlin relations. We shall chart the ebb and flow of the rumors, mixed with fact, which reflect the political importance of this subject in the world's capitals.

[16] Leoni, *"Spia del Vaticano!"* (Roma, 1959).

Rumors of diplomatic moves on the religious question began to appear in the neutral and Allied press within a few months. The religious issue was raised by the United States ambassador at Moscow in October 1941, on instructions from President Roosevelt. Shortly afterward *Anti-Religioznik* ceased to appear. In November, Swiss newspapers attributed to "American propaganda" reports of a rapprochement between the Vatican and the Kremlin. On January 20, 1942 Swiss correspondents reported from Rome concerning a meeting alleged to have taken place on that subject between Harry Hopkins and Archbishop Godfrey, then apostolic delegate in London. Hopkins was the special envoy of President Roosevelt. German newspaper, cited by the same sources, quoted the archbishop as denying this report.

One of the most unusual rumors of this kind to get currency in the world press during the war cropped up in the spring of 1942. On March 3, at a time when the military fortunes of the Allies were at their lowest ebb, a report was issued from Rome by an independent news agency, Agenzia Radio Urbe, which asserted that Generalissimo Stalin had written a letter to the Pope. Further details were added in later dispatches. In the alleged communication, the Soviet chief asked the Pope to examine the question of diplomatic relations. He was cited as referring to the approaching diplomatic relations with Japan and as asking for the same treatment for the Soviet Union.

Although the agency's story was denied by Vatican spokesmen and the *Osservatore Romano* ignored it completely, it provided material for speculation for several weeks. The *New York Times* dignified it by publishing a circumstantial account of the letter in a telephoned Berne dispatch under date of March 17. The dispatch stated that, official denials notwithstanding, the Soviet generalissimo had indeed sent Pius XII a personal manuscript letter which was generally interpreted as respectful to the Catholic Church. The letter dwelt, it was reported, on the religious policy of the Soviet Union.

The immediate source of the *Times* story may have been a series of dispatches from the Roman correspondent of the *Corriere del Ticino* of Lugano and published in that Swiss newspaper in the issues of March 13, 14, 16, and 22. This journal, whose story was given wider circulation by the Nazi radio, asserted without any qualification that the letter had been confirmed as authentic and that it was being examined by various Vatican bodies. Along with this letter, said the correspondent, there was also being examined a series of documents defending the religious policy of the Soviet Union. This documentation, it was said, reached the Vatican through "a great power now allied with Russia in the war." The Soviet government was asserted to have pointed out that "freedom of religion" is amply recognized, in line with the promise made to the United States at the time of the 1933 recognition. It denied that the Union of Militant Atheists was government-inspired. This group, it said, had merely solicited the protection of the government for its own propaganda primarily based on the diffusion of "scientific tracts."

Did this story, which got such publicity in the world press, including the *London Times* as well as the *New York Times*, have any foundation in fact? Or was it simply and literally a "March tale"? We do know from Sherwood's biography of Harry Hopkins and Langer-Gleason, and from the wartime correspondence of President Franklin D. Roosevelt with Pius XII, that the United States was particularly anxious about the anti-religious policy of the Soviet Union. Washington was worried, among other things, about the reaction of the papacy toward allied assistance to the Communist regime in the form of Lend-Lease. The Vatican's announcement of forthcoming diplomatic relations with Japan was an annoyance to Washington and London. Did the Allies plant this report as a means of making the Soviet Union more acceptable to the West and thus do, in reverse, what the Axis propagandists had sought to do six months earlier?

This latter interpretation has been given the episode by Rev. F. A. Cavalli, of the Jesuit-edited *Civiltà Cattolica*. In his view, the story was a hoax engineered by the Allies, specifically by the English. In an article published after the war (May 21, 1949), he pointed out that the effect of the rumored Stalin letter was sufficient to show from what side the story emanated: "To judge from the contents, which tended to undermine the propaganda claims of the Axis to the effect that the war against

Russia was a crusade of Christianity against atheistic communism, the information must have come from an Anglo-Saxon source." It was characteristic of British "humor," said the Roman writer, to argue that, if the Pope could have relations with Japan, he could do no worse by having the same relations with the Soviet Union.[17]

Nothing more was ever heard of this alleged personal letter of Generalissimo Stalin to Pope Pius XII. Before it trailed off into oblivion, however, Vatican sources alluded to it indirectly in a defense of the newly-formed relations with Japan. The Vatican Information Office declared in its bulletin *Corrispondenza* that there was a great difference between Japan and the USSR. In non-Christian Japan, Catholicism was one of the four officially recognized religions. Furthermore, the relations between the Imperial House, the government, and the Holy See had long been cordial. In the Soviet Union, on the other hand, which was by tradition a Christian country, the rulers of that country had long proclaimed and carried on a war against God and every form of religion.

As the war entered a new phase and it appeared that the Red Army would hold its own against the Wehrmacht, yet other rumors of Vatican-Kremlin relations entered the world press. On February 17, 1943 an AP dispatch from Berne quoted Swiss news agencies as reporting that Vatican sources denied categorically a published report that the Pope had consented to receive a special Soviet delegation. On the same day a DNB (German) dispatch declared that the Vatican had denied allegations, attributed by DNB to Tass, that the Vatican was preparing to receive a delegation of Soviet diplomats.

The dissolution of the Comintern, announced on May 22, kindled the fire anew. For instance, the Washington correspondent of the *London Times* on May 25 cabled his paper about a "persistent report" of a "concordat." The dispatch suggested that Archbishop Spellman of New York, who was at that moment in Turkey, on a world tour to visit U.S. troops (for whom he was the Catholic military vicar), might be an intermediary for such a purpose. Similar rumors were carried by the *New York Times* of May 27 and 28.

[17] Cavalli, *Civiltà Cattolica, loc.cit.*

In reality, during all this period of flux in the military fortunes of Soviet Russia, the Vatican's efforts at winning the cooperation of the Kremlin in purely humanitarian matters, particularly for prisoners of war, were meeting with complete failure. The Soviet Union had not been a party to the Red Cross Geneva Conventions and refused entry of foreign observers to their prison camps. There is not on record the meeting of any papal envoy with Soviet authorities at any time during the war. Though there is little published evidence to this effect, it can be assumed that the papal suggestions and ideas were conveyed either by neutral diplomatic channels, such as Switzerland, or through the Soviets' own allies, especially the United States.

The year 1944 was a turning point in the war and also marked a new phase in relations between Rome and Moscow. In this year the Red Army, pressing the weakened Wehrmacht, entered into the lands of traditionally or largely Catholic peoples: Poland, Czechoslovakia, and Hungary. For the second time it also entered Lithuania from which it had been obliged to retreat after June 1941. In June, Rome itself was occupied by Allied troops and this opened up a new source of news. Inevitably, the question of future Vatican policy toward the Soviets was raised by Allied correspondents in Rome. In the course of an unprecedented press conference, the Vatican spokesman, Msgr. Jacques Martin, noted that there had been no relations with the Russians since the First World War. He then added: "Certain developments are noted here with interest. We believe certain signs of change can be observed. For the Vatican there are, as yet, strictly speaking, no new facts."[18]

This reply reflected the grave uncertainty of that extremely fluid period of world politics. The military success of the Soviet Union had won much sympathy in a war-weary Allied populace. They hoped to see a new Russia emerge from the experiences of the war. Yet, the Allies had to contend with the extreme suspicion of the Kremlin. The charge voiced suddenly by *Izvestia* on July 22, 1944 of an Anglo-American attempt at a separate peace with the Nazis was a warning of the state of Stalin's mind. *Izvestia* had already in January launched a bitter

---

[18] *Tablet* (London), June 17, 1944.

attack on the Vatican. Yet all in all, as the Vatican spokesman had said, there were encouraging developments in the Soviet Union. It was the desire of everyone to see them go farther. The inclination everywhere was to explore every possible avenue of rapprochement with a nation that for years had been a pariah in the international community.

The return to Western Europe of old-time Communists in exile for years in the Soviet Union provided an additional new source of rumors. One of the returnees was Palmiro Togliatti, the secretary of the Communist party in Italy. He became a member of the provisional government and promptly set about establishing a position for the party. He found those who were willing to explore the possibility that the war may have perhaps made it possible to collaborate with the Communists. Among facts of note was his visit of July 13, 1944 to Msgr. Montini, the papal substitute secretary of state.

An article published in *Foreign Affairs* at the beginning of 1945, and therefore referring to the situation as of late 1944, may be significant. Its author was Don Luigi Sturzo, founder of Christian Democracy in Italy, whose contacts with civil and clerical circles in Italy were close. Don Sturzo attributed many of the rumors to the activity of Togliatti:

"Many recently believed that the Communist leader Togliatti, a member of the present Italian government, had presented a plan for closer relationship between the USSR and the Holy See to the Christian Democratic leader de Gasperi, also a member of the Italian Government, and that either jointly or separately they had discussed the matter with the papal Under Secretary of State, Msgr. Montini. But the existence of such a plan was later denied by the official Vatican organ, *Osservatore Romano*. Since then the Moscow press has twice attacked the Vatican, accusing it of following a pro-Fascist policy in the past and of continuing such a policy."[19]

[19] Sturzo, in *Foreign Affairs*, 1946. Don Sturzo may have been referring to a denial issued by *Osservatore Romano*, which in its issue of August 14-15 denied what it termed "unfounded rumors," which it attributed to Reuters. These were to the effect that the Russian government "in a political move without precedent have sent a memorandum to the Vatican proposing coordinated action between Moscow and the Holy See in the postwar, for the solution of moral and social problems." The original story had been first published by the *London News Chronicle*.

In a commentary written for Religious News Service at this point in the war, an expert on Russian religious affairs examined the basis for such an agreement. Professor N. S. Timasheff, of Fordham University, cited as significant a Vatican comment reported from Rome on August 11, 1944 by the Associated Press. According to this dispatch the Vatican spokesman stated that, although doctrinally conciliation was impossible, it "is not impossible to imagine from the practical standpoint that Stalin might at any moment take up a surprise position before which the Vatican itself must be prepared." Professor Timasheff also quoted an unidentified Moscow official who, when asked about a report of such an agreement, said, "If such an agreement is reached, you won't know about it." On September 6, however, the *Osservatore Romano* denied that the Soviet Union was making overtures to the Vatican.

On March 11, 1945 came another denial from the Vatican press office. This time *il Tempo*, an anti-Communist liberal daily of Rome, claimed that negotiations for an agreement were going on with the collaboration of the United States and the support of Great Britain. A *New York Times* Rome dispatch noted that the denial was not published by the *Osservatore Romano* itself and that the subject had, in fact, been on everyone's tongue. On March 14, Tass itself joined in with its own denial.

For once there was more than smoke. In February, a close adviser of President Roosevelt, Edward J. Flynn of New York, a Catholic, went to Yalta for the Crimean conference, and proceeded afterward directly to Moscow. On March 21, Flynn arrived in Rome from the Soviet capital. Within the space of a few days he saw the Pope not once, but twice. The purpose of the Flynn mission has never been officially revealed. Religious News Service, however, in a dispatch datelined London, April 5, gave some details which it claimed to have from a reliable source. According to RNS, Flynn's mission was to raise at Moscow three matters of importance for religion: (1) permission for the Holy See to send priests immediately to East European countries then under Red Army occupation; (2) approval for the reopening of Church institutions in these areas; (3) assurances in regard to Soviet intentions toward Italian prisoners in the Soviet Union.

No practical results emerged from the Flynn mission, if indeed the trip really had such a purpose. Queried about this visit, Foreign Minister V. M. Molotov was subsequently quoted by RNS as saying that the Vatican's own attitude toward the Soviet Union would have to be known before anything could be said on the specific points reportedly raised by Flynn.[20] In the background of these scattered bits of information and tendentious rumors in a time of wartime censorship lay a great drama: the future course of Soviet policy toward the West. The Vatican was not alone in its hopes, hesitations, and doubts. Men were soon recalling what Sir Winston Churchill had said on October 1, 1939 when he described Soviet policy as "a riddle wrapped in a mystery inside an enigma." For the Church, the Stalin riddle did not long keep its mystery. By the end of 1945 the Kremlin had displayed its intentions by carrying on a program of forced schism among the Eastern-rite Catholics in union with Rome, as well as by bitter anti-Vatican propaganda. As far as Eastern and Central Europe was concerned, the ruler of the Kremlin did not wish to share his political control with the Western powers, nor his ideological monopoly with the Pope of Rome. As the postwar decade unfolded, bringing fresh episodes of pressure on the Church, the possibility of an understanding steadily receded into the background.

In the nearly half-century after the Bolshevik Revolution of 1917, the Soviet Union and the Holy See officially never came closer than they did in 1922. The peripheral contacts at the Genoa conference failed to develop. The record of these four decades, scanty though the information is, does not bear out the impression that the Vatican rejected every idea of rapprochement simply out of intolerance or pique. In Vatican diplomacy, the line of conduct is determined by the same considerations that govern any other kind of diplomacy. It is predicated upon the sincere desire of the other party for a lasting understanding

[20] The interest of the Soviet Union in the Vatican at this time was indirectly manifested by the publication in *Bolshevik* (April 1945) of an article by Morris Stein, former Soviet ambassador to Italy. The Vatican, he said, was a world power, despite its lack of territory.

that respects in good faith the basic interests of all concerned. The Catholic Church has adapted itself to living in peace with many different forms of government. These governments have, in turn, learned to adapt their own system to the exigencies of their Catholic citizens. In time the Holy See may conceivably reach some form of *modus vivendi* or accommodation with the Soviet Union. If the Church's basic liberties are respected and it is allowed to carry on its mission without crippling restrictions, there is no reason to exclude the possibility of a form of diplomatic relations between the two which can be described as at least officially "normal."

The struggle of Church and State in the countries bordering on the Soviet Union, where a regime of the so-called "popular democracies" was installed after the Second World War under Moscow's instigation, has served to bring out the nuances of Vatican policy toward an officially unbelieving regime. The Vatican did not at once withdraw its diplomatic representatives when the Marxist-Leninist regimes came to power. It did not take the initiative of diplomatic rupture but left that move to the Communist-controlled regimes, which thereby assumed responsibility for the break.

In these Soviet-style democracies the population is very largely Catholic. It is not therefore difficult to imagine an evolution of circumstances out of which diplomatic relations might be restored. Overwhelmingly Catholic Poland, for instance, with its intense loyalty to the Holy See, will sooner or later edge closer to normal relations with the Vatican. In this eventuality the Communist government will find itself carried by forces which it cannot control.

Such a stable understanding seemed quite remote even after the death of Stalin and the liberalization which ensued. Nevertheless, there are indications that the terms of such an accommodation have been studied in the Vatican. We have already instanced the three points on religious freedom in Soviet Russia which the Holy See presented at Genoa in 1922. These were conditions of recognition. Presumably, if accepted and observed, they could have led to diplomatic relations between Rome and Moscow. In the light of subsequent experience these three rather elementary points require a more elaborate development.

"Freedom of religion" in the Soviet Union has been so transformed from its original meaning that a new formulation of these essential rights has become necessary. Freedom of religion should not be a formula by which religion is left to wither on the vine. It must embody a substantive body of sovereign tasks to be performed by and through religious leaders under conditions of real independence.

In an address delivered by radio in 1956 Pius XII himself appears to have sketched the main lines of Catholic thought on the possible conditions of peace with the Kremlin. On the occasion of the Katholikentag at Cologne, on September 2 of that year, the Pope hinted at the minimum conditions for coexistence with the Communist State (not with Communist ideology). In the same breath with which he warned against possible entrapment by Moscow's "coexistence" propaganda, the Holy Father left open the possibilities of some kind of negotiations:

"There is coexistence in Truth. We have on a previous occasion [*Christmas, 1955*] spoken of this, so We only add thereto these remarks: The Catholic Church does not force anyone to belong to it. For itself it asks, however, *freedom to live in the state according to her constitution and her laws, to minister to her faithful and to be able to preach openly the gospel of Jesus Christ*. This, We say, is its indispensable basis for any honorable coexistence." (*Italics supplied.*)

In other words, the Church does not demand that the State necessarily modify its own official ideology as a condition for normal relations. Even from the atheistic Soviet Union it does not exact as a condition *sine qua non* the ending of Marxism-Leninism. That the Pope was referring to the problems of the popular democracies and the Soviet Union is clear from his allusion to the idea of "coexistence," a word which at that phase of international developments was a favorite one with Moscow's spokesmen and propagandists.

The Church demands only the right to teach the catechism to the faithful, particularly to the young, and to administer the sacraments; it must at the same time have the right to preach the gospel, not merely to its own adherents but also to those not of the household of the faith—in other words, to evangelize and proselytize. In these stipulations other conditions are implied: the Church's own existence as a society or organization having its own constitution and laws must be recognized at least implicitly. Not the least of its requirements for free existence worthy of the name is the union of the bishops and faithful with the source and symbol of unity which is Rome.

Such conditions are not exorbitant. They are largely fulfilled in virtually every other part of the world outside the Communist orbit. As Count Giuseppe Dalla Torre has expressed it, "The Catholic Church asks from the Communist countries nothing more nor less than it asks from other countries where separation of church and state exists."[21] From the record, the Soviet system seems far removed from the desire or even capacity of according this kind of freedom to the Church. A long period of struggle and of evolution seems therefore indicated for the future. The past, perhaps, offers a clue to the future. The most stormy and difficult chapters in Vatican diplomatic history have been in the century before the First World War, in the areas now under Soviet hegemony. Diplomatic relations between imperial Russia and the Holy See, while tense and often meager of results, were not impossible or entirely without object. At times relations were even cordial. A common interest in resolving otherwise insoluble problems kept the two parties together. What the course of Vatican-Kremlin relations may be in the second half of the 20th century is subject to too many variables to permit confident prediction. Neither party concerned in this dramatic duel will wish to initiate negotiations, or seem to, but both will be equally pushed by the exigencies of events from which neither Church nor State can really dissociate itself, whether it wishes to or not.

[21] Dalla Torre, in *United Nations World*, 1949.

CONCLUSION

IN A SOCIAL GATHERING, it is said, to maintain an agreeable atmosphere guests should avoid discussing religion or politics. This advice was not meant for writers of books but its wisdom should not be lost on them, particularly on those congenital nettle-graspers who write on both subjects at one and the same time. In the field of Church-State relations not only is broad agreement difficult to achieve but objectivity is a rare quality likely at any moment to fail either the writer or the reader, or both.

From the standpoint of these hazards, the study of Church-State relations as a diplomatic problem has much to recommend it. Like Ariadne's thread, Vatican diplomacy is a tenuous but no less sure guide through the labyrinth of Church-State relations. The facts are simple and present for all to see, for diplomacy of its very nature is a public institution. By its nature, too, it is the bond between two independent societies differing in kind as well as in number. Diplomacy speaks with authority and authenticity the language of international society. The *lingua franca* of international intercourse, it is comprehensible to all, regardless of form of government and social ideals. When it acts as the bridge not merely between two political societies but between a civil and a religious society, it tells much about that relationship.

But behind procedures, principles inevitably are to be found at work. In the operation of diplomacy, many disciplines are called into play: international law, constitutional law, domestic as well as foreign policy. When, as in the case of Vatican diplomacy, the political aspect of these relations has a religious pendant, an additional set of factors enters: canon law, theology, culture, conscience. In both cases, history is ever present with its experience and instruction. As a result, diplomacy is not merely a technical organ of intercourse; it reveals implicitly the very principles upon which international society is built. It portrays on a wide canvas, if in lesser detail, what might otherwise be overlooked or obscured when studied in its purely national, local, or contemporary segment.

Because the institution of diplomatic representation links both practice and theory, the light it throws in the field of Church-State relations is less subject to the extremes of error. The English historian Geoffrey Barraclough, in writing about contradictory versions of the medieval empire presented by scholars, points out that much depends upon the viewpoint. If you regard only pure facts you are likely to get one conclusion, whereas if you start from theory you are likely to get quite another. "The political historian," he says, "tends to portray realities that have no value, while the political philosopher and the historian of ideas is apt to deal with a scheme of values that have no reality." If we apply this warning to the present subject, it appears that one will not get the true picture of contemporary Church-State relations by regarding Vatican diplomacy as merely a play of material interests or a contest of power. By the same token, the theoretician who comes to this subject with nicely formalized theories on what he thinks ought to be the relations of the sacred and the profane in our day is likely to spin a purely doctrinaire system out of all relation to reality. Diplomacy, with its deep roots in both reality and theory, can help the reader to avoid both extremes.

Some general conclusions have by this time no doubt presented themselves to the reader of their own accord. One of these may be the realization that Church and State are not, and never have been, entirely separated from each other in the sense that either wished or could ignore the other. Church and State are not two pyramids standing unmoved next to each other in the same Egyptian desert for uncounted centuries, their grandeur equaled only by their aloofness. On the contrary, these two societies act and interact, influence and are influenced. To assume otherwise is to bar any fruitful probe into a question that needs constant interpretation and reinterpretation.

Another observation is that, whatever else it is, Vatican diplomacy is an accepted and well-established institution even in those circles not at all suspect of partiality to the Holy See. This establishes the assumption that there is some basic and entirely consistent exigency to which it corresponds. The rational explanation of Vatican diplomacy may be difficult to discover, and perhaps this present study will not entirely satisfy the curious.

It is certain, however, that the phenomenon has some valid explanation, or at least that it can teach many lessons to the inquirer.

Another observation will also have spontaneously arisen in the mind of the reader familiar with the Church's system of the "two societies" as expounded in public ecclesiastical law. In Vatican diplomacy we have a clear instance of the confrontation of the two perfect societies which Leo XIII described with such preciseness in his 1886 encyclical *Immortale Dei*. The two societies deal with one another through the same instrument which the states employ among themselves, in their capacity of sovereign powers, as the medium of their formal relationships. In international law, the states acknowledge each other's mutual sovereignty not only in formal agreements, such as a treaty of peace or alliance, but also in the exchange of formally accredited representatives. This process is most jealously reserved to the restricted company of sovereign powers. As the ambassador is the herald of the State's political sovereignty, so the papal nuncio is the herald of the Pope's spiritual sovereignty. Both represent a perfect society, each supreme and independent in its sphere.

But once one has gotten beyond these elementary observations, papal diplomacy remains an enigma on several counts. For some, papal diplomacy is an inexplicable deviation from the secularization of international law. The integration of Church diplomacy into the framework of the modern law of nations appears to them as a regrettable retrogression in the march of progress toward a future where troublesome questions joining religion and politics no longer intrude.

To resolve this puzzle, recourse is had to various hypotheses. The chief one is that the states do not in fact recognize the Pope as a religious potentate so much as the temporal sovereign of the State of Vatican City. This viewpoint, quite natural to a generation accustomed to think in purely secular terms, attributes the diplomatic capacity of the Holy See to at least the fiction of the temporal or civil power. It is assumed accordingly that the Pope is able to use (or usurp) diplomatic channels for the conduct of religious affairs because he happens to be, for reasons incidental or not to his religious role, the temporal sovereign of the State of Vatican City.

Such an explanation is difficult to reconcile with the data of history. It is incompatible, for instance, with the fact that for sixty years in the lifetime of many now living, the Pope was without recognized temporal sovereignty. During this period (1870-1929), the governments continued in increasing numbers to accredit their diplomatic representatives at the Holy See. This was not regarded by the Kingdom of Italy (the most important rival of the papacy on this very matter) as a recognition of the civil sovereignty of the Pope. For their part, the governments stressed their right to have an ambassador at the Vatican precisely because the Pope was a religious leader with whom they had important affairs to transact at the highest level.

There were other, briefer, periods which momentarily revealed that the states were more concerned with the Pope diplomatically as pontiff than as king. In 1808 when Napoleon's troops were occupying Rome the envoys remained at their post in the Eternal City and received, in fact, instructions from their home governments to remain in normal relations with the Pope—this despite the fact that, to all intents and purposes, the papal states were extinguished. Their mission, as diplomats, had a primarily religious object. A comparable situation arose in 1848, when Pius IX was making his vain effort to introduce constitutional reform into the papal states. During a short period there were two secretaries of state, one for secular affairs and the other for ecclesiastical affairs. Faced with this clear demarcation of competences, the states showed by their conduct that they regarded the religious side of their envoy's work as more basic and important than the purely temporal side. They maintained closer contact with the secretary of state for religious affairs and thereby taught themselves as well as others, if any instruction was needed, that the Pope's right of legation was due more to his religious role than to his political status.

But the judgment implicit in these governmental acts at certain crucial moments of papal history is explicit in multiple declarations down the centuries of modern diplomacy. There was a clear awareness of the double title by which the Pope enjoyed diplomatic representation. The kings of France regularly instructed their ambassador-designate that he was to have a twofold task at Rome. He was to deal equally with the Pope as sovereign prince of considerable territories and also as sovereign Pontiff of the Catholic Church. On either score, his mission was a diplomatic one.

As a result of combined historical and theoretical developments, by the time of the Lateran Treaty the Pope's right of legation as a religious chief was widely recognized in international law. It is true that, for various reasons, the ecclesiastical side of papal diplomacy was obscured in certain instances. The Protestant rulers, for instance, found it convenient to nickel-plate their diplomatic negotiations with the Pope on ecclesiastical matters by pointing out that the Pope was, after all, also a royal sovereign. In virtually every instance, however, this presented a false picture. The only exception was the case of the United States (for the years 1848-1868). As the instructions issued to the first United States chargé d'affaires pointed out, most of the other states represented at Rome dealt with the Pope as head of the Catholic Church. And this was when the Pope was ruler not of the one thousand inhabitants of Vatican City but of three million subjects at the center of the Italian peninsula.

Papal writers, too, expressed themselves at times as though the diplomatic relations of the papacy betokened civil sovereignty primarily. This stress upon the temporal power dates from the loss of the papal states in 1870, particularly after the Roman question reached its highest intensity at the turn of the century. Echoes of this point of view still crop up in some Catholic writings influenced by the polemical literature created in the controversy preceding the 1929 Lateran settlement. These were debating points, of some value in themselves, but they did not touch off the essence of papal diplomacy. The temporal power is indeed a guarantee, even an indispensable guarantee in the state of international law up to now, of the papal independence. By no means does it constitute the basis of papal diplomacy. The view adopted throughout this study is that this diplomacy is an expression of the spiritual sovereignty and as such quite independent of any connection with the primarily symbolic State of Vatican City.

Even aside from the religious character of the Pope, the papacy's world status as an international juridical personality presents another enigma for specialists of international law. The kind of authority exercised by the Holy See is something distinct. It is not the mere "juridical capacity" of other non-territorial subjects of international law. The vitality of Vatican diplomacy suggests that what is involved here is something more than a mere "moral authority" of a religious leader whose world "prestige" commands respectful attention.

In the course of these pages we have not hesitated to use the word "sovereignty" to describe the essence of the moral and religious authority of the Holy See. Such a use of this privileged term is bound to outrage some legal theoreticians. As it is commonly employed, sovereignty implies almost universally a political authority. To term the Church's authority a "spiritual" sovereignty seems to be a contradiction in terms and at most a figure of speech.

Yet sovereignty is an old word of which the modern jurists have no monopoly. In treating of diplomacy it is difficult to avoid using the word with which this institution is traditionally linked. There is no other concept more apt to describe the phenomenon before us. In Vatican diplomacy are found the same attributes to be found in political sovereignty, namely, an entire independence toward outside societies and auto-determination in internal affairs. Too many profound conflicts, too many treaties of peace, lie in the diplomatic archives for this fact to escape notice or be challenged. The Vatican is not like the other non-territorial international personalities: mere instruments created by the members themselves as an extension of their joint power, to serve a common, if higher, political cause. The Church is a separate society whose goals are not subordinated to those of the political community. The Pope exercises the prerogatives of sovereignty in his diplomacy because his authority possesses the elements of independence that the State expects and supposes in those with whom it deals in its own diplomacy. In treating with the papacy at the diplomatic level, the State here experiences a familiar echo of its relations to the other states. Why not describe this "moral authority" with the only word which matches the reality?

The use of "spiritual sovereignty" as a term can also be justified from the history of the struggle of Church and State.

In the 17th and 18th centuries sovereignty was regarded as indivisible. This was stressed notably when the royal power in religious matters was in question. Such a contention is no longer maintained. Sovereignty is indeed divisible, regardless of the arguments once used and once believed so conclusive and logical. If sovereignty can be divided, it can be partitioned, that is, shared by both the State and the Church. It would be arbitrary to allege that the Pope's share in this sovereignty should not be styled sovereignty but something else. To say that the authority of the Church, over what was once claimed by the State as its own prerogative, does not deserve to be called sovereignty, simply because it concerns religion and not politics, is only to use words to conceal what really exists. If in the 17th and 18th centuries men were arguing that the eagle cannot have two heads, one does not answer the difficulty in the 19th and 20th centuries by saying that there are indeed two heads but that one of them, representing the Church, is not that of an eagle.

Far from introducing dangerous ambiguities, the acceptance of "spiritual sovereignty" as a legitimate and meaningful expression would help to clear away the dilemma that mystifies the international lawyers. Without that key to the inner significance of Vatican diplomacy, the student will remain fated to grapple in vain with a phenomenon it has no means of comprehending.

Perhaps the general reader would be more enlightened if Vatican diplomacy were explained in terms of liberty rather than in terms of sovereignty. In the end, liberty is the acid test of sovereignty. When one considers the rampant regalism of the 18th century on the eve of the French Revolution, can it be said that the Church was then really sovereign? In the century following the Revolution, the Catholic Church reputedly had a nostalgia for the old system of Church-State relations. But even in the days of the Restoration, when much was made of the "union of the altar and the throne," did any Catholic spokesman seriously advocate a return of the kind of "protection" afforded by the Catholic monarchs? This kind of sponsorship by the prince had brought the Church to an extreme of weakness and subjection not seen in centuries. The Catholic regalists

(Gallicans, Febronians, and Josephinists) used their special privilege as protectors of the Church not for the advantage of the Church but in order to enslave her. It is significant that many of the condemnations of Pius IX in his 1864 Syllabus are directed not against the tenets of the liberal State of the 19th century but against those of the regalist State of the 18th.

In the last century, the Church finally broke away from the shackles that the old regalism had imposed upon it. The course of this development, as reflected in the changing function of papal diplomacy at this time, is depicted in several chapters of this study. It is a paradox that the Holy See was able to break loose from its bonds in the very century of the much-denounced liberal State and in large part thanks to the principles of that liberal State. Church history needs rewriting from this point of view. The last century, too often studied in isolation and in the eyes of its contemporaries, deserves to be looked at in the light of the evils that had preceded in the century before, as well as in the light of the advantages that have accrued to the Church in the century after. Today's papal diplomacy has one simple objective: to maintain the liberty of the Church as a perfect society vis-à-vis that other perfect society whose own autonomy it in turn recognizes, whether Catholic or not.

In these chapters we have had occasion to stress that the Holy See is something in a class by itself. It is unique diplomatically both as a religious institution and as an institution within international law. But this note of singularity should not be sounded too loud or too long. Vatican diplomacy is not a being from another planet or a misbegotten offspring of religion and politics. Despite the exceptional status of the Holy See it is not at all alien to contemporary trends in institutions and ideas. In the international legal order now emerging, the Holy See appears less strange than it did to men of a half-century ago. Legal theory has moved along rapidly, thanks to the acceleration induced by the two world wars. Not only states but also contractual organizations without any territorial basis are admitted to the once exclusive company of international persons. From a system in which only states were admitted to juridical capacity, the liberalization of the law of nations has proceeded to a point where this capacity is extended to non-territorial institutions, such as the United Nations, and even to individuals. The Holy See, once an ugly duckling in international law, meets with more comprehension when put in the company of the intergovernmental organizations such as the United Nations and the autonomous specialized agencies which cluster about the world peace agency.

The field of human rights exemplifies one of the more specific directions of this trend. The movement for "the international protection of human rights" finds some striking applications in the case of the Holy See. Here, too, governments attribute to an international body outside their own jurisdiction some authority over their own citizens. Human rights are no longer an "internal affair," as was once said also of Church affairs. Boris Mirkine-Guetzévitch described this process as "the transposition of the rights of man and of the citizen from the domain of constitutional law to the sphere of international law." This development lifts the problem of freedom from the level of purely domestic law and makes it an international concern. As a result, not only is the constitutional power of the State limited in regard to its own citizens, but this limitation or renunciation or sharing of jurisdiction is made in favor of an international organ. The movement is yet in its initial stages, but the trend is clear. In the words of Lauterpacht, "The constant expansion of the periphery of human rights—an enduring feature of legal development—cannot stop short of the limits of the state."

But what the lawyers project into the immediate future is already an accomplished fact in the case of the Holy See. For within the sphere of religious freedom and for the specific benefit of Catholics (the only religious group organized internationally whose supreme head is outside the national boundaries), the State has long since adopted what is now advertised by the most advanced legal theorists as the inevitable law of the future. It was not necessary to await the creation of the first international agency for human rights. There already was one, the Holy See, to which the State accorded a legitimate concern over the particular area of human rights touching the consciences of its Catholic citizens. This acknowledgment of participation it seals and confirms by taking the step of entering into diplomatic relations with the supreme organ of Catholicism, over matters it once contended were within its exclusive domestic jurisdiction.

Nor is the Holy See completely without parallel even in the religious world. The Catholic Church differs from most non-Catholic religions in possessing a supreme authoritative organ to which the civil power, with good or bad grace, can address itself for concrete decisions. But the Holy See is not a solitary specimen in other respects. One of the corollaries of religious freedom is that the State must acknowledge that its citizens can have a loyalty beyond and above national interests. In this vital stake the Catholic Church has no monopoly. The primacy of conscience is a tenet of the Christian (and non-Christian) world generally. The only difference for non-Catholic denominations is that for the most part this primacy is not polarized by the existence of a qualified supreme organ able to act as the keeper of that conscience.

The State's pledge of respect for conscience entails for it many moments of difficult decision. If the primary loyalty of the citizen is and ought to be beyond the State, tension is inevitable when the interests conflict. The religious community is not limited to man-made territorial boundaries. It speaks not only to the citizen but to the man. This is not necessarily out of harmony with national purposes, at least with the higher interests and ideals of the nation. But it can bring a radical and revolutionary criticism to bear on national egoism and therefore on policy.

What should be the State's policy in the face of resistance to its "sovereign" will by those whose immunity it has sworn to respect on the grounds of freedom of conscience? "The state," says William Ernest Hocking, whose thought we are taking the liberty of adapting, "has no choice but to accept this possibility which—in spite of all efforts to make a firm line between the standards of politics and morals—effectively limits its freedom of action to courses that do not massively violate the conscience of its people."

Such a situation is verified for religion as such, or at least for those who hold that one must obey God rather than man. It is a constant problem for the State, for it is idle to pretend that religious freedom can be a reality in a State without self-denial on the part of the powers that be. In the case of the Catholic Church, the resistance of conscience is likely to be much more "massive" than in the case of other denominations less compactly organized under legitimate pastors. Historically, the State finds a remedy for its self-imposed handicap by seeking to deal with the Holy See and thereby search for a compromise which will secure a solution without doing violence to consciences.

In short, the modern State must accept a dual loyalty on the part of its citizens. If it is not lack of due loyalty to the civil power to admit the primacy of conscience, it is not wrong for a Catholic to look for guidance to that religious authority which he personally accepts as the keeper of his conscience. It might be alleged that such matters should be strictly between the State and the citizen, without the necessity of introducing a third, extraneous, agent. But the primacy of conscience means nothing if the State is entitled to select and choose the precise religious norms or tribunals by which its citizen is to be guided. Freedom of conscience implies freedom to organize religious life in the form consistent with one's belief. If the citizen recognizes the Pope of Rome as such a guide, the State has no choice but to bow and to make its calculations on that basis. It may be added that when such international organs as the World Council of Churches assume a comparable role of authoritative guide, the State will in all consistency need to take that into account. In the meantime, the civil power is not acting in a discriminating fashion when it accredits its diplomatic representatives to the only religious authority which affords peremptory guidance to consciences.

Some representatives of Protestant groups, particularly those stemming from the tradition of the Nonconformists in England, find it objectionable in principle for the State to take cognizance, in any form whatever, of religious bodies. But this viewpoint is based upon historical experience that is limited both as to time and as to place. It is so incomplete and so riddled with unstated premises as to distort the elements of the problem out of all proportion and so render solution and comprehension more difficult than need be. A study of Vatican diplomacy and its lessons of the past five centuries of what are called modern times, through a dozen major political and religious crises, may perhaps restore a somewhat more realistic and illuminating perspective to one of the central problems of man's existence on this earth, the compatibility of his sacred and his secular concerns.

BIBLIOGRAPHY

DIRECTORIES

Almanach de Gotha. Annuaire généalogique, diplomatique et statistique. Gotha, 1763-   . (Diplomatic lists not cited before 1803.)
Annuaire pontifical catholique. Albert Battandier, ed. Paris, 1898-
Annuario pontificio. Roma, 1860-1870; 1912-
Bittner (Ludwig) und Gross (Lothar), ed. *Repertorium der diplomatischen Vertreter aller Länder seit dem westfälischen Frieden (1648).* I Band (1648-1715), Berlin, 1936. II Band (1716-1763), Friedrich Hausmann, ed., Zürich, 1950
La Gerarchia della Chiesa e la famiglia pontificia. Roma, 1872-1911
Notizie per l'anno. . . . In Roma nella stamperia di Galeazzo Chracas, presso s. Marco al Corso. 1716-1798; 1807-1808; 1818-1859. (The Diplomatic Corps in Rome is listed only after 1792.)

BOOKS

Abt, Hans. *Die Schweiz und die Nuntiatur. Eine Richtigstellung.* Zürich, 1925
Accioly, Hildebrando. *Os Primeiros nuncios no Brasil.* S. Paolo, 1949
Ackermann, August. *Die Schweiz und Rom. Ihre wechselseitigen Beziehungen in Vergangenheit und Gegenwart.* Freiburg (Schweiz), 1940
Adair, E. R. *The Extraterritoriality of Ambassadors in the Sixteenth and Seventeenth Centuries.* London, 1929
Adamow, E. *Die Diplomatie des Vatikans zur Zeit des Imperialismus* (Tr.). Berlin, 1932
Ago, Roberto. "Occupazione bellica dell'Italia e Trattato Lateranense," in *Istituto di diritto internazionale e straniero della università di Milano. Communicazioni e studi.* Milano, 1946. Vol. II, pp. 131-172
Albion, Gordon. *Charles I and the Court of Rome.* London, 1935
Almedingen, Martha Edith. *The Catholic Church in Russia Today.* New York, 1923
Ammann, Albert M. *Abriss der ostslawischen Krichengeschichte.* Wien, 1950
Anzilotti, Dionisio. *Corso di diritto internazionale.* 3 ed., Roma, 1928; 4 ed., Padova, 1955
————. *Cours de droit international* (Tr.). Paris, 1929
[Apponyi, Count Albert.] *The Memoirs of Count Apponyi.* London, 1935
Artaud de Montor, Marquis. *Histoire du pape Pie VII.* Paris, 1836, 2 v.
————. *Histoire du pape Léon XII.* Paris, 1843. 2v.

Artaud de Montor, Marquis. *Histoire du pape Pie VIII*. Paris, 1844

Ashley, The Hon. Evelyn. *The Life of Henry John Temple Palmerston 1848-1865 with selections from his speeches and correspondence*. 2 ed., London, 1876. 2v.

Aubert, Roger. *Le Pontificat de Pie IX*, Paris, 1952

Audisio, Guglielmo. *Idea storica e razionale della diplomazia ecclesiastica*. Roma, 1864

——. *Diritto pubblico della Chiesa e delle genti Cristiane*. Roma, 1863, 3v.

Aureli (Guido) e Crispolto (Crispolti). *La Politica di Leone XIII da Luigi Galimberti a Mariano Rampolla*. Roma, 1912

Auswärtige Amt. Die grosse Politik der europäischen Kabinette, 1871-1914. Sammlung der diplomatischen Akten des Auswärtigen Amtes. Berlin, 1926. 40v.

Baisnée, Jules A. *France and the Establishment of the American Catholic Hierarchy*. Baltimore, 1934

Balladore-Pallieri, Giorgio. *Il Diritto internazionale ecclesiastico*. Padova, 1940

——. *Diritto internazionale pubblico*. 5 ed., Milano, 1948

Bangen, Johann Heinrich. *Die römische Kurie. Ihre gegenwärtige Zusammensetzung und ihr Geschäftsgang*. Münster, 1854

[Banning, Emile et al., éd.] *La Belgique et le Vatican. Documents et travaux législatifs concernant la rupture des relations diplomatiques entre le gouvernement Belge et le Saint-Siège, précédés d'un exposé historique des rapports qui ont existé entre eux depuis 1830*. Bruxelles, 1880-1881. 3v.

Bannon (Francis) and Dunne (Peter Masten). *Latin America. An Historical Survey*. Milwaukee, rev., 1958

Barraclough, Geoffrey. *The Medieval Empire. Idea and Reality*. London, 1950. The Historical Association, General Series: G 17.

Bastgen, Hubert. *Die römische Frage. Dokumente und Stimmen*. Freiburg i. Br., 1917-1919. 3v.

——. *Forschungen und Quellen zur Kirchenpolitik Gregors XVI (Veröffentlichungen zur Kirchen- und Papstgeschichte der Neuzeit, Bd. 1)*. Paderborn, 1929

——. *Bayern und der Heilige Stuhl in der ersten Hälfte des 19 Jahrhunderts*. München, 1940. 2v.

Baumgarten, Paul Maria (ed.). *Der Papst. Die Regierung und Verwaltung der Heiligen Kirche in Rom. Neuarbeitung des Werkes: Rom, das Oberhaupt, die Einrichtung und die Verwaltung der Gesamtkirche. Herausgeber Leo-Gesellschaft in Wien*. München, 1904

Becker, Jerónimo. *Relaciones diplomáticas entre España y la Santa Sede durante el siglo XIX*. Madrid, 1908

Benson, Oliver E. *Vatican Diplomatic Practice as affected by the Lateran Agreements*. Liège, 1936

Berutti, Christophorus M. *De curia Romana. Notulae historico-exegetico-practicae.* Romae, 1952

Bettanini, Antonio M. *Lo Stile diplomatico. Propedeutica allo studio della diplomazia.* Milano, 1930

Beyens, Baron (Napoléon E.). *Quatre ans à Rome, 1921-1926.* Paris, 1934

Biaudet, Henry. *Les Nonciatures apostoliques permanentes jusqu'en 1648. (Etudes romaines publiées par l'expédition historique finlandaise à Rome.* Vol. I, No. 1 in *Annales Academiae scientiarum fennicae.* Ser. B. 2), Helsinki, 1910

Binchy, Daniel A. *Church and State in Fascist Italy.* Oxford, 1941

Bindel, Victor. *Le Vatican à Paris (1809-1814).* Paris, 1942

von Bischoffshausen, Sigismund. *Papst Alexander VIII und der wiener Hof (1689-1691).* Stuttgart und Wien, 1900

Bluntschli, Johann Kaspar. *De la responsabilité et de l'irresponsabilité du pape dans le droit international.* A. Rivier, tr. Paris, 1876. (Broch.)

Boggiano-Pico, E. *La Città aperta di Roma.* Rome, 1943

Bompard, Raoul. *Le Pape et le droit des gens.* Paris, 1888

Boudou, Adrien. *Le Saint-Siège et la Russie.* Paris, 1922. 2v.

Brezzi, Paolo. *La Diplomazia pontificia. Istituto per gli studi di politica internazionale.* Milano, 1942

Broderick, John F. *The Holy See and the Irish Movement for the Repeal of the Union with England, 1829-1847.* Rome, 1951

Brück, Heinrich. *Geschichte der katholische Kirche in Deutschland im neunzehnten Jahrhundert.* Mainz, 1889. 3v.

Brusa, Emilio (ed.). *Del diritto internazionale. Lezioni del Professore Ludovico Casanova . . . con introduzione e note copiossissime dell'Avvocato Emilio Brusa.* 3 ed., Firenze. 1876. 2v.

Bryce, Lord. *Studies in History and Jurisprudence.* Oxford, 1901

Buder, Christian Gottlieb. *De legationibus obedientiae Romam missis liber singularis.* Jena und Leipzig, 1737

[Burke, Edmund.] *Correspondence of Edmund Burke and William Windham.* J. P. Gilson, ed. Cambridge, 1910

Bury, John B. *History of the Papacy in the 19th Century.* London, 1930

Calvo, Carlos. *Le Droit international théorique et pratique.* 5 éd., Paris, 1896. 6v.

Cammeo, Federico. *Ordinamento giuridico dello Stato della Città del Vaticano.* Firenze, 1932

Casoria, Giuseppe. *Concordati e ordinamento giuridico internazionale.* Rome, 1953

Charles-Roux, François. *Huit ans au Vatican, 1932-1940.* Paris, 1947

Charykov, N. V. *Glimpses of High Politics Through War and Peace. 1855-1929.* London, 1931

Cheke, Marcus. *The Cardinal de Bernis.* New York, 1959

de Claparède, Arthur. *L'Essai sur le droit de représentation diplomatique d'après le droit international moderne* (thèse). Genève, 1875

[Cochin, Denys.] *Denys Cochin, 1914-1922. La Guerre—le blocus— l'union sacrée.* Paris, 1923

Coleman, William J. *The First Apostolic Delegation in Rio de Janeiro and its Influence in Spanish America. A Study in Papal Policy, 1830-1840.* Catholic University, Washington, 1950

[*Collectio Lacensis.*] *Acta et decreta sacrorum conciliorum recentiorum.* Freiburg i. Br., 1890. 7v.

Commons, House of. *British Parliamentary Papers. Correspondence Respecting the Relations existing between Foreign Governments and the Court of Rome. LIX (1851)*

―――. *Correspondence Respecting the Affairs of Rome, No. 1 (1870-1871). LXXII (1871)*

Conci, Francesco. *La Chiesa e i vari stati. Rapporti—concordati— trattati—per una storia del diritto concordatario.* Napoli, 1954

[Consalvi, Ercole Cardinale.] *Memorie del Cardinale Ercole Consalvi.* Mario Nasalli Rocca di Corneliano, ed. Roma, 1950

―――. *Mémoires du Cardinal Consalvi . . . avec une introduction et des notes.* J. Crétineau-Joly, ed. Paris, 1864. 2v. (A third edition of 1895 in a single volume omits some documentary material.)

Conte a Coronata, Matthaeus. *Institutiones juris canonici. Introductio. Jus publicum ecclesiasticum.* 3 ed., Romae, 1947

Cordier, Henri. *Histoire des relations de la Chine avec les puissances occidentales 1860-1900.* Paris, 1901-1902. 3v.

Costantini, Celso (Cardinale). *Con i missionari in Cina (1922-1933).* Roma, 1946. 2v.

―――. *Ultime foglie. Ricordi e pensieri.* Roma, 1954

Des Houx, Henri. *Souvenirs d'un journaliste français à Rome.* 2 éd., Paris, 1886

des Michels, Jules Alexis. *Souvenirs de carrière (1855-1886).* Paris, 1901

Despagnet, Frantz. *Cours de droit international public.* 4 éd., Paris, 1910

Devoti, Joannes. *Institutionum canonicarum libri IV.* Bassani, 1843. 4v.

Dietze, Hans Helmut. *Die päpstlichen Nuntien.* Frankfurt-Main, 1944

Dittrich, Kurt. *Die preussische Gesandtschaft beim Vatikan.* Berlin, 1918

Doeberl, Ludwig. *Maximilian von Montgelas und das Prinzip der Staatssouveränität.* München, 1925

Duclos, Paul. *Le Vatican et la seconde guerre mondiale.* Paris, 1955

Duguit, Léon. *Traité de droit constitutionnel.* Paris, 1925. 5v.

Durry, Marie-Jeanne. *L'Ambassade romaine de Chateaubriand.* Paris, 1927

Dvornik, Francis, "Church and State in Central Europe" in *The Soviet Union: Background, ideology, reality. A Symposium.* Waldemar Gurian, ed. Notre Dame, 1951, pp. 195-216

Eckhardt, Carl Conrad. *The Papacy and World Affairs as Reflected in the Secularization of Politics.* Chicago, 1937

Egan, Maurice Francis. *Recollections of a Happy Life.* New York, 1924

Ehler (Sidney Z.) and Morrall (John B.). *Church and State Through the Centuries. A Collection of historical documents with commentaries.* Westminster, 1955

Ellis, John Tracy. *Cardinal Consalvi and Anglo-Papal Relations, 1814-1824.* Washington, 1942

Engel-Jánosi, F. *Oesterreich und der Vatikan 1846-1918.* Graz-Wien-Köln, 1958

Epstein, Klaus. *Matthias Erzberger and the Dilemma of German Democracy.* Princeton Univ. Press, 1959

Esperson, Pietro. *Diritto diplomatico et giurisdizione internazionale marittima col commento della disposizione della legge italiana del 13 maggio sulle relazioni della Santa Sede colle potenze straniere.* Roma-Torino-Firenze, 1872-1876. 3v.

Farini, Luigi Carlo. *The Roman State from 1815 to 1850.* Translated by Rt. Hon. W. E. Gladstone. London, 1851. 4 v.

Fauchille, Paul. *Traité de droit international public. Huitième édition, entièrement refondue, complétée et mise au courant, du Manuel de droit international public de M. Henry Bonfils.* Paris, 1921-1926. 4v.

Favre, Jules. *Rome et la République française.* Paris, 1871

Febronius, Justinus (pseud., von Hontheim, Johann Nikolaus). *Justini Febronii, jurisconsulti, de statu ecclesiae et legitima potestate romani pontificis, liber singularis ad reuniendos dissidentes in religione catholica compositus.* Bullioni, 1763

Feiertag, Loretta Clare. *American Public Opinion on the Diplomatic Relations between the United States and the Papal States (1847-1867).* Washington, 1933

Feller (Abraham H.) and Hudson (Manley O.) (ed.). *A Collection of the Diplomatic and Consular Laws and Regulations of Various Countries.* Washington, 1933. 2v.

Ferrata, Domenico Cardinale. *Mémoires.* Roma, 1920. 3v.

Figgis, John Neville. *Churches in the Modern State.* London, 1913

Foster, John W. *A Century of American Diplomacy. 1776-1876.* Boston, 1900

———. *The Practice of Diplomacy as Illustrated in the Foreign Relations of the United States.* New York, 1906 de Franciscis, Pasquale (éd.). *Discours de notre très saint-père le pape Pie IX* (Tr.). Paris, 1875-1876. 3v.

Friedberg, Emil. *Der Staat und die Bischöfswahlen in Deutschland.* Leipzig, 1874

Galter, Albert. *The Red Book of the Persecuted Church* (Tr.). Westminster, 1957

Garsou, Jules. *Les Relations extérieures de la Belgique (1839-1914).* Bruxelles, 1946

Gasquet, Francis Aidan. *Monastic Life in the Middle Ages; with a note on Great Britain and the Holy See, 1792-1806.* London, 1922

Gebhardt, Bruno. *Wilhelm von Humboldt als Staatsmann.* Stuttgart, 1896-1899. 2v.

Geffcken, Heinrich. *Léon XIII devant l'Allemagne* (Tr.). Paris, 1892. (Broch.)

Genêt, Raoul. *Traité de diplomatie et de droit diplomatique.* Paris, 1931-1932. 3v.

——. *Malte et son destin.* Paris, 1933

Gerbrandy, P. S. *Eenige Hoofdpunten van het Regeeringsbeleid in London gedurende de Oorlogsjaren 1940-1945.* 's Gravenhage, 1946

von Gierke, Otto. *Natural Law and the Theory of Society. 1500 to 1800. Translated with an introduction by Ernest Barker.* Cambridge, 1950

Giobbio, Alfredo. *Lezioni di diplomazia ecclesiastica.* Roma, 1899-1901. 3v.

Del Giudice, Vincenzo. *La Questione romana e i rapporti tra stato e Chiesa fino alla conciliazione.* Roma, 1947

——. *Manuale di diritto ecclesiastico.* Milano, 1949

Goulmy, P. J. L. M. *Nederland naar het Vaticaan.* Nijmegen, 1915

——. *'s Pausen Diplomatie en de Nederlanden,* Utrecht, 1917

Goyau, Georges. *Le Vatican. Les Papes et la civilization. Le Gouvernement central de l'Eglise.* Paris, 1895

Graham, Robert A. *The Rise of the Double Diplomatic Corps in Rome. A Study in Diplomatic Practice (1870-1875).* The Hague, 1952

[Gregory XVI.] *Gregorii Papae XVI, Acta.* Romae (ed. Vanutelli), 1901-1904

Greville Memoirs, The. A Journal of the Reign of Queen Victoria from 1847 to 1852. London, 1885

Grimaldi, Felix. *Les Congrégations romaines, guide historique et politique.* Sienne, 1890

Guariglia, Raffaele. *Ricordi. 1922-1946.* Napoli, 1950

Guggenheim, Paul. *Traité de droit international public.* Genève, 1954. 2v.

Guizot. *Mémoires pour servir à l'histoire de mon temps.* Paris, 1865. 8v.

Hackworth, Green. *Digest of International Law.* Washington, 1940-1943. 7v.

Hales, E. E. Y. *Pio Nono. A Study in European politics and religion in the nineteenth century.* New York, 1954

———. *The Catholic Church in the Modern World.* New York, 1958

Halperin, Samuel William. *Italy and the Vatican at War.* Chicago, 1939

[Hamilton, J. A.] *Reminiscences of James A. Hamilton.* New York, 1869

Hanotaux, Gabriel (éd.). *Rome. Avec une introduction et des notes.* Paris (1888-1911-1913) (*Recueil des instructions données aux ambassadeurs et ministres de France depuis les traités de West-phalie jusqu'à la Révolution française.* Vols. VI, XVII, XX). 3v.

Hanus, Franciscus. *Church and State in Silesia under Frederick II (1740-1789).* Catholic University, Washington, 1944

———. *Die preussische Vatikangesandtschaft, 1747-1920.* München, 1953

Hayes, Carleton J. H. "Medieval Diplomacy" in Walsh, E. A. (ed.), *The History and Nature of International Relations.* New York, 1922

Hayward, J. *Pie IX et son temps.* Paris, 1948

Heffter, A. W. *Das europäische Völkerrecht der Gegenwart.* 7 Aufl. bearb. von J. Heinrich Geffcken. Berlin, 1881

Hegel, Eduard. *Die kirchenpolitischen Beziehungen Hannovers, Sachsens und der nord-deutschen Kleinstaaten zur römische Kurie, 1800-1846.* Paderborn, 1934

d'Herbigny, Michel. *La Tyrannie soviétique et le malheur russe.* Paris, 1923

Hershey, Amos S. *Diplomatic Agents and Immunities.* Washington, 1919

———. *The Essentials of International Public Law.* Rev. ed., New York, 1927

Hertling, Ludwig. *A History of the Catholic Church* (Tr.). Westminster, 1957

Heston, Edward L. "Papal Diplomacy: Its Organization and Way of Action" in *The Catholic Church in World Affairs,* ed. Waldemar Gurian and M. A. Fitzsimons, Notre Dame, 1954

von der Heydte, Friedrich August. *Völkerrecht. Ein Lehrbuch. Bd. I.* Köln, 1958

———. *Die Geburtsstunde des souveränen Staats.* Regensburg, 1952

Higgins, Pearce. *Studies in International Law.* Cambridge, 1928

Hill, David Jayne. *A History of Diplomacy in the International Development of Europe.* London: Vol. I, 1921; Vol. II, 1924; Vol. III, 1914

Himly, Auguste. *Histoire de la formation territoriale des états de l'Europe Centrale.* Paris, 1876. 2v.

de Hinojosa, Ricardo. *Los Despachos de la diplomacia pontificia en España. Memoria de una mision official en el archivo secreto de la Santa Sede. Tomo Primero.* Madrid, 1896

Hochfeld, Herbert. *Die Rechtspersönlichkeit des Heiligen Stuhles im Völkerrecht vom Untergang des Kirchenstaates bis zum Schaffung der Città del Vaticano (1870-1929).* Diss. Hamburg, 1930

Holloran, Mary P. *Church and State in Guatemala. (Studies in History, Economics and Public Law. Columbia University. No. 549.)* New York, 1949

Hollôs, Franz Tibor, "Die katholische Weltkirche und ihre Diplomatie" in *Verfassung und Verwaltung in Theorie und Wirklichkeit. Festschrift für W. Laforet.* München, 1952

Hudal, Alois. *Die deutsche Kulturarbeit in Italien.* Münster, 1934

———. *Die oesterreichische Vatikanbotschaft, 1806-1918.* München, 1952

von Huebner, Baron Joseph. *Sixte-Quint* (Tr.). Paris, 1882. 2v.

Hugues de Ragnau, Edmond. *The Vatican. The Center of Government of the Catholic World.* New York, 1913.

[Hull, Cordell.] *The Memoirs of Cordell Hull.* New York, 1948. 2v.

Hunt, Gaillard (ed.). *Journals of the Continental Congress 1774-1789.* Washington, 1904-1937. 34v.

Von Hutten-Czapski, Bogdan Graf. *Sechzig Jahre Politik und Gesellschaft.* Berlin, 1935. 2v.

Hyde, Charles Cheney. *International Law. Chiefly as Interpreted and Applied by the United States.* 2 rev. ed., New York, 1947

[Ickes, Harold L.] *The Secret Diary of Harold Ickes.* New York, 1953-1955. 3v.

Imbart de LaTour, Joseph. *La Papauté en droit international.* Paris, 1893

Jacini, Stefano. *Il Tramonto del potere temporale nelle relazioni degli ambasciatori austriaci a Roma (1860-1870).* Bari, 1931

Jannacone, C. *I Fondementi del diritto ecclesiastico internazionale.* Milano, 1936

Johnson, Humphrey. *Vatican Diplomacy in the World War. With foreword by Count de Salis.* Oxford, 1933. (Broch.)

Karttunen, Liisi. *Les Nonciatures apostoliques permanentes de 1650 à 1800. (Etudes romaines publiées par l'expédition historique finlandaise à Rome. Vol. II, No. 3 Annales Academiae scientiarum fennicae,* Ser. B. 5.) Genève, 1912

Kelsen, Hans. *The Law of the United Nations.* London, 1950

von Kienitz, Erwin Roderich. *Die Gestalt der Kirche. Einführung in Geist und Form des kirchlichen Verfassungsrechts.* Frankfurt-Main, 1937

Kissling, Johannes B. *Geschichte des Kulturkampfs im deutschen Reich.* Freiburg i. Br., 1913

Kölle, Friedrich. *Betrachtungen über Diplomatie.* Stuttgart und Tübingen, 1838

Kühn-Steinhausen, Hermine. *Die Korrespondenz Wolfgang Wilhelms von Pfalz-Neuburg mit der römische Kurie.* Köln, 1937

La Brière, Yves de. *Les Luttes présentes de l'Eglise.* Paris, 1913-1924. 6v.

———. *l'Organisation internationale du monde contemporain et la Papauté souveraine.* Paris, 1924-1927-1930. 3v.

———. *L'Eglise et son gouvernement.* Paris, 1935

Laemmer, Hugo (ed.). *Monumenta Vaticana historiam ecclesiasticam saeculi XVI illustrantia. Appendix* II. *Informatione del secretario et secreteria di Nostro Signore et di tutti gli offitii che da quella dependono del Sgr. Giovanni Carga. 1574.* Friburgi, 1861

von Lama, Friedrich. *Papst und Kurie in ihrer Politik nach dem Weltkrieg.* Illertissen, 1925

Lambruschini, Luigi Cardinal. *La Mia Nunziatura di Francia. A cura Pietro Pirri. Diarie et memorie.* Bologna, 1934

Lampert, Ulrich. *Die völkerrechtliche Stellung des Apostolischen Stuhles.* Trier, 1916

———. *Kirche und Staat in der Schweiz.* Freiburg (Schweiz). 1929-1939. 3v.

Langer, William L. *European Alliances and Alignments.* 2 ed., New York, 1950

Langer (William L.) and Gleason (S. Everett). *The Challenge to Isolation, 1937-1940.* New York, 1952

———. *The Undeclared War, 1940-1941.* New York, 1953

Laski, Harold. *Studies in the Problem of Sovereignty.* New Haven, 1917

Latreille, André. *Napoléon et le Saint-Siège, 1801-1808. L'Ambassade du Cardinal Fesch.* Paris, 1935

Lauterpacht, H. (ed.). *International Law. A Treatise by L. Oppenheim.* 8 ed., New York, 1955. 2v.

———. *Recognition in International Law.* Cambridge, 1947

———. *International Law and Human Rights.* New York, 1950

Lawrence, T. J. *The Principles of International Law.* 5 ed., Boston, 1910

[Lebzeltern, Louis de.] *Mémoires et papiers de Lebzeltern.* Emmanuel de Lévis-Mirepois, Prince de Robech, éd. Paris, 1949

Lecler, Joseph. *L'Eglise et la souveraineté de l'État.* Paris, 1946. (Tr., *The Two Sovereignties,* New York, 1952)

———. *Histoire de la tolérance au siècle de la Réforme.* Paris, 1954. 2v.

Lector, Lucius (pseud.) [Mgr. Joseph Guthlin.] *Le Conclave. Origines, histoire, organisation, législation ancienne et moderne.* Paris, 1894

Lector, Lucins (pseud.). *L'Election papale*. Paris, 1896

Lefebvre de Béhaine, Edouard. *Léon XIII et le Prince de Bismarck*. Paris, 1898

Lefêvre, Joseph. *Analecta Vaticano-Belgica*. 2e Série: *Nonciature de Flandre, IX. Documents relatifs à la juridiction des nonces et internonces des Pays Bas pendant le régime autrichien (1706-1794)*. Bruxelles-Rome, 1950

————. *Nonciature de Flandre, VIII. Documents relatifs à la juridiction des nonces et internonces des Pays Bas pendant le régime espagnol (1596-1706)*. Bruxelles-Rome, 1943

————. *Nonciature de Flandre, VII. Documents relatifs à l'admission aux Pays Bas des nonces et internonces*. Bruxelles-Rome, 1939

LeFur, Louis. *Le Saint-Siège et le droit des gens*. Paris, 1930

Lehmann, Max (ed.). *Preussen und die katholische Kirche seit 1640. Nach den Acten des geheimen Staatsarchives*. Leipzig, 1878-1902. 7v. *(Publikationen aus dem k. preussischen Archiven*. Bde. 69-75.) Continued by H. Granier, ed.: Achter und Neunter Theil (Bde. 76-77). Leipzig, 1902. 2v.

Leslie, Shane. *Henry Edward Manning. His Life and Labours*. New York, 1921

Lesourd, Paul. *L'Ambassade de France près le Saint-Siège sous l'Ancien Régime*. Paris, 1925

Leturia, Pedro. *Der Hl. Stuhl und das spanische Patronat in Amerika. Das Ende des spanischen Patronats in Amerika und die Enzyklika Leos XII vom 24 Sept. 1824*. Diss. München, 1925

————. *Bolivar y Leòn XII*. Caracas, 1931

[Loftus, Lord Augustus.] *The Diplomatic Reminiscences of Lord Augustus Loftus. Second Series, 1862-1879*. London, 1894. 2v.

Loiseau, Charles. *Politique romaine et sentiment français*. Paris, 1923

Lucas, Edward. *The Life of Frederick Lucas, M.P.* London, 1886. 2v.

de Luise, Gaspare. *De jure publico seu diplomatico Ecclesiae Catholicae*. Romae, 1877

Maass, Ferdinand. *Der Josephinismus. Quellen zu seiner Geschichte in Oesterreich 1760-1790. (Oesterreichische Akademie der Wissenschafter in Wien. Fontes rerum austriacarum. Zweite Abteilung. Diplomataria et acta*. Bde. 71, 72, 73). Wien, 1951-1956. 3v.

McCullagh, Francis. *The Bolshevik Persecution of Christianity*. London, 1924

Madelin, Louis. *La Rome de Napoléon. La Domination française à Rome de 1809 à 1814*. 3 éd., Paris, 1906

Magnini, Leo. *Pontificia Nipponica: Le relazioni tra la Santa Sede e il Giappone attraverso i documenti pontifici*. (Bibliotheca Missionalia, nn. 5, 6.) Roma, 1947-1948. 2v.

de Maistre, Joseph. *Du pape*. Lyon, 1819. 2v.

[Mamachi, Thomas Maria.] *Thomae Mariae Mamachii . . . Epistolarum ad Justinum Febronium Jurisconsultum de ratione regendae*

Christianae reipublicae, deque legitima Romani pontificis auctoritate. Romae, 1776-1778. 3v.

Manfroni, Giuseppe. *Sulla soglia del Vaticano. 1870-1891. Dalle memorie.* Bologna, 1920. 2v.

De Marchi, Giuseppe. *Le Nunziature apostoliche dal 1800 ai 1956.* Roma, 1957

Maritain, Jacques. *The Things That Are Not Caesar's.* New York, 1931

du Marsais. *Exposition de la doctrine de l'Eglise gallicane par rapport aux prétentions de la cour de Rome.* Paris, 1817

de Martens, Charles. *Manuel diplomatique.* Paris, 1822

————. *Le Guide diplomatique.* 4 éd., Paris, 1851. 2v.

————. *Guide diplomatique.* Éd. F. H. Geffcken. 5 éd., Leipzig, 1866

Martens, Fédor Fédorovich. *Traité de droit international* (Tr.). Paris, 1886. 3v.

————. *Recueil des traités et conventions conclus par la Russie avec les puissances étrangères; publié d'ordre du ministère des affaires étrangères.* St. Petersburg, 1874-1909. 15v.

Martens, Georges Frédéric. *Cours diplomatique, ou tableau des relations extérieures des puissances de l'Europe.* Berlin, 1801. 3v.

Martin, Jacques Paul. *La Nonciature de Paris et les affaires ecclésiastiques de France sous le règne de Louis-Philippe (1830-1848).* Paris, 1944

Martin, Victor. *Les Cardinaux et la curie. Tribunaux et offices. La Vacance du Siège Apostolique.* Paris, 1930

Mater, André. *La République au conclave et l'alliance avec Rome en régime de separation. Le Conclave de Venise. 1794-1799-1800.* Paris, 1923

Mathieu, François-Désiré Cardinal. *Le Concordat de 1801. Ses origines—son histoire.* Paris, 1903

Mattingly, Garrett. *Renaissance Diplomacy.* Boston, 1955

de Maulde-La-Clavière, René. *La Diplomatie au temps de Machiavel.* Paris, 1892-1893. 3v.

Mecham, J. Lloyd. *Church and State in Latin America.* Chapel Hill, 1934

Meier, Otto. *Zur Geschichte der römisch-deutschen Frage.* Bde. I-III, 1, Rostock, 1871-1874; Bd. III, 2, Freiburg i. Br., 1885

————. *Ueber den päpstlichen Hof. Vortrag gehalten in Evangelischen Vereine zu Berlin am 17 Januar 1870.* Berlin, 1870. (Broch.)

————. *Die Propaganda in England. Zur kirchenrechtlichen Beleuchtung der Bistumsfrage.* Leipzig, 1851

Michie, Alexander. *The Englishman in China during the Victorian Era.* London, 1900. 2v.

Mills, J. Saxon. *The Genoa Conference.* London, 1922

Ministère des affaires étrangères. Documents diplomatiques français (1871-1914). 1ère série (1871-1900), 1929-1947, 11 tomes; *2e série (1901-1911)*, 1930-1948, 10 tomes; *3e série (1911-1914)*, 1929-1936, 11 tomes. Paris

Ministère des affaires étrangères. La Politique extérieure de l'Allemagne, 1870-1914. Documents officiels publiés par le ministère allemand des affaires étrangères. Paris, 1927-1939. 32v. (Translation of portions of *Die Grosse Politik.*)

Ministero degli affari esteri. Documenti diplomatici relativi alla Questione Romana communicati dal ministero degli affari esteri nella tornata del 19 dicembre 1870. Camera dei deputati. Sessione 1870-1871. Prima della XI legislatura. Doc. n. 46. Roma, 1871

Mirbt, Carl. *Die preussische Gesandtschaft am Hofe des Papstes.* Leipzig, 1899. (Broch.)

——. *Quellen zur Geschichte des Papsttums und des römischen Katholizismus.* 4 Aufl. Tübingen, 1924

Miruss, Alexander. *Das europäische Gesandtschaftsrecht.* Leipzig, 1847

Mollat, G. *La Question romaine de Pie VI à Pie XI.* Paris, 1932

Montini, Giovanni Battista. La *"Responsio super nuntiaturis" di papa Pio VI. Appunti delle lezioni. Pontificio Istituto "Utriusque Juris" S. Apollinare. Anno accademico 1936-1937.* Editrice Studium, Roma, 1936. (Mimeo.)

[Monts, Anton Graf.] *Erinnerungen und Gedanken des Botschafters Anton Graf Monts.* Berlin, 1932

Moody, Joseph N. (ed.). *Church and Society. Catholic Social and Political Thought and Movements 1789-1950.* New York, 1953

Moore, James Bassett. *A Digest of International Law.* New York, 1906, 8v.

Morelli, Emilia. *La Politica estera di Tomasso Bernetti segretario di stato di Gregorio XVI.* Roma, 1953

Morgan, Thomas B. *The Listening Post. Eighteen Years on Vatican Hill.* New York, 1944

[Moroni, Gaetano.] *Dizionario di erudizione storico-ecclesiastica da St. Pietro sino ai nostri giorni. Compilazione di Gaetano Moroni.* Venezia, 1840-1879. 109v.

Mourret, F. *The Papacy* (Tr.). London, 1931

Mowat, R. B. *Diplomacy and Peace.* London, 1935

Muller, Joseph (ed.). *Das Friedenswerk der Kirche in den letzten drei Jahrhunderten. Erster Band: Die Friedensvermittelungen und Schiedssprüche des Vatikans bis zum Weltkrieg. 1598-1917.* Berlin, 1927

Murray, John Courtney, "On the Structure of the Church-State Problem," in *The Catholic Church in World Affairs,* ed. Waldemar Gurian and M. A. Fitzsimons. Notre Dame, 1954

Napoléon Ier. *Correspondance. Publié par ordre de l'Empereur Napoléon III.* Paris, 1858-1869. 32v. (2 éd., Paris, 1858-1870. 32v.)

Nava, Santi. *Sistema della diplomazia.* Padova, 1950

Newton, Lord. *Lord Lyons. A Record of British Diplomacy.* London, 1913. 2v.

Niboyet, J.-P. *L'Ambassade de France au Vatican (1870-1904).* Paris, 1912

Nicolson, Harold. *Diplomacy.* New York, 1939

[Niebuhr, B. G.] *The Life and Letters of Barthold George Niebuhr, with essays on his character and influence by the Chevalier Bunsen and Professors Brandis and Lorbell* (Tr.). New York, 1852

Nielsen, Fredrik Kristian. *The History of the Papacy in the XIXth Century* (Tr.). New York, 1906. 2v.

Nippold, Friedrich. *The Papacy in the 19th Century* (Tr.). New York, 1900

Noack, Friedrich. *Das Deutschtum in Rom. Seit dem Ausgang der Mittelalter.* Berlin-Leipzig, 1927. 2v.

Nys, Ernest. *Le Droit international. Les Principes, les théories, les faits.* Bruxelles, 1912, nouvelle éd., 3v.

Odier, Pierre. *Des privilèges et immunités des agents diplomatiques en pays de Chrétienté.* Paris, 1890

Ojetti, Ugo (ed.). *Ambasciate e ambasciatori a Roma.* Milano-Roma, 1927

de Olivart, Marquis. *Le Pape, Les Etats de l'Eglise et l'Italie. Essai juridique sur l'état actuel de la Question Romaine.* Paris, 1897. (Extract tr. from Vol. 4, *Del Aspecto internacional de la Cuestione Romana.* Barcelona, 1893-1895. 4v.)

Ollivier, Emile, *L'Eglise et l'Etat au Concile du Vatican.* Paris, 1879. 2v.

——. *Nouveau Manuel de droit ecclésiastique français. Textes et commentaires.* Paris, 1886

O'Reilly, Bernard. *John MacHale, Archbishop of Tuam. His Life, Times and Correspondence.* New York, 1890. 2v.

Orlando, V. E. *Miei Rapporti di governo con la Santa Sede.* 2 ed., Milano, 1944

Ottaviani, Alaphridus. *Institutiones juris publici ecclesiastici.* 2 ed., typis polyglottis vaticanis, 1947-1948. 2v.

Pacca, Bartolomeo Cardinal. *Oeuvres complètes* (Tr.). Paris, 1845. 2v.

Parker, Thomas M. *Christianity and the State in the Light of History. The Bampton Lectures.* London, 1955

Paro, Gino. *The Right of Papal Legation.* Catholic University of America. Studies in Canon Law, n. 211. Washington, 1947

Parsons, Wilfrid. *The Pope and Italy.* New York, 1929

Pasquazi, Josephus. *Jus internationale publicum.* Vol. 1, *De jure pacis.* Romae, 1935 von Pastor, Ludwig Freiherr. *The History of the Popes from the Close of the Middle Ages* (Tr.). St. Louis, 1899-1953. 40v.

————. *Tagebücher-Briefe-Erinnerungen.* Heidelberg, 1950

Patin, Wilhelm. *Beiträge zur Geschichte der deutsche-vatikanischen Beziehungen in den letzten Jahrzehnten. Als Manuscript gedruckt—nur fur den Dienstgebrauch. Quellen und Darstellungen zur politische Kirche.* Berlin, 1942

Paz, Carlos. *Bolivia en Roma.* La Paz, 1923

Pernot, Maurice. *L'Eglise catholique et la politique mondiale.* Paris, 1924

Perugini, Angelus. *Concordata vigentia notis historicis et juridicis declarata.* Romae, 1934

Pinheiro-Ferreira, Sylvestre. *Supplément au guide diplomatique de M. le Baron Ch. de Martens.* Paris, 1833

Piola, Andrea. *La Questione Romana nella storia e nel diritto da Cavour al Trattato del Laterano.* Padova, 1931

[Pius VI.] *Sanctissimi Domini Nostri Pii papae VI responsio ad metropolitanos Moguntinum, Treverensem, Coloniensem et Salisburgensem super nuntiaturis apostolicis.* Romae, 1789

[Pius VII.] *Correspondance authentique de la cour de Rome avec la France, depuis l'invasion de l'Etat romain jusqu'à l'enlèvement du souverain pontife, suivie des pièces officielles touchant l'invasion de Rome par les Français et des lettres de N.S.P. le pape, Pius VII.* 4 éd., Paris, 1814

[Pius IX.] *Pii papae IX pontificis maximi acta.* Roma, 1854-1878. Prima pars, 7v.; Seconda parte, 2v.

Plischke, Elmer. *Conduct of American Diplomacy.* New York, 1950

Portalis, J. E. M. *Discours, rapports et travaux inédits sur le concordat de 1801 et les articles organiques.* Paris, 1845

del Pozzo, Ferdinand. *Catholicism in Austria; or, an Epitome of the Austrian Ecclesiastical Law, with a dissertation upon the rights and duties of the English government with respect to the Catholics of Ireland.* London, 1827

Pradier-Fodéré, Paul. *Cours de droit diplomatique.* Paris, 1881. 2v.

————. *Traité de droit international public Européen et Américain.* Paris, 1885-1891. 5v.

de Pradt, Dominique. *Du congrès de Vienne.* 2 éd., Paris, 1815. 2v.

[Prosch, Felix.] *Festschrift Felix Prosch zum 70 Geburtstag,* Paderborn, 1923. (P. 168-195, Herman von Granert, "Wilhelm Uhden, der erste deutsche Vertreter Preussens beim päpstlichen Stuhl; die Schicksale des Kirchen-staates unter Papst Pius VI.")

Purcell, Edmund Sheridan. *Life of Cardinal Manning, Archbishop of Westminster.* London, 1896. 2v.

Quacquarelli, Antonio. *La Ricostituzione dello Stato Pontificio. Con una memoria inedita "Il mio secondo ministero" del Card. Pacca.* Città di Castello, 1945

Quadrotta, Guglielmo. *Il Papa, l'Italia et la guerra*. Milano, 1915

Randall, Sir Alec, *Vatican Assignment*. London, 1956

Rinieri, Ilario (ed.). *Corrispondenza inedita dei cardinali Consalvi e Pacca nel tempo del congresso di Vienna (1814-1815)*. Torino, 1903

Rivier, Alphonse. *Principes du droit des gens*. Paris, 1896. 2v.

Rivière, Jean. *Le Problème de l'Église et de l'État au temps de Philippe le Bel*. Paris, 1926

Rogers, Francis M. (ed.). *The Obedience of a King of Portugal*. Tr. with commentary. University of Minnesota Press, 1958

Rommen, Heinrich A. *The State in Catholic Thought*. St. Louis, 1945

Rothan, G. *Souvenirs diplomatiques. L'Allemagne et l'Italie, 1870-1871*. Paris, 1885. 2v.

Rouët de Journel, M.-J. *Nonciatures de Russie. Nonciature de Litta, 1797-1799*. Città del Vaticano, 1943

————. *Nonciatures de Russie. Nonciature d'Arezzo, 1802-1806*. Rome, 1922-1927. 2v.

————. *Intérim de Benvenuti, 1799-1803. Studi e testi*. Cité du Vatican, Bibliothèque Vaticane, 1957

Rousset de Missy, Jean. *Mémoires sur le rang et la préséance entre les souverains de l'Europe et entre leurs ministres représentans*. Amsterdam, 1746

Saint-Simon, Louis de. *Mémoires*. Paris, 1879-1930. 41v.

Salandra, Antonio. *Italy and the Great War. From Neutrality to Intervention* (Tr.). London, 1932

Salata, F. *Per la storia diplomatica della Questione Romana. I. Da Cavour alla Triplice Alleanza*. Milano, 1929

Salvatorelli, Luigi. *La Politica della Santa Sede dopo la guerra*. Milano, 1937

Satow, Sir Ernest. (Ed., Sir Neville Bland). *A Guide to Diplomatic Practice*. 4 ed., London, 1957

Savino, Paolo. *Diplomazia ecclesiastica*. Roma, 1952

————. (ed.). *La Pontificia Accademia ecclesiastica. 1701-1951*. Prefazione, Mons. Paolo Savino. Città del Vaticano, 1951

Scaduto, Francesco. *Guarentigie pontificie e relazioni tra Stato et Chiesa (legge 13 maggio 1871). Storia, esposizione, critica, documenti, bibliographia*. Torino. 1 ed., 1884; 2 ed., 1889

Scharp, Heinrich. *Wie die Kirche regiert wird*. Frankfurt-Main, 1950

von Schlözer, Kurd. *Römische Briefe (1864-1869)*. 2 Aufl. Stuttgart, 1913

————. *Letzte römische Briefe (1882-1894)*. Stuttgart, 1924

Schmidlin, Josef. *Papstgeschichte der neuesten Zeit (1800-1922)*. München, 1933-1939. 4v.

Segreteria di stato. Expositio documentis munita earum curarum quas S.P. Pius IX assidue gessit in eorum malorum levamen quibus in ditione Russica et Polona Ecclesia Cattolica afflictatur. Romae, 1870. (Papal White Book on relations with Russia, first published in 1866.)

Segreteria di stato. Il Congresso di Vienna del 1815 e la precedenza dei rappresentanti pontificii nel corpo diplomatico. Relazioni del cardinale Ercole Consalvi segret. di stato e ministro plenipotentiario del Sommo Pontefice Pio VII al cardinale B. Pacca, camerlengo di S.R.C., pro-segretario di stato. Roma, Tipografia Vaticana, 1899

Segreteria di stato. Istruzione relativa al diritto di precedenza dei rappresentanti pontificii nel corpo diplomatico. Roma. Tipografia Vaticana. [April 1900]

Sencourt, Robert. *The Genius of the Vatican.* London, 1935

Sereni, Angelo Pietro. *The Italian Conception of International Law.* New York, 1943

Sforza, Carlo. *Diplomatic Europe since the Treaty of Versailles.* New Haven, 1928

Sherwood, Robert E. *Roosevelt and Hopkins.* New York, 1948

von Sickel, Theodor. *Römische Erinnerungen.* Wien, 1947

Simon, Alois. *La Politique religieuse de Léopold Ier.* Bruxelles, 1953

Soderini, Eduardo. *Il Pontificato di Leone XIII.* Milano, 1932-1933. 3v.

Soglia, Joannes Cardinalis. *Institutiones juris publici ecclesiastici.* 6 ed., Paris, 1853

Spada, Giuseppe. *Storia della rivoluzione di Roma.* Roma, 1869

Steed, Henry Wickham. *Through Thirty Years, 1892-1922. A Personal Narrative.* New York, 1924. 2v.

Stock, Leo Francis (ed.). *United States Ministers to the Papal States. Instructions and Dispatches 1848-1868. American Catholic Historical Association. Documents: Volume I.* Washington, 1933

———. *Consular Relations between the United States and the Papal States. Instructions and Dispatches. American Catholic Historical Association. Documents: Volume II.* Washington, 1945

Stokes, Anson Phelps. *Church and State in the United States.* New York, 1950. 3v.

Strang, Lord (ed.). *The Foreign Office.* London, 1955

Stuart, Graham. *American Diplomatic and Consular Practice.* New York, 1936

Sturzo, Luigi. *Church and State* (Tr.). New York, 1939

[Stutz, Ulrich.] *Kirchliche Rechtsgeschichte; auf der Grundlage des Kirchenrechts von Ulrich Stutz, von Hans Erich Feine. Bd. I: Die katholische Kirche.* Weimar, 1950

Tarquini, Camillo. *Juris publici ecclesiastici institutiones.* 11 ed., Romae, 1887

Taylor, Myron C. (ed.). *Wartime Correspondence between President Roosevelt and Pope Pius XII. With an introduction and explanatory notes by Myron C. Taylor.* New York, 1947

————. *Correspondence between President Truman and Pope Pius XII. With an introduction by Myron C. Taylor, Personal Representative of the President of the United States to His Holiness Pope Pius XII.* (Private printing, 1953. Reproduced in *Catholic Mind*, Oct. 1953)

du Theil, Joseph. *Rome, Naples et le Directoire. Armistices et traités, 1796-1797.* Paris, 1902

Thureau-Dangin, Paul. *Histoire de la Monarchie de Juillet.* 2 éd., Paris, 1890. 6v.

Toynbee (Arnold J.) and Boulter (V. M.), ed. *Survey of International Affairs 1929.* London, 1930. (Part v. "Relations between the Sovereign National States and the Papacy"; i, "The Settlement of the Conflict between the Papacy and the Kingdom of Italy," pp. 422-478)

Twiss, Sir Travers. *The Letters Apostolic of Pope Pius IX considered with reference to the Law of England and the Law of Europe.* London, 1851

Ullmann, Walter. *The Growth of Papal Government in the Middle Ages. A study of the ideological relations of clerical to lay power.* London, 1955

Vali, F. A. *Servitudes of International Law.* 2 ed., London, 1958

Vandenbosch, Amry. *Dutch Foreign Policy Since 1815.* The Hague, 1959

Wagnon, Henri. *Concordats et droit international; fondement, élaboration, valeur et cessation du droit concordataire.* Gembloux, 1935

Wallace, Lillian Parker. *The Papacy and European Diplomacy, 1869-1878.* Chapel Hill, 1948

Watters, Mary. *A History of the Church in Venezuela, 1810-1930.* Chapel Hill, 1933

Wehberg, Hans. *Das Papsttum und der Weltfriede.* M. Gladbach, 1915

von Weiszäcker, Ernst. *Erinnerungen.* München, 1950

Wharton, Francis. (ed.). *The Revolutionary Diplomatic Correspondence of the United States.* Washington, 1889

Wilbaux, Théodore. *La Question du Vatican au point de vue du droit à la représentation diplomatique.* Bruxelles, 1879. (Broch.)

Williams, Michael. *The Catholic Church in Action.* Completely revised by Zsolt Aradi. New York, 1958

Winter, Eduard. *Der Josephinismus und seine Geschichte. Beiträge zur Geistesgeschichte Oesterreichs, 1740-1848.* Brünn-München-Wien, 1943

Winter, Eduard. *Russland und die slawischen Völker in der Diplomatie des Vatikans, 1878-1903.* Berlin, 1950

Woodward, E. L. *Three Studies in European Conservatism. Metternich, Guizot, the Catholic Church in the Nineteenth Century.* London, 1929

———. *War and Peace in Europe, 1815-1870.* London, 1931

Wynen, Arthur. *Die päpstliche Diplomatie, geschichtlich und rechtlich dargestellt.* Freiburg i. Br., 1922

Zaccaria, Franciscus Antonius. *Antifebronius vindicatus seu suprema Romani Pontificis potestas adversus Justinum Febronium ejusdemque vindicem Theodorum a Palude iterum adserta et confirmata.* Caesenae, 1771

Zacher, Albert. *Aus Vatikan und Quirinal. Bilder von nebeneinander der beiden Höfe.* Frankfurt-Main, 1901

Zallinger zum Thurm, Jacobus. *Institutionum juris naturalis et ecclesiastici publici libri v.* Augusta, 1784

Zechlin, Walter. *Diplomatie und Diplomaten.* Stuttgart-Berlin, 1935

ARTICLES AND ESSAYS

Albion, Gordon, "England and the Holy See. A Survey of Diplomatic Relations," *The Month*, January 1939, pp. 74-78

Alcock, Sir Rutherford, "France, China and the Vatican," *Nineteenth Century*, xx, Nov. 1886, pp. 617-632

Anon., "La Doppia Rappresentanza diplomatica in Roma," *Civiltà Cattolica*, giugno 20, 1871, pp. 5-15

Anon., "Germans and the Vatican City State," *The Tablet*, Sept. 18, 1943

Anon., "La Politique allemande et le protectorat des missions catholiques," *Revue des deux mondes*, t. 149, 1 sept. 1898, pp. 5-41

Anon., "Prisoners of the Vatican; the wartime life of the Diplomatic Corps," *The Tablet*, April 14, 1944

Anon., "Il Protettorato cattolico della Francia nell' Oriente et nell' Estremo Oriente," *Civiltà Cattolica*, ott. 27, 1904, pp. 257-276

Anzilotti, Dionisio, "La Condizione giuridica internazionale della Santa Sede in seguito agli accordi del Laterano," *Revista di diritto internazionale*, xxi (1929), pp. 165-176

Bachelet, Vittorio, "L'Organisation administrative du Saint-Siège et de la Cité du Vatican," *Revue internationale des sciences administratives*, n. 2, 1955, pp. 231-274

Baldwin, Simeon E., "The Mission of Governor Taft to the Vatican," *Yale Law Journal*, xii, Nov. 1902, pp. 1-7

Bettanini, Antonio M., "Il Fondamento giuridico della diplomazia pontificia," *Revista internazionale di scienze sociale e discipline ausiliarie*, ott. 1908, pp. 193-231

Binchy, David, "The Vatican and International Diplomacy," *International Affairs*, Jan. 1946, pp. 47-56

Bonghi, Ruggero, "Le Gouvernement italien et la Papauté," *Revue des deux mondes*, 1 mai 1873

Borenius, Tancred, "The Vatican and Finland," *The Tablet*, Feb. 10, 1940

Breycha-Vauthier, A. C., "L'Ordre S. M. Jérosolymitain de Malte. Evolutions récentes autour d'une ancienne organisation internationale," *Zeitschrift für ausländischen öffentliches Recht und Völkerrecht*, März, n. 3/4 (1956), pp. 500-522

Brusa, Emile, "La Juridiction du Vatican," *Rev. de dr. int. de lég. comp.*, xv (1883), pp. 113-145

Cansacchi, Giorgio, "Il Diritto di legazione attivo et passivo dell'-Ordine di Malta," *Diritto internazionale*, 1940, pp. 58-81

Cavalli, F., "Le Relazioni diplomatiche tre la S. Sede e il Giappone, 1922-1942," *Civiltà Cattolica*, maggio 21, 1959, pp. 393-408

Charles-Roux, François, "La Situation internationale du Saint-Siège," *Le Monde français*, avril 1946, pp. 531-543

————. "Souvenirs de la Cité vaticane," *Revues des deux mondes*, 15 nov. 1942

Cumbo, H., "The Holy See and International Law," *International Law Quarterly*, ii (1948-49), pp. 603-620

Dalla Torre, Giuseppe, "The Vatican's Conditions for Peace with Communism," *United Nations World*, Oct. 1949

Degert, Antoine, "Le Clergé de France et les origines de la diplomatie française," *Revue d'histoire de l'eglise de France*, ix (1923), pp. 321-346

Delos, Joseph T., "Le Traité du Latran et la situation juridique nouvelle de la Papauté," *Rev. gén. de dr. int. pub.*, 36 (1929), pp. 452-478

Farran, C. d'Olivier, "The Sovereign Order of Malta in International Law," *International and Comparative Law Quarterly*, April 1954, pp. 217-234

Farrell, John T., "Background of the 1902 Taft Mission to Rome," *Catholic Historical Review*, xxxvi (1950), pp. 1-32.

de Gabriac, Marquis, "Souvenirs d'une ambassade auprès du pape Léon XIII (1878-1880)," *Revue des deux mondes*, 1 jan., 15 jan., 1901, pp. 52-80, 287-314

Gaselee, Sir Stephen, "British Diplomatic Relations with the Holy See," *Dublin Review*, Jan. 1939, pp. 1-19

Gebhardt, Bruno, "Wilhelm von Humboldt und die Anfänge der preussischen Gesandtschaft in Rom," *Forschungen zur brandenburgischen und preussischen Geschichte, herausg. von A. Naudé*, Bd. 7, Leipzig, 1894, pp. 363-376

Genêt, Raoul, "La Société des Nations et le droit d'ambassade actif et passif," *Revue de droit international et de législation comparée,* XVI (1935), pp. 527-573

Goller, E., "Vorgeschichte der Bulle *Provida Solersque," Freiburger Diözesan-Archiv.* LV (1927), pp. 143-216; LVI (1928), pp. 436-613

Goss, Edward F., "The Taft Commission to the Vatican, 1902," *Records of the American Catholic Historical Society,* Dec. 1935, pp. 184-201

Goyau, Georges, "La Conférence de La Haye et le Saint-Siège," *Revue des deux mondes,* t. 154 (1899), pp. 590-611

Graham, Robert A., "The Vatican's role in international law," *America,* Sept. 30, 1950, pp. 669-671

——, "The Vatican in world diplomacy: France," *America,* Nov. 10, 1951, pp. 149-150

——, "Protestant states at the Vatican," *America,* Nov. 17, 1951, pp. 175-177

——, "If relations, why diplomatic?" *America,* Nov. 24, 1951, pp. 205-207

——, "The Papacy in the diplomatic world," *America,* Dec. 1, 1951, pp. 252-254

——, "The Vatican's policy on U.S. relations," *America,* Feb. 28, 1953, pp. 591-592

Guariglia, Raffaele, "La Mia Missione presso la Santa Sede et la questione di Roma città aperta," *Nuova anthologia,* agosto-sett, 1946

Gwynn, Denis, "Vatican Diplomacy and Peace," *Dublin Review,* April-May-June 1940, pp. 233-250

Hasting, Martin F., "United States-Vatican Relations," *Records of the American Catholic Historical Society of Philadelphia,* March-June (LXIX), 1958, pp. 20-55

von der Heydte, F. A., "Die Stellung und Funktion des Heiligen Stuhles im heutigen Völkerrecht," *Oesterreichische Zeitschrift für öffentliches Recht,* II (1950), pp. 572-586

Hubbard, Gustave, "Des relations diplomatiques entre les états et les églises," *La Justice internationale,* août-déc., 1904

Hughes, Philip, "The International Action of the Papacy," *The Tablet,* 1940, Nov. 2, 9, 16, 23

Ireland, Gordon, "The State of the City of the Vatican," *Am. Journal of International Law,* XXVII, i (1933), pp. 271-289

Krauske, Otto, "Die Entwickelung des ständigen Diplomatie vom fünfzehnten Jahrhundert bis zu den Beschlüssen von 1815 und 1818," *Staats-und socialwissenschaftliche Forschungen,* Leipzig, VI (1885), pp. 1-246

Kunz, Josef L., "The Status of the Holy See in International Law," *American Journal of International Law,* XLVI (1952), pp. 308-314

La Brière, Yves de, "Le Traité du Latran et le nouvel Etat Pontifical," *Rev. de dr. int. et de lég. comp.,* X (1929), pp. 123-158

———. "La Condition juridique de la Cité du Vatican," *Recueil des cours de l'Académie de droit international de La Haye*, t. 33 (1930, iii), pp. 117-165

———. "Le Ministère pontifical des affaires étrangères," *Revue de droit international*, xv (1935), pp. 340-346

———. "La Diplomatie vaticane et sa légende," *Etudes*, t. 239 (1939), pp. 674-681

Lecler, Joseph, "L'Idée de séparation entre l'Eglise et l'Etat," *Etudes*, 20 déc., 1930, pp. 664-694

Louis-Jaray, Gabriel, "La Papauté, la Triple Alliance et la politique extérieure de la France," *Questions diplomatiques et coloniales*, t. xvii (1904), pp. 561-576

Magnin, E., "Affaires ecclésiastiques extraordinaires, Congrégation des," *Dictionnaire de droit canonique*, éd. R. Naz, Paris, 1935—. i., col. 252-259

Marraro, Howard R., "The Closing of the American diplomatic mission to the Vatican and efforts to revive it," *Catholic Historical Review*, xxxiii (1948), pp. 423-447

Martini, A., "La Diplomazia della Santa Sede e la pontificia Accademia ecclesiastica," *Civiltà Cattolica*, 19 maggio 1951, pp. 372-386

Mecham, J. Lloyd, "The Papacy and Spanish American Independence," *Hispanic American Historical Review*, ix (1929), pp. 154-175

Méjan, François, "Le Rôle des nonces apostoliques," *La Revue administrative*, janv.fév., 1954, pp. 14-33

Miko, Norbert, "Die diplomatischen Beziehungen zwischen England und dem Heiligen Stuhl im 19. Jahrhundert," *Zeitschrift für katholische Theologie*, Bd. 82 (1956), pp. 206-225

Murphy, Joseph J., "The Pontifical Diplomatic Service," *The [American] Ecclesiastical Review*, xli (1909), pp. 1-8

Nys, Ernest, "Le Droit international et la Papauté," *Rev. de dr. int. et de lég. comp.*, x (1878), pp. 501-538

Pierantoni, Augusto, "Il Papato e la rappresentanza diplomatica," *l'Italia moderna*, marzo 1907, pp. 5-31

Siotto Pintor, Manfredi, "Les sujets du droit autres que les états," *Recueil des cours de l'Académie de droit international de La Haye*, t. 41 (1932, iii), pp. 247-361

Randall, Sir Alec, "British Diplomatic Representation at the Holy See," *Blackfriars*, Sept. 1956, pp. 356-363

Renaud de Moustier, "La France et le protectorat des missions dans l'Empire chinois," *Le Correspondant*, 25 juin, 1886, pp. 957-976

Richard, P., "Origines et développement de la secrétairerie d'état apostolique, 1417-1823," *Revue d'histoire ecclésiastique* (Louvain), 1910, pp. 56-72, 505-529, 728-754

Richard, P., "Origines de la nonciature de France," *Revue des questions historiques,* xxxiv (1905), pp. 102-147

———. "Origines des nonciatures permanentes," *Revue d'histoire ecclésiastique,* vii (1906), pp. 52-70

Rouët de Journel, M.-J., "Three Papal Nuncios in Russia," *Thought,* xxviii (1953), pp. 325-353

Schücking, Walter, "Le Développement du pacte de la Société des Nations," *Recueil des cours de l'Académie de droit international de La Haye,* t. 20 (1927, v), pp. 351-458

Serafini, Alberto, "Le Origini della pontificia segreteria di stato e la *Sapienti Consilio* del B. Pio X," *Apollinaris,* xxvi (1952), pp. 167-239

Shiels, W. Eugene, "Church and State in the First Decade of Mexican Independence," *Catholic Historical Review,* xxviii (1942), pp. 206-228

Smith, H. A., "Diplomatic Relations with the Holy See, 1815-1930," *The Law Quarterly Review,* xlviii, July 1932, pp. 374-393

Sturzo, Luigi, "The Vatican's Position in Europe," *Foreign Affairs,* Jan. 1945, pp. 211-221

Stutz, U., "Die päpstliche Diplomatie unter Leo XIII," *Abhandlung der preussischen Akademie der Wissenschaften, Jahrgang 1925, Phil-Hist. Klasse, Nr.* 3/4., Berlin, 1926

Suliak, Hassan, "Die Beziehungen der islamischen Staaten zum Vatikan," *Aussenpolitik,* Okt. 1956, pp. 653-657

Temperley, Harold, "George Canning, the Catholics and the Holy See," *Dublin Review,* July 1933, pp. 1-12

Ullmann, Walter, "The Development of the Medieval Idea of Sovereignty," *The English Historical Review,* Jan. 1949 (ccl), pp. 1-33

Verdross, Alfred, "Die Stellung des Apostolisches Stuhles in der internationalen Gemeinschaft," *Oester. Arch. für Kirchenrecht,* 3 (1952), pp. 54-68

Woodward, E. L., "The Diplomacy of the Vatican under Popes Pius IX and Leo XIII," *Journal of the British Institute of International Affairs,* iii-iv (1924), pp. 452-457

Wright, A., "Argentina and the Papacy, 1810-1827," *Hispanic American Historical Review,* xviii (1928), pp. 15-42

Wright, Herbert F., "The Status of the Vatican City," *American Journal of International Law,* Vol. 38 (1944), pp. 452-457

Van Zuylen, Baron Pierre, "La Première Mission du Vicomte Vilain XIIII à Rome," *La Revue générale,* t. 124, 15 juillet 1930, pp. 31-48

ENCYCLOPEDIAS

"Ambassadeurs auprès du Saint-Siège." *Dictionnaire d'histoire et de géographie ecclésiastiques,* Paris, 1912—, ii, col. 1015-1030, signed: P. Richard

"Diplomatie pontificale." *Catholicisme. Hier, aujourd'hui, demain,* III, col. 859-862, signed: M. Noiret

"Gesandtschaften am päpstlichen Hof." *Die Religion in Geschichte und Gegenwart, zweite Auflage,* Tübingen, 1927-1931, II, col. 1075-1076, signed: Mirbt

"Gesandtschaftsrecht, päpstliches." *Lexicon für Theologie und Kirche, zweite Auflage,* 1930-1938, IV, col. 448-450, signed: H. Bastgen

"Legate." *Catholic Encyclopedia,* IX, pp. 118-120, signed B. Cerretti

"Legaten und Nuntien." *Realencyclopädie für protestantische Theologie und Kirche, dritte Auflage,* XI, pp. 340-345, signed: H. F. Jacobson, v. Schulte

"Legates and Nuncios, Papal." *The New Schaff-Herzog Encyclopedia of Religious Knowledge,* VI, pp. 440-441, signed: J. F. Schulte

"Le Pape. La Diplomatie pontificale." *Dictionnaire de théologie catholique,* XI, col. 1916-1928, signed: Victor Martin

"Nuntius." *Lexikon für Theologie und Kirche, zweite Auflage,* VII, col. 644-646, signed: K. Guggenberger

"Nuntius." *Staatslexikon, fünfte Auflage* (Freiburg, 1926-1932), III, col. 1642-1646, signed: E. Schneider

"Nunziatura apostolica; Nunzio apostolico." *Enciclopedia cattolica,* VIII, col. 2022-2024, signed: Dino Staffa

"Pouvoir pontifical. III: Le Droit de souveraineté du Saint-Siège." *Dictionnaire apologétique de la foi catholique,* IV, col. 97-102, signed: de la Brière

INDEX

Abdul-Hamid II, 85

Abeken, Heinrich, quoted on changed role of Prussian legation, 300n

Abyssinia, 104. *See also* Ethiopia

Accademia ecclesiastica di nobili, 10

Acta Apostolicae Sedis, official papal gazette, promulgation of decrees through, 295f; attitude of Czarist authorities, 295f

Ad dominici gregis custodiam, papal bull, 57

ad extra, legatio, 262. *See also* legation, right of external

ad intra, legatio, 262. *See also* legation, right of internal

Adrian VI, names lay nuncio, 123f

Agency, imperial Austrian, in Rome, for ecclesiastical affairs, 293

agréation, 29, 120

Aix-la-Chapelle, Congress of, 164

Albania, 148

Alexander I, of Russia, 65f, 166

Alexander II, of Russia, 68

Alexander III, of Russia, 68

Alexander III, Pope, 125, 145

Alexander VI, 100f, 116, 129

Alexander VII, 128

Alexander VIII, 120

Alfonso I, of Aragon, 101

Almanach de Gotha, 27

Alsace-Lorraine, 20

Ambassadors accredited to pope, 99-114
  diplomatic corps: 17-21; caliber of personnel, 21-23; increase after First World War, 25; from non-Catholic states, 19, 114n, 150; opened to non-Catholics, 40f; first Protestants, 42-44; Consalvi account, 45; royal honors as distinguishing mark, 103; ecclesiastics as envoys to pope, 110, 111-13; Antonelli quoted, 113; cardinals never of ambassadorial rank, 110; religion of, 113f, 114n; at conclave, 107f; suppression of, proposals, 30f, 32-34, 207, 210, 285f; distinct from envoys accredited to Italy, 110f; in wartime, *see* privileges and immunities
  dual temporal and ecclesiastical function: France, 106; Lebzeltern quoted on, 134n, 138; attempted

separation, 138f; French instructions, quoted, 163; Visconti-Venosta, quoted, 205; status in international law, 186f, 190f, 193, 201, 204-6, 207, 214, 219, 310
  to pope as spiritual sovereign: Upper Rhine states, 56-58; Buchanan quoted, 85f; Humboldt case, 52f, 138, 161f; Farini quoted, 139; Jacobini quoted, 214, 336f; Leo XIII quoted, 219; Pithou, 254; d'Aubeterre instructions, 257; Van Zuylen quoted, 287; Nys quoted, 287n; Bunsen quoted, 289; Rossi mission, 281-83; Brühl mission, 291; Abeken quoted, 300n
  to pope as temporal sovereign: France, 39; Prussia, 50, 52f; United States, 83f; United States relations to Vatican State, 140, 336f, 344; Archb. McNicholas, 344f; letters of credence. 345n; critique, 345-47

ambaxiatores, 101

American Relief Administration for Russia, 356, 363, 366

Amiens, 1802 Treaty of, 26

Amoudru, J. B., 370n

Ampthill, Lord, 73. *See also* Russell, Odo

Ancient City, 4

d'Anethan, Baron, foreign minister, envoy in Rome, 302

anticlericalism, 14, 198n, 302, 341

antifebronians, 225-27

antireligious laws in Soviet Union, 371

Antonelli, Card. Giacomo, sec'y of state, 112f, 137, 140; not a priest, 141; personal career, 142n; on concordats as treaties, 232; on Church as perfect society, 233, 235; on nuncios distinguished from ambassadors, 235

Anzilotti, Prof. Dionisio, quoted on nuncio, 200

Apocrisarii, 115, 145, 265

Apostolic Briefs, Section for, in Secretariat of State, 143

apostolic delegate, as title of papal nondiplomatic envoy, 126; "religions, nonpolitical" mission, 126

apostolic delegate and envoy extraordi-

nary, as title of papal envoy, discontinued, 82
apostolic legate, *see* primate
appel comme d'abus, 255
Aquinas, St. Thomas, on state as *communitas perfecta*, 230f; Tarquini's definition of *societas perfecta* mistakenly attributed to, 231
Archetti, special papal envoy to Russia, 38, 65, 166
Ardighello, Pietro, 130
Arezzo, special papal envoy to Russia, 65, 166
Argentina, 19, 21, 26, 82
Aristotle, on "perfect community" and "imperfect community," 229
Arles, Archb. of, case of, 256
Arnim, Harry von, sent to Rome by Bismarck as instrument of new Prussian policy, 288
Arntz, Prof. E. R. N., quoted on papal sovereignty, 198
Artaud de Montor, quoted, 24, 42f
Assumption, Pius XII proclaims dogma, 298
atheism in Soviet Union, 349f, 352
d'Aubeterre, Marquis, 108, 161, 257
Aubin, semi-official British agent, 72f
Audisio, Guglielmo, quoted on Church as "state," 221
Aufsichtsrecht (jus cavendi, jus defensionis et praecautionis), 261
Australia, 19
Austria, 19, 20, 26; absolutism of, 228; abolishes Placet, 292f; Vatican embassy seized by Italy, 317
L'Avenir of de Lamennais, condemned, 152
Avignon, 109
Axis, envoys in wartime, 320; anti-Bolshevik crusade, 372f
d'Azeglio, Massimo, on concordat, 233
Azpuru y Ximenes, Thomas, ecclesiastic as envoy of Spain, 110

Baden, Grand Duchy of, 54, 56; concordat dispute, 232f
Badoglio, armistice of Gen., 317
Baluffi, Gaetano, papal envoy, 80
banquiers expéditionnaires, 256f
Barthou, French foreign minister, 358
Barzio de Barzii, pioneer papal envoy, 116, 119
Basel, Council of, on cardinals, 110
Baudrillart, Card. Alfred, supports Axis anti-Bolshevik crusade, 372

Bavaria, 110, 278; envoys at Vatican in wartime, 308
Belgium, 19, 20; ruptures relations with Holy See, 192-94; constitution, 279; as "separation state," 284-88; Catholics oppose Vatican mission, 285f; Mission of Vilain XIIII, 285; Treaty of London of 1831, 285; Vatican mission in wartime, 321
Bellarmine, St. Robert, on indirect power, 160
Benedict XIII, 122f
Benedict XIV, denies red hat to Turin nuncio, 123
Benedict XV, quoted on papal diplomacy, 13; British and coronation, 77; and Card. Gasparri, 128; protests to Italy, 315-17; aid to Russia and Genoa conference, 355-57; intervention for Russian Orthodox, 362
Berg, 263
Berne, wartime diplomatic correspondence through nunciature, 324
Bernetti, Card., secretary of state, 135; deacon, 141
de Bernis, Card., last envoy of ancien regime, 37, 39; as ecclesiastic, 110
de Bernis, Count Archbishop, rejected as nuncio to Czar, 66
Beust, Count von, quoted on right of legation of Austria, 207f
Biaudet, cited on origin of nunciatures, 114
Bichi, Vincenzo, Portugal protests recall as nuncio without promotion to cardinalate, 121-23
bishops, governmental permission needed to leave country, 251, 298
Bismarck, Prince von, esteem of papal diplomacy, 22; on the importance of imponderables, 159; proposal to exact papal pledge of non-interference, 159; on need for temporal power of pope, 177; protest to Italy over papal encyclical, 209f
Bock, Nicholas, quoted on Czarist policy, 295n
Bofondi, Card., secretary of state, 137
Bohemia, 117
Bolivia, 19, 21, 82
Bologna and Ferrara, papal fiefs, 103
Bolshevik Revolution, 354
Bompard, Raoul, quoted, against papal legal status, 191f

Bonald, Card. de, criticizes Gallican book, 279f
Bonaparte, Joseph, ambassador in Rome, 41
Boncompagni, Card., 38
Bonetti, papal delegate in Ottoman empire, 92, 94
Bonghi, Ruggero, 306f
Boniface VIII, 129; on direct power, 160
Borgongini-Duca, nuncio to Italy, 321
Borromeo, St. Charles, pope's secretary, 128
Bossuet, on necessity of temporal power, 176; events vindicate, 182
Bourbons, politico-ecclesiastical policies, 253
Brandenburg, Elector, 42
Brazil, 19, 21, 26, 79, 82f
Bremen, 57
British legation, represents other Commonwealth members, 19; personnel, 22n; no reciprocity, 23, 78n; story of relations, 69-78; inaugurated by Sir Henry Howard, 77f; made permanent by Lloyd George, 78; minister not a Catholic, 114n
Bruehl, Frederick William, Prussian envoy, 291
Brusa, Emile, quoted on legal status of pope, 198n
Brussels, nunciature, 118
Bryce, Lord, quoted on sovereignty, 188
Buchanan, U.S. secretary of state, statement of policy, 83f, 336
Budkiewicz, Constantine, trial and execution, 364
Bulgaria, 148
Bull of Circumscription, for Prussia, 57, 289; for German principalities, 57
Bulwer, Henry Lytton, foreign secretary, 299
Bunsen, Christian Karl von, Prussian envoy, 60; quoted on Niebuhr, 289; Cologne troubles, 290f
Buonfiglio, agent of Württemberg, 56
Burckhardt, John, diarist of Roman court, 102
Burgundy, 118
Burke, Edmund, quoted on relations with pope, 69f
Burma, 19
Bussi, Antonio, on papal mission, 124

Buttrick, George A., letter from President, 328, 343
Buturlin, Czarist envoy, 67
Byzantine-Slav rite, Catholics of, 351n, 354, 367
Byzantium, Emperor in, 145

Cacault, François, French envoy, anecdote on pope, 24; in Rome, 39
Cadorna, Gen., 53
Caesaropapism, 220n
camera secreta, 129
Campbell, Sir John, 72
Campo, Marquis de, 124
Canada, 19, 72
"Cannes Resolutions," 358n
Canning, foreign secretary, consults on relations with pope, 72; quoted on recognition of Latin American republics, 79
canon law, cited, 13, 142, 143, 145, 146f, 151, 153, 266
Canossa, Ludovico di, first nuncio to Paris, 116
Canterbury, 115
Caprara, Card. Giambattista, nuncio in Vienna, 38; in Paris, last *legatus a latere*, 116; protests Organic Articles, 268
cardinal nephew, system of, 130-32
Cardinals, College of, as senate of Church, 145
Carrere, Jean, cited, 313
Carroll, Archb. John, 335n
Casoni, Card., sec'y of state, 44
Cassini, Czarist agent, 67
Castelfidardo, battle, 181
Castiglione, Balthasar, lay envoy of pope, 124
Castile, 118
Castile and Leon, 101
Castlereagh, foreign secretary, letter to Consalvi, 71; role at Vienna on precedence, 169-71
Catherine II, of Russia, 38, 65, 66, 166
Catholic Church,
vicissitudes of: political predominance in 13th century, 157-59; weakness after Western schism in 15th century, 129; brilliance of Roman Court in 16th and 17th centuries, 105f; growing disdain of Catholic absolutist princes, 190; Versailles, 161f; Vienna, humiliating voyage of Pius VI, 258; Civil Constitution of the Clergy and the

concordat, 173; secularization in Germany, 53; Napoleon abolishes papal states, 173; carries Pius VII into captivity, 174; restoration of temporal power by Congress of Vienna, 172; de Pradt's prognostications, 53f; troubles in Papal States, 180f; paradoxical rise of papal authority throughout Europe, growth of centralization in Church, 283, 297f; signs of times in 1854, British agent's analysis of papal gains, 299f; laicism replaces regalism as threat to Church, 301f; ultramontanism triumphant at Vatican Council, 215f; fall of papal states, 181; restoration of temporal power by Lateran Treaty, 181f; *constitution of*: a "perfect society," 215f, 218; as a "state," 218; not a *collegium*, 225; Leo XIII quoted, 218f; Devoti quoted, 226f; independence of, 227; Piux IX, on perfect society, quoted, 233f; Antonelli quoted, 233; St. Pius X quoted, 246f; André Mater quoted, 240f; Consalvi quoted, 220n
Catholic states, 17, 19
Catholics in the United States, and Vatican relations, 347
Cavalli, F. A., quoted on rumors of relations with Russia, 376f
Cavour, Camillo, raises Roman question, 180f; views on pope in wartime, 306; Siccardi law, 232; on "free Church in free State," 296
Cavourians, lose power in 1876, 195; conception of spiritual sovereignty in Law of Guarantees, 200, 203-7; their views close to Vatican's, 211
centralization in the Church, 299. *See also* ultramontanism
Central Powers, 77; envoys' departure from Rome, 309f, 312
Ceremonial Congregation, 147; sets protocol for envoys, 150
Ceylon, 19
Chaix d'Est-Ange, councillor of state, defense of neo-Gallicanism, 274f; on indivisibility of sovereignty, 275
Champs de Mai, 145
Charitable Donations and Bequests Act, 74
Charlemagne, form of rule, 115; ruler of united Christendom, 177; Na-

poleon's conception of himself as new, 174, 179
Charles V, emperor, 124
Charles VI, emperor, 104
Charles VII, emperor, 104
Charles-Albert, of Sardinia, 232
Charles of Lorraine, praises Placet, 258f
Charles-Roux, François, French diplomat, on envoys in wartime, 319; on wartime diplomatic communications, 324
Charles-Theodore, Elector, asks for nuncio, 263
Charykov, N., Czarist diplomat, on Vatican diplomacy, 22
Chekib Effendi, Ottoman envoy, 85
Chery-Bey, Ottoman envoy, 95
Chicherin, Soviet foreign minister, on concordat with Russia, 355n; episode with Archbishop Signori in Genoa, 357f; on religious freedom in Soviet Union, 359; rumors concerning, 359-62; tart reply to papal intervention for Orthodox, 362; acknowledges Vatican relief offer, 362; withdraws privileges of Vatican relief mission, 366n
Chile, 19, 21, 26, 81
China, 20; Empire, 85f; Republic, 90; envoy at Vatican, 321
Churchill, Sir Winston, on Stalin and the pope, 25; on Soviet enigma, 381
churchmen, as envoys, 109f
Church-State relations, 3, 6
Ciacchi, Card., 138
Cicognani, Amletto, apostolic delegate, 332
Cieplak, Archb., trial by Bolsheviks, 364
Ciofani, Matteo, Prussian agent, 48
Circumscription, Bull of, for Prussia, 57, 289; for German principalities, 57
city states, 4
Civil Constitution of the Clergy, 39f, 173
civil diplomacy, definition, 32
civil power, 160
Civil War (U.S.), 84
Civiltà Cattolicà, on the Vatican in time of war, 307
Civitavecchia, 45, 209
Clemenceau, Georges, 3f
Clement VII, 104, 124, 131f

Clement VIII, 131
Clement X, 132
Clement XI, 47, 121f
Clement XII, 122
Clement XIII, 107
Clement XIV, 222
Clermont, Bishop of, 279
Code for Ecclesiastical Affairs Respecting Foreign Religions, Russia, 296
coercion by the State in religion, Card. Manning on, 78n
coexistence with communism, Pius XI on, 350; conditions, 383
Collegial System, applied by Febronius to Catholic Church, 223; in Germany, 260, 277f. *See also*, Episcopal System, Territorial System
collegium, Pius IX on Church as, 234; Pufendorf and Collegial System, 223f, 260; in Febronianism, 223; Mammachi cited, 225; draft canon at Vatican Council, cited, 230n
Cologne, Archb. of, as *legatus natus*, 115; protests Munich nunciature, 263f
Cologne, nunciature, 262f, 117, 119; Pacca as nuncio, 264
"Cologne Troubles," 289-92
Colombia, 19f, 20, 26. *See also* New Granada
Coltrolini, Giovanni Antonio, Prussian agent in Rome, 46-49
Comintern, dissolution, 377
Comité National, protest to pope over Russian "concordat," 361, 363
communication, diplomatic, in time of war, 307, 310, 312, 322-25; Charles-Roux, quoted, 324-25
communication with Rome restricted by state, justification of system, 250f; Saint-Simon quoted, 255f; Louis XIV relaxes, 256; at end of ancien régime, 257; penal code prohibits unauthorized, 272; in Prussia, 278; unrestricted in Belgium, 384-86; unrestricted in Prussia, 288; Netherlands, 292; Bavaria, 292; in Austria, 292f; in Württemberg, 293; restrictions maintained in imperial Russia, 294-96
communism, Pius XI on, 350
Communist bloc countries, 21
concession theory of Law of Guarantees, 201, 207. *See also* Esperson, Pietro

conclave, of 1831, 80; ambassadors at time of, 107f
concordat, in definition of papal diplomacy, 12; antedated by papal diplomacy, 15f; *jus foederis* distinguished from *jus legationis*, 16
concordat, legal nature of, disputed, 185f; Hubbard denies, 190; Bompard denies, 191; canonists on, 236f; civil lawyers on, 236f; canonists and civil lawyers reverse opinions, 236; as treaty, Card. Antonelli quoted, 232f; as internal and revocable legislation, d'Azeglio quoted, 233; Pius IX on contractual nature, 233; postwar multiplication, 18, 237; replaces Placet, 252. *See also*, convention, *modus vivendi*
concordats, French of 1801, 88, 116, 190, 302; Austrian of 1855, 292, 301; Netherlands of 1827, 57, 285; Sardinian of 1841, 295, 232; Russian of 1847, 295, 232; of Baden of 1859, 233; Italian of 1929, 237, 296; Pius XI on, 237; alleged concordat with Soviet Union, 355n, 360f, 377; German of 1933, 24, 56; Spanish of 1953, 219; Dominican Republic of 1954, 219
"concordat states," listed, 20
Congo, 20
Congregatio extraordinaria praeposita negotiis ecclesiasticis orbis catholici; Congregatio a negotiis ecclesiasticis extraordinariis; Congregatio super negotiis ecclesiasticis regni Gallorum; see, Extraordinary Ecclesiastical Affairs, Congregation for
congregations, Roman, 12
Consalvi, Card., sec'y of state, account of first Protestant envoys admitted at Rome, 42-45; and Niebuhr, 59; correspondence with Castlereagh, 71, 71n; visitor in London, 71; not a priest, 141; secures recognition of nuncio's precedence at Vienna, 164-71; secures restoration of Papal States, 172; on Church as perfect society, quoted, 220n; Ollivier contrasts with Portalis, 269n; on primary ecclesiastical function of nuncio, quoted, 294n
Consistorial Congregation, 143, 145f, 147, 148

Constance, Council of, 102

Constans, French envoy to Constantinople, 94

constitution, of Prussia, 277, 288; of Belgium, 279, 284; Belgian constitution and *Mirari Vos*, 284n; United States, 336f, 347; of Catholic Church, *see* Catholic Church

constitutional reform of Papal States, 134-38; 140

Continental Congress, Second, replies to papal message, 335f

convention, with imperial Russia in 1847, 68; Rumania, 20. *See also* concordat

Coquille, Guy, 269n

Corsica, 101

Corsini, Lorenzo (Clement XII), 120

Corte amendment to Law of Guarantees, 306f

Cort Van der Linden, on papal influence, 62

Costantini, Card. Celso, apostolic delegate in China, 90

Costa Rica, 19f, 26, 82

Council, Congregation of, 147, 149

Council of Trent, Congregation of, 146

courier in wartime, diplomatic, 312

Cracas (Chracas), Roman almanach, 47. *See also Notizie per l'anno*

Crétineau-Joly, cited, 141f

Crispolti, Filippo, on pope in time of war, 307

Croatia, and Placet, 301

crusade, anticommunist urged by Axis, 372f; supported by Card. Baudrillart but ignored by Pius XII, 372f

Cuba, 19

curia Romana, 144

Cyprus, 148

Czarist Government, 22; Church-State policies, 66-68, 152, 253, 294f; proposed changes on eve of war, 295f

Czechoslovakia, 20; *modus vivendi*, 20

Dalai Lama, pope as a, 89

Dalberg, Karl Theodore von, 54, 56

Dalla Torre, Guiseppe, on conditions of peace with Soviet Union, 384

Dante Alighieri, Italian battleship, famous supper in Genoa harbor, 356, 358

David, Emperor of Abyssinia, 104

deanship of nuncio, *see* precedence

Declaration of the Gallican Clergy of

1682, 279. *See also* Liberties of the Gallican Church

Decretals, as source of canon law, 226

"Defenders of the Faith," Catholic kings as, 106

Della Genga, Card., papal envoy at Regensburg, 56

Delos, José, quoted on basis of papal sovereignty, 202n

Denmark, 19, 118

Depretis, Agostino, 194, 211

Derby, Earl of, 73

De salute animarum, papal bull, 59f, 289

Des Prats, Francisco, believed first permanent nuncio, 116

Devoti, Giovanni, quoted on Church as a "state," 221; on respective spheres of Church and State, quoted, 226f; no *status in statu*, 226

diplomacy, authenticity of papal, 7f; in Renaissance, 8; as key to Church-State relations, 8; defined in general, 8f; Nicolson quoted, 8; Calvo quoted, 9; ecclesiastical diplomacy defined, 9-11; by Giobbio, 10; by Pinchetti-Sanmarchi, 10; by Savino, 10f; as an art, 11; as an institution, 11f; protocol of, 11

diplomatic agents, classification of, 164; privileges and immunities, 11, 196, 208, 214, 305f; in First World War, 306-10, 314f, 317; in Second World War, 318-21, 325

diplomatic corps at Vatican, 25. *See also* ambassadors

diplomatic missions, personnel of, 21f, 22n

Diplomatic Relations Act, 75f

diplomatic relations with Soviet Union, conditions, 382-84

diplomatic representation linked with sovereignty, 217

diplomatics, 9

Directory, 39f, 173

Discours sur l'unite de l'Eglise of Bossuet, 176-79

Divini Redemptoris, encyclical, 371

Dodecanese Islands, 148

Dolci, Archb., apostolic delegate in Constantinople, 95

Dominican Republic, 19f; concordat, 219

Dominis, Marco Antonio de, quoted

on nuncios in 16th century, 265; corrected, 267

Dowager Empress of China, 89

droit d'annexe, 280

Drost zu Vischering, Archb. Clemens August von, of Cologne, imprisoned by Prussia, 291

Dubourg, Bishop of New Orleans, 336n

Du Congrès de Vienne, of de Pradt, 54

Duguit, Léon, constitutionalist, quoted on "Catholic fact," 15

du Marsais, Marquis, quoted on nuncios as ambassadors, 256f

Dunn, John George, emissary of Empire of China, proposes exchange of envoys, 87-89

Dupin, André, *Manuel* denounced by French bishops, 279f

Eastern Europe, 18, 20, 27; crisis of Church in, 297

Ecclesiastical Affairs, Section for Extraordinary, in Secretariat of State, 142; Section for Ordinary, 142, ecclesiastical diplomacy, as bona fide diplomacy, 7f; defined, 9-11; by Giobbio, 10; by Pinchetti-Sanmarchi, 10; by Savino, 10f; as an art, 11; as an institution, 11f

Ecclesiastical Titles Act, 300n

L'Eclair, cited on relations with Ottoman Empire, 94

Ecuador, 19f, 26, 81f

Egypt, 148. *See also* United Arab Republic

Eldon, Lord, 72

elections bring anticlericals to power, Italy in 1876, 194; France in 1877, 192; Belgium in 1878, 192

Elizabeth, Statute of Queen, 42, 69, 72. *See also praemunire*

El Salvador, 19-21, 26. *See also* San Salvador

Emancipation Act of 1829, 297

embassy, right of, *see* legation, right of

Empress of China, Dowager, 89

Ems, Punctuation of, 264f

England, *nuncii et collectores* in, 118; Pius IX reestablishes hierarchy, 300n. *See also* Great Britain

entrée, of ambassador in Rome, 106

Episcopal System, 259f. *See also* Collegial System, Territorial System

Erastianism, *see* regalism

Eritrea, 148

Erskine, Msgr. (Card.) Charles, mission to England, 38

Erzberger, Matthias, proposals for solution of Roman question, 313

Espen, Bernhard van, Janenist canonist, on Placet, 258

Esperson, Pietro, interpretation of Law of Guarantees, 194-97, 211f; and Mancini, 194; comment by Anzilotti, 200; by Rolin-Jacquemyns, 197; by Brusa, 198n

espionage trials, in wartime, 313f

Estonia, 20

Ethiopia, 20, 23n, 148

Eugene IV, 101

exclusivum, 80, 107

excommunication, of princes, 158

Exequatur, 296. *See also* Placet

Expectancy, right of, 105

external legation, right of, 215. *See also* internal legation

external mission of nuncios, 125. *See also* internal mission

Extraordinary Ecclesiastical Affairs, Congregation for, 135, 147f, 151-53; as "miniature consistory," 151

Fabbri, lay minister in papal states, 139

Farini, quoted on envoys to pope, 139

Favre, Jules, foreign minister, concern for papal policy in Levant, 86f, 95; quoted against churchman as French envoy in Rome, 111; rejects Italy's hints in this sense, 111

Febronianism, 222-27, 264-67. *See also* regalism

Febronians, 227. *See also* regalists

Febronius, Justinus (Bishop Johannes Nikolaus von Hontheim), 222-27; rejects monarchical nature of papal power, 222; and Collegial System, 222; denies Church is a "state" or *societas perfecta*, 223f; influenced by Pufendorf, 223f; quoted on nuncios as exclusive envoys to princes, 265; Pastor on, 224

Federal Council of Churches, 328, 334

Fenestrelle, prison fortress, 179

Feodorov, Leonidas, Exarch, 351n, 354, 367

Ferdinand II, 81

Ferdinand the Catholic, 100

Ferrara and Bologna, papal fiefs, 103

Ferretti, Card. Gabriele, sec'y of state, 137

Fesch, Card. Joseph, French minister in Rome, 110

Florence, 114

Flynn, Edward J., Moscow visit, rumors of negotiations, sees Pius XII, 380f

Fontainebleau, Pius VII imprisoned at, 152; concordat, on right of legation, 175

Foreign Correspondents Association, Pius XII addresses, quoted, 6

France, 3, 18-20, 26, 33; after Revolution, 39-41; separation, 240; rupture with Vatican, 241; renews relations, 241f; politico-ecclesiastical system of, 160-63, 253-57, 267-75; king of France as "Eldest Son" of Church, 255. *See also* Gallicanism, Convention, Directory, Napoleon, Organic Articles, Liberties of the Gallican Church, Portalis, Pithou

Franchi, Archb., Alessandro, papal envoy to Turkey, 86f

Francis I, 86, 105

Francis II, 104

Francis Joseph II, 292

Frankfurt-Main, plenipotentiaries of free city, 57; Congress of, 57

Franklin, Benjamin, 335f

Franzoni, Card. Giacomo Filippo, head of Propaganda, 75

Frederick I (Frederick III, Elector of Brandenburg), royal title not recognized by Rome, 47

Frederick II (the Great), 38; quoted on Roman agent, 46f; policy towards Catholics, 49, 51, 58; Bismarck on his Roman agent, 112

Frederick William I, advised not to reply to papal letter, 41f, 45f

Frederick William III, 38, instructions to Humboldt, 50-52; reasons to seek entente with Rome, 58; death ends Cologne Troubles, 291

Frederick William IV, abolishes Placet, 288; heals quarrel with Church, aids completion of Cologne Cathedral, 291f

"Free Church in a Free State," as understood in Belgium, 284; Cavour's use of phrase, 296; Montalembert, 296

"freedom of religion," 383

Frère-Orban, government of, 192f

Freycinet, French foreign minister, protests to Holy See against project of papal nuncio to China, 87f

Friars Lands, question of in Philippines, 341f

Frizon, Bishop Alexander, shot by Soviets, 370

Fundamental Statutes for the Temporal Government of the State of the Holy Church, promulgated by Pius IX, 137

Fustel de Coulanges, quoted on distinction of religion and politics introduced by Christianity, 4

Gabrielli, Card. Giulio, sec'y of state, protest on violation of Quirinal, double status of pope and his secretary, 133f

Gaeta, 140

Gallagher, Louis J., 363, member of Vatican Relief Mission, 363

Gallicanism, 105, 161, 253-57; theological and political, 254f; Hanotaux on, 267; neo-Gallicanism, 268. *See also*, regalism, France, Liberties of the Gallican Church, Declaration of the Clergy of France, Organic Articles

Gamberini, Card. Antonio Domenico, minister of the interior, 135

Gambetta, on anticlericalism not an article for export, 341

Garibaldi, Antonio, papal chargé in Paris, quoted on paradoxes of freedom of the press, 280n

Garrau and Salicetti, French envoys at Treaty of Tolentino, 39f

Gasparri, Card. Pietro, sec'y of state, 128, 237, 357; agreement with Soviet representative on relief mission, 361n; telegrams to Chicherin and Lenin on religious persecution of Orthodox, 362

Gelasius I, Pope St., on "two powers," 4, 231n

Genêt, cited on Order of Malta, 27

Genoa, Republic of, 103; Conference, 355-61; letter of Pius to Archbishop, 356; memorandum of Pius XI, 357-60; Chicherin-Signori incident, 356f; Pizzardo mission, with three proposals for Russian treaty, 357; reaction of Supreme Allied Council, 358; reaction of Chicherin, 359; explanation of *Osservatore Romano*, 359; reaction of Russian emigré circles, 360-62

George III, 38

George, Lloyd, announces permanency of Vatican legation, 78; at Genoa Conference, 357f

Gerbrandy, Prof. P.S., on Netherlands Vatican policy in wartime, 63

Gerlach, Rudolf von, trial for espionage, 313f

Germany, 20f; politico-ecclesiastical system of princes, 259f; concordat of 1933 and precedence of nuncio, 171; question of envoys at Vatican in World War I, 308-11; in World War II, 320; Nazi policy during occupation of Rome, 317. *See also* Prussia, Bavaria, Baden, Württemberg

Giobbio, Alfredo, on papal diplomacy, 10f; pope in wartime, 307

Giustiniani, Card. Alessandro, barred from papacy by Spain, 80

Gladstone, concern over doctrine of infallibility, 159

Godfrey, Arch. (Card) William, 375

Gorky, Maxim, 356

Gortchakoff, Czarist chancellor, on nunciature in Russia, 234f

Goyau, Georges, on work of Congregation for Extraordinary Ecclesiastical Affairs, 153

Graz, Archb. of, as *legatus natus*, 115

Great Britain, 20f; Erskine mission, 39; severe prohibitive legislation, 42; Burke quoted on need for relations with pope, 69f; historian quoted on false position forced upon the Government, 70; Pius VII hopes for minister in Rome, 71; Consalvi bids for official recognition, 71n; stratagems of foreign secretary to avoid incurring penalties of *praemunire*, 72-75; Irish troubles bring issue to a head, 74-76; Lord Russell's Diplomatic Relations Act, 75f; crippling amendment barring ecclesiastics as papal envoys in London, 76; Act repealed, 76; diplomatic crisis at outbreak of First World War, 76f; Sir Henry Howard dispatched "on special mission" on occasion of coronation of Benedict XV, 77; instructions of Lord Grey, 77; permanent legati on in 1920, 78; Card. Manning's opposition to a nuncio, 78n

Great Soviet Encyclopedia, 361n

Greece, relations with Rome blocked by France, 90n, 148

Gregory I (the Great), and system of consistories, 145

Gregory VII, receives embassies of obedience, 104; and *legatus missus*, 116

Gregory XIII, and embassy of obedience of Rudolf II, 105; gives nunciatures organized status, 117; no cardinal nephew, 131

Gregory XVI, recognizes New Granada and other Latin American states, 81; enunciates policy of recognition of new regimes, 81n; attempts constitutional reform in papal states, 134; Sardinian concordat, 232; condemns de Lamennais, 279; quoted on freedom of Church in United States, 338n

Greville, Lord, quoted on need for English agent in Rome, 75

Grey, Sir Edward, instructions to British envoy, 77f

Grotius, Hugo, system of Church-State relations, 259f; writes "handbook of regalism," 259. *See also* Territorial System

Guarantees, Law of, rejected by pope, 183, 190, 192; Mancini's minority interpretation, 194; interpretation by Esperson (*see* Esperson, Pietro), 194-98; by Rolin-Jacquemyns, 197; by Brusa, 198n; the law as intended by its makers, 203-7; parliamentary explanations of Visconti-Venosta, 204-6; official interpretation communicated to foreign governments, 206f; Count von Beust affirms Austria's right of legation, 207f; Bismarck tests Cavourians' conception of Law of Guarantees, 208-10; Martinucci case introduces new conception of Law of Guarantees, 192, 213f; contemporary doctrine in relation to the two interpretations, 200; Lawrence, quoted on, 200; provisions on Placet, 296; provisions for time of war, 305-17; policies of Italy, 307-13; Article II, 308-10; protest on Law of Guarantees in wartime, by Benedict XV, 315-17

Guariglia, cited on diplomatic communication in wartime, 325

Guatemala, 19, 21, 82

Guizot, quoted on Church-State lessons of Rossi mission, 281-84
Gustavus III, 37f

Hackworth, Green, quoted on diplomatic agents, 330f
Häffelin, Card. Casimir, envoy of Bavaria, 60, 110
Haiti, 19f, 26, 82
Hanotaux, Gabriel, 93; on Gallicanism, 267
Hanover, 54, 56, 277
Hapsburgs, politico-ecclesiastical policy, 253, 257-59; services to Church, 258. *See also* Josephinism
d'Harcourt, Count Bernard, French envoy, 87, 111; Duke Eugene, French envoy, 139
Hardenberg, Prince von, 44, 58-60
Harding, Pius XI letter to President, 363n
Henry II, of England, 125
Henry VII, of England, 100
d'Herbigny, Michel, secret mission to Soviet Union, 368-70
Hermes, German philosopher condemned by Rome, 297
Hertslett, E., précis of papal-British relations, 70f; Hertslett, L., 73f
Herzan von Harras, Card. von, Hapsburg envoy, 110
Hesse-Darmstadt, 54; Hesse-Kassel, 54, 56
Hinduism, 84
Hippisley, John Coxe, 69f
Historical Sciences, Pius XII to Congress of, 160
Hitler, Adolf, 318f
Hobbes, Thomas, cited by Rousseau on unity of power, 251
Hohenlohe, Card. Gustav Adolf zu, proposed by Bismarck at Prussian envoy, 111-13
Holy Office, Supreme Congregation of the, 130, 147, 149
Holy Places in Palestine, 340
Holy See, agreement with United Nations on terminology, 346n; distinction from State of Vatican City, 346n. *See also* pope, Vatican, Court of Rome, international law
Hommer, Bishop, of Trier, deathbed revelation, 291
Honduras, 19-21
Hontheim, Johannes Nikolaus von, *see* Febronius, Justinus

Hood, Admiral, 69
Hoover, Herbert, 356, 363
Hopkins, Harry, 375
Howard, Sir Henry, 77, 95, 339
Hubbard, Gustave, quoted on legal status of pope, 189-91
Hull, Cordell, 332
Humboldt, Alexander von, naturalist, 48
Humboldt, William von, first Prussian envoy, his arrival related by Consalvi, by Artaud de Montor, 42f; questions of his credentials, 43f; his instructions, 50-52; his view of his mission, 52f; departure, 53; at Congress of Vienna, 169
Hungary, 19; and Placet, 301

Ickes, Harold, 347
ideological conflict with Soviet Union, 350
Ildephonsus, Court of St., 80
Immaculate Conception, solemn definition by Pius IX, Spain objects to unauthorized promulgation, 193; ceremony in Rome, comments on ultramontanism by British agent, 298-301
Immortale Dei, encyclical, 208, 226, 228
Impensa Romanorum Pontificum, papal bull, 56
imperium et sacerdotium, 5, 271
Index of Prohibited Books, 147
India, 20
indirect power, of popes, 158f; Lambruschini anecdote, 159n; St. Robert Bellarmine on, 160; Tarquini comments, 228
Indonesia, 20, 64
Infallibility and right to depose sovereigns, 158-69
Innocent III, 145
Innocent VIII, 129-31, 145
Innocent X, 131
Innocent XI, 109, 132
Innocent XII, 120f, 132
Innocent XIII, 122
Inquisition, 146
internal mission of nuncios, 125. *See also legatio interna, legatio ad intra*
International Court of Justice, advisory opinion on United Nations, 29
International Labor Organizations, 187
international law, 8, 11, 13; seculariza-

tion, 14. *See also* ambassadors, nuncio, Law of Guarantees, right of active and passive legation, Holy See as subject of international law, privileges and immunities

internuncio, 23, 126n; first permanent, 171; not always a bishop, 23n; question of precedence in Netherlands, 171

Ionian Islands, 148

Iraq, 148

Ireland, 19, 21, 74, 76, 118

Isabella, of Spain, 100

Islam, as official religion, 21

Isvolsky, Alexander, Czarist envoy, 22, 69

Italinsky, Andrei J., first Czarist envoy, 67

Italy, 19, 21, 26, 296; concordat, 237; and Pius XII, 339. *See also* Roman Question, Law of Guarantees, ambassadors in wartime, temporal power

Jacobini, Card. Ludovico, sec'y of state, quoted on papal sovereignty, 214; quoted on role of nuncio, 294n

Japan, 20f, 64, 84, 96; Second World War, 375-77

Jaricot, Pauline, 149

Jervoise, Clarke, British semi-official agent, 73

Jesuits, 52, 76, 125, 295; Guizot's appeal to Rome, 281-83; 357

John II, of Castile and Leon, 101

John III, of Sweden, 125

John V, of Portugal, 121-23

John VI, of Portugal, 79

John XXII, 146

John XXIII, 17

Joseph I, 104

Joseph II, 38, 258, rescript on nuncios, 263f, 267; attitude on nunciature dispute, 266

Josephinism, 229; and Hapsburgs, 257-59, 261; Portalis and, 271, 292. *See also* regalism

Journal des débats, cited, 93

Juliers, 263

Julius II, 104, 119, 129

jura majestatica circa sacra, 261f

jurisdictionalism, *see* regalism, Josephinism, Placet

jus cavendi, 261

jus circa sacra, 260, 262, 281, 296

jus defensionis, 261

jus foederis, 16, 234

jus in sacra, as understood by Grotius, 260

jus legationis, 16, 236. *See also* legation, right of active and passive; legation, external and internal

jus primarum precum, 105

jus protectionis seu advocatiae, 261

jus reformationis, 261

jus supremae inspectionis, 261

Justinian, emperor, 115

Kalnocky, Austrian envoy, instructions to, 113

Kamenetz, diocese of, 353f

Kaunitz, Prince von, Austrian chancellor, 38

Kennedy, Joseph B., represents U.S. President at papal coronation, 326

Kessler, Bishop Joseph, 354

King, Rufus, U.S. minister to papal states, 83f; 326

Knyphausen, Baron von, reply on correspondence with pope, 41

Kölle, Frederick, Württemberg chargé d'affaires, 56; quoted on excellence of papal diplomacy, 22

Kölner Wirren, 289. *See also* "Cologne Troubles"

Kulturkampf, 25; Bismarck's protests to Italy bring test to conception of Law of Guarantees, 208-10

Kurakin, Czarist envoy at Vienna, letter to on status of nuncio, 66

La Brière, Yves de, quoted on apostolic delegate in Constantinople, 96; quoted on basis of papal sovereignty, 182n

La Fontaine, quoted, 218n

laicism succeeds regalism, 301f

Lambruschini, Card. Luigi, sec'y of state, policy on Latin American states, 80f; anecdote on indirect power, 159n; 290

Lamennais, Félicité de, case of, 152, 279, 285, 297

Lampert, Ulrich, cited on Roman question, 313

Lanza, head of government, 194, 204f, 213

Lateran Accords, treaty and concordat, 237. *See also* Lateran Treaty

Lateran Treaty, establishes State of Vatican City, ends Roman question, 15, 25, 181f; precedence of nuncio provided, 171; Article 12 on envoys at Vatican, in wartime, 318-20, 323f; question of communication, 318; Article 24 on inviolability of territory, 318; Charles-Roux quoted, 319; on pope's moral and spiritual mission, 340

Latin American states, 19, 23

Latour-Maubourg, Count de, 108, 282

Latvia, 20

Launay, Count de, Italian envoy in Berlin, Bismarck complains to about papal attacks, 111

Laval, Pierre, Stalin's famous remark to on papal "division," 25

Lavardin, Marquis de, French ambassador, descent upon Rome, 109

Lawrence, Prof. T. L., quoted on Law of Guarantees, 200

League of Nations, international personality and right of legation, 28f, 187. *See also* United Nations

Lebanon, 20, 26, 148

Lebzeltern, Louis von, quoted on dual character of pope, 134n

Lecler, Joseph, quoted on two societies, 231n; quoted on Grotius, 259; on secularization of state, 261f

Lector, Lucius, cited on conclave, 107

Lefebvre de Béhaine, French ambassador, 87f

Lega, Card., 151

legates, papal, species of, 115-17; laymen as, St. Stephen, 125; Henry II, 125

legatio ad extra, 262; *ad intra*, 262

legatio externa, 125; *interna*, 125. *See also* right of external and internal legation, 248f

legation, right of active and passive, *legal capacity to exchange diplomatic representatives*: 17; limited to concert of Europe, denied to Turkey, China, 85; token of sovereignty, independence and equality, 102f, 105, 217f; bracketed with war- and treaty-making rights, 29; La Fontaine quoted on ambitions of lesser princes, 218n; exercise by Order of Malta, 26f; by League of Nations, 28f; by United Nations, 29f

Of Holy See: not to be confused with right of concordat, 16; renewal of credentials at accession John XXIII, 17; controversy over

legal nature, 186f; challenged by Esperson, 195, 197; by Bompard, 195; defended by Arntz, 198; questioned by Nys, 199; defended by Anzilotti, 200; in Belgium, 192f; Visconti-Venosta defends, 205f; Austrian view, 207f; Lima challenge, 202; present dominant theory, 200f; Leo XIII quoted, 209; in Russia, 234; distinction between internal and external right of legation, states reverse their views between 18th and 19th century, 248f; wartime issues, 313; in Lateran Treaty, 318-20; United States, 343; contrast with Malta and United Nations, 26-30. *See also* ambassadors, nuncio

legationes obedientiae, 104

legatus missus, 115f; *a latere*, 116f. *See also* nuncio

legatus natus, 115, 117

Leist, Court Councillor, 56

Lend-Lease to Soviet Union, Roosevelt concern over Vatican's attitude, 347f, 376

Lenin, Card. Gasparri's telegram to, 362

Leo I (the Great), 115

Leo X, 117, 129f

Leo XII, 72, 80f, 159n

Leo XIII, 33, 69, 85, 87, 94, 128; on Church as perfect society, 218f

Leoni, Pietro, in Soviet Union, 374

Leonini, Angelo, 116

Leopold I, Emperor, 47, 104, 120f

Leopold II, Emperor, 258

Leopold I, of Belgium, 286f

letters of credence of envoys at Vatican, 345n

letters-patent, 43

Liberals in Belgium, 192f

liberal state, 279

Liberia, 20

Liberties of the Gallican Church, 161, 253-55, 270, 279. *See also* Pithou, Declaration of the French Clergy

Li Hung-chang, viceroy, 87

Lisbon, as First-Class Nunciature, 121

Lithuania, 19f, 378

Litta, papal envoy to Russia, 65, 166

Litvinov, Maxim, foreign minister, 356, 365

Lizakevitz, Russian agent, 67

Lobanov, envoy and foreign minister, 23

Lodzinski, Bishop, 354

Loftus, Lord Augustus, 177

London, Treaty of, Nov. 15, 1831, 285

Lopes de Mendoza, Inigo, first envoy of Spain, 100

Lorenza, Senor de, envoy of Latin American states, 82

Louis XI, 100

Louis XIII, 104

Louis XIV, 106f, 109, 161, 250

Louis XVI, 110

Louis Philippe, 108, 281

Louis the Pius (Ludwig I), 115

Lübeck, 57

Lucerne, nunciature, 262f

Luck-Zhitomir, 353

Luetzow, Count von, Austrian envoy, 138

Lugano, Central Powers envoys in residence, 310, 312f

Lunéville, Treaty of, 49, 54

Lusatia, 117

Luxembourg, 19-20

Lvov, Prince, head of Provisional Government, 354

Lyons, Lord, career of, 22. *See also* Richard B. Lyons

Lyons, Richard B., semi-official agent, 73; his diplomatic report of 1854 on increased influence of papacy, 298-301

Macchi, Giuseppe, papal envoy in Latin America, dispute on precedence, 212

MacHale, Archb., and Irish question, 75

Madrid, as first class nunciature, 33, 121; privileges, 120; tribunal, 294n

Maglione, Card. Luigi, sec'y of state, 319

Mainz, Prince-Archb. of, and nunciature dispute, 263, 265; Dalberg, 54, 56

Maistre, Count Joseph de, quoted on pope as not "foreigner," 249

Malecki, Anthony, 370n

Malta, Island, 72f

Malta, Order of, 19, 21, 26-28; basis of its right of legation, 27; contrast with Holy See, 28

Mamachi, Thomas, quoted against Febronius, 225

Mamiani, Terenzio della Rovere, forms government, 137-39; dismissed by Pius IX, 141

Mancini, S., amendments to Law of

Guarantees rejected, 194; his interpretation becomes the official one, 194

Mankowski, Bishop Peter, 354

Manning, Card., criticizes Vatican diplomacy, 31n; opposes nunciature in London, criticizes use of coercion in religion, 78n

Marchetti, Count Giovanni, papal foreign minister "for secular affairs," 137-39

Maria I, 104

Maria Theresa, 259

Maritain, Jacques, quoted, 202n

marriage legislation in Prussia, controversy, 290-91

Marschall, Baron Adolf Hermann von, German envoy in Turkey, efforts to break French diplomatic monopoly, 92f

Martens, Charles de, author of diplomatic guide, 11

Martens, F. F., quoted on Czarist politico-ecclesiastical policy, 66

Martin V, 102

Martin, Jacques, quoted on Soviets, 378

Martin, Victor, quoted on papal secretaries, 129, 145

Martinucci Vincenzo, lawsuit against Holy See, 213-14; Brusa quoted on case, 198n

Massimi, Marquis Camillo, lay papal envoy, 41, 124

Mastai-Ferretti, Card. Giovanni Maria, *see* Pius IX

Mater, André, lay canonist, quoted on Church as perfect society, 240

Mathieu, Card., quoted on psychology of theologians and diplomats of the Church, 153n

Matulionis, Bishop Theophilus, 370n

Maxima quidem, allocution of Pius IX, 234

Maximilian, Emperor of Mexico, 80

May Laws, 209

McCullagh, Francis, quoted on Bolsheviks and Vatican relief mission, 366n

McNicholas, Archb. John, quoted on U.S.-Vatican relations, 344f; view discussed, 345

Mecklenburg, 57

Medici, Giulio de', 130. *See also* Clement VII

memorandum of powers on reform of papal states, 180

Mercier, Card., rejects criticisms of Russian emigrés, 361n

Merezhkovsky, Dmitry, open letter to pope on Bolsheviks, 361

Merry del Val, Card. Rafael, sec'y of state, 94, 128

Metternich, Prince, Austrian chancellor, and Restoration, 235; Belgium, 287

Mexico, 19, 80, 82

Meyendorf, Baron Felix, Russian chargé, offends Pius IX, 68

Minghetti, Mario, 213

ministero degli affari esteri secolari, 137, 139

Minsk, diocese, 353f

Minto, Lord, 75

Miollis, Gen., French commander occupies Rome, 52; arrests Pius VII, 133f

Mirari vos, and Belgian Constitution, 284n

Mirbt, Carl, quoted, 51, 57f, 291

"mixed questions," 231f, 271f

Mocenni, Mario, papal envoy in dispute on precedence, 211, 213

modus vivendi, 20. *See also* concordat, convention

Mohammed V, 94

Mohilev, Archb. of, 353

Molotov, V. M., foreign minister, attacks Vatican, 371; on Flynn visit to Moscow, 381

Monaco, 19

Monarchy of July, 1830 Constitution, 279; surveillance of correspondence with Rome, 279

Mondragone, students of, Pius XI speaks of "negotiating with the devil," 351

Montalembert, 296

Montalto, Card., 131

Montegelas, Maximilian, Bavarian chancellor, denounces "two powers," 278

Monti, Baron, 315

Montini, Card. Giovanni Battista, substitute sec'y of state, defense of papal diplomacy, 31f; visited by Togliatti, 379

"moral authority" of pope, 243f

Moscow trial of Catholic clergy, 364f; 370n; reaction of Pius XI, 364f

Muelenaere, de, foreign minister, 286

Muench, Aloisius, Bishop of Fargo, nuncio in Bonn, 23

Muenster, Bishop of, 58, 290

Mühlberg, Otto von, Prussian envoy, leaves Rome, 310

Multis gravisbusque, allocution of Pius IX, 233

Mundelein, Card., 347

Munich, nunciature requested by Prince Elector, 263f. *See also* nunciature dispute

Murray, Archb., 75

Muslim states, 21, 84, 334

Mussolini, 317

Naples, 110, 118, 123

Napoleon I, 24, 26, 52, 133, 174, 272

Napoleon III, 274

Narkomindel, 369

Nassau, 56; Nassau-Usingen, 54

National Catholic Welfare Council, 344f

National Catholic Welfare Conference, 366

nationalization of Church property in Russia, 354f

Nazar Aga, envoy of Persia, 85

Neo-Gallicanism, 268

nepotism, abolished, 130-32

Netherlands, The, 20f, 57; résumé of relations, 61-64; politico-ecclesiastical policies, 284; question of communication with Rome, 292; abolishes Placet, 292

neutrality of Vatican City, 317

Neveu, Bishop Pie Eugène, 370n

New Granada, 80. *See also* Colombia

New Zealand, 19

Nicaragua, 19f, 26

Nicholas I, 68

Nicholas II, 295n, 353

Nicolson, Harold, 8

Niebuhr, Barthold Georg, Prussian scholar and envoy, 59f, 289f

Niko, M. S., Yugoslav envoy, 321n

Nilsson, Lauritz, 125

Nina, Card. Lorenzo, sec'y of state, 193

Nobile theatro di Apollo, 141

Nobis profecto, allocution of Benedict XV, 315f

non-Christian states, 84

Normanby, Lord, 75

Norway, 19, 118

nunciature dispute, 262-67; Joseph II, 266. *See also* nuncio

nunciatures, first class, 121. *See also*
Lisbon, Madrid, Paris, Vienna

nuncio, papal envoy with rank of
ambassador,

origins and characteristics: 115-
26; *nuntii et collectores*, 118; usually an archbishop, 23; ecclesiastics as nuncio, 123-25; English
law bars ecclesiastics, 76; laymen
as nuncio, 123; "political mission"
defined, 126; precedence over other
ambassadors, in Vienna regulation,
19, 23f, 164-72; in Berlin, 171;
Card. Manning opposes nuncio in
London, 78n; Belgian bishops cool
to project, 287. *See also* papal
legate, *legatus missus*

*dispatched by pope both as tem-
poral and religious sovereign*: conceded by Gallicans, Josephinists,
Febronians, 267; denied by de
Dominis, 265; Consalvi on primacy
of spiritual role, 294n; Arntz on,
198; other opinions, 189n; Secretariat of State affirms spiritual
priority, 212f; Congress of Vienna
proposals, 167f; Maritain quoted,
202n

*distinguished from secular am-
bassador*: Antonelli quoted, 235;
Secretariat of State document, 211f;
Fontainebleau concordat, 175

*assimilated by governments to
"mere ambassador"*: Russia, 66f,
234f; France, 256f, 335f; Saint-
Simon quoted, 256; by Guizot, 160,
262, 284

*dual diplomatic and internal
mission*: internal mission denied
by Febronius, 265; *Responsio*, 266;
denied in Punctation of Ems, 264;
denied by prince-archbishops, 262f;
imperial rescript, 263; Organic
Articles denies, 269; Consalvi rejects Spanish proposal, 294n; Jacobini rejects second Spanish proposal, 294n

real diplomatic status debated,
negative view held by Hubbard,
190; by Bompard, 191; by Esperson, 195f; affirmative view dominant, 186-88; Arntz, 198; Anzilotti,
200; Visconti-Venosta, 206f, 210;
Secretariat of State, 211; diplomatic corps dispute in Lima, 211f;
Vienna regulation, 164

obedience, embassies of, 104
Offices of Roman curia, 154
Oldenburg, 54, 57
Olivart, Marquis de, rejects "honorary
sovereignty," 202
Ollivier, Emile, contrasts Consalvi with
Portalis, 269n
Ompteda, Baron von, 56
"On Atheistic Communism," encyclical,
371
Orange, Prince of, 167
oratores, 101
Ordinary Ecclesiastical Affairs, section
of, in Secretariat of State, 142
Organic Articles, 267-69, 279; on Placet,
268; denies jurisdiction of nuncios,
269; Card. Caprara protests, 268;
Protestants in, 268f; comparable
articles in Prussian constitution,
277; Portalis defense of, 268-73
Oriental Church, Congregation for,
147f, 150
Orlando, Victor Emmanuel, policy on
position of pope in wartime, 307-
11, 314f
Orsini, Card. Domenico, envoy of
Naples, 110
Orthodox in Russia, 354; suspicions
towards Vatican, 361f
Osservatore Romano, quoted on envoys
in wartime, 311
ostensibile notificatorium, 43
Ottaviani, Card., quoted on diplomacy
and public ecclesiastical law, 220
Oudinot, Gen., relieves Rome, 180

Pacca, Card. Bartolomeo, nuncio and
pro-sec'y of state, 47, 172, 177, 264
Pacelli, Card. Eugenio, nuncio and
sec'y of state, 128f, 295n, 365, 368.
See also Pius XII
Paderborn, 58, 60, 130
padrone, 130
Palatinate, 262
Palestine, 148; Holy Places in, 340
Palmerston, Lord, 72, 171
Pamphili, Card. Doria, pro-sec'y of
state, 133
Panama, 19, 26
Pancirolo, Card., 131
papal (Vatican) diplomacy, 7f; defined,
11f, 32; antedates concordat system, 16; denounced by Card. Manning, 31n. *See also* other entries
under Vatican diplomacy
papal supremacy *in temporalibus*, 158

Papée, Polish envoy in wartime, 321

Paraguay, 19, 21, 26, 82

Paris, second Treaty of, 58; Conference of 1856, 85, 180; as first-class nunciature, 121

Parma, 27

pase regio, 293f

passive legation, right of, *see* legation, right of

Patrimony of St. Peter, 181

patronato real, 79f

Paul I, of Russia, 65f, 166

Paul II, 100

Paul III, 130, 146

Paul IV, 104

Pauline privilege, 147

Pekin, church building in, dispute over, 89

Pelagius II, 145

Penal Code of 1810, French, prohibits unauthorized communication with foreign religious leaders, 272

Penitentiary, Sacred, 146

"perfect society," as key concept in public ecclesiastical law, 220; used sooner by diplomats than by canonists, Consalvi quoted, 220n; not necessarily expressed in formula of Pope St. Gelasius I, 231n. *See also* Catholic Church, constitution of

Pernot, Maurice, quoted, 93, 152, 242-44

Persia, Shah of, sends special envoy, 85

"personal representative," 328-30

persona non grata, persona grata, 30, 120, 123; Bunsen relieved, 291

personality, international, of Holy See, generally conceded today, 184f, 188; distinct from international personality of State of Vatican City, 186. *See also* sovereignty, right of legation

Peru, 19f, 26, 82

Peter the Great, 354

Petre, semi-official British agent in Rome, 73f

Philippines, 19

Pieracchi, Francesco, 124

Pimentel, Bernardino, lay nuncio, 123f

Pinchetti-Sanmarchi, definition of papal diplomacy, 10, 212

Piranesi, Francesco, 37

Pithou, Pierre, father of Gallicanism, 161, 253-55, 269n, 280. *See also* Gallicanism

Pius IV, 117

Pius (St.) V, 131

Pius VI, 37, 39, 45, 70, 151, 163, 215, 258; *Responsio*, 265f

Pius VII, 43, 45, 57, 59, 71f, 133

Pius VIII, 80; brief on marriages in Prussia held up, 290

Pius IX, 84, 135f; quoted on necessity of temporal power, 182; quoted on Church as perfect society, 233f; calls Pellegrino Rossi, 282; and Card. Antonelli, 142n

Pius (St.) X, allegedly wishes to abolish papal diplomacy, 33f; 77, 94, 128, 142f, 146; quoted on politics and religion, 245f

Pius XI, 25, 128; quoted on sovereign parties to concordat, 237; on communism, 350, 371; on negotiating with the devil, 351; Genoa Conference, 356-60; sends relief mission, 363; allocution on Moscow trials, 364f; on Vatican Russian policy, 366f; calls for prayers for Russia, 371

Pius XII, quoted on world concerns of Holy See, 6; on coexistence with communism, 350f; and Italy, 339; rejects Axis-sponsored anti-Bolshevik crusade, 372f; quoted on conditions for peace with Soviet Union, 383f. *See also* Pacelli

Pizzardo, Card. Giuseppe, at Genoa Conference, 357, 359n, 360n, 361n, 362

Placet, governmental approval of papal decrees, 50f, 56n, 223, 229, 250, 252, 258, 268, 275, 278, 279f, 288, 294, 292, 293f, 296, 301. *See also* regalism

Poincaré, Raymond, 91

Poland, 19-21, 118, 123, 382; envoy in Vatican, 321

Polizeistaat of 18th century, 252, 279, 289, 301

Polk, James K., 82f

Pontifical Commission for Russia, 371

Pontificia Accademia ecclesiastica, 31

pope, his authority in the Catholic Church, 215f; as "foreign ruler": significance, 249, 249-52, 257; de Maistre quoted, 249; Penal Code, 272, 296; as secular prince: 50, 52f, 133f, 163, 167, 174, 198, 238, 337, 344

 as both temporal and spiritual sovereign: 13, 39, 50, 52f; Sir

Henry Howard to pope as head of Church, 77; ignored by British even as temporal prince, 70, 73; United States only as temporal sovereign, 83f; to pope as head of Christendom, 106; two roles, 133f, 134n; Farini quoted, 139; two-fold foundation today, 158; spiritual sovereignty, 161; instructions for French ambassadors, 163; at Congress of Vienna, recognition of religious role, 164, 167f; Schoenbrunn decree allows spiritual sovereignty, 174; Napoleon quoted, 174; Leo XIII, 219; Portalis quoted on dual role, 273; Consalvi quoted, 337; United States, 344, 346n; Brusa quoted, 193n; Arntz, 198; Law of Guarantees, 203; Visconti-Venosta quoted, 205; Secretary of State quoted, 212f

"popular democracies," relations with Holy See, 382

Portalis, J.-E.-M., French minister of worship, neo-Gallicanism of, in Organic Articles, 268-73; contrasted with Consalvi, 269n

Portugal, 18-21, 26, 33, 104, 118

Posen, 58

Possevino, 125

Poubelle, French envoy, 93

Pradt, Dominique de, quoted on aftermath of Napoleonic era, 54

praemunire, 42, 69, 73

Prague, 115

precedence, of pope, 27f; of nuncio, 101, 163f, 211; of internuncio, 171. *See also* nuncio

primacy of spiritual, 158

primacy of jurisdiction of pope, 216, 262

primate, 115

privileges and immunities, diplomatic, 196, 208, 214, 305f; in First World War, 306-10, 314f, 317; Second World War, 318-21, 325

privileges of Catholic monarchs, 120f

promulgation of papal decrees, Chaix d'Est Ange on, 274f. *See also* Placet

Propaganda, *see* Propagation of the Faith, Congregation for the, 148

Propaganda, Congregation, 74f, 88, 94, 148, 150

Propagation of the Faith, Society for the, 149

Protestantism, 5; as guide for judging papal diplomacy, 238f

Protestants at Rome, 14

Protestant states, jurisdiction of, in religious matters, 259f; and Organic Articles, 268f

protocol for Catholic and non-Catholic envoys in Rome, 150

Provida solersque, Bull of Circumscription, 57

Provisional Russian Government, 353f

Prussia, gains territory through secularization decree, 58, 113, 277; Cologne troubles, 288-92; changed role of Roman legation, 300n

Public Ecclesiastical Law, defined, 220, 222; "new science" defended, 227; as a weapon against the Church, 227f

public power, *see* sovereignty

Pufendorf, Samuel, Collegial System, 223; quoted on church not a state, 224, 260

Punctation of Ems, 264f

Quadrotta, Guglielmo, 95; quoted on wartime diplomats, 308f

Quanta cura, encyclical of Pius IX, 273, 293

Quelen, Archb. de, 279

Quirinal, 133

Radek, Karl, 354

Radio Vatican, in wartime, 324f

Rampolla, Card. Mariano del Tindaro, 93, 128; as nuncio in Spain protests *pase regio*, 294

Rapallo Pact, 357

Raumer, Carl Georg von, memorandum on Prussian envoy, 60

Rechtstaat, Austria abandons *Polizeistaat* for, 301

reciprocity of diplomatic representation, 23, 27, 60, 78n, 285

recognition, Gregory XVI expounds policy, 81n

Red Cross Geneva conventions, 378

regalism, as system of state control of Church, 229, 249, 251-53; 257, 259, 279, 287, 298; succeeded by laicism, 301f. *See also* Josephinism, Febronianism, Gallicanism, jurisdictionalism, Grotius, Pufendorf

Regensburg, Diet of, 54

Regout, I. H. W., Netherlands envoy, 63

Reichsdeputationshauptschluss, 54. *See also* secularization decree

Reims, Arch., papal letter to, 94; as *legatus natus*, 115

Reinhold, Johann Gotthard von, Netherlands agent, 57

religion and politics, of Romans, 3-5; in Muslim and Orthodox countries, 341

Religious, Congregation for, 147-49

Rense, declaration of, 104

Responsales, 115, 265

Responsio, Brief of Pius VI, on papal envoys with ecclesiastical jurisdiction, quoted, 265f; on nuncios as diplomats, 266. *See also* right of internal legation

revolution, French, 38f; in Latin America, 79f; Roman, 149; Belgian, 279; American, 335; in Russia, 353

Rex est Imperator in regno suo, 102, 103n

Riario, Count de, Prussian agent, 46

Richard, P., quoted on first envoys in Rome, 101f

Richelieu, 9

Riga, Treaty of, 351n, 359n; Litvinov-ARA agreement on Russian relief, 356

Rinieri, Ilario, 10

Rites, Congregation of, 147, 149f

Ritter von Grünstein, Baron Otto von, Bavarian envoy, 311

Rochechouart, Card. de, French envoy, 162

Rolin-Jacquemyns, Gustave, attacks pope's legal status, quoted, 193f; rejects Esperson interpretation of Law of Guarantees, quoted, 197; Brusa agrees with rejection, 198n

Roman Curia, 12, 144

Roman question, settled definitively by Lateran Treaty, 15; raised by Cavour at Paris, 180f; dramatization, 183; implications for international law, 184; Erzberger's wartime proposals for solution, 313; French and Belgians reticent, 313. *See also* Lateran Treaty, temporal power

Roman Republic, 173

Romanum decet pontificem, papal decree on nepotism, 132

Roosevelt, Franklin Delano, sends Myron C. Taylor to Pius XII, 326-

29; decision on Tittmann as chargé d'affaires, 332; why he adopted formula of "personal representative," 342f; concern for Vatican's attitude on aid to Russia, 347f; raises religious issue with Soviets, 375

Ropp, Edward de, Archbishop of Mohilev, negotiations with Provisional Government, 353f; arrest and exile, 354; proposals to Bolsheviks on religious freedom, 335, 358; letter of Patriarch Tikhon to, 362

Rospigliosi, Card., sec'y of state, 128. *See also* Clement IX

Rossi, Pellegrino, special mission to Rome as French envoy, 281-84; unusual career, 282; Guizot's comment on significance of Rossi mission, 283; as papal minister, 139, 282; assassination, 282

Rota, 146

Rousseau, J. J., quoted on indivisibility of sovereignty, 251

royal honors, as symbol of sovereignty, 102

Rudolf II, 105

Rudolf IV, Duke of Austria, and origins of Josephinism, 258

Rumania, 20

Rumiantzev, Czarist chancellor, quoted on nuncio's status at Russian court, 66

rupture of diplomatic relations, with France, 33, 189, 191; with Portugal, 33, 122; with Russia, 68f; with Belgium, 192; not tantamount to religious rupture, 18; not tantamount to denial of papal sovereignty, 302

Russell, Lord John, prime minister, 76f

Russell, Odo semi-official British agent, 22, 73, 75. *See also* Ampthill, Lord

Russia, Czarist relations with papacy, 65-69; control of communication of pope with Russian Catholics on Caesaropapist principles, 66-68; Martens quoted, 66; Rumiantzev quoted on nuncios, 66; first Czarist envoy arrives, 67; his instructions on control of communication, 68; papal rejection quoted, 68; concordat of 1847, 68; negotiations for a nunciature, 234f; rupture of relations, 68; restoration of relations through Isvolsky, 69; Czarist Placet retained until regime's end, 294-96; abortive moves towards revision, 295n; Provisional Government, 353. *See also* Soviet Union

sacerdotium et imperium, 5, 228, 271
Sacraments, Congregation of, 147, 149
Sacro vergente anno, Pius XII letter to peoples of Russia, 372f
St. James, Court of, 23
St. John of Jerusalem, 27. *See also* Malta, Order of
Saint-Simon, Duc de, quoted, 106f, 120, 255f
Salandra, 310, 315
Salicetti and Garrau, French plenipotentiaries, 39
Salzburg, archb. as legatus natus, 115; nunciature dispute, 263
Salisbury, 73
Salis, Count de, British envoy, 78
San Domingo, 82. *See also* Dominican Republic
San Marino, 19, 26
San Salvador, 82. *See also* El Salvador
Sanuto, Marino, 102
Sapienti consilio, St. Pius X reorganizes Roman curia, 142, 146
Sardinia, 101, 152, 180f; dispute with Holy See, 232f
Satow, Sir Ernest, author of diplomatic guide, 11
Savino, Paolo, his definition of papal diplomacy, 10
Savoy, Duke of, 103; House of, 203
Saxony, Duchy and Grandduchy of, 57
Sazonov, Czarist envoy, 23; foreign minister, 295n
Scaduto, Francesco, on Law of Guarantees in wartime, quoted, 308f
Schmedding, Johann Heinrich von, quoted on politico-ecclesiastical system of Prussia, 277f
Schmitz-Grollenberg, 57
Schoenbrunn, decree of Napoleon abolishes temporal power, 173f
Schutz- und Vögtei Recht (jus protectionis seu advocatiae), 261
Scotland, 118
secret agreement on mixed marriages in Prussia, 290f
Secretariat of State of His Holiness, 12; development and characteris-

tics, 127-43; document on precedence of nuncio, 212f
secretarius domesticus, 129f
Secularization, decree of 1803, 27, 53, 58, 175f; of international law, 14, 30, 163, 196, 198n; of civil life, 301f
Ségur, Louis Philippe de, 39f
Seminaries and Universities, Congregation for, 148, 150
separation of Church and State, characteristic of Christian era, 3-6; separation states, 18-20; in France, 3, 240; André Mater quoted on consequences of, 240; relation to diplomatic relations, 242f; in Belgium, 284, 286; in Soviet Union, 354, 359, 368; in United States, 167, 337
Siam, 85
Siccardi Law, 232f
Sicily, 101, 118, 152
Siglo Futuro, El, on nuncio, 294n
Signature, Apostolic, 146
Signori, Archb. of Genoa, relations with Chicherin, 355n, 356-60
Silesia, 46
Simmons, Sir L. Lintorn A., British special envoy, 73
Sinai peninsula, 148
Sixtus IV, 116
Sixtus V, 131n, 146
Sloskans, Bishop Boleslas, 370n
Smith, H. A., quoted on British relations, 70
societas perfecta, as ecclesiastical public law term, 220. *See also* Catholic Church, constitution: civil state as perfect society, 224
Soglia, Card. Giovanni, sec'y of state, 139, 221
Sollicitudo ecclesiarum, encyclical of Gregory XVI, 81
Somaglia, Card. Giulio Della, sec'y of state, 72
Sonnino, 310, 315
sovereigns, Catholic, as protectors of religion, 271. *See also jus protectionis*, 261
Sovereignty, early exercise by popes, 157; classic conception of European concert of sovereign states, 187, 196; Bryce on controversies, 188; argument on indivisibility of, as anti-papal weapon, 224f, 227-29; Rousseau quoted on, 251f, 261;

Portalis on, 269-72; abdication of sovereignty claims in religious matters, 299; question of spiritual sovereignty, 15; as basis of Law of Guarantees, 197, 201; Card. Jacobini quoted on, 214; as problem of international law, 248; of domestic constitutional law, 248, 252; concurrence of political and spiritual sovereignty, 158, 247f, 252. *See also* right of legation

Soviet Union, and Holy See, 349-84; Catholic statistics, 351n; famine relief, 356f; anti-Bolshevik emigrés, 360, 369; religion, 375f; seeks Vatican recognition, 369f; rumors of diplomatic relations, 356, 365; Lend-Lease, 347f

Spada, quoted, 138

Spain, 19-21, 26, 33, 100, 293f; concordat of 1953, 219

Spellman, Archb. (Card.) Francis, 377

Spiegel, Archb. Ferdinand, 290f

spiritual sovereignty, *see* sovereignty

Stalin, 24; attacks Vatican, 371; alleged letter to Pius XII, 375-77, 380

State of Vatican City, *see* Vatican City, State of

status in statu, Devoti quoted, 226

Storer, Bellamy, 338n

Stremeyer, on abolition of Austrian Placet, 301

Sturzo, Luigi, quoted, 379

Sublime Porte, 85

"survival theory" of papal diplomacy, 238f, 245

Sweden, 19, 118

Switzerland, 21, 23, 167

Syllabus Errorum of Pius IX, 273, 293, 297

Synod Roman, 145

Syria, 148

Tablet (London), cited on British relations with Rome, 76

Tacci-Porcelli, apostolic delegate in Turkey, 94

Taft, William Howard, mission of Gov., 341f

Talleyrand, 58, 268

Tarquini, Card. Camillo, systematizes doctrine of Church as perfect society, 228, 232; defines *societas perfecta,* 229, 230n; quoted on reasons for new approach, 228

Taylor, Myron C., mission of, interpretation, 326-48; diplomatic status as seen in Washington and Rome, 327f; wartime visit, 322

Tanara, Sebastiano Antonio, Vienna nuncio chosen from *terna,* 121

Tejada, Ignacio de, first envoy of New Granada, 80

temporal (territorial) power of papacy, stress on Roman question in 19th century, 15; origins in 8th century, 157; unchallenged in century before French Revolution, 173; plots against, 173; Roman Republic, 173; Napoleon suppresses papal states, 173; his arguments, 174; restored by Congress of Vienna, 172; subsequent vicissitudes, 180f; papal arguments on need of temporal power, 175-80; Bossuet's classic formulation, 176f, 179; considerations of Card. Pacca, 177-79; Bismarck on pope's need for his own state, 177; Pius XI quoted, 182; not the precise juridical point in the debate on international status of papacy, 201f

terna, list of three names of prospective nuncios, 121

Territorial System, 259f. *See also* Collegial System, Episcopal System

Tevfik, Pasha, foreign minister, 92

Thrace, 148

Thun, Count, Austrian minister of worship quoted on end of Placet, 292f

Thureau-Dangin, Paul, quoted on growth of ultramontanism, 283

Tikhon, Orthodox Russian Patriarch, arrested, 361; letter of thanks for appeal of Pius XI for Orthodox, 363; Pizzardo appeals for, on behalf of pope, 362; Stalin permits election of successor, 373

Timasheff, N. S., quoted on Vatican-Soviet relations, 380

Tiraspol, diocese of, 354

Tittmann, Jr., Harold, aide to Myron C. Taylor, Italy questions status in wartime, 321f; moves with family into Vatican, 327; revelation of *Osservatore Romano* on his appointment as chargé d'affaires, 330-32; Roosevelt papers, 332f; State Department and, 333

Togliatti, Palmiro, Italian communist,

returns from Soviet Union, 379; sees Msgr. Montini, 379

Toledo, bishop as *legatus natus*, 115

Tolentino, Treaty of, 39f, 124, 172

toleration, religious, rising tide of at end of 18th century, 37; in imperial Russia, 352

totalitarian states, Pius XI, 351

Transjordania, 148

Trent, Council of, 116, 119

Tribunals of Roman Curia, 154

Trier, Prince Archb. of, and nunciature dispute, 263, 265; Bishop Hommer, accepts secret Prussian pact, 290; deathbed recantation, 291

Triple Entente, 76f

Truman, Harry S., renews Taylor mission, 327

Tsungli Yamen, imperial Chinese foreign office, 87

Türkheim, Baron von, plenipotentiary of Baden, 57

Turin, nunciature closed, 123

Turkey, blocked from having relations with Vatican, 85f, 148

Tydeman, Dutch parliamentarian, 62

Twiss, Sir Travers, quoted on Placet, 300n

"Two powers," Pope St. Gelasius on, 4, 158, 226; as residing in one subject in Middle Ages, 231n; not popular in 17th and 18th centuries, 251; conception of, denounced by Montgelas, 278. *See also* sovereign, indivisibility of

"Two swords" of Boniface VIII, 158

Uhden, William von, Prussian agent in Rome, 48

ultramontanism, growth of, 215f, 283, 297f; 299f, 301

United Arab Republic, 20; as Muslim state, 334

United Nations, 26, 29f; right of legation, 28f; international personality, 29, 185; compared to Holy See, 29f; accord with Holy See on terminology, 346n

United States, 15, 19, 167; relations with papal states, 82-84; with Vatican, 326-48; Catholic Church in, 297; tribute of Gregory XVI, 338n; separation of Church and State, 337; bases of relations with papacy, 338-44

Universities and Seminaries, Congregation of, 148

Upper-Rhine states, plenipotentiaries, 57f

Urban VIII, 104

Uruguay, 19, 21, 82

"usurpation theory" of papal diplomacy, 238f, 245

Vanutelli, Card. Vincenzo, 69

Vásquez, Canon Pablo Francisco, Mexican envoy not received, 80

Vatican City, State of, 28; no foreign minister, 140; not basis of diplomacy, 238; residence of envoys in wartime, 319-23; use of radio in wartime, 324f; Fundamental Law, 345; no mention of, in credentials, 345n; term discontinued in United Nations usage, 345n. *See also* Lateran Treaty, temporal power

Vatican Council (1869-1870), 111, 159; settles dispute on primacy of jurisdiction, 215f; defines Infallibility, 301; draft canons against Collegial System, on Church as perfect society, 230n; use of Placet by states on decrees, 301

Vatican diplomacy, "ordinary and particularly apt instrument," 13, 316; criticisms of, 30f; defended by Card. Montini, 31f; alleged intentions of St. Pius X, 33f; symbol of Church-State relationship, 218. *See also* ecclesiastical diplomacy, papal diplomacy, right of active and passive legation

Vatican Relief Mission to Russia, 360, 363, 364-67; no diplomatic status, 363, 366n

Vatican vs. Quirinal, 183. *See also* Roman Question, Law of Guarantees

"Vatican," usages, 346n

Venaissin, 109

Venezuela, 19, 20, 82; envoy challenges precedence of papal envoy, 211

Venice, 100, 103f, 114, 118, 123, 129

Ventura, Gioacchino, 75

Viborg, Manifesto of, 353

Vicars Apostolic, early title of papal representative, 115

Vienna, Congress of, 24, 26; establishes precedence of nuncio, 164, 171; restores temporal power to pope, 171. *See also* nuncio, precedence of

Vienna, first class nunciature, 33, 120f, 262f

Vilain XIIII, special Belgian envoy, 285-87; his reasons for opposing Rome mission, 285f

Visconti-Venosta, Emilio, foreign minister, and Cavourians' conception of papal spiritual sovereignty under the Law of Guarantees, 194, 204-10, 296; quoted in defense of spiritual sovereignty as an international right, in Chamber, 204f; in Senate, 205f; circular for foreign governments on spiritual sovereignty, 206f; reply to Bismarck protest, quoted, 209f; Martinucci case reverses his interpretation, 213

Visscher de Celles, Count de, Netherlands envoy, 57

Vladivostok, diocese created, 355n

Vogüé, Count de, French envoy to Turkey, 87f

Vorkuta, 374

Vorowski, Vaclav, Bolshevik negotiator in Italy, 356; assassinated, 361n

Waldeck, Prince of, 57

Walsh, Edmund A., 359n; relief mission to Russia, 361n, 363

Weiszäcker, Ernst von, German envoy, 320

Welles, Sumner, 332

Western Schism, 129

Westphalia, Treaties of, 105, 119, 163

White Russian exiles, denounce Vatican on Bolsheviks, 353

Wilbaux, Theodore, quoted against papal sovereignty, 192f, 198

William the Conqueror, attitude on papal legates, 116

Wiseman, Bishop (Card.) Nicholas, 75

Wolsey, Card., 116

World War, First, 3, 15; Netherlands, 61-63; Great Britain, 77f; envoys during, 305-17. *See also* ambassadors in wartime

World War, Second, Netherlands, 63f; envoys during, 317-25; United States, 339; Soviet Union, 371-81. *See also* ambassadors in wartime

Württemberg, 54, 56; abolishes Placet, 293

York, Archb., as *legatus natus*, 115

Young Turks, movement, 94

Yugoslavia, 20; envoy in wartime, 321

Zaccaria, Francesco Maria, quoted on nature of Church, 225

Zallinger zum Thurm, Jakob, quoted on nature of Church, 221; defends new public ecclesiastical law, 227

Zoglio, Giulio Cesare (Card.), nuncio, 263

Zuylen, Pierre Van, quoted on relations with pope, 287